Come Fly with Me

The Rise and Fall of Trans World Airlines

DANIEL L. RUST AND ALAN B. HOFFMAN

Missouri Historical Society Press

St. Louis

Distributed by University of Chicago Press

ISBN 979-8-9855716-3-9

Library of Congress Cataloging-in-Publication Data
Names: Rust, Daniel L., 1970- author. | Hoffman, Alan B., 1946- author.
Title: Come fly with me : the rise and fall of trans world airlines /
    Daniel L. Rust and Alan B. Hoffman.
Description: St. Louis : Missouri Historical Society Press, [2023] |
    Includes bibliographical references and index. | Summary: "This book
    recounts how three larger-than-life personalities-Charles Lindbergh,
    Howard Hughes, and Carl Icahn-shaped Trans World Airlines (TWA) and
    determined its fate. The only comprehensive history of TWA and its
    predecessors, this book traces the airline from its origins in the 1920s
    to the 21st century. It's the story of how powerful, strong-willed
    individuals created and ultimately destroyed an American icon that had
    deep roots in Kansas City and St. Louis, Missouri"-- Provided by
    publisher.
Identifiers: LCCN 2023010636 | ISBN 9798985571639 (paperback)
Subjects: LCSH: Trans World Airlines--History.
Classification: LCC HE9803.T7 R88 2023 | DDC 387.706/573--dc23/eng/20230727
LC record available at https://lccn.loc.gov/2023010636

Distributed by University of Chicago Press
Designed by Steve Hartman
Cover image: TWA brochure, ca. 1962, Alan Hoffman Collection
Printed and bound in the United States by Modern Litho

CONTENTS

INTRODUCTION

Three larger-than-life personalities—Charles Lindbergh, Howard Hughes, and Carl Icahn—shaped the history of Trans World Airlines (TWA) and determined its fate. This book is the story of how powerful, strong-willed individuals created and ultimately destroyed an American icon with deep roots in St. Louis and Kansas City, Missouri.

Lindbergh plotted the routes, selected the equipment, and piloted the first eastbound flight of TWA's predecessor Transcontinental Air Transport (TAT). After TAT merged with Western Air Express to become TWA in 1930, the airline made Kansas City its corporate and operational headquarters. TWA called itself "The Lindbergh Line" throughout the decade, trading on the world-famous aviator's charisma and credibility. TWA was a leader in developing new technology, including the DC-2—the first modern airliner—and conducting groundbreaking flight research. But the airline abruptly distanced itself from Lindbergh after he became a controversial figure on the eve of the Second World War.

Howard Hughes took over the cash-strapped airline in 1939 and marketed it as "The Airline of the Stars." Working closely with TWA and Lockheed Aircraft officials, he helped create the Constellation—the first successful pressurized, high-altitude, high-speed airliner. Drawing on the airline's wartime international experience, Hughes succeeded in making TWA the first US airline with both domestic and international routes, but his obsessive desire for control led to a crisis that ultimately cost him the business he helped build.

Airline deregulation upended the entire industry in 1978. In response TWA created a St. Louis hub, and Lambert Airport became one of the nation's busiest and most congested airports—as well as the center of a protracted battle over expansion. Initially greeted as the airline's financial savior, financier Carl Icahn acquired TWA amid the "greed-is-good" culture of the 1980s. He moved the corporate headquarters to Mount Kisco, New York, and merged TWA with St. Louis's thriving Ozark Air Lines, eliminating it as a competitor.

Icahn battled with TWA's unions as he used the airline for his own financial benefit, leaving TWA a shell of its former self. But an unlikely coalition—including TWA's unions, Republican senator John Danforth, and

Democratic representative Dick Gephardt—worked together to remove Icahn in 1993. After Icahn's ouster TWA relocated its corporate headquarters to St. Louis and continued expanding Lambert as a hub.

TWA's employees fought to stave off a shutdown and liquidation through two painful bankruptcies in the 1990s, but Icahn's damage ran deep. Just as the company began to recover, the 1996 tragedy of Flight 800 dealt a mortal blow. American Airlines purchased TWA in 2001 with the stated intention of retaining the airline's jetliners, personnel, and St. Louis hub, but in the wake of the September 11 terrorist attacks former TWA employees found themselves first in line for layoffs as American struggled to avoid bankruptcy.

Yet TWA's legacy lives on. The airline pioneered technological advances that made air travel safe and appealing. No other airline so caught the public's attention and imagination, and none so fully captured the spirit of air travel in the United States and beyond. From its 1930s genesis, TWA brought air travel from the domain of well-heeled elites to a flying experience for the masses, exemplified by Frank Sinatra's iconic 1958 song and album, *Come Fly with Me.* Its artwork depicted Sinatra extending his hand in an invitation to fly TWA to distant lands—exactly the atmosphere TWA sought to create. Throughout its life TWA beckoned America to come flying, and America responded.

Chapter 1
IN THE BEGINNING: 1920–1929

The US Post Office Department's airmail service was not just TWA's ancestor. It was the forerunner of every legacy airline in the country. Efforts to use the newly invented airplane to carry mail throughout the United States started in 1911. During an aviation meet on Long Island in September of that year, the US Post Office authorized pioneer aviator Earle Ovington to carry mail pouches between a temporary flying field in Garden City, New York, and the post office in Mineola, New York. In one week Ovington carried a total of 32,415 postcards, 3,993 letters, and 1,062 circulars.

Flying the Mail

Although small-scale experiments like this one were suspended when America entered World War I, interest in airmail service kept growing.[1] In May 1918 the US Post Office took steps to establish a transcontinental airmail service. A few months later it acquired 100 DH-4 aircraft from the Army Air Service to use as mail planes, and soon mail was being transported between Washington, DC, and Philadelphia. On September 8, 1920, transcontinental airmail became a reality when operations commenced between San Francisco and Omaha.[2] In just four years the US Post Office had created a coast-to-coast network of electric lights so that mail could be transported at night.[3]

By 1925 the US Post Office was carrying nearly 14 million letters and packages annually via aircraft. The nation's railroad industry was paying attention. Holding contracts to move mail on its rail networks, railroads perceived the US Post Office's airmail service as a competitive threat from the public sector and lobbied Congress to privatize airmail in America. The Contract Airmail Act of 1925, also known as the Kelly Act, authorized the US Post Office to accept competitive bids from private companies seeking to operate feeder lines that branched from its existing coast-to-coast service. When the first 12 Contract Airmail (CAM) routes were offered to bidders in the fall of 1925, Postmaster General Harry S. New declared, "Upon the result of this enterprise depends the future of aerial transport in the United States."[4] His statement would prove prophetic, for airmail contracts subsidized—and later became—the basis of airline service in America.

Western Air Express

Harry Chandler, owner of the powerful *Los Angeles Times*, and James A. Talbot of Richfield Oil wielded considerable political and financial influence in California. They cofounded Western Air Express (WAE) in 1925 "to establish, maintain, lease and operate air transport services, and airlines and systems, for the interstate and intrastate air transportation of passengers, mails, express and freight, and for each and every object and purpose for which aircraft and air service may be available and useful."[5] During the initial round of airmail contracts, the Post Office awarded to WAE Contract Airmail Route 4, between Los Angeles and Salt Lake City via Las Vegas, Nevada.

Chandler and Talbot selected Harris M. "Pop" Hanshue as president of WAE. Like many aviation pioneers, Hanshue was a colorful character: an automobile dealer, a car racer, and a shrewd businessman. He was determined to make WAE the dominant carrier between the West Coast and Denver and even envisioned extending its service all the way to the East Coast.[6] "This commercial airline will cut more than 40 hours from the present fastest schedule between the populous and rich California region and Chicago," Hanshue said shortly before WAE began flying. "It will bring Los Angeles and adjacent communities within 30 hours by airmail of New York City." He also foresaw carrying passengers.[7]

WAE began operations on April 17, 1926, with a fleet of six Douglas M-2 mail planes but only four pilots—known as the "Four Horsemen" because they rode horses to work—to fly them. Unlike the war surplus DH-4s used by the Post Office and many other airmail contractors, the M-2 was a purpose-built mail carrier. In what would be the first of many connections between Hollywood and the airline industry, actress Claire Windsor was the recipient of the first package delivered by WAE.[8]

Flying Passengers

Just one month after starting airmail operations, WAE began flying passengers. One person could fit into an open cockpit by sitting on mailbags—still the priority cargo. Ben Redman paid $90 (about $1,550 in 2023) to be WAE's first passenger on a 9:30 a.m. flight from Salt Lake City to Los Angeles's Vail Field with an intermediate stop at Las Vegas. The high desert terrain required pilot Charlie James to fly at altitudes as high as 12,000 feet without oxygen. More than 200 others braved the trip over the next seven months, sometimes making unscheduled rest stops in the Mojave Desert.[9]

One of those hardy pioneer air travelers was Maude Campbell, WAE's first woman passenger. The airline turned her $180 round-trip flight from Salt Lake City to Los Angeles into a media event. Campbell was outfitted with a flight suit, then given cotton to stuff in her ears for hearing protection,

Western Air Express president Harris "Pop" Hanshue was a pioneer of the airmail era and had great aspirations for establishing WAE as a passenger carrier. Photograph, ca. 1926. From J. E. Frankum, Legacy of Leadership, *1971.*

a leather helmet, and a parachute. The toilet facilities were a tin can, which she declined to use. "I waited until we got to Las Vegas," she said. "It was the only thing to do." Despite the cotton, she arrived at Los Angeles somewhat deafened. Hanshue greeted her with a bouquet of flowers as cameras snapped.[10]

Another early air traveler, Colonel Thurman Bane, gave a detailed account of flying on WAE in October 1926. After donning a flight suit and parachute, he climbed into "a most roomy and comfortable cockpit," which he shared with 178 pounds of mail. The plane departed Los Angeles at 7:45 a.m., pushed through fog, and headed for the Cajon Pass following the Union

Pacific railroad line. It crossed the pass at 8:05 a.m.—"very close to the tops of the trees"—and flew out over "miles and miles of [desert], flat and sandy on the left with miles of barren mountains on the right." At 9:30 a.m. they entered rougher country, "nothing but mountains, millions of them, ridge after ridge in every direction." Passing 11,000-foot Mount Charles, the pilot began the descent to Las Vegas, where they landed at 9:55 a.m., 2 hours and 10 minutes after leaving LA.

By 10:30 a.m. they were airborne again, the pilot noting where Boulder Dam (later renamed the Hoover Dam) would be constructed. An hour later they passed Zion National Park. Bane suggested that passengers should have maps pointing out interesting features on the ground—a practice airlines adopted and followed for many years. By now, Bane noted, "The top of my head is starting to freeze." After noon the pilot asked if he was hungry. "It is a little too rough to eat," he thought. "I don't like to place too much confidence in my stomach in such a rough sea."

At 2:00 p.m. the pair approached the Great Salt Lake and began descending, passing over the Mormon Temple and Tabernacle, Bane's ears "ringing as usual when coming down from a few thousand feet rapidly." They landed at 2:15 p.m., exactly 6.5 hours after leaving Los Angeles—a trip that would have taken more than a day by rail. "Like all other airmen," Bane said, "I have dreamed of an airline like this for the past 10 years."[11]

Although transporting passengers wasn't yet profitable, Hanshue said that it could be if combined with a reasonable volume of mail or parcels. The chief dangers he identified were "inefficient, incompetent operation with unfit equipment" and economically unsound undertakings. He urged the government to regulate the airworthiness of equipment and personnel under the Air Commerce Act of 1926. And, making a recommendation that would come back to haunt him, Hanshue advocated "empowering the Post Office Department to prevent letting contracts for routes impossible for either economic or natural reasons."[12]

The Model Airway

When the Daniel Guggenheim Fund for the Promotion of Aeronautics created a "Model Airway" between San Francisco and Los Angeles and selected WAE to operate it, it was a breakthrough for the company. WAE received $180,000 from the Guggenheim Fund, which it used to purchase a fleet of 12-passenger Fokker F-10 Super trimotors that would fly the route. Service began on May 26, 1928.

Hanshue moved WAE's passenger service to Alhambra Airport, northeast of downtown Los Angeles. The airline built a spacious, modern terminal structure that reflected the upscale service it aimed to provide, as

"Pop" Hanshue greets Maude Campbell, WAE's first woman passenger, upon her arrival in Los Angeles, June 1926. Collection of SFO Museum, Gift of Barbara A. Dawson.

well as a large, hexagonal-shaped maintenance hangar. Passengers could take limousines to the airport, and on board the plane they were served box lunches from LA's Pig 'n' Whistle cafeteria. In addition to providing airmail services, the Model Airway gave WAE valuable experience in operating scheduled passenger air transit. WAE hired Herbert Hoover Jr.—son of the newly elected president—to assist in developing a sophisticated infrastructure, including its own weather observation stations, two-way radio communications with aircraft, and an extensive ground-based telephone and teleprinter communications system. A weather reporting service was implemented along the California air route that all pilots in the area who had on-board radios could use. WAE also supported efforts to develop the first aircraft radio compass, which became the basis for the automatic direction-finding equipment that has been used by commercial airlines and the military for decades.[13]

Although the Model Airway operated for just over a year, it demonstrated the value of weather reporting and communications, and it laid the foundation for safe and reliable passenger air service. There were no weather-related accidents during the Model Airway's existence—a remarkable achievement. The United States Weather Bureau (today the National Weather Service) took over its weather reporting functions on July 1, 1929, and eventually extended them across the entire country, forming the backbone of the aviation and weather forecasting service that has existed ever since.[14]

THE FIRST AIRLINERS

Dutchman Anthony Fokker designed and manufactured the famous Fokker fighter planes that Germany used in World War I. After the war Fokker established an American subsidiary to producc commercial aircraft for the US market. In 1928, Fokker created the F-10, a capable trimotor design with 12 passenger seats.

Fokker faced competition from the Ford trimotor. Henry Ford wanted to add aviation to his industrial empire, and in 1926 he produced the Ford Model 4, which enjoyed considerable success with the early airlines. The more powerful Ford Model 5 came two years later and could carry up to 15 passengers. Unlike the Fokkers, which featured a wooden wing and fabric-covered fuselage, the Fords were made of sturdy all-metal construction.

The Fokker and Ford trimotors were state-of-the-art airliners in the late 1920s, but the Fokkers quickly disappeared after a TWA F-10 carrying beloved football coach Knute Rockne crashed when its wooden wing structure failed. The Fords were replaced the next decade by the faster and more comfortable twin-engine Boeing 247 and DC-2.

Standard Airlines

As WAE prepared to carry mail and passengers, Los Angeles–area pilots Jack Frye, Paul Richter, and Walter Hamilton pooled their resources to form Aero Corporation of Los Angeles. The new company ran a flying school and acquired the rights to sell Fokker airplanes. After operating an air charter service, Frye and his partners established Standard Airlines as a subsidiary of Aero Corporation and succeeded in persuading WAE investor Harry Chandler to provide financial backing. In November 1927 three weekly flights began operating from Los Angles to Phoenix and Tucson, using Fokker planes and employing Aero Corporation's flying school graduates as pilots. Because the Fokkers lacked lavatories suitable for women, flights routinely made a brief "rest stop" at a remote gas station with two crude outhouses along a stretch of desolate desert highway.[15]

With financial backing from Harry Chandler, Standard Airlines began operating three flights per week between Los Angeles and Tucson via Phoenix in November 1927. This 1929 timetable cover depicts one of the carrier's Fokker aircraft. Schwantes-Greever-Nolan Collection.

Despite its primitive facilities, Standard suceded in attracting a Hollywood clientele looking for sunny weather in Arizona. In February 1929, Standard extended its route east to El Paso, Texas, where—at least in theory—passengers could connect with the Texas and Pacific Railway and continue on to the East Coast. On this somewhat tenuous basis Standard announced the inauguration of "America's First Transcontinental Air-Rail Travel Route" and attracted the attention of Hanshue, who was entertaining similar ambitions.[16]

Maddux Air Lines

A successful Los Angeles–area Lincoln automobile dealer, Jack L. Maddux was another enterprising western aviation entrepreneur. In November 1927 he purchased a Ford Model 4 trimotor passenger plane and began raising capital to start his own airline. Described as a "rugged, stubborn pioneer all his life in different fields,"[17] Maddux's approach to generating financial backing was nothing if not creative. He offered scenic flights over LA to wealthy acquaintances and business contacts in his new "Air Yacht." His wife organized preflight luncheons for the businessmen and their spouses. The flights were so successful that within two months more than 600 passengers had flown in the Ford, and Maddux had secured the needed financing to launch his airline. Maddux inaugurated air service between Los Angeles and San Diego on November 1, 1927, and even persuaded Charles Lindbergh, the most famous pilot on earth, to serve as "honorary chief pilot" for the occasion.[18] Along with Lindbergh, Maddux also hired Navy pilot Daniel W. "Tommy" Tomlinson as head of airline operations. Under Tomlinson's leadership Maddux established a number of innovations that later became industry standards, such as a system for rotating pilots between air and ground duties.[19]

Charles Lindbergh hoped that flying from New York to Paris would spark interest in aviation. He succeeded beyond his wildest dreams. Photograph by Sensor Studio, 1927. Missouri Historical Society Collections.

Even without an airmail contract, Maddux's passenger service was thriving. In April 1928 he began offering two daily flights from Los Angeles to San Francisco, and by year's end his fleet had grown to eight Fords and two single-engine Lockheed Vegas. In 1929, Maddux added daily service to Phoenix and supplemented his fleet with eight Ford Model 5 trimotors—becoming a serious rival to WAE and Standard.[20]

The Coming of Lindbergh

Who was Charles A. Lindbergh, the aviator who took the world by storm following his historic transatlantic flight in May 1927? He was born in 1902, the son of Minnesota congressman Charles A. Lindbergh and Evangeline Land Lindbergh. After his parents became estranged, young Charles was shuttled between his father in Washington, DC, and his mother in Detroit. He spent summers at his father's farm in Little Falls, Minnesota, where he was "a good woodsman, an excellent marksman, and an ingenious do-it-yourself improviser."[21] He was also skilled at working with machinery and learned to drive a car before reaching his teens. This background imbued him with a strong sense of independence and self-confidence—traits he retained throughout his life.

Lindbergh enrolled in the University of Wisconsin's engineering department, but formal study bored him and failed to satisfy his restless imagination. Faced with such poor grades that he risked expulsion, he decided to drop out of college in the first half of his sophomore year to learn to fly. "I longed for open earth and sky," he wrote. "The fascination of aircraft had mounted to form an irresistible force in my mind. Was a life of flying to be renounced because it shouldered danger? I chose a school in Nebraska and enrolled in a course for the spring."[22] Lindbergh went on his first flight on April 9, 1922, at the Nebraska Aircraft Corporation in Lincoln, but the company closed before Lindbergh could solo. For the next year Lindbergh was a wing walker, parachute jumper, and mechanic for barnstorming pilots before he bought his own plane. In April 1923, Lindbergh traveled to Georgia's Souther Field, where a private dealer sold war surplus aircraft. Lindbergh bought a Curtiss JN-4 "Jenny" and essentially taught himself to fly it.

Lindbergh barnstormed around the Midwest during the summer of 1923 with meager results. In September he flew to St. Louis for the International Air Races at Lambert Field. After the races he sold the Jenny and stayed in St. Louis to teach flying. During the winter he was accepted for flight training by the Army Air Service, where he learned to fly fast and powerful military planes. On March 14, 1925, he received his Army wings and a commission in the Army Air Service Reserve.[23]

Back in St. Louis, Lindbergh kept busy instructing, carrying passengers, and taking a few barnstorming trips. He also joined the 110th Observation Squadron of the 35th Division Air Service of the Missouri National Guard and became its engineering officer. For the first time he had a permanent home and a settled life. Lindbergh's activities brought him into contact with several St. Louis businessmen, including banker Harold Bixby, insurance executive Earl Thompson, and broker Harry Knight. These men saw fliers as more than acrobats and daredevils; they believed that aviation had a future.

In the fall of 1925, Robertson Aircraft Corporation, the principal operator at Lambert, was awarded Contract Airmail Route 2 between St. Louis and Chicago, via Springfield and Peoria, Illinois, and offered Lindbergh the position of chief pilot. He organized the Robertson service, laid out the route, and hired the other pilots.[24] Over the winter of 1925 and 1926, Robertson modified several surplus DH-4s and was ready to commence operations by springtime. Lindbergh flew Robertson's first airmail service between Chicago and St. Louis on April 15, 1926—celebrated today as the first flight of one of the companies that would later form American Airlines.

While flying mail over the Illinois countryside, Lindbergh considered seeking the Orteig Prize: New York hotelier Raymond Orteig was offering $25,000 to whoever completed the first nonstop flight between New York and Paris. Lindbergh believed most businessmen thought of aviation in terms of "barnstorming, flying circuses, crashes, and high costs,"[25] but he believed aviation had far greater potential, and a nonstop flight to Paris could prove it.

He approached the St. Louis businessmen he'd met while working at the airport, starting with Albert Bond Lambert and Earl Thompson. Winning the Orteig Prize, Lindbergh explained, would advance aviation and publicize St. Louis. With Thompson's assistance he formed a syndicate of St. Louis business leaders and aviation figures, and ultimately raised $15,000 for the project.

As potential rivals prepared to attempt the Paris flight, Lindbergh contacted Ryan Airlines, which offered to build a modified version of its mail carrier that fit Lindbergh's budget and deadline. Lindbergh worked closely with the team at Ryan designing the aircraft, and he flew it for the first time in late April 1927. After a hurried flight test program, he left San Diego for New York on May 10, stopping only in St. Louis for fuel and to unveil the newly named *Spirit of St. Louis* to his financial backers. Hurrying on to New York, he set a transcontinental speed record of 21 hours, 20 minutes. The San Diego–to–St. Louis leg was the longest nonstop solo flight that had been made to date in the United States.[26]

Lindbergh's record coast-to-coast flight caught the public's imagination and proved he was a serious contender for the Orteig Prize. As rival pilots with greater recognition and better finances were stymied by accidents and legal squabbles, Lindbergh saw his chance on May 20. He took off from Long Island's Roosevelt Field in the rain at 7:52 a.m. Navigating entirely by dead reckoning—using rudimentary information such as compass courses, wind speed, and landmarks to determine location—he reached his intended landfall in Ireland, then landed at Le Bourget Airport in Paris, 33.5 hours after takeoff. Neither he nor his St. Louis partners could have dreamed of the significance this flight would have.

After a week's rest in Paris, Lindbergh flew to Brussels and on to London, where his arrival almost ended in tragedy after crowds broke through police lines and surged onto Croydon Aerodrome's runway as he was landing. His European sojourn concluded when, as commander in chief, President

Calvin Coolidge ordered him to return to the United States. In New York he was greeted by a delirious crowd estimated at 3 to 4 million—close to half the city's population.[27] On July 20 he took off from New York on a goodwill tour of all 48 states, which lasted until October. Lindbergh was now a media superstar and aviation's most sought-after figure. He had succeeded brilliantly where others with much greater resources had failed.

Growing Western Air Express

Harris Hanshue moved aggressively to expand WAE beyond its original airmail route and West Coast passenger service. In December 1927 he acquired Colorado Airways, which held the airmail contract connecting Pueblo, Colorado Springs, and Denver with the US Post Office's transcontinental airmail route at Cheyenne, Wyoming. That hundreds of miles separated WAE's eastern terminus at Salt Lake City from all of these cities was no deterrent for Hanshue. In 1928 he went on to purchase Pacific Marine Airways, an operator of seaplanes between Los Angeles and nearby Catalina Island.[28]

The following year WAE inaugurated passenger service between Los Angeles and Albuquerque, and then onward to Kansas City via Amarillo and Wichita. It also added a north-south route connecting Albuquerque with Denver and El Paso. By purchasing West Coast Air Transport in late 1929, the line extended its reach north from San Francisco to Portland and Seattle. West Coast Air offered spectacular views of mounts Shasta, Jefferson, Hood, and St. Helens, but without a mail contract it consistently lost money.[29] Then in May 1930, WAE acquired Standard Airlines, adding a southern route to Dallas and gaining Jack Frye, Paul Richter, and Walter Hamilton, all of whom would prove to be highly capable airline executives. Frye had already arranged for connections with Southwest Air Fast Express (SAFE), the New York Central Railroad, and the Texas and Pacific Railway, allowing—at least on paper—a 70-hour transcontinental air-rail service.[30]

The airline also added two four-engine Fokker F-32s—the world's largest passenger airliner at the time—to its growing fleet of passenger and mail carriers. This ungainly fabric-covered plane, with its engines suspended beneath high wings, could carry up to 32 passengers. But it was too large for the air-travel demand, and it was already obsolete when WAE put it into service in the spring of 1930. The death of Notre Dame football coach Knute Rockne in a Fokker F-10 crash sealed the airliner's fate. WAE retired the F-32 after only six months of operation.[31]

Western Air Express now spanned the continent and boasted the country's most extensive air network. But it had become unwieldly. WAE used a variety of different aircraft—many of them open-cockpit mail planes unsuited to carrying passengers—and operated over a hodgepodge route system. Although it had a handful of mail routes, the contracts weren't enough to subsidize its unprofitable passenger services. The 1929 stock market crash and the onset of the Great Depression brought even more financial strain to Hanshue's air empire. WAE also gained a potent rival, one that would eventually take over the airline with help from the government.

The Birth of Transcontinental Air Transport

Charles Lindbergh sought to establish a coast-to-coast passenger airline with customer appeal. After unsuccessfully approaching Henry Ford, he and three of his *Spirit of St. Louis* partners—Harold Bixby, Harry Knight, and Bill Robertson—reached out to Clement Keys.

Keys, a New York investment banker, was one of the first businessmen to grasp the potential of aviation. After World War I he took the helm of the Curtiss Aeroplane and Motor Company, and it soon became the nation's leading aircraft manufacturer.[32] Keys moved beyond building airplanes in 1925, when he founded North American Aviation for the purpose of financing and promoting airlines and aviation-related businesses. That company spawned National Air Transport, which was awarded CAM 3, the contract airmail route between Chicago and Dallas. Up until now Keys had concentrated on airmail, but he recognized the commercial potential of an air service that treated passengers as more than cargo.

Transcontinental Air Transport (TAT) was formed in May 1928 with $5 million in capital stock. Keys served as president, Paul Henderson as vice president, and Lindbergh as head of its technical committee.[33] Keys assembled a blue-chip investor group including Curtiss, Wright Aeronautical, National Air Transport, and the Pennsylvania Railroad. Bixby and Knight sat on TAT's board of directors.[34]

Henderson outlined TAT's operational concept in a meeting with Keys, Lindbergh, and Chester Cuthell, a lawyer and director of several aviation businesses. After stating that the Pennsylvania Railroad had been interested in aviation for some time, Henderson sketched out his plan for the air route and rail connections. The Pennsylvania Railroad would carry passengers overnight in Pullman cars from New York City to Columbus, Ohio. Then TAT would fly passengers during daylight hours to Indianapolis, St. Louis, Kansas City, Wichita, and Dodge City, where they would transfer to the Santa Fe Railway for the night segment to Las Vegas, New Mexico. The next day passengers would fly on to Los Angeles via Albuquerque; Winslow, Arizona; and Kingman, Arizona.[35]

Lindbergh pointed out that there wasn't an airport on the route with facilities for transport service, and Keys assured him that they would only begin operations when prepared to do so. Lindbergh, the technical committee chair, made several transcontinental trips to survey the route and identify possible airport sites. Afterward, the route was adjusted to substitute Waynoka, Oklahoma, and Clovis, New Mexico, for the western rail connections. The technical committee concluded that TAT would have to construct its own airports at Kingman, Winslow, Clovis, and Waynoka. Work began in late 1928.[36]

Asking the railroads to support passenger air service may seem strange today, but rail passenger service had never been very profitable, and rail carriers were more concerned about competition for their mail and express service. In fact, the railroads viewed TAT as rail travel that included some incidental air travel. Meanwhile, TAT's leadership hoped the public's familiarity with the comforts of travel by rail would add to the appeal of its service, stressing that passengers would enjoy Pullman cars and beds at night.[37]

W. W. Atterbury, president of the Pennsylvania Railroad, confidently declared that "the railroads will remain, of course, the backbone of the nation's transportation system." However, Atterbury had watched with growing alarm as his company's passenger revenues declined in the face of increasing competition from other modes of transportation. In the late 1920s he saw potential for the Pennsylvania Railroad to play a leading role in offering a hybrid air-rail transcontinental passenger service.[38]

Making TAT a Reality

TAT opened a temporary office in Washington, DC, in the fall of 1928 to begin planning for operations under Paul Henderson's leadership. TAT took full advantage of Lindbergh's fame and prestige to promote its service, calling itself "The Lindbergh Line." It also hired Amelia Earhart, the era's most famous woman aviator. She promoted air travel by speaking with women's groups and writing articles about how to best enjoy the experience of flight and what to wear while traveling.[39]

To keep stockholders, directors, and railroad officials apprised of its progress, TAT published a newsletter called *TAT Plane Talk*. The airline also created its own proprietary weather observation and reporting network, and it hired experienced meteorologists to staff its principal airports. Weather stations were sited both on the TAT airway and away from it to provide more complete coverage of conditions. The Pennsylvania and Santa Fe railroads operated many of these stations using their own wire systems. Radioed weather reports would be transmitted from the stations to aircraft in flight. TAT proclaimed itself "the only air transport company which owns and operates such a bureau."[40]

TAT divided its system into eastern and western divisions. Municipalities in the more populous eastern division stepped up to support TAT's services.

Columbus, Ohio, floated a bond issue to purchase land and construct runways, hangars, and paved ramp areas. The city built an elegant structure adjacent to the Pennsylvania Railroad tracks at Columbus Airport to allow passengers to walk directly from the train to the airport terminal. This historic and architecturally significant building still exists, as does the large hangar constructed for TAT. The citizens of St. Louis, Kansas City, and Wichita also passed bond issues to support TAT's airport facilities.[41]

TAT funded and constructed most of the airports, terminal structures, and facilities in its sparsely populated western division. Lindbergh chose tiny Waynoka, Oklahoma, as an airport site because it was suitably located to transfer passengers to and from the Santa Fe Railway. TAT purchased land from local farmers and constructed runways of plowed soil mixed with oil. The airline also built a large hangar, measuring 120 feet by 200 feet, along with a radio station and weather observation facility.[42] To carry passengers the 5 miles between the airport and the Santa Fe station in Waynoka, it used the Aerocar: an automobile that pulled a luxuriously equipped 14-passenger trailer (conveniently manufactured by Clement Keys's Curtiss Aeroplane company). Waynoka's Santa Fe depot was an imposing structure that included a hotel and a Fred Harvey restaurant, where westbound TAT passengers could enjoy dinner before boarding their sleeping cars for the overnight rail link to Clovis, New Mexico. (The Waynoka passenger depot, hotel, and restaurant complex still exists and has been restored as an air-rail museum that holds artifacts from its TAT days.)[43]

The Santa Fe terminal at Clovis also had a Harvey House restaurant that served breakfast to TAT passengers headed west and dinner to those traveling east. TAT bought the abandoned town of Blacktower, about 5 miles away, and converted its unused railroad station into an air terminal dubbed Portair, complete with a mile-long runway and large hangar, where its planes could be serviced and maintained overnight. As at Waynoka, an Aerocar ferried passengers between the railroad and the airport. Because Clovis and Portair were in different time zones, westbound travelers would arrive by train at Clovis at 8:20 a.m. central standard time and depart from Portair by plane at 8:10 a.m. mountain standard time.[44]

Farther west, TAT leased a pre-existing airfield in Albuquerque. At more than 5,000 feet above sea level, Albuquerque was TAT's second-highest airport. TAT improved the airport's runways and extended the longest to 4,000 feet. It erected a Spanish pueblo-style terminal building with a Fred Harvey restaurant and other amenities.[45] TAT built a similarly styled passenger terminal and an aircraft hangar at Winslow's airfield, and it constructed two runways at Kingman—one nearly a mile long.[46] TAT established Grand Central Air Terminal at Glendale as its Los Angeles facility.

A large passenger terminal, two paved runways, and extensive hangar and support facilities already existed on the site.[47]

Under Lindbergh's leadership TAT bought 10 all-metal Ford trimotors for a total of $813,000, including spare engines and parts. TAT boasted that it reduced the planes' seating capacity from 12 to 10 so that "tea and luncheon can be served aloft in an aerial dining car service." One was designed as a "flying office" for TAT executives.[48] The Fords were durable and reliable, but like their contemporaries, noisy and uncomfortable. Although heat could be directed to the cabin, it was insufficient to keep passengers from shivering in the winter months. Cruising around 100 mph, the planes rarely flew higher than a few thousand feet above the ground. The Fords bounced around in turbulence and often made passengers airsick. Despite these limitations, it was hoped that the Ford name would convey a sense of familiarity and safety to the public.

In addition to teletype and telegraph, radio played a critical role in TAT's operations. The company constructed two 128-foot-high radio towers near each airport with a radio direction finder that could determine a plane's bearing from the station. Each plane was equipped for two-way voice and Morse code radio communication with the ground stations, whose range allowed continuous communication with aircraft in flight. The airborne radios were also available to passengers for "essential business or emergency use."[49] These facilities were ahead of their time, anticipating capabilities that would not become common for nearly another decade.

Even though the air-rail arrangements did not include night flying, TAT provided for night operations from the outset—delays and early winter sunsets made some night operations inevitable. Standard airport lighting consisted of obstruction lights, boundary lights, approach lights, flood lights, and "ceiling lights" used to determine cloud heights. Each airport had a rotating beacon to alert pilots to its location and guide them to it.[50] Plans were also made to light the airway with beacons, and TAT embarked on an ambitious lighting program. In all, TAT spent more than $3 million of its initial $5 million capitalization on aircraft and infrastructure.[51]

The company put great care and consideration into selecting pilots. Once again Lindbergh spearheaded the effort, with the assistance of Paul F. Collins—an experienced pilot who flew 7,000 hours in the First World War— as an airmail pilot and chief test pilot for Ford. After a nationwide search TAT recruited an initial cadre of 32 first pilots and second pilots, who averaged 3,000 hours flight time. Even the second pilots were all graduates of Army Air Service training at Kelly Field in San Antonio, Texas, making them better qualified than most civilian-trained pilots.[52]

Each TAT flight also featured a third crew member: the courier. The predecessors of flight attendants, couriers were responsible for passenger comfort. They served snacks and lunch, comforted those who became airsick, and handled baggage on the ground. Contrary to later practice, TAT's cabin staff were all men and wore uniforms inspired by those of naval officers.[53]

During flights between St. Louis and Kansas City, couriers served lunch on an upscale table service with lavender tablecloths and napkins. The fare included cold meats, sandwiches, salad, coffee, tea or milk, and fruit. Passengers ate breakfast and dinner aboard trains and at Fred Harvey restaurants at overnight stops.[54] The total coast-to-coast fare ranged from $337 to $403 (about $6,000 to $7,000 in 2023), depending upon the class of rail service purchased. The air portion accounted for $290 (about $5,000 in 2023), including all meals, and a $5,000 life insurance policy as air travel was not covered in standard policies.[55]

Before carrying any paying passengers, TAT staged a two-week, full-scale dress rehearsal in June 1929. Company directors, railroad officials, news reporters, and others tried out the air-rail experience. Pilots succeeded in avoiding severe storms, thanks to weather information from the ground. Over those two weeks TAT aircraft flew more than 50,000 miles and carried 261 passengers. Satisfied with the outcome, Charles Lindbergh wrote to Clement Keys on behalf of the technical committee that TAT was ready to start a regular passenger schedule between New York and California on July 8.[56]

As TAT prepared to begin operations, Lindbergh sent a telegram to General Atterbury expressing his confidence in the hybrid transcontinental transportation system. "From a technical standpoint, the system is ready for operation," he wrote. "Every precaution which modern methods have developed has been taken for the safety of our passengers and I feel confident that we can start operation today with a system which combines the elements of safety, comfort and rapidity of travel in the highest degree."[57]

Westward Ho

Elaborate ceremonies at Pennsylvania Station heralded TAT's inaugural service on July 7, and they were broadcast over the radio. A TAT trimotor was brought into the station, where Amelia Earhart christened it the *City of New York*. Congratulatory telegrams arrived from numerous public officials, including New York governor Franklin D. Roosevelt and New York City mayor Jimmy Walker. Across the country in Los Angeles, Lindbergh pressed a button to toll a bell at Penn Station. At that moment the *Airway Limited*, a new Pennsylvania passenger train created to serve the eastern leg of the journey, began its trip to Columbus, Ohio.[58]

The *Airway Limited* departed at 6:05 p.m. and arrived at Columbus at 7:55 a.m. Some 3,000 spectators turned out to witness the event in a light rain, but covered walkways protected the passengers' walk from the train to the adjacent Port Columbus Airport terminal. The passengers boarded two waiting trimotors—the *City of Columbus* and the *City of Wichita*—to begin the air segment of their transcontinental journey. With the TAT weather service reporting clearing skies to the west, the two planes departed for Indianapolis at 8:15 a.m.[59]

One of the passengers was Marguerite Salomon of the New York Chamber of Commerce, who flew in the *City of Wichita*. She found her seat with a reclining back and an ashtray in the armrest "surprisingly comfortable." The cream-colored ceiling, lavender walls, and chrome paneling with curtains at the windows made the interior "bright and cheerful, very homelike." A thick carpet, deep purple, covered the floor. Each seat was equipped with a reading light and call button to summon the courier. Outside conditions were dark and dismal, but the courier assured her that the weather would clear.[60]

Once airborne, Salomon felt little sense of speed. "This must be the strange magic of air travel," she wrote. "It's not rough. It's smooth and level. Even the trembling has stopped." The courier handed her a map of the United States showing the route they would follow and interesting sights to look for. "There's a washroom in the rear of the cabin," the courier said. "It's perfectly all right for you to walk around. It won't throw the plane off balance. Are you comfortable? Would you like a pillow? Care for a magazine?"[61]

Passing over Dayton, Ohio, home of the Wright brothers, the second pilot left the cockpit to chat with passengers. He informed Salomon that they were flying at an altitude of 3,000 feet at 100 mph with a slight tailwind. Soon the Fasten Belts sign illuminated, and the plane began its descent to Indianapolis. "There's really nothing to this landing business," Salomon decided. The aircraft seemed to ride an invisible slide from sky to earth, leveled off near the ground, and touched down with hardly a bump.[62]

Following a 15-minute stop at Indianapolis, the flight proceeded to St. Louis. While crossing into Illinois, Salomon took a short nap, awakening to find the sky had cleared as predicted. After a crew change at St. Louis the plane headed to Kansas City, and passengers enjoyed lunch of cold chicken, potato salad, and a cup of hot consommé, plus iced tea and strawberry shortcake for dessert.[63]

After another brief stop at Kansas City, it was on to Wichita. The flight encountered turbulence over the sweltering Kansas plains, and some passengers became airsick. Salomon found that reclining her seat helped. There was enough time on the ground at Wichita for passengers to deplane for a quick cup of coffee and a sandwich before departing for Waynoka.

A covered walkway protected passengers from the elements as they traveled between the waiting TAT Ford trimotor and Lambert Airport's terminal around 1930. Missouri Historical Society Collections.

En route Salomon was allowed to come forward to see the pilots flying the airplane and was impressed by the number of instruments. She noted that they were flying at 109 mph at an altitude of 5,000 feet. The flight arrived at Waynoka just before 6:30 p.m., having covered 980 miles by air. Here the passengers boarded a 14-passenger Aerocar—furnished much like the interior of the aircraft—to travel the 4 miles to the Santa Fe Railway station. They dined at the Harvey House restaurant before boarding sleeping cars for the overnight rail trip to Clovis, New Mexico.[64]

Heading East

Charles Lindbergh piloted the first eastbound flight from Los Angeles. One of the passengers was his new wife, Anne Morrow Lindbergh. She had already been swept up in his nonstop aviation and business career, and she was tired: The couple had just flown from the East Coast in an open-cockpit, single-engine Curtiss Falcon biplane. At Grand Central in Los Angeles on the morning of July 8, California governor Clement Calhoun Young and his wife sat with TAT officials in a little circle below the bandstand. A crowd estimated at 30,000 turned out for the festivities. After a few speeches, actress Mary Pickford climbed a ladder and cracked a bottle on the plane's nose to christen the *City of Los Angeles*, while Gloria Swanson did the honors for the *City of Philadelphia*.[65]

TAT's first eastbound flight departing Los Angeles on July 9, 1929, with Lindbergh at the controls. From J. E. Frankum, Legacy of Leadership, *1971.*

Now departing from Los Angeles on the *City of Los Angeles* with Charles at the controls, Anne found the trimotor the height of luxury, "beautifully comfortable and businesslike," especially after enduring the rigors of the open-cockpit Falcon. This plane's interior was painted a cool gray-green and had adjustable leather seats, little green curtains, and blue shaded lights. The courier shouted in her ear (to be heard over the din of the engines) that he would provide anything she wanted. Anne cataloged the aircraft's conveniences and comforts—"soup in the middle of the morning 'served aloft' and lunch, of course, and 'lemonade or tea' in the afternoon."[66]

One of Anne Lindbergh's fellow passengers on the eastbound flight was Vera Darling, who published an account of her experience in *The World's Work* magazine. She admired the interior furnishings, from "the polish of the panels on the walls to the electric cigar lighters, individual lamps with parchment shades, and sliding glass windows" that opened in flight for ventilation. Silk shades and soft curtains graced the windows. Passengers hung their coats in a compartment that could also accommodate golf bags. Hats, reading materials, and other small items could be stashed in racks along the walls above the rear seats. All of it, wrote Darling, provided "a subtle feeling of confidence."[67]

Upon landing in Kingman, Arizona, the passengers walked under a cover from the plane to the terminal. They lunched on cold chicken or tongue, salad with sliced pineapple (no dressing but cream cheese on the side), white and brown bread, sliced grapefruit, and cake served on metal plates and lavender linen tablecloths, all washed down with hot coffee.[68] The Lindberghs flew on to Winslow, where they boarded the inaugural westbound flight to return to LA, where Anne met Amelia Earhart, one of the passengers.

California, Here We Come

The westbound passengers ate breakfast at the Santa Fe Railway station in Clovis before boarding another Aerocar for the 5-mile drive to the TAT Portair air terminal. The departing Ford trimotor roared across the Portair landing field for an on-time departure for Albuquerque at 8:10 a.m., but disaster nearly ensued when an engine failed moments after takeoff. The pilots put the plane back on the ground, but it veered off the runway and—despite heavy braking—its left wing struck the TAT hangar. Shaken but unhurt, the passengers were ushered off the damaged trimotor. After a half-hour delay, the passengers departed uneventfully in a replacement plane.[69]

The aircraft climbed to 9,000 feet above sea level as it flew over mountainous terrain on its way to Albuquerque. Because of decreased atmospheric pressure at this altitude, the courier dispensed chewing gum and advised the passengers on how to best clear their eustachian tubes. On the ground at Albuquerque, Salomon felt better after taking an aspirin with a cup of coffee. En route to Winslow, Arizona, passengers enjoyed aerial views of the Petrified Forest and the Painted Desert. Salomon called it "some of the most beautiful scenery in the world," the desert "a symphony of tans in different shapes and color values."[70]

At Winslow the westbound passengers met Charles Lindbergh, who would pilot one of the westward flights back to Los Angeles—though not Salomon's, to her disappointment. Her flight to Kingman was also uneventful except for a brief rain shower that pelted the Ford's metal skin and gave her a sight she had never seen before: a complete circle rainbow, "like a bullseye target reflected on the ground below."[71]

The final leg from Kingman to Los Angeles was the longest of the trip, taking over 3 hours. The plane flew through a fog bank near Los Angeles. "Look out the window," wrote Salomon. "Nothing but fog." She wondered whether there were "any other flyers lost up in this thick soup." She could now appreciate all the instruments she had seen in the cockpit and imagined the pilots were "earning their salt." In reality, no blind-flying instruments existed at this time, and entering fog or clouds risked disorientation and loss of control.

At some locations TAT passengers transferred from train to plane via the Aerocar, as depicted in this 1929 photograph. Gerald Balzer Collection, Greater St. Louis Air and Space Museum.

The flight quickly emerged from the fog into bright sunlight, and soon the Pacific Ocean came into view. Salomon's plane circled over Los Angeles so that Lindbergh's flight could land first.[72] Both planes taxied up and stopped in front of another welcoming crowd. From Los Angeles, passengers could take an Aerocar into the city and then an overnight train to San Francisco or fly there the next morning on Maddux Air Lines.

Tragedy on Mount Taylor

Despite TAT's emphasis on safety, tragedy struck less than two months later. At 10:20 a.m. on September 3, 1929, the westbound *City of San Francisco* departed Albuquerque for Winslow with three crew and five passengers on board. Although TAT's weather service reported no adverse weather over the route, showers and thunderstorms moved into the region shortly after the flight departed. It was scheduled to reach Winslow by 1:15 p.m. but never arrived, and ground stations received no radio reports from the missing plane. Based upon reported sightings, search parties began to assemble. As many as 1,000 people—including Zuni, Hopi, Navaho, and Apache, as well as cowboys and prospectors—joined in, lured by a $10,000 reward from TAT. More than 100 civilian and military pilots also took part. TAT suspended regular operations and sent several of its planes to assist in the effort. Charles and Anne Lindbergh took off from New York and headed for New Mexico to lead the search.[73]

Rain delayed the efforts for several days, but on September 7 an eastbound WAE flight spotted wreckage on the south slope of Mount Taylor, an 11,300-foot mountain located 50 miles west of Albuquerque. The pilot flew over the area and identified the plane by the registration number on its smashed wing. After landing at Albuquerque, the WAE pilot reported his findings before guiding three other planes back to the crash site. [74]

Hampered by difficult terrain and wet conditions, searchers finally reached the aircraft. They found a debris field stretching 250 yards through thick forest. The Ford's rugged metal structure had been shredded by trees and a post-impact fire. Passengers' remains removed from the crushed cabin were identified based on jewelry and dental records. Crew and passenger wristwatches read 11:01 a.m., about 40 minutes after the plane's departure time. [75]

The crash site was near the Albuquerque-to-Winslow route, so the plane was not badly off course or lost. The debris field was oriented northwest, and its 250-yard length indicated that the pilot did not lose control but rather flew into the mountain without seeing it.

The Mount Taylor crash was one of the first significant air carrier accidents in the United States. Although the Aeronautics Branch of the Department of Commerce regulated aviation activity, a formal accident investigative body and procedures had not yet been established. The government sent an investigator to New Mexico, but Assistant Secretary of Commerce for Aeronautics William P. MacCracken announced that no report on the investigative findings would be made "in accordance with the Department's policy." This did not sit well with Congress, where New Mexico senator Sam Bratton announced that he would request a Senate investigation. Bratton pointed out that the statute creating the Bureau of Air Commerce expressly provided for public disclosure, and the Senate adopted a resolution calling on Secretary of Commerce Robert P. Lamont to furnish a statement of the cause. In response, Lamont stated, "It is obvious that the airplane encountered a severe thunderstorm in the vicinity of Mount Taylor, during which it collided with the slope of the mountain."

The statement added that the department would not attempt to determine legal responsibilities, nor would it investigate accidents for the purpose of finding remedial measures for future operations.[76] The whole tenor of the proceeding was cavalier and dismissive despite the loss of life, the high profile of TAT, and the importance of determining what happened as fully and accurately as possible.

The question remains how and why the crash happened. It's likely that the pilot was surprised by the suddenly developing storms, and he inadvertently entered the clouds. In that case it would have been prudent to reverse course, fly back into the clear, and return to Albuquerque or land at one of TAT's emergency fields. Why the pilot failed to do this is unknown, but the fact that the inaugural westbound flight penetrated a fog bank suggests that TAT's pilots were willing to try flying blind, without instruments or navigational aids. After the accident TAT shifted the Albuquerque-to-Winslow route to the south, away from Mount Taylor.[77] Still, weather would continue to bedevil early airline operations until reliable and effective blind-flying instruments and radio navigational aids became standard.

TAT's Struggles

An accident a few months later at Indianapolis resulted in the death of a Philadelphia businessman, whose widow filed a wrongful death suit seeking the then-unheard-of sum of $150,000.[78] The adverse publicity from crashes affected bookings and revenue, but TAT spared no effort or expense to promote the safety, reliability, and luxury of its service. TAT added a new amenity in October 1929, when in-flight motion pictures were shown for the first time. Passengers watched the week's newsreel and cartoons on the westbound segment between Columbus and Waynoka, but no amenities could overcome the fact that the Fords were slow, noisy, and far from comfortable.[79] The stock market crash of October 1929 and the uncertainty that followed was a further blow to TAT's fortunes.

In an attempt to recover from these setbacks, in November 1929, TAT merged with Maddux Air Lines, with which it had previously partnered to extend its transcontinental service north from Los Angeles to San Francisco. Jack Maddux took over as president of the merged airline, now known as TAT-Maddux.[80] But TAT was never profitable and, despite the Maddux merger, sustained increasing losses. The airline slashed fares to $160 in January 1930, which increased traffic by 450 percent. To accommodate the additional demand, the airline bought four 18-passenger Curtiss Condors, putting them into service between Columbus and Waynoka. The fabric-covered biplane with external bracing wires was a step backward from the all-metal Fords, and its flying characteristics were unpleasant for passengers. TAT's losses continued to mount.[81]

Looking back in 1952, TWA president Ralph Damon said, "TAT was long on prestige, short on profits, and at the end of 18 months, the operation showed a loss of $2,750,000. It was sad proof that an airline could not survive at that time without the government financial aid of an airmail contract, and that average John Q. Public had not learned the advantages of air travel."[82] Of course, TAT's service was not aimed at John Q. Public but at an affluent elite willing to pay for a high level of luxury.

Even after merging with Maddux, TAT faced effective competition in the west from WAE, which had an extensive network of mail and passenger service from Los Angeles north to Seattle and east to Kansas City. Through arrangements with another airline and railroads, WAE could even offer transcontinental service—albeit somewhat inconvenient and cobbled together. But with the onset of the Great Depression, both WAE and TWA needed airmail contracts to provide reliable cash flow and support their unprofitable passenger services—a need that would drive them, reluctantly, into each other's arms.

Chapter 2
"THE LINDBERGH LINE": 1930–1939

Newly inaugurated president Herbert Hoover appointed Ohio attorney Walter Folger Brown postmaster general in 1929. At the time it was a position of considerable power and influence, and Brown, an experienced Republican politician, intended to use it to strengthen and promote the fledgling American air transport industry. He sought to establish efficient and financially sound transcontinental routes through airmail contracts.[1] The route structure he created lasted for decades, but his controversial methods shook the young industry to its core.

Walter Folger Brown and the Spoils Conferences

Brown formed a plan for a national system based on three transcontinental airmail routes. Rather than renew the original mail contracts awarded in 1925 under the Kelly Act, he extended them temporarily for six months in November 1929, allowing him to gain control over the industry as he plotted his course.[2] Next, Brown successfully lobbied Congress to amend the Kelly Act; this gave him broad discretion to extend existing contracts, award new ones, and consolidate routes "when in his judgment the public interest will be served thereby."[3]

Now armed with far-ranging power, Brown convened a series of meetings with air carriers in his Washington office, which the press would later dub the "Spoils Conferences." He laid out his goal to establish two new transcontinental airmail routes in addition to the former US Post Office route between New York and San Francisco: a central route from New York to Los Angeles via St. Louis and Pittsburgh, and a southern route from Atlanta to Los Angeles via Dallas.[4]

The industry was already consolidating. United Aircraft Corporation succeeded in wresting control of National Air Transport away from Clement Keys in early 1930, thereby giving it control of the former Post Office route and paving the way for coast-to-coast airmail and passenger service by a single carrier. Keys approached Hanshue about a possible merger between

WAE and TAT. Hanshue responded warily, suggesting that the companies join forces to provide transcontinental service, with each company supplying equipment but operating independently. Touting WAE's regional experience and expertise, his real interest was maintaining its independence. "If we permit ourselves to become absorbed in a national system," he wrote to Keys, "we ultimately would lose our identity and control and our local interest." But that was fine by Keys, and he made sure that the postmaster general was aware of Hanshue's rebuff.[5]

The Shotgun Marriage

Brown wanted each transcontinental route to be operated by a single carrier rather than by groups of companies with connections, so he suggested that carrier executives meet and find a solution. When they were unable to agree, Brown flexed his statutory muscle to force outcomes. He awarded the southern route to American Airways, and he pressed Hanshue to merge WAE with TAT and receive the central route. Hanshue resisted, but Brown was adamant and responded by suggesting a three-party merger among TAT, WAE, and Pittsburgh Aviation Industries Corporation (PAIC).[6]

PAIC had been formed by a group of Pittsburgh businessmen who were concerned that their community had been left out of both the US Post Office's transcontinental airmail route and TAT's air-rail service. PAIC investors included members of the wealthy and influential Mellon family who financed the effort out of their own pockets as a civic duty. They incorporated PAIC in November 1929 and elected Richard H. Robbins, a Harvard classmate of Hanshue, as president. PAIC began flying between New York and Pittsburgh via Philadelphia the following month with two single-engine biplanes. This service scarcely qualified it as an airline, but it did allow PAIC to claim "pioneer rights" to the route—a claim given more heft by the Mellons' political connections and clout.[7]

As TAT had never operated east of Columbus and WAE had not operated east of Kansas City, there was an element of reason to Brown's demand that the three should combine into a single transcontinental carrier. Hanshue had little leverage. His directors could read the handwriting on the wall, and he was unable to sway them. Eventually all three companies agreed to Brown's proposal, and a merger agreement—which was soon known as the "shotgun marriage"—was signed on July 15, 1930.[8] On October 1, Postmaster Brown delivered the wedding present by awarding the new airline CAM 34, the central transcontinental airmail route between New York and Los Angeles.

Brown completed his plan when he awarded the southern transcontinental route to a joint venture between American Airways and

Southwest Air Fast Express. He gave the lucrative routes between New York and Florida to Eastern Air Transport, thus single-handedly creating the "Big Four" US airlines—United, TWA, American, and Eastern—that would dominate the nation's air carrier industry for the next 50 years. But Brown's forceful methods would have major consequences.

The Birth of TWA

A new corporation—Transcontinental and Western Air Inc.—was formed on July 24, 1930. TAT and WAE each held 47.5 percent of its stock (and contributed their equipment and other assets) while PAIC held 5 percent. The new airline, known from its inception as TWA, acquired most of WAE's fleet and 500 of its employees, including Jack Frye and Paul Richter. It also acquired TAT's Ford trimotors, employees, and infrastructure.[9] Hanshue reluctantly agreed to become TWA's first president after the merger. However, he also continued to operate the original WAE route between Los Angeles and Salt Lake City, which had not been included in the merger, and WAE— rather than TWA—remained the focus of his interest. This conflict hampered TWA's early operations and rankled its board of directors.

TWA convened its first board meeting in New York on October 2, 1930. The directors elected Hanshue president, Maddux vice president, and Keys chairman. The board also formed an executive committee chaired by Daniel M. Shaeffer. After addressing the mechanics of transferring the business and properties of TAT and WAE to TWA, the board appointed Frye vice president of operations with Tomlinson as his assistant. The board designated Lindbergh chairman of the technical committee, a continuation of the position he had held at TAT, with an annual salary of $10,000 (about $182,000 in 2023), plus 25,000 shares of TWA stock.[10] TWA also adopted "The Lindbergh Line" tagline, invoking Lindbergh's credibility and prestige—important assets during a period when air travel was neither overly reliable nor safe.

Upon its formation, TWA divided itself into an eastern division, between New York and Kansas City, and a western division, from Kansas City to San Francisco. Frye assumed responsibility for the New York–Columbus segment of the eastern division, and Richter became the superintendent of the western division.

TWA inaugurated all-air, coast-to-coast passenger service on October 25, 1930. The westbound flight departed from New Jersey's Newark Airport at 6 a.m. and traveled west via Philadelphia, Harrisburg, Pittsburgh, and Columbus. From Columbus it followed the former TAT route onward to Kansas City, where it stopped for the night. Passengers reboarded the next morning for Wichita, Amarillo, Albuquerque, Winslow, Kingman, and finally

Los Angeles. Eliminating the costly and burdensome rail connections cut the total coast-to-coast time from 48 to 36 hours, still including the overnight stop in Kansas City. On TWA's first day of operation, it carried 94 passengers and 3,289 pounds of mail.[11] The railroads probably didn't yet feel threatened by the development, for crossing the continent in a Ford trimotor was an arduous experience.

Although Hanshue was the company's president, he had little interest in the job or in TWA. In January 1931 director and executive committee member J. C. Cowdin wrote a scathing letter to Keys, Hanshue, and Shaeffer detailing the shortcomings of the airline's management. He found the operating costs "all out of proportion or necessity to our probable revenue," and in a shot at Hanshue, insisted that the principal salaried officers should "disassociate themselves from the activities of any other companies of similar nature and devote their entire time, thoughts and energies to the welfare of this company." He also objected to the sharing of TWA assets and resources with WAE, which was charging TWA to use its facilities in Los Angeles.[12]

The criticisms were well founded. General Motors, a major investor, became concerned about TWA's management and elected Ernest R. Breech as director to serve as its eyes and ears. Breech had risen from chief accountant for Yellow Truck & Coach Manufacturing Company to the General Motors executive suite. He advised GM that "Hanshue is really not operating as a president" and that some of the directors were meddling in the affairs of the company. "We're going to have to get hold of this thing or it's going to go broke," Breech said. "It has no top-management direction." He recommended a smaller board with an executive committee that had no conflicts of interest, and that Hanshue be sent back to California "to run Western Air Express, which is what he wants to do." Hanshue did so, resigning in July 1931 after a bout of pneumonia. TWA's directors elected Richard Robbins of PAIC as his successor.[13]

After an aggressive lobbying campaign by the Kansas City Chamber of Commerce, the city was chosen as TWA's central base for operations, overhaul, and maintenance. Located squarely in the middle of the country, Kansas City was almost equidistant from New York and Los Angeles on TWA's transcontinental route. A press release announcing the move noted that the city was "within 12 hours' flying time of any point on the company's system."[14] TWA constructed a new two-story art deco headquarters and maintenance facility at the municipal airport, close to the downtown business district. TWA would remain closely associated with Kansas City for the rest of its life.

The Rockne Crash

On the morning of March 31, 1931, TWA Flight 5, flown by one of the Fokker F-10 trimotors TWA had inherited from WAE, departed Kansas

City for Wichita and points west in stormy, threatening weather. One of its six passengers was beloved Notre Dame football coach Knute Rockne, who was on his way to Hollywood to serve as a consultant on an upcoming film. Weather had already delayed the departure by an hour, but a report showed it would clear. The pilot, Robert Fry, took off and headed southwest.[15]

As Flight 5 approached Wichita, the TWA radio operator called in. The copilot, Jesse Mathias, his voice distorted by static, replied that he could not talk because he was "too busy." When Wichita queried the crew's intentions, Mathias answered, "I don't know." There were no further communications with the flight. Witnesses on the ground saw the Fokker emerge from the clouds and its right wing suddenly fail. The plane nosed over and dove into the ground, killing everyone on board. Eyewitnesses claimed they saw bodies fall out of the plummeting aircraft.[16]

Rockne's death caused a great public outcry, and the Aeronautics Branch of the Department of Commerce launched a more thorough accident investigation than the casual effort that followed TAT's Mount Taylor crash. But statements released to the public were contradictory, based on incomplete and inaccurate information. It was first believed that the pilot had overstressed the airplane in turbulence. The focus then shifted to icing, but no evidence supported that theory.[17]

Even before the accident the Aeronautics Branch had received reports that the Fokkers' wooden wing spars were breaking down and separating from their plywood surface midflight. Eventually the investigation determined that the crash was caused by structural failure resulting from moisture that deteriorated the plane's wing glue. Five weeks after the accident the government grounded all Fokkers built before 1930 and imposed a rigorous inspection process that effectively required dismantling and rebuilding their wings—a remedy that was economically impracticable. The accident shattered public confidence in wooden aircraft structure and abruptly ended the Fokkers' airline service. TWA stripped theirs of engines and other useful equipment before burning the aircraft in a field near the Kansas City maintenance base.[18]

TWA fell back on its sturdy all-metal Fords, but the negative publicity that came from the death of the legendary coach did nothing to assuage the public's fear of flying. TWA also acquired several single-engine Lockheed Vegas and Orions, plus Consolidated Fleetsters. Although faster than the lumbering Fords, they could carry no more than six passengers over short routes in cramped conditions. TWA also bought a small fleet of Northrop Alpha mail planes that could carry a few passengers, but TWA never used them for that purpose. And it acquired three powerful, high-performance Northrop Gamma mail planes later used for high-altitude research.

A Fokker F-10 trimotor leaves New York on TWA's inaugural westbound flight, October 25, 1930. Knute Rockne's 1931 death in a Fokker trimotor ended the wooden-winged airliners' passenger carrying service in the United States. From J. E. Frankum, Legacy of Leadership, *1971.*

But these single-engine planes compiled a miserable safety record: Of the 14 Alphas TWA owned, 9 were written off in crashes. Two of its three Orions were lost to crashes within six months, and one of the three Gammas was lost a few months after delivery.[19] Like other airlines, TWA badly needed safer and more capable multiengine planes.

In January 1932, Clement Keys resigned as a TWA officer and director in the aftermath of a massive misappropriation of funds from his investment firm. He sold his TWA stock to General Motors in an effort to make good on the losses, thereby increasing GM's control over TWA.[20] Following Keys's departure the directors elected Ernest Breech to replace him as chairman in June 1932.[21]

FLYING BLIND

Early pilots navigated by dead reckoning: following compass courses and headings, using time, distance, and wind to compute their location. They also followed landmarks such as roads, railroads, and rivers. Flying in clouds or fog not only risked getting lost, but also could easily cause disorientation and loss of control or collision with terrain, as happened at Mount Taylor.

To become viable businesses, airlines needed to fly in all weather—day and night—as did the military, which spurred development of new technology. Famed racing pilot and aeronautical engineer Jimmy Doolittle demonstrated the first totally "blind" flight by using new gyroscopic instruments in September 1929, and TWA began equipping its passenger and mail plane fleet with these tools a few years later.

While gyroscopic instruments allowed pilots to maintain control without seeing the ground or the horizon, there remained the problem of navigating from point A to point B in instrument weather conditions—that is, when there are clouds or other obstructions to visibility that make it difficult or impossible to navigate by visual reference. The lighted transcontinental airway created by the US Post Office was the first navigational aid for night flight. TWA lighted its own route from Los Angeles to Wichita, turning it over to the government in February 1932.[22] But lights could not penetrate clouds. Radio provided the answer in the form of a four-course, low-frequency radio range consisting of four transmitter towers: two transmitting *A* in Morse code (dit-dah) and two transmitting *N* (dah-dit). The interference of the radio signals created four narrow bands, or "beams," where the *A* and *N* signals merged into a steady tone, which were aligned on preset compass courses. The pilot flew the beam by listening and keeping the tone steady. The on-course tone changed subtly to an *A* or an *N* if the aircraft began to veer off course.

The radio range could also be used to land in instrument weather conditions. Upon reaching the destination, the plane flew an approach that led it over the cone of silence—the dead spot directly above a radio range station where nothing can be heard, which confirms that the aircraft has passed the station. Then the pilot followed a compass heading to the runway while descending at a fixed rate until the runway lights came into view. If the pilot did not see the lights when a prescribed minimum altitude was reached, he executed a missed approach, climbed back up, and tried again. If he still could not find the airport, the flight diverted to an alternate airport where the conditions were better.

Although primitive by today's standards, the low-frequency range was a giant step forward. It required no special on-board equipment other than a radio receiver, and it provided a veritable highway in the sky. With an effective range of about 150 miles, the stations made coast-to-coast instrument flight possible. They allowed the airlines to fly reliably and safely to their destinations in all weather and to land through clouds as low as 300 feet above the surface.

The government began installing low-frequency radio ranges in 1929, and by the end of the 1930s there was a nationwide network comprising more than 200 stations.[23] Together, gyroscopic flight instruments and the radio ranges enabled planes to fly safely in virtually all weather.

The other radio navigation aid was the radio beacon, a transmitting station that broadcast a continuous signal—the radio equivalent of a beacon of light. An airplane equipped with a directional "loop" antenna could determine the relative direction of the radio beacon from the plane, and the pilot could point the aircraft toward the beacon and fly to it. Radio beacons did not need the extensive infrastructure required by the radio ranges, and loop-equipped planes could even use commercial broadcast stations for navigation (which also allowed pilots to enjoy entertainment in flight).

New Planes for New Times

Thanks to the development of instruments and radio navigation aids, TWA was able to eliminate the overnight stop at Kansas City on its transcontinental schedule in 1932.[24] The westbound flight from New York now took 28 hours, and flying eastbound from Los Angeles took 24 hours. The schedule proudly proclaimed it the "new fastest coast-to-coast service."[25] But traveling a full day on a Ford or Fokker trimotor remained a grueling ordeal. Even though airlines now had the ability to fly in all weather, they still needed faster, safer, more comfortable planes to carry their passengers.

In 1931 the Boeing Airplane Company produced for the US Army the B-9: an all-metal twin-engine bomber with retractable landing gear. The cash-strapped Air Corps bought only two of them, but Boeing used the B-9 design to create the Model 247, the first modern commercial airliner, in 1932. United Air Lines, a subsidiary of United Aircraft and Boeing's corporate sister, immediately ordered 60 of the 247s, effectively monopolizing production and putting other airlines at a disadvantage.[26]

In April 1932, TWA's president Richard Robbins briefed the executive committee on the airline's need for modern passenger planes. He pointed out that the Fords were three years old and had already exceeded their original estimated service life. Plus, the Fokkers were being removed from service in the wake of the Rockne crash. With Boeing production committed to United, he estimated it would take 18 months to design, build, and test a suitable new aircraft, and another 6 months to produce the fleet of 15 that TWA needed to fly its transcontinental schedule.[27]

To this end Robbins formed an advisory committee led by Lindbergh, Frye, and Tomlinson to study TWA's needs and draw up specifications for a new passenger liner. On August 2, 1932, Frye wrote to five manufacturers requesting proposals for "ten or more" all-metal, 12-passenger trimotor aircraft "with comfortable seats and ample room" and a range of 1,000 miles at 150 mph. Because of the high surface elevations of TWA's Arizona and New Mexico stations, the proposal stipulated that "This plane, fully loaded, must make satisfactory take-offs, under good control at any TWA airport on any combination of two engines." [28] It was destined to become one of the most famous documents in aviation history.

Donald Douglas, president of Douglas Aircraft Corporation in Santa Monica, California, agreed to meet with TWA in New York to present a proposal for a larger, faster, more capable twin-engine plane known as the DC-1—Douglas's first commercial design.[29] For the next three weeks the TWA and Douglas teams negotiated, hammering out detailed specifications for the new airliner. In addition to carrying 12 passengers—two more than the Boeing 247—the DC-1 also had a taller fuselage profile so that adults could walk upright through the length of the cabin. Douglas promised it would be 15 to 20 mph faster than the Boeing, cruising at nearly twice the speed of the lumbering Fords it would replace.[30]

Lindbergh insisted that the new plane must be able to take off from the highest airports on TWA's route even if it lost power on one engine—an entirely reasonable requirement, but more demanding for a twin-engine than a trimotor aircraft. Lead engineer Arthur Raymond was confident the requirement could be met, and Donald Douglas authorized the team to proceed.[31]

After meeting with the Douglas team in New York, the TWA technical committee presented its analysis and conclusions to the executive committee on September 20, 1932. The technical committee recommended contracting with both Douglas for the DC-1 and General Aircraft Manufacturing for the

GA-38 trimotor. General Aircraft Manufacturing was controlled by General Motors, which also owned a substantial interest in TWA. (GM was later required to divest its TWA stock as a result of the 1934 reforms that separated ownership of the airlines and aircraft manufacturers. It also required Boeing and United to sever their relationship.) That both projects were allowed to proceed suggests TWA was not convinced that a twin-engine aircraft could satisfy the engine-out takeoff requirement, and it wanted a trimotor fallback in case the Douglas came up short.

Arthur Raymond of Douglas returned from New York on TWA, stopping off in Kansas City for a few days to discuss final revisions to the specifications. He then boarded another TWA Ford for Los Angeles. Flying coast to coast on a Ford trimotor was an experience he would never forget—and it crystallized what the new design would need to make air travel viable. "The thing vibrated so much it shook the eyeglasses right off your nose," he recalled. "In order to talk with the guy across the aisle, you had to shout at the top of your lungs. The higher we went to get over the mountains, the colder it got inside the cabin. My feet nearly froze. The lavatory was so small that you could barely squeeze through the door. The leather-upholstered, wicker-back chairs were about as comfortable as lawn furniture." Back at Santa Monica he told Douglas, "We've got to build comfort and put wings on it. Our big problem is far more than just building a satisfactory performing transport airplane."[32]

Douglas engineers and draftsmen began working on plans and blueprints even before they returned from New York. Scale models were tested in the new California Institute of Technology wind tunnel. Different wing, stabilizer, and tail configurations were tested to determine the optimum aerodynamic design for the airplane. A full-scale fuselage mockup was constructed to create the cockpit and interior designs. A cutaway drawing of the Boeing 247 was posted in the engineering office with the direction, "Don't copy it! Do it better!"[33]

On June 22, 1933, the DC-1 emerged from the Douglas factory. Measuring 60 feet long with an 85-foot wingspan, at that time it was the largest twin-engine aircraft ever built in the United States. Nine days later it made its first flight. With all 800 Douglas employees watching, chief Douglas test pilot Carl Cover took off shortly after noon. Almost immediately, one engine—then both of them—sputtered and failed. Disaster seemed imminent, but Cover managed to coax enough power from the engines to circle back for a safe landing. It turned out the carburetors were improperly mounted, which interrupted fuel flow to the engines. The fault was corrected, and the test program proceeded.[34] Flight tests soon demonstrated its superiority over the Boeing 247—as well as all other airliners then in service.

Created in response to a request from TWA, Douglas designed and built a single copy of the DC-1, depicted here in 1933. Douglas later modified the design and renamed it the DC-2. From J. E. Frankum, Legacy of Leadership, *1971.*

To comply with Lindbergh's single-engine requirement, on September 11, 1933, the DC-1 took off from Winslow, Arizona—TWA's highest airport—and one engine was immediately shut down. The plane continued climbing, and after reaching 8,000 feet, it flew 240 miles to Albuquerque on one engine. The single-engine demand now satisfied, Douglas handed the DC-1 over to TWA two days later.[35] Cruising at 180 mph, it was nearly twice as fast as TWA's Fords, and it was quieter and far more comfortable for passengers.

Undoing the Spoils, Canceling the Contracts

While the DC-1 was being tested a political storm was brewing in the nation's capital. The small airlines left out of the 1930 Spoils Conferences were frustrated by Brown's favored treatment of the largest and best-financed carriers, but their complaints had gained little traction during the Hoover administration. After Franklin D. Roosevelt was inaugurated in March 1933, with a new Congress that was firmly under Democratic control, politicians became more sympathetic to the claims of those shunned by Brown. The airline structure created by the former postmaster general would soon become the subject of controversy and scandal.

In September 1933 the Senate created a special committee chaired by populist Alabama senator (and future Supreme Court justice) Hugo Black to investigate airmail and shipping contracts, which soon became a forum for the grievances of the disfavored airmail claimants. Airlines were subpoenaed for all records relating to their airmail contracts. TWA's Washington, DC, counsel, William P. MacCracken, advised that the subpoena's broad scope include attorney-client privileged materials, which he refused to provide. MacCracken had previously served as Walter Brown's deputy during the

Spoils Conferences, adding fuel to the allegations of conflict and impropriety. However, the TWA directors voted to waive the privilege and directed MacCracken to produce everything requested.[36] Black's committee eventually assigned blame to all parties involved in the Spoils Conferences: It blamed Congress for giving the former postmaster general Brown so much power, Brown for misusing that power, and the airlines for participating in and profiting from it. It also recommended competitive bidding for airmail contracts and reducing or eliminating subsidies.[37]

The committee's revelations led to an investigation by the Interstate Commerce Commission and the US Post Office. On February 4, 1934, Attorney General Homer Cummings delivered a report to Roosevelt concluding that the airmail contracts awarded by Brown were "highly irregular and interfered with the freedom of competition contemplated by the statutes." Acting on orders from the president, Postmaster General James Farley canceled all existing airmail contracts on February 9. Roosevelt, reassured by the secretary of war that the military could take over, ordered the Army Air Corps to fly the mail starting on February 19.[38] It was a precipitous action that would have tragic consequences.

TWA's directors convened a special Sunday meeting on February 18 to consider the airline's situation now that all airmail contracts had been canceled by the US Post Office Department. TWA president Richard Robbins recommended that the airline limit its flying schedule "until the plans of the Administration in Washington become more concrete." The board directed TWA management to "arrange for a meeting with the President of the United States for the purpose of explaining TWA's position in the matter and submitting to the President a prepared statement for his further consideration of the facts involved." [39] But there is no record that such a meeting occurred or that this direction was ever acted upon.

The board also authorized Robbins to "reduce the personnel either by furloughing them or laying them off indefinitely."[40] Robbins responded by issuing a notice stating, "Effective February 28th, 1934, the entire personnel of T. & W. A. is furloughed," even though TWA was still free to operate passenger service.[41] It reflected the airline's continuing dependence on airmail revenue and may have been a bid to get the Roosevelt administration's attention by putting employees out of work during the depths of the Depression.

Jack Frye saw an opportunity to capture public attention and turn it in TWA's favor. He recruited World War I ace Eddie Rickenbacker—the vice president of Eastern Air Lines, who was skilled at attracting press coverage—to serve as his copilot on a symbolic final transcontinental mail flight to demonstrate the airlines' capabilities. Even before Frye and Rickenbacker departed from Los Angeles, three Army pilots had died while attempting to reach their assigned airmail stations. Rickenbacker angrily proclaimed it "legalized murder." The quote made headlines nationwide and ensured their flight would attract maximum publicity.[42]

At 10 p.m. on February 18, Frye and Rickenbacker took off from Los Angeles in the DC-1 with TWA's last load of eastbound airmail. Racing against a major winter storm and stopping only twice, they landed at Newark 13 hours later, having set a new transcontinental speed record.[43] Their gesture defiantly proved the capabilities of the US airline industry, which would soon starkly contrast with the Army's.

The Army Air Corps was utterly unprepared and unequipped for the mission thrust upon it. It had only 200 officers and 400 enlisted men to fly 27,000 miles of airmail routes—a task that took 7,000 airline personnel to fill. Accustomed to flying mainly in daylight and good weather, Army pilots lacked the training and experience needed for such intensive operations, and they were unfamiliar with the routes they were now called upon to fly. Most of the Army's planes were single-engine fighters and observation planes with limited instrumentation, range, and payload capacity. Only modern, multiengine aircraft were capable of flying safely at night and in bad weather. To make matters worse, the winter conditions during February and March 1934 were particularly severe.

Deaths increased dramatically during this new mission: In just a little over a month, 12 Army pilots died in 66 crashes. Amid mounting public outcry, on March 10, Roosevelt ordered the Army to stand down, pending adoption of more effective safety measures. For nine days the country had no airmail service.[44] After operations resumed the Army's safety record improved, but it was still wholly unprepared for the task.

THE ARMY FLIES THE MAIL

The Army lost eight planes in its first week of mail service. Five pilots died, and six were critically injured. Ira Eaker, who would later command the 8th Air Force strategic bombing campaign against Germany in World War II, was a captain at the time. He was assigned to fly the mail route between Los Angeles and Salt Lake City in a single-engine, open-cockpit biplane capable of carrying only 50 pounds of mail. The Army soon made a twin-engine B-1 bomber available to him, but as the only pilot in his squadron qualified on the large plane, he had to fly it every day for a week.[45]

Robert L. Scott also flew the mail in 1934 and described the experience in his wartime bestseller, *God Is My Co-Pilot.* Having received little military training or experience with night and instrument conditions, he sought instruction from airline pilots. One night after flying from Chicago to Cleveland, Scott learned that the pilot who was scheduled to take the mail on to Newark was sick, so he volunteered to do it. He took off heading east into deteriorating weather. Following advice from airline pilots, he climbed to get above the weather, finally emerging from the clouds at 18,000 feet into a clear sky filled with stars. Then his radio failed, and he had no way to determine his location. As the sun was rising, he chanced a descent through the clouds on instruments and managed to find the Scranton, Pennsylvania, airport. After landing to refuel he continued on to Newark.[46] Scott was later assigned to fly a Martin B-10, a new twin-engine bomber with retractable landing gear. It was much larger and more complex than the single-engine open-cockpit fighters he was used to, but Scott received no instructions on how to fly it.[47]

Postmaster General Farley, who had opposed canceling the airmail contracts, now acted to extricate FDR and the country from its consequences. On April 20, 1934, he convened a meeting of the air carriers to bid on temporary mail contracts, pending enactment of new airmail legislation by Congress. Although airlines that had participated in the Spoils Conferences and their executives were barred from bidding, Farley indicated that this could be avoided by forming new corporations with different leaders to apply for the new contracts. This meant Richard Robbins had to resign as TWA's president.

In his place the board elected 29-year-old Jack Frye, with an annual salary of $13,500 (about $307,000 in 2023), as TWA's president and Paul Richter as vice president of operations to succeed Frye in that position.[48] It capped a banner year for Frye, one in which he had also set two transcontinental speed records. Frye and Richter would remain in their posts for the next 13 years.

In the aftermath of the airmail debacle, Congress passed the Black-McKellar Airmail Act of 1934, which authorized the US Postal Service to award airmail contracts, gave the Interstate Commerce Commission the

Jack Frye was TWA's president from 1934 to 1947. A record-setting pilot and an innovative leader, he pushed TWA to the forefront of aviation technology. From J. E. Frankum, Legacy of Leadership, *1971.*

power to set airmail rates, and gave the Bureau of Air Commerce regulatory authority over the airways and air safety. It marked the beginning of federal regulation of the airline industry. But its most important reform was outlawing the holding company structures that had allowed common ownership and control of aircraft manufacturers and suppliers—and their airline customers.

The act's reforms ended General Motors' aviation empire and forced the disposition of its airline interests, including TWA. Ernest Breech persuaded John D. Hertz, who had owned the Yellow Cab Company and was a partner in the Lehman Brothers investment house, to acquire an 11 percent stake in the airline—enough to gain control. Hertz had little interest in aviation and was mainly devoted to cutting costs. But Frye and Richter were determined to keep TWA at the forefront of burgeoning aviation technology, and they were willing to make the needed investments to accomplish that goal. It put them on a collision course with Hertz that would shape the airline's future.[49]

The Arrival of the DC-2

After building a single copy of the DC-1, Douglas modified the design to carry 14 instead of 12 passengers and called it the DC-2. In May 1934 the first DC-2 emerged from the Douglas plant at Santa Monica and made its inaugural flight. TWA put it into service only one week after taking delivery.[51] A few months later TWA began transcontinental DC-2 operations. Its DC-2s quickly set several airline speed records, including a transcontinental flight in 13 hours; a flight from Los Angeles to Kansas City in 6 hours, 40 minutes; and a flight from Chicago to New York in 3 hours, 10 minutes. TWA could now claim service "which no other competitor can approach—the Shortest, the Fastest, the Finest. The Shortest Route Coast to Coast. The Fastest Service Coast to Coast and the Finest equipment ever built."[52]

To publicize the DC-2, TWA invited aviation writer Wayne Parrish to experience it for himself. Parrish swam in the Atlantic Ocean before boarding the westbound flight at Newark in the afternoon. He reported that the airliner was as smooth as a fast train and had comfortable reclining seats. Darkness settled in over Ohio, and Parrish rested through the night before seeing the sun rise again over northern Arizona. After arriving in Los Angeles, he bathed in the Pacific Ocean less than 24 hours after taking a dip in the Atlantic. Author George Reiss also compared a transcontinental DC-2 flight to the same trip by rail, noting that if he left New York on Sunday afternoon he would not arrive until Thursday—even on the fastest railroad schedule. By contrast, his TWA flight departed Newark on Sunday afternoon and arrived the following morning. His airfare was $162.50 (about $3,700 in 2023) versus $134.50 for the train. "For an extra $27 I have saved four days," he wrote.[53]

TWA proclaimed that "the Douglas luxury liner is the fastest multi-motor passenger plane in the world [and] can fly fully loaded on only one of its 710 horsepower Wright Cyclone engines." With memory of the Rockne crash still fresh in Americans' minds, acknowledging safety concerns was imperative. The public response exceeded TWA's expectations, and passenger volume soared.[55]

The arrival of TWA's DC-2s also set off a competitive battle for airplanes and passengers. American and Eastern soon followed TWA in ordering DC-2s, and United Air Lines now struggled to survive with its 10-passenger Boeing 247s that were outclassed in speed, comfort, and operating economy.

While the DC-2 was a great technological advance, it was tricky to land and handle on the ground. Its retractable landing gear and flaps were raised and lowered manually via a hydraulic pump, which took considerable strength and effort. The brakes were also operated manually by pulling on a handle extending from the instrument panel while using the rudder pedals for directional control. Cabin heat was supplied by a steam boiler unit behind the cockpit—an onerous duty that fell to the copilot.[56]

In addition to their cockpit responsibilities, TWA copilots now also assumed passenger service duties. TWA's president Robbins considered them crucial to winning over customers and instructed copilots to make passengers feel at home by anticipating their wants, telling them, "You are the host, and your passengers are your guests."[57] At least one passenger was impressed. "Your co-pilots, I think, do an excellent job," wrote Eastern Air Lines' director of public relations after an early transcontinental DC-2 flight. "They come out of their compartments at frequent intervals, speak a word to each passenger and, if the time is proper, serve their lunches or supply pillows all around. They seem to sense exactly what a passenger desires without imposing themselves."[58] But copilots hated the job, and it interfered with their cockpit activity. A better arrangement was needed.

Hostesses in the Sky

Setting records and establishing new performance standards in passenger comfort, the DC-2 was a great leap forward—and it necessitated a new kind of crew member. United had introduced women stewardesses on its flights in 1930, and American followed suit in 1933. But TWA held back, based at least in part on surveys purporting to show that 80 percent of its passengers preferred to be attended by copilots. The reality was emphatically to the contrary, however, as reflected by the favorable reactions of United and American passengers, and TWA could no longer ignore this competitive advantage.[59] In July 1935, TWA's board authorized women attendants on all flights at a monthly cost of $11,186.[60] Reportedly Frye—now TWA's president—disliked the term "stewardess," so he issued an order that the women on flights would be called "hostesses" because "they're serving our guests."[61] Like other airlines, TWA initially required that its hostesses be registered nurses, believing that they'd make disciplined, respected professionals who could reassure passengers in bad weather and assist when flights were delayed or canceled.[62]

TWA ran newspaper ads seeking hostesses in September 1935. Each hostess was required to be a registered nurse between 21 and 26 years old; be 5 feet to 5 feet, 4 inches tall; and weigh between 100 and 118 pounds. Of the 2,000 applicants, 30 were selected.[63] The first hostess class began in Kansas City on October 23, 1935. Trainees were not paid a salary but received $2.50 per diem for living expenses. Their instructor was LeRoy Rainey, a TWA copilot who made no effort to disguise his chauvinism and lack of enthusiasm for this role. One trainee recalled Rainey telling the class, "If you haven't found a man to keep you by the time you're 28, TWA won't want you, either."[64]

Along with ticketing and hostess duties, trainees studied flight theory, meteorology, and scenic points of interest along TWA routes, as well as how to operate the cantankerous DC-2 heating system. They learned the planes' layouts and where items were stored. Outside the cabin they learned how to make train reservations, transport passengers to the nearest station, buy their tickets, and get them to their destinations when flights were canceled. On top of that, the new hostesses were subject to constant critical appraisals of their conduct and appearance, which were often highly subjective and without criteria or guidance.[65]

Their uniform, selected by Frye, consisted of a soft gray flannel suit with a fitted jacket and a long-sleeve red silk blouse and a skirt that hit 11 to 12 inches below the knee. At all times hostesses wore an overseas-style hat bearing the company logo; the jacket was required only while passengers were boarding or deplaning.[66]

The first hostess class graduated on December 6, 1935. Regulations limited time in the air to 110 hours a month. They further stipulated the kind of makeup and nail polish hostesses could wear on the job and that they could not accept gratuities.[67] There was just one hostess per flight aboard TWA's DC-2s. An hour before the first daily departure she swung into action, checking the plane's interior for cleanliness and provisions. Back in the terminal the hostess coordinated with the passenger agent, checked the passenger count, and ensured enough meals were available. She then returned to the plane to welcome passengers aboard and help them fasten their seat belts. Once airborne, the hostess's responsibilities included assisting mothers traveling with infants and young children. Hostesses were admonished to be "pleasant and cheerful with your fellow employees and create an atmosphere of good nature and congeniality," but not to "succumb to the temptation of becoming too jovial with each other."[68] Even though hostesses took over cabin-attendant and customer-relations functions that copilots hated, they still had to tolerate demeaning jokes and pranks by the all-male cockpit crew.[69]

The first hostesses confronted many new challenges, chief among them safety-related responsibilities in an era when flying was still hazardous

Dressed in prewar, military-style uniforms, TWA's first hostess class posed for this photograph on December 6, 1935. From J. E. Frankum, Legacy of Leadership, *1971.*

and accidents were not uncommon. In April 1936 a DC-2 crashed into a mountainside near Uniontown, Pennsylvania, throwing hostess Nellie Granger out of the plane. After assisting injured passengers, she went to seek help. She walked 11 miles before reaching a farmhouse, where she called TWA's Pittsburgh office. She then led rescuers back to the crash site. In a front-page article about the incident, the *New York Times* reported, "The flying hostess may well expect a career of romance and adventure, for it is a fascinating life that goes along with hazards strikingly illustrated in the experience of Nellie Granger, plucky heroine of the recent crash of the big transport plane on a mountain near Uniontown, Pennsylvania." Five years later Granger had to evacuate another TWA plane that made a wheels-up landing.[70] Although accidents became less frequent over time, the skills and resourcefulness required of hostesses remained, even if largely unrecognized and underappreciated by the public.

Flying Faster and Higher

TWA became an industry leader in aviation technology during the 1930s. As TWA's chief technical expert, Tommy Tomlinson was a groundbreaker. Among many other feats, in April 1935 he took the DC-1 to a new transcontinental record time of 11 hours, 5 minutes, and a month later he set a speed record of 169 mph over a closed course, also in the DC-1.[71] Frye and Tomlinson successfully persuaded the TWA board to finance construction

As TWA's vice president of research from 1935 to 1941, D. W. "Tommy" Tomlinson, pictured here ca. 1936, spearheaded TWA's high-altitude research and flew many of the missions himself. From J. E. Frankum, Legacy of Leadership, *1971.*

and installation of an experimental precision instrument landing system (ILS) at the Kansas City airport and the installation of an ILS receiver in the DC-1 to test it.[72]

Beginning in early 1935, TWA sponsored experimental stratospheric flights by Wiley Post, the one-eyed Oklahoma pilot who flew the single-engine Lockheed Vega *Winnie Mae* around the world with a navigator in eight days in 1931. (He'd repeat the feat flying solo two years later.) Both flights had been dogged by bad weather that Post hadn't been able to climb above. These experiences awakened his interest in high-altitude flight, and he began preparing a serious investigation of its possibilities.[73]

Post planned to attempt long-distance flights in the stratosphere, at altitudes as high as 50,000 feet—far above any level believed attainable at the time. Doing so required a high-altitude pressure suit that didn't yet exist, so he worked with the B. F. Goodrich Company to develop and test several prototypes. With their heavy metal helmets and bulky design, they looked more like undersea divers' suits, but they provided a suitable oxygen supply and environment that allowed Post to fly at altitudes above 40,000 feet.

TWA arranged for Post to carry airmail on his stratospheric flights and had him sworn in as a TWA airmail pilot. On March 5, 1935, Post took off in

Tomlinson flew this Northrop Gamma, pictured in front of Lambert Airport in 1936, as part of his high-altitude research. David Ostrowski Collection, Greater St. Louis Air and Space Museum.

the *Winnie Mae* from Burbank, California, headed for New York. The *Winnie Mae* reached ground speeds above 300 mph, propelled by powerful high-altitude winds (later identified as the jet stream) that reached up to 150 mph. After running out of oxygen Post landed at Cleveland, having flown at an average ground speed of 279 mph.[74]

Post's pioneering high-altitude efforts were cut short when he was killed in an August 1935 crash in Alaska along with humorist Will Rogers. TWA then began its own high-altitude research. Tomlinson was appointed chief engineer in 1936 and led a department responsible for developing new planes, engines, and equipment, and for conducting ground and flight tests in support of that mission.[75]

Tomlinson flew in the DC-1 modified with superchargers in a series of long-distance flights at high altitudes, including a nonstop flight of 1,100 miles from Kansas City to New York, during which he skirted thunderstorms by flying above 35,000 feet. "It was concluded as a result of these tests that air transport operations involving continuous cruising above 20,000 feet could be safely carried out," Tomlinson reported. "Observed weather conditions support the conclusion that 90 to 95% of 'bad weather' is cleared when flying at 20,000 feet. Any severe conditions involving turbulence above this level may be avoided by flying around the storm center."[76]

Tomlinson also embarked on a series of high-altitude flights in a single-engine Northrop Gamma. One reached an altitude of 36,000 feet, and he reported being "in poor mental condition" owing to the limitations of the onboard oxygen supply. "With our present knowledge, 20,000 feet appears to be the top economical limit," Tomlinson concluded. "In fact, it looks as though revolutionary improvements in power plants and propulsive methods will have to come before the dream of passenger transports flying through the stratosphere can come true."[77] He was right. Not until the arrival of jet airliners more than 20 years later would commercial flights above 30,000 feet be feasible.

THE BIRTH OF AIR TRAFFIC CONTROL

The Air Commerce Act of 1926 put the secretary of commerce in charge of regulating air safety in the United States. Because the nascent airlines depended upon airmail contracts for economic viability, their business growth and development was largely controlled by the US Post Office. With increased passenger service and planes capable of flying in all weather conditions at speeds approaching 200 mph, a more comprehensive, integrated system was needed.

In 1929 the City of St. Louis hired Archie League, the country's first air traffic controller, to operate Lambert Airport's control tower. He used radio to communicate with planes in the air and on the ground. Other cities followed suit. Soon airlines began establishing their own radio networks to convey information to their planes, such as weather reports and estimated arrival times. But this arrangement relied upon telephones or telegraphs, which were awkward and inefficient. The airlines recognized the need for centralized communication, and together with the military they called for a system of uniform air traffic control and compliance.

As the Bureau of Air Commerce studied possible solutions, some airlines—including TWA, United, and American—entered into inter-airline agreements to enhance safety at airports and on heavily traveled air routes. The bureau's director, Eugene Vidal, hosted an aviation conference in November 1935 to discuss airway traffic control. From this came the recommendation that "flight control officers" be located at strategic points along the federal airways to prevent "traffic confusion which might result in collisions." They would "direct and coordinate the progress of all flights" to ensure their safe and orderly arrival at airports. In addition, flight control officers would be stationed at Chicago, Cleveland, Newark, Detroit, Pittsburgh, and Washington, DC. Airport control towers would continue to be responsible for air traffic control at their airports.[78]

In December 1935 the airlines pooled their resources to create the first Airway Traffic Control Station at Newark. Early controllers kept track of planes' positions by using maps and blackboards. They had no direct radio link with aircraft. Instead, they used telephones to contact airline dispatchers, airway radio operators, and airport traffic controllers, who in turn provided information to the controllers and relayed their instructions to pilots via their company radio networks. Controllers moved markers (known as "shrimp boats") representing aircraft across the map as flights progressed based on telephone contacts with airline dispatchers. Airport control towers kept the airway centers advised of operations at their terminals.[79]

Two additional centers later opened in Chicago and Cleveland. The Bureau of Air Commerce took over these facilities in July 1936. It was the origin of a nationwide federal network of air traffic control centers that quickly grew to include facilities at Detroit, Los Angeles, San Francisco, and Washington, DC. Earl Ward, an American Airlines employee who had played a key role in devising the system, became the first chief of airway traffic control for the Bureau of Air Commerce.[80]

The bureau also established federal civil airways between terminal airports. Each airway included the airspace within a 25-mile radius around airports on the route and 25 miles to each side of the line connecting the terminal airports. The air traffic control centers assumed responsibility for coordinating traffic on the airways.[81]

The Plane That Changed the World

The DC-2's heyday was short lived. American Airlines offered sleeper service on overnight flights, but the DC-2's fuselage was too narrow for berths, so American president C. R. Smith asked Donald Douglas for a bigger version. Although Douglas reportedly thought that sleeping on planes would prove "about as popular as silent movies," the company responded by creating the Douglas Sleeper Transport, known as the DST, and a non-sleeper version, the DC-3.[82] TWA was aware that Douglas was developing the new airliner, but Tomlinson recommended against purchasing it, believing the plane was overweight and underpowered and would have stability issues. TWA opted not to order DSTs or DC-3s in August 1935, a mistake that cost the airline early delivery positions and put it a year behind its competitors.[83]

A crowd of curious onlookers at the Kansas City airport in the mid-1930s surveil a busy ramp featuring a TWA DC-2 and a DC-3 "Skysleeper" bearing the words "The Lindbergh Line." Greater St. Louis Air and Space Museum.

The new plane flew for the first time on December 17, 1935, and American put the DC-3 into scheduled service between Chicago and New York only six months later. The 21-passenger DC-3 had 50 percent more capacity than the DC-2 with similar performance and operating costs, making it the first airliner capable of profitable passenger operation without an airmail subsidy. United, which had suffered great competitive disadvantage with its Boeing 247s, moved to recover by placing early orders for DC-3s and DSTs. TWA, which had led the way with the DC-2, now had to play catch-up, vying with Eastern and United for DC-3s as quickly as Douglas could build them.

TWA ordered 10 DC-3 "Skysleepers" and 8 DC-3s in 1936, but they weren't put into service until June 1937—a year after American, with whom it competed on the New York–Los Angeles transcontinental route. TWA's president Jack Frye had to persuade Douglas to substitute DC-3s for some DC-2s the airline already had on order.[84] TWA's Skysleepers were designated DC-3Bs, a version unique to the airline. They were equipped with eight seats that converted to double berths in the forward half of the cabin and seven reclining lounge chairs to the rear.[85] The berths were curtained off much like railway sleeper accommodations are today. They also had separate dressing rooms for men and women.

As part of a determined effort to make flying more appealing, TWA hired famed industrial designer Raymond Loewy to create interiors for the new planes that would also match the redesign of TWA's ground facilities, uniforms, and brochures.[86] "We feel confident that this fleet will set new standards of luxury and comfort in air travel," TWA's 1936 annual report predicted. TWA's westbound transcontinental Skysleeper Flight 7 departed Newark at 5:15 p.m. and arrived at Los Angeles at 7:25 a.m. the next morning, stopping at Chicago, Kansas City, and Albuquerque. Eastbound Flight 6 left Los Angeles at 4:30 p.m. and reached Newark at 10:40 a.m. with the same intermediate stops. The one-way transcontinental fare was $160 for a berth (about $3,500 in 2023) and $155 for a seat.[87]

Donald Douglas's dismissal of domestic airline sleeper service proved correct. The short flight segments between landings and takeoffs made in-flight sleeping difficult, and Skysleeper service never gained widespread popularity. TWA eliminated it from domestic flights with the coming of World War II, although it was retained for long overseas flights during the postwar period. TWA continued adding DC-3s to its fleet and eventually acquired more than 100, using them until they were replaced with modern equipment in the early 1950s.

The DC-3's combination of good performance and good economics made it the world's dominant airliner prior to the Second World War. By 1941, 80 percent of the airliners in US domestic scheduled service were DC-3s.[88] As war approached the military ordered modified DC-3s as Army C-47 and Navy R5D transports, which served in every wartime theatre with the United States and its allies. More than 10,000 were made before production ceased in 1945. The DC-3 transformed air travel into a viable business.

Airline Regulation

The rapid growth of airline service during the 1930s made it clear that a more comprehensive regulatory framework was needed. In response Congress passed the Civil Aeronautics Act of 1938, which created the

Walking across a rain-soaked apron in 1937, passengers board a TWA "Sky Club" DC-3. The DC-3 made carrying passengers profitable and changed the world. Greater St. Louis Air and Space Museum.

Civil Aeronautics Authority and made it responsible for the airlines' economic regulation, including airline fares and routes, as well as for air safety. The administrator of aviation carried out the safety policies of the Civil Aeronautics Authority, air traffic control, and the airways system. The Authority also assumed control over airline mergers and acquisitions, and it granted permanent certificates to the existing airlines.[90]

In 1940, Congress modified this arrangement by splitting the Authority into the Civil Aeronautics Administration (CAA) and the Civil Aeronautics Board (CAB). The CAB was given the dual tasks of economic regulation of the airline industry and accident investigation. Charged with developing "a confident, ambitious and expanding industry," it did just that for nearly 40 years.[91]

The CAB treated the airline industry as a public utility: The airlines could neither add new routes nor abandon existing ones without CAB approval, and the CAB rigidly controlled the fares they charged. The CAB sought to guarantee the airlines a 12 percent return on investment, kept fares relatively high, and discouraged discounting. Unable to compete on fares or routes, the airlines instead competed for customer satisfaction and loyalty. TWA became an industry leader in this effort.

During the 1930s the airlines relied heavily on business travelers, who made up three-fourths of their passengers.[92] But TWA also promoted leisure travel and emphasized the glamour of Hollywood. TWA sales personnel scoured the movie industry for business and kept tabs on passengers arriving by ocean liners in New York, Los Angeles, and San Francisco, seeking celebrities who might be persuaded to travel onward by air. But stars themselves could be problematic: There was actress Sonja Henie, who regularly complained about being charged for the hundreds of pounds of excess baggage she brought on board, and Columbia Pictures president Harry Cohn, who always insisted on a lower berth on TWA's Skysleeper. Headaches notwithstanding, TWA accommodated their demands because of the star power their patronage wielded. [93]

Despite the airlines' efforts to woo passengers, the general public remained skeptical about the safety of air travel. In May 1935 a TWA DC-2 crashed while attempting to land in heavy fog, killing 5 of the 13 on board, including New Mexico senator Bronson Cutting. A 1936 survey by *Fortune* showed that more than 75 percent of Americans would rather travel by train than by air, principally because of safety concerns. "It will be many a year," the magazine predicted, "before the airlines will be able to persuade a large part of the public aboard one of their passenger planes." Although air travel became more common throughout the decade, 400 to 700 million Americans used the railroads in the 1930s, while fewer than 1 million traveled by air. [94] The railroads were slow but familiar, while air travel retained an aura of uncertainty and danger.

TWA sought to change this attitude by stressing the new advances in comfort and technology. "Now these giant silvery birds that wing at 200 miles per hour carry up to 21 passengers in all the luxury of a smart club lounge," it proclaimed after the introduction of the DC-3. "Vibration is a thing of the past and, more wonders, these powerful planes have sleeping compartments— roomy berths with soft, downy mattresses—that enable the modern air passenger to sleep away the miles to the other side of the continent." TWA also touted the DC-3's 1,000 hp Wright Cyclone engines as "[the] nation's mightiest motors [that] speed you at 200 miles an hour." [95] (That was a bit of an exaggeration—the DC-3 actually cruised at 180 mph.)

The airline also emphasized safety. "Every 400 hours these great engines are changed. . . . Nothing is left to chance. Every nut, bolt and screw, as well as engines, instruments, propellers and the most minute details of the plane are subjected to expert examination." [96] But accidents continued to stoke fear. In March 1938, TWA Flight 8, eastbound from San Francisco, disappeared in a storm and came down in a remote, mountainous area. The snow-covered wreckage was not located until June. Although the cause was never definitively established, facts suggest that the pilot tried to turn back in the storm but became lost due to static interference with his radio reception, and the plane was brought down by icing conditions in the clouds. [97]

In September 1938 a devastating hurricane struck New England, crippling road and rail transportation—and bringing TWA and other airlines an unexpected opportunity to curry favorable attention. The airlines suddenly had more demand than they could supply. The air route between New York and Boston was swamped with travelers wanting to fly, and the airlines happily obliged. At TWA's Newark terminal, there were no reservations or ticketing. Passengers showed up, paid the fare, and were allowed to board the next available flight. For the first time large numbers of travelers discovered the speed and convenience of flying, and passenger demand stayed high—even after the crisis eased. [98] Its success demonstrated the public's appetite for cheap, convenient, frequent air service and foreshadowed the popular East Coast air shuttle service that would appear 30 years later.

Reaching New Heights

Jack Frye understood that there was much work to be done to improve both the safety and comfort of air travel. Tomlinson's pioneering high-altitude research flights showed that flying above 16,000 feet would clear most weather except thunderstorms, which could be avoided, and that above 20,000 feet, higher airspeeds were possible too. While airplanes could reach those altitudes, passengers could not. Flying above 10,000 feet required oxygen, and the airlines had no interest in making passengers wear oxygen masks. Carrying passengers higher into the sky would require a pressurized cabin with heating and air conditioning to cope with the temperature extremes.

TWA was particularly affected by these limitations. Its routes crossed high desert and mountainous terrain, so the airline's management was eager for the development of a high-altitude airliner.[99] In 1935, Boeing produced the Model 299, the prototype of the B-17 Flying Fortress—the first four-engine American bomber to enter production and the most famous American bomber of World War II. Boeing invited Tomlinson to fly one of the early B-17s, and he was impressed with its potential. Tomlinson discussed his findings with Frye and vice president of operations Paul Richter, who agreed that TWA should explore the possibility of a pressurized four-engine airliner based on the B-17. Frye contacted Boeing, which was interested in pursuing a new commercial development after falling short with the 247. Using the B-17's wing and tail, Boeing engineers designed a new fuselage to create the Model 307 Stratoliner: It was the world's first pressurized airliner, capable of flying at altitudes up to 20,000 feet comfortably and without the need for oxygen. Frye saw the Stratoliner as the means to the high-altitude air travel that TWA envisioned, and in January 1937 he signed a contract for six of the new planes, at a cost of nearly $2 million, to be delivered in 1938.[100] Pan American followed suit with an order for four Stratoliners for its South American routes.

TWA's Stratoliners could carry 33 passengers by day—with 16 berths and nine reclining chairs available at night—at a high level of luxury. TWA again engaged Raymond Loewy to design the interior and contracted with Chicago's Marshall Fields department store to provide the furnishings. Frye was optimistic that the four-engine Stratoliner could propel TWA to the forefront of the airline industry, and TWA touted the advantages the Stratoliners would deliver over the DC-3s flown by its competitors. But all was not well, for trouble was brewing over TWA's management. John Hertz became a director in October 1937, and at his insistence the board voted to cancel an order for two additional Stratoliners placed only a month before.[101] It was a harbinger of conflict.

TWA's finances were strained by its DC-2 and DC-3 purchases. It lost nearly $1 million in 1937 (equivalent to about $21 million in 2023).[102] Alarmed, Hertz directed progress payments on the Stratoliners to be withheld, leading Boeing to cancel the contract in June 1938.[103] The board ordered Frye to try to renegotiate the Stratoliner contract or sell some of the planes to American or United Air Lines, neither of which was feasible.[104]

The Stratoliner controversy roiled TWA for most of 1938. Matters came to a head in December, when Hertz ordered TWA to terminate the contract and file suit against Boeing, which promptly filed a counterclaim for nonpayment.[105] By early 1939, Frye and Richter were increasingly at odds with Hertz about TWA's direction and future. The dispute flared into the open at a board meeting, where Richter erupted after Hertz questioned his recommendation to install full feathering propellers on all TWA planes as a safety measure.[106] Knowing nothing about the subject and having no basis to challenge Richter's technical judgment, Hertz backed down. Nevertheless, the growing tension between the pilot-executives and the Hertz-dominated board threatened to tear the airline apart.

"The Lindbergh Line" No Longer

TAT and TWA both used the slogan "The Lindbergh Line," proudly trumpeting the role of the world's most famous and trusted flier as their chief technical consultant. "TWA routes, surveyed by Col. Charles A. Lindbergh, are model highways of the air," the airline proclaimed in 1937.[107] Throughout the decade Lindbergh devoted much time and energy to exploring international routes to the Far East, Europe, and Latin America for Pan American—then the sole American international carrier and later a bitter rival of TWA. He and his wife, Anne Morrow Lindbergh, pioneered a northern route to Asia in 1931. Anne's account of the trip in her book *North to the Orient* brought both the romance and the potential benefits of international air travel to the public eye. Then, in 1932, the Lindberghs were devastated by the kidnapping and murder of their child Charles Jr. and sickened by the press attention and sensationalized coverage of Bruno Hauptmann's murder trial. Charles Lindbergh resigned as TWA's technical director in January 1935, citing "personal matters [which] will make it impossible for me to maintain the close association with operation which I would want to maintain if I continued my present connection."[108] To escape the media and threats to their safety, he and Anne fled the United States for England in December 1935.

After settling there Lindbergh received an invitation from Hermann Göring, the chief of Nazi Germany's newly unveiled air force, the Luftwaffe, to visit and inspect its military air capabilities. The invitation was instigated by Major Truman Smith, the US military attaché in Berlin, who hoped that Göring's eagerness to show off Germany's new air arm and Lindbergh's prestige could yield valuable intelligence for America. Smith encouraged Lindbergh to accept. For their part, the Germans saw it as an opportunity to use Lindbergh for propaganda purposes.

Lindbergh flew to Berlin in July 1936 and spent a week visiting German factories and airfields, observing the latest in airplanes and technology. He was Göring's guest of honor at a formal luncheon in Berlin, where he attended the opening of the 1936 Olympics. He made a speech stressing the destructive power of military aviation and expressed the hope that "we do not destroy the very things we wish to protect," a sentiment that was well received back in the United States.[109] But Lindbergh also developed a budding admiration for Hitler's Germany. While acknowledging "many reservations," he wrote to Major Smith that "the condition of the country, and the appearance of the average person I saw, leaves with me the impression that Hitler must have far more character and vision than I thought."[110]

And Lindbergh went even further. "Europe, and the entire world, is fortunate that a Nazi Germany lies between Communistic Russia and a demoralized France," he said, adding that Germany was "especially anxious to maintain a friendly relationship with England" with no "intention of attacking France for many years, if at all," and had "a sincere desire for friendly relations with the United States."[111] In doing so he crossed the line from an objective observer to an unwitting accomplice of the Third Reich.

Lindbergh returned to Germany in 1937, where he again inspected factories and airfields—including the secret Luftwaffe test facility at Rechlin, where he was shown the new Messerschmitt 109, Germany's front-line fighter aircraft. He reported, "Germany is once more a world power in the air. Her air force and industry have emerged from the kindergarten stage." He also told his friend and colleague Dr. Alexis Carrel, "Hitler is apparently more popular than ever in Germany . . . he has done much for Germany."[112]

Anne and Charles Lindbergh traveled together to Germany in the fall of 1938, a tense time. They considered wintering in Berlin, and Anne spent her days house hunting while Charles made the rounds of the country's air industry and military airfields. While attending a function at the US embassy in October 1938, Göring unexpectedly presented Lindbergh with a medal commemorating his 1927 New York–to–Paris flight. Along with the medal was a proclamation signed by Adolf Hitler. Lindbergh gave it little thought— he had received dozens of medals since 1927—but Anne presciently called it "the Albatross."[113] Lindbergh stubbornly refused demands to return it. His blindness to the implications of his actions undermined the public admiration and respect he had enjoyed since his historic flight.

Lindbergh crossed paths with Tommy Tomlinson while in Berlin. As part of the German charm offensive, both were allowed to fly in Germany's newest four-engine airliners, the Focke-Wulf Fw 200 (which had recently made a record-setting flight from Berlin to New York) and the Junkers Ju 90.[114] The Nazi regime was so intent on impressing Lindbergh that it even allowed him to fly the Messerschmitt 109. After familiarizing himself with its flying characteristics, he wrung it out in aerobatic maneuvers and declared that the plane handled "beautifully."[115]

During Kristallnacht, on November 9, 1938, mobs burned synagogues and destroyed thousands of Jewish-owned shops and homes, just as the Lindberghs were searching for a house in Berlin. Dozens of German Jews were murdered, and thousands more were imprisoned. Kristallnacht opened the eyes of the outside world to the new realities of Nazi Germany and ended the Lindberghs' plans for staying there. Lindbergh was baffled by it. "I do not understand these riots on the part of the Germans," he confided in his journal. "It seems so contrary to their sense of order and their intelligence in other ways. They undoubtably have a difficult Jewish problem," he continued, "but why is it necessary to handle it so unreasonably? My admiration for the Germans is constantly being dashed against some rock such as this."[116] He expressed no concern or sympathy for the victims. These private sentiments showed a blindness to the vicious anti-Semitism of the Third Reich and to his apparent unawareness that he was lending it prestige and credibility.[117]

Lindbergh could have cleared the air by returning the medal and denouncing the Nazi regime. But, proud and self-righteous, he could not bring himself to do so. He had transformed himself into a lightning rod and a symbol of growing American division over the threat of Nazi Germany, an object of controversy and scorn. *The New Yorker* wrote sarcastically, "With confused emotions, we say goodbye to Colonel Charles A. Lindbergh, who wants to go and live in Berlin, presumably occupying a house that once belonged to Jews."

The decline in Lindbergh's standing was not lost on TWA. The airline began removing "The Lindbergh Line" slogan from its advertising and publicity in December 1938. Jack Frye asserted that it was merely "a routine change," but the *Kansas City Star* reported, "It is known that the reason for the dropping of the Lindbergh identity is mounting complaints against the heroic Atlantic flyer to live in Germany."[118] In 1939, TWA replaced "The Lindbergh Line" with "The Transcontinental Line" on its planes and removed a large portrait of the aviator from its offices. It was the end of TWA's relationship with Lindbergh, never to be revived.

Enter Howard Hughes

As TWA divorced itself from one famous aviator, it was about to become engaged to another. In 1938, Howard Hughes was at the peak of his success and popularity as a pilot, filmmaker, and celebrity. Hughes was almost as well known as Lindbergh and widely admired for his aviation accomplishments. Above all, he commanded vast personal wealth through his control of the Hughes Tool Company, which produced equipment essential to the booming oil industry.

Howard Robard Hughes Jr. was born on Christmas Day in 1905, in Houston, Texas. His father, Howard Sr., made a fortune by inventing an effective oil drilling bit in 1908, which quickly became the industry standard. Howard Sr. bought out his partners in 1912, before the gusher of wealth began, and became the sole owner of the future Hughes Tool Company. He died in 1923, two years after his wife, leaving 18-year-old Howard Jr. in control of Hughes Tool and its enormous wealth to be used however he pleased.

Hughes moved to Hollywood in 1925 to try his hand at moviemaking. His first two films had little impact, but in 1928 his third picture, *Two Arabian Knights*, won an Academy Award. Now established in the film industry—though by no means part of its establishment—Hughes turned his attention to making *Hell's Angels*, a World War I flying epic. He lavished all his financial resources, creativity, and obsessiveness on it, amassing an armada of World War I aircraft and replicas and an army of pilots to fly them.

Hughes's obsessive perfectionism compelled him to shoot scenes over and over. When the technology to make sound movies was perfected during the lengthy filming of *Hell's Angels,* Hughes proceeded to reshoot the entire film with sound and a new script—and he cast the just-discovered 18-year-old Jean Harlow as its leading lady, launching her on the road to stardom. Hughes's quest for spectacular aerial sequences resulted in several crashes and four deaths. When finally released in 1930, *Hell's Angels* was a sensation, but it failed to earn a profit because Hughes had spent nearly $4 million (about $73 million in 2023) making it—an astronomical amount by filmmaking standards of the day. But it also made Hughes the king of Hollywood.

The Aviator

Hughes began taking flying lessons during the production of *Hell's Angels*. After a stunt pilot refused to perform a flying scene he considered too dangerous, Hughes flew it himself—and crashed, sustaining serious injuries. Hughes was an intuitive and innovative engineer, and he formed the Hughes Aircraft Company as a division of Hughes Tool to create the world's fastest airplane. Its first product was the H-1 Racer. It was the most advanced high-performance aircraft anywhere when it appeared in 1935, faster than the contemporary German Messerschmitt 109 military fighter, which also debuted that year. On September 13, 1935, Hughes set a world absolute speed record of 352 mph in the Racer, besting the existing record by 40 mph.[119]

On January 19, 1937, he flew the Racer, now fitted with extended wings for long range, from Los Angeles to Newark. Reaching altitudes above 20,000 feet while breathing oxygen through a tube, he attained ground speeds as high as 370 mph before a malfunction in the oxygen system forced a descent. "This is a tricky ship to handle," he told reporters after landing. "You have to have a clear head to bring it down all in one piece." Its flight time of 7 hours, 28 minutes, at an average speed of 330 mph, set a record that stood for 10 years.[120]

Hughes was now ready to tackle his most ambitious aviation feat: circling the globe in record time. The existing mark of a little over seven days had been set in 1933 by Wiley Post. Hughes planned to break Post's record by a wide margin to demonstrate the advances in aviation and its modern capabilities. Tapping into his significant wealth, he spent two years preparing and spared no expense. He bought a new Lockheed 14—a fast, 14-passenger twin-engine airliner—fitted it with more powerful engines and extra fuel tanks, installed all the latest navigation and radio equipment, and equipped it with emergency gear and survival provisions in case of a remote forced landing. Hughes then recruited an experienced four-man crew—a copilot, navigator, radio operator, and flight engineer—to accompany him on the flight and make sure all went as smoothly as possible. He also hired a professional meteorologist to provide ground-based weather reports and forecasts.

As part of his publicity campaign, Hughes arranged with Grover Whalen, the head of the 1939 New York World's Fair, to name the plane *New York World's Fair 1939* and make the flight a goodwill gesture.[121] On July 10, 1938, Hughes took off from Brooklyn's Floyd Bennett Field and flew to Paris in 16 hours, 38 minutes—half of Lindbergh's 1927 flight time.[122]After refueling he flew to Moscow, then across desolate Siberia to Yakutsk; Fairbanks, Alaska; and Minneapolis, Minnesota. Hughes landed back at New York only three

Thanks to his record flight and Hollywood exploits, Howard Hughes's fame eclipsed Charles Lindbergh's by 1938. From J. E. Frankum, Legacy of Leadership, *1971.*

days and 19 hours after departing, having cut Post's time more than in half. (But he did modestly call Post's solo flight "the most remarkable flying job ever done."[124])

A month after the circumnavigation Hughes flew the Lockheed nonstop from Los Angeles to New York in 10.5 hours, at altitudes above 20,000 feet, to show the potential of high-altitude commercial flight. "Ultimately transport operations will be conducted at altitudes around 30,000 feet," he predicted, saying that passengers would receive oxygen "by direct injection into the cabin," without using masks, and that air travel would prove to be "not only the fastest but the safest and cheapest means of transportation."[125] Both forecasts would prove correct. Hughes was named the outstanding American aviator of 1938 by the National Aeronautic Association and received the prestigious Harmon Aeronaut Trophy for aviation achievement.[126]

Hughes Comes Aboard at TWA

By the end of 1938, Jack Frye was at loggerheads with Hertz and the Lehman Brothers. At this point Frye made a decision that would shape TWA's destiny for the next two decades. Frye knew Hughes as a fellow pilot and had invited him to fly one of TWA's first DC-2s in 1934. Paul Richter also knew Hughes, having served as a stunt pilot in *Hell's Angels*. Frye and Richter flew to Los Angeles, met with Hughes, and spelled out the impasse at TWA. Hughes expressed interest, requested a list of TWA shareholders, and began buying TWA stock. By May 1939, Hughes was TWA's largest stockholder, with nearly 100,000 shares, and he threatened Hertz and Lehman with a proxy fight and a possible hostile takeover. Never having had much enthusiasm for aviation, Hertz readily negotiated a buyout of his interest in the airline.[127]

On May 19, 1939, the board accepted the resignations of Hertz and seven other Hertz-aligned directors, then formed an executive committee to run the airline, which included Frye and Richter. Hughes never became an officer or director of TWA. Instead he installed Noah Dietrich, his right-hand man who managed Hughes Tool Company and kept the money flowing, on TWA's board and executive committee to look after Hughes's interests.[128] Negotiations with Boeing resumed, leading to a contract for five Model 307B Stratoliners in September 1939.[129] Two months later the board, now firmly in Hughes's grasp, agreed to a $2.5 million loan from Hughes Tool to provide the needed financing.[130] For the next 20 years Hughes would control TWA, using Hughes Tool to fund the airline and give him unchallenged autonomy during a period that would often be stormy.

Chapter 3
THE AVIATOR: 1940–1949

Under the leadership of Jack Frye and Paul Richter in the 1930s, TWA had emerged as a pioneer in aviation technology and entered the 1940s with another high-profile pilot-leader. By 1939, Howard Hughes had gained control of TWA. After distancing itself from Charles Lindbergh, TWA's new slogan became "The Airline Run by Flyers." With Hughes, Frye, and Richter in charge, it was literally true. Hughes fully supported Frye and Richter in moving ahead with the Stratoliner contract: five for TWA and one for his own personal luxury transport.

This 1939 timetable cover proudly proclaimed TWA as "The Airline Run by Flyers"—a slogan that was true for much of the airline's existence. Schwantes-Greever-Nolan Collection.

A New Pilot for TWA

The Stratoliner was both the world's first pressurized airliner and the first four-engine American airliner flown in scheduled passenger operation. Before putting the Stratoliner into service, the airline subjected it to proving flights over its entire route system, and crowds showed up at each stop to view the plane and its interior. In May a Stratoliner was displayed to the public at Bolling Field in Washington, DC, and 100,000 people came to see it. TWA sent the Stratoliner on a transcontinental "dress rehearsal," carrying a group of passengers selected from the press and business worlds. When they were delivered, every TWA Stratoliner was given the name of a Native American tribe: Cherokee, Comanche, Zuni, Apache, Navajo.[1]

The Boeing Stratoliner, the world's first pressurized airliner, entered TWA service in 1940 as World War II raged in Europe. TWA now used the slogan "The Transcontinental Line" instead of "The Lindbergh Line." From J. E. Frankum, Legacy of Leadership, *1971.*

TWA inaugurated scheduled Stratoliner service on its cross-country route on July 8, 1940. Hollywood stars Tyrone Power and Paulette Goddard were among the passengers. The new craft shortened the flight time between New York and Los Angeles to 14 hours westbound and 12 hours eastbound, stopping in Chicago, Kansas City, and Albuquerque.[2] The plane could comfortably carry 33 passengers by day and at night converted to 16 berths and nine reclining seats. It flew above most weather, rather than through it. Frye and Richter had achieved their goal of providing service far superior to TWA's competitors, and the traveling public responded enthusiastically.

TWA invited Wayne Parrish—the writer who in 1934 had chronicled his swims in the Atlantic and Pacific oceans within 24 hours of each other—to experience the Stratoliner. Parrish marveled at flying close to 20,000 feet with greater smoothness and comfort than at lower altitudes on other airliners, and he felt less tired at the end of the coast-to-coast journey. Frye saw to it that each Stratoliner passenger received a certificate stating the date of the flight and that he or she was part of "a small group of distinguished air travelers who have participated in the historical development of the science of upper-level flight." A more tangible benefit was a significant decline in airsickness among Stratoliner passengers.[3]

TWA expanded its route network by negotiating to purchase the stock of newly formed Marquette Airlines for $350,000, adding Marquette's airmail contract and passenger service. It began flying Marquette's routes with TWA planes in August 1940. The CAB finally approved the deal in April 1941, which was consummated two days before the attack on Pearl Harbor.[4] It would be 45 years before TWA acquired another airline.

Creating the Constellation

The Stratoliners were the only four-engine airliners in airline service before World War II. Yet even before Stratoliners began flying for TWA, Hughes and Frye had set their sights on a revolutionary new plane that would make every other existing airliner obsolete. Along with the major carriers, TWA had participated in a project with Douglas Aircraft to develop the DC-4E, an advanced four-engine airliner. However, the plane was too large and too expensive, and its performance was underwhelming. TWA dropped out of the project, and no airline bought it.

After gaining control of TWA, Hughes surveyed his new domain. The coast-to-coast route laid out a decade earlier—anchored by cities like Kansas City, Wichita, and Albuquerque—was short on big, traffic-generating centers between the coasts. Because routes could only be changed after acquiring CAB permission, a difficult and uncertain process, Hughes believed the answer was a fleet of large, fast, high-altitude planes with transcontinental range that would outstrip anything the competition could offer. He also believed that cultivating an aura of glamour and prestige would create a marketing buzz for the airline. An exciting new plane meshed well with this approach.[5]

In an 8-hour long-distance call, Hughes and Frye hammered out specifications for an airliner capable of carrying 50 passengers and 6,000 pounds of cargo coast to coast at 250 to 300 mph above 20,000 feet.[6] Lockheed Aircraft Corporation accepted the challenge. It had already begun preliminary design work for a new four-engine airliner called the L-44 Excalibur. Like the Stratoliner, it would be pressurized to fly above the weather and at higher speeds   up to 275 mph. But it was initially designed to carry only 32 passengers, so it generated little interest.[7]

Lockheed developed a new model, incorporating features of its P-38 twin-engine fighter, which promised the highest performance of any production airplane of the time. Known as the Constellation, the plane's design featured a scaled-up version of the P-38's wing and tricycle landing gear, plus an elegantly curved fuselage with a triple tail that allowed it to fit inside existing hangars. (Contrary to popular belief, Hughes did not design the Constellation, but he was involved in every aspect of its development.[8])

Hughes's obsession with secrecy permeated the project. To keep the Constellation concealed from competitors, Lockheed created a fictitious airplane, known as the "Lockheed Model 27," as a cover for the work that was actually being done, and even assigned it the name of the abandoned Excalibur project to further the deception.[9] The TWA representative at Lockheed was required to assume a made-up name and use coded references in correspondence with Hughes and with TWA. Hughes was known as "God" and Frye as "Jesus Christ."[10] The plane's true identity—the Model 49 Constellation—would only later be revealed.

TWA and Lockheed negotiated a series of agreements in June and July 1939 for nine Constellations for $405,000 each and an additional 21 at a price of $425,000.[11] The total order was later increased to 40 aircraft.[12] Possessing the funds to finance the purchase internally, Hughes Tool Company—rather than TWA—bought the planes. "Howard Hughes agreed to contract for these planes," Frye explained, "committing himself for several million dollars, giving TWA an option on them, but with no obligation on TWA's part to purchase them."[13] This arrangement maintained secrecy, avoided conventional financing, and gave Hughes complete control—a modus operandi he would follow for the next two decades.

Lockheed built a mockup of a proposed interior in a shed at Burbank Airport. Hughes inspected it and turned his thumbs down, insisting that designer Raymond Loewy create the interior. Hughes made appointments with Loewy, forcing him to change his schedule and wait, only to fail to appear when Loewy arrived.[14] Detailed design and development of the Constellation proceeded under cover. Meanwhile, Lockheed took on an increasing volume of military contracts after World War II began and came under growing governmental oversight. Eventually an impending military inspection of Lockheed's production facilities made the aircraft's disclosure inevitable. In June 1941, TWA and Lockheed unveiled the Constellation to the world.

Pan American's founder and CEO Juan Trippe immediately wanted Constellations for Pan Am's international routes—an order Lockheed welcomed to ensure the project's commercial viability. After Hughes extracted a promise from Lockheed president Robert Gross that the Constellations would not be sold to TWA's domestic competitors, Pan Am placed an order for 40 of them.[15] It was the start of an intense and sometimes bitter competition between these rival airlines.

TWA Goes to War

TWA's 1940 annual report stated that the airline "stands ready to assist in the national defense."[16] In May 1941, Tommy Tomlinson, a Navy reserve pilot, took a leave of absence after being called to active duty. The Army Air Force already had its eye on TWA's Stratoliners as long-range military transports, and TWA's directors adopted a resolution "offering the resources and experience of the Company in furtherance of the National Defense."[17]

Army Air Force chief Henry H. "Hap" Arnold asked TWA to establish a school for overseas ferry crews. In response TWA created one at Albuquerque. Known as Eagle's Nest, it eventually trained more than 1,000 Army personnel for long-range overwater operations. TWA also created a training center for Army Air Force mechanics at Kansas City and a modification center for B-25 medium bombers in Kansas City, Kansas.[18]

After Pearl Harbor the Army requisitioned TWA's Stratoliners, designating them C-75 transports. It removed their pressurization systems and luxurious interiors, installed additional fuel tanks to increase their range, painted them olive drab, and pressed them into long-range transport service. Despite their military garb, the planes retained their TWA Native American names. TWA created the Intercontinental Division (ICD) to operate the Stratoliners for the Army's Air Transport Command and contracted with the War Department to "hire and train all personnel, procure necessary facilities and supplies, and secure necessary certificates of convenience and necessity, licenses and permits essential to providing air service on a worldwide basis for the United States Army."[19]

The ICD set up shop at the newly opened Washington National Airport and was led by Otis Bryan, a respected veteran TWA captain. It operated under military command and faced wartime hazards, including hostile enemy action. German submarines stationed along the North Atlantic air route to Britain transmitted false radio signals to lure aircraft off course. The first ICD Stratoliner flight departed Washington, DC, on February 26, 1942, bound for Egypt with a load of badly needed munitions for British forces in North Africa. Within weeks, ICD's routes stretched all the way to India. ICD also began regular flights across the North Atlantic to Great Britain via Canada, Greenland, and Iceland.[20]

From its earliest days the ICD was tasked with carrying priority cargo and VIP passengers. It carried Army Chief of Staff George Marshall, General

Dwight Eisenhower, Army Air Force Chief Henry "Hap" Arnold, Chief of Naval Operations Ernest King, and Admiral John Towers to meet with their UK counterparts in London and plan their Allied war strategy in May 1942.[21]

Based on ICD's early success, the Army Air Force selected TWA to undertake the first overseas operations of the new four-engine Douglas C-54 transport in late 1942. Bryan commanded part of the first presidential flight in history, taking Franklin Roosevelt to the Casablanca Conference in January 1943, and to the Cairo and Tehran conferences in November 1943. In February 1945, Bryan flew Roosevelt to Yalta in the first special presidential aircraft, a modified C-54 irreverently called the *Sacred Cow*. Its features included a presidential stateroom and a specially designed elevator to accommodate the president's disability without the need for ramps and other ground support.[22] The confidence that the ICD had established through its wartime record was evinced by the trust the White House placed in Bryan.

TWA's last military flight took place in April 1946. During wartime ICD completed over 9,000 transoceanic flights and flew some 42 million air miles. Forty-four TWA personnel and nine TWA planes were lost, including one shot down in error by British fighters protecting a convoy over the South Atlantic. [23]

By 1944 the Army had amassed a large fleet of C-54s, and the TWA Stratoliners, now weary from intensive use, were returned to the airline in June 1944.[24] TWA refurbished the planes and returned them to transcontinental service in April 1945.

The Home Front

In 1940, TWA carried more than a quarter million passengers—an increase of 57 percent over 1939. TWA ordered 15 additional DC-3s in the spring of 1940, but only 4 were delivered to the airline; the US military took the rest.[25] While TWA and the other airlines were committed to the war effort, demand for commercial air travel skyrocketed. The end of automobile production and rationing of gasoline, tires, and other necessities made highway travel difficult. Railroads were overwhelmed with passenger traffic. Before the war, air travel had been dominated by business travelers and a handful of wealthy individuals, but it was now a vital mode of transportation for all who could find seats. By 1943 the airlines were carrying 1.5 million more passengers than they had in 1939 using half the number of aircraft.[26] A priority system was established to ensure that the most important air travel needs were met:

1. White House personnel and others working directly for the president
2. Military and civilian pilots assigned to ferry aircraft from place to place
3. Military and other government personnel and civilians whose air travel was deemed essential to the war effort
4. Military cargo for the War Department

Those without priority (and some priority 3 travelers) flew standby. Those with higher priority could bump those below them, including at intermediate stops. Every seat on every flight was routinely filled, and the airlines stopped advertising and promotional efforts.[27]

One wartime passenger who enjoyed priority status was actress Carole Lombard, who in January 1942 returned to Los Angeles after a hugely successful cross-country war bond drive in which she had raised more than $2 million. A gifted comedian, she had recently completed filming *To Be or Not to Be*, a dark comedy set in wartime-occupied Poland.

On January 16, Lombard boarded TWA Flight 3 in Indianapolis, accompanied by her mother and an MGM press agent. During a stop in Albuquerque, she was asked to relinquish her seat for military personnel, but, anxious to be reunited with husband Clark Gable, she asserted her priority status and was allowed to stay on the flight, which proceeded to Las Vegas. Shortly after takeoff from Las Vegas, Flight 3 struck Potosi Mountain, an 8,500-foot peak northwest of the airport, killing everyone on board.

The accident happened at night in clear weather, and the Civil Aeronautics Board found it was caused by pilot error: Although the available radio range facilities were operating properly, the plane was badly off course. There was speculation that the captain had left the cockpit to converse with Lombard, leaving an inexperienced copilot at the controls, but no hard evidence of this ever came to light. Nonetheless, Gable never made a claim against TWA.[28]

Despite the adverse publicity from the Lombard crash, demand for air travel remained high throughout the war. It exposed a broad swath of the public to the airlines for the first time and paved the way for the postwar air travel boom.

The Constellation Arrives

TWA sold its rights to the first 40 Constellations to the US government in December 1941, with the right to repurchase them within six months after hostilities ended, and Pan American entered into a similar contract for its Constellations.[29] But the Army desperately needed combat planes and cargo transports, and the new state-of-the-art passenger plane—designated the C-69—did not figure prominently in its war plans.

The Constellation remained TWA's great hope for the postwar period. That it was controlled by the Army Air Force in the meantime was no obstacle for Hughes. He ensured that TWA retained the contractual right to conduct initial flight testing before the C-69 was delivered to the Army. Using this authority, on April 17, 1944, Hughes and Frye flew the second Constellation—temporarily bearing TWA markings—from Burbank to Washington, DC, in 6 hours, 58 minutes, at an average ground speed of 331 mph. The flight broke all existing transcontinental speed records.[30]

Howard Hughes and Jack Frye arrive in Washington, DC, on April 17, 1944, after their record-setting Constellation flight. From J. E. Frankum, Legacy of Leadership, *1971.*

After arriving in Washington, Hughes proceeded to take "Hap" Arnold, cabinet members, and congressmen on local flights around the DC area to showcase the Constellation.[31] Arnold was infuriated to find the Army's aircraft painted in TWA markings and used as a promotional tool, but Hughes was unfazed, having succeeded in publicizing himself and his airline.[32]

Hughes's bravado using wartime government resources would come back to haunt him. Among those whom Hughes took on these joyrides was Missouri Democrat senator Harry Truman, chairman of the Senate Special Committee to Investigate the National Defense Program, which was formed to oversee wartime production, and Maine Republican senator Owen Brewster. Truman had lived in Kansas City, TWA's home base, and had no problems with Hughes. But after the war Brewster would take over as the committee's chairman and become Hughes's nemesis.

Howard Hughes shows off the Constellation to senators and other officials at Washington, DC, in April 1944. Hughes is eighth from the left. To his right is senator and future president Harry S. Truman. Senator Owen Brewster, who later became Hughes's bitter adversary, is at Truman's right. Jon Proctor Collection.

Two Kind Words

TWA continued its commitment to flight research during World War II. In November 1943 the Army loaned the airline a B-17 bomber to carry out weather research, and Captain Robert Buck stepped up to fly into areas of snow, take measurements, and test different types of equipment. Buck was familiar with the problems surrounding static-electricity buildup on aircraft radio antennas when flying through snow and near thunderstorms, weather that interfered with low-frequency radio navigation and voice communications. Now his job was to help solve them.[33]

Mechanics at TWA's Kansas City maintenance base removed unneeded military equipment from the B-17 and installed specialized devices to accurately measure the static phenomena. Buck and the crew named their loaned bomber *Two Kind Words*. After fitting it with testing instruments and embarking on a series of proving flights, they departed for Alaska. A B-17 flown by civilians, outside of military operations and rules, raised military eyebrows everywhere it went, but Buck and his crew quickly learned to adapt, get the support they needed, and carry on with their mission.[34]

They looked for and flew in bad weather anywhere they could find it, from the north slope of Alaska to the Panama Canal. In addition to static, they studied weather and icing on the aircraft structure and propellers. They captured snow for analysis and tested different antenna sizes and materials. They flew through thunderstorms in Florida and the tropics, finding them less violent than those in the American Midwest. Their work led to the static discharge devices that became common on all aircraft. They also found that the bomber had a serious carburetor icing problem and warned the Army about it.[35]

One flight took the B-17 some 1,700 miles from the Aleutian Islands in Alaska to Midway Island, a tiny dot in the Pacific. They found the conditions they were looking for, passing through five weather fronts before being greeted by Navy fighters. Then they returned home to Kansas City with their hard-earned data for analysis. Buck relinquished the bomber and became TWA's chief pilot.[36]

Hughes, the Flying Boat, and the XF-11

Although Hughes remained intensely interested in the Constellation, he was also preoccupied with two airplanes produced by the Hughes Aircraft division of Hughes Tool Company. The most famous was the monstrous flying boat irreverently known as the *Spruce Goose*, which came out of an effort to mass produce cargo vessels to replace the Allied merchant ships that German U-boats were sinking at an alarming rate. To avoid drawing on supplies of scarce aircraft metals, the enormous flying boat—known as the H-4 Hercules—was designed to be made of wood. Despite the derisive *Spruce Goose* nickname, it was constructed using a patented process called Duramold, which used several layers of birch veneer laminated with urea-formaldehyde glue.[37] Hughes built a gigantic hangar in Culver City, California, where the HK-1 prototype would be constructed. Reportedly the largest wood structure in the world at the time, the hangar measured 750 feet long, 250 feet wide, and 100 feet high.[38]

While Hughes was attempting to get the flying boat project up and running, he pursued another government contract for a military version of a twin-engine, all-wood plane he had been developing called the D-2. Having previously but unsuccessfully offered the D-2 to the Army as a fighter, Hughes assigned his public relations chief, John W. Meyer, to cultivate Army Air Force Colonel Elliott Roosevelt—the president's son—who headed a group charged with developing a new, high-performance reconnaissance aircraft.[39]

Elliott Roosevelt visited the West Coast in August 1943, where Meyer wined and dined him. Meyer even set him up with actress Faye Emerson, whom Roosevelt would later marry. After Roosevelt returned east, Meyer continued to host him at New York night clubs. As Hughes had hoped, Roosevelt recommended purchasing an all-metal reconnaissance version of the D-2, designated the XF-11. In September 1943, General Arnold authorized a production contract for 100 XF-11s, a decision that Arnold later said was against his better judgment and the advice of his staff.[40]

By late 1943 the flying boat was in serious trouble and far behind schedule. The XF-11 was an additional burden, competing for limited Hughes Aircraft resources. While all of this was unfolding, Hughes crashed his Sikorsky S-43 amphibian flying boat. Two crew members died. Although Hughes was not seriously injured, the accident shook his self-confidence as a pilot.[41]

Meanwhile, the Allies had gained the upper hand against the U-boat menace, which deprived the flying boat of its raison d'être. In February 1944 the War Production Board halted work on the flying boat. Hughes immediately flew to Washington, where he spent several weeks working feverishly to save the project. He enlisted Jesse Jones, the powerful head of the Reconstruction Finance Corporation, to intercede directly with the president on behalf of the flying boat. Jones persuaded FDR that the giant plane should be completed, and that the money already spent on it would be lost if the contract were canceled. However, the contract was scaled back to the one plane under construction at a total of $18 million. Because more than $13 million had already been spent, Hughes would have to spend his own money to finish the job.[42]

During this same period Hughes lavished time and energy on his latest film, *The Outlaw*. His constant interference had led the director to quit, leaving Hughes to take over and divert his attention away from the flying boat and the XF-11—a project funded by the public.

International Aspirations

Drawing on TWA's ICD experience, Hughes and Frye submitted a bold bid to the CAB for an around-the-world route network in June 1944. But TWA's overseas aspirations faced formidable opposition from Juan Trippe's Pan American. Pan Am was the only US international carrier at the time, and Trippe was determined to keep it that way. He lobbied Congress aggressively for so-called "Chosen Instrument" legislation, under which there would be only one US international airline, owned by all the domestic carriers but operated by Pan Am. The legislation failed to gain support, however, and in 1944 the CAB announced that it would accept applications for postwar international routes.[43]

Amid the flying boat crisis, Hughes suffered a breakdown in the summer of 1944. He began repeating himself in conversation and became increasingly obsessed with minor details. He disappeared for an extended period, leaving even Noah Dietrich and TWA management in the dark. Then he resurfaced and threw himself back into his projects with renewed gusto.[44]

On July 5, 1945, the CAB authorized TWA to serve Paris, Rome, Athens, Cairo, Jerusalem, and onward to India and Ceylon (Sri Lanka). It then approved a second route to Lisbon, Madrid, Algiers, and across North Africa to Cairo, and a connecting route to Madrid and Rome.[45] Pan American also received extensive overseas route authority, and American Overseas Airlines—a new international subsidiary of American Airlines—was awarded routes to London and Northern Europe.[46] After the war TWA would become the principal competitor of Pan American Airways, sparking an intense rivalry between the airlines and their strong-willed leaders.

TWA in the Postwar Era

British aviation writer Peter Davis called the Constellation "the secret weapon of American air transport," but that was an overstatement—the war years had largely erased its head start.[47] Flight testing of the military C-69 had uncovered problems that the Army Air Force had little interest in correcting. Meanwhile, industry leader Douglas secured government funding for a stretched, pressurized, and more powerful version of the DC-4, designated the XC-112. First flown in early 1946, it became the prototype for the postwar DC-6 airliner.

By 1944 the Constellation design was already five years old. The DC-6 was newer and superior in many respects, and American and United placed large orders for them. TWA and Lockheed faced a strong competitive threat from the DC-6, and Lockheed feared that Douglas would win the race for postwar airline sales. Lockheed president Robert Gross asked Hughes for relief from the TWA commitment to allow sale of early-production Constellations to other airlines. Hughes initially refused, but eventually he was persuaded that keeping Lockheed committed to the airplane was in TWA's interest and relented.[48]

Robert Rummel, TWA's vice president of engineering, reviewed the C-69 flight test data and determined that the Model 049 Constellation would fall far short of Lockheed's contractual guarantees and that the military C-69s were ill-suited to airline operations. This finding led to a series of meetings with Lockheed's senior management and engineering staff to hammer out the capabilities of the Constellation in airline service.[49]

TWA wanted to start flying Constellations as soon as possible but needed to update the design. Lockheed proposed a threefold approach: the original C-69–based Model 049 Constellation; an improved, "gold plated" model to meet the challenge of the DC-6; and an "ultimate" version that might be jet- or turboprop-powered. TWA hoped to take only a few of the first-generation Model 049 Constellations as a bridge to the "gold plated" version, which would have more powerful engines, greatly improved systems, and increased fuel capacity and range for transatlantic routes.[50]

When TWA officials and engineers met with Lockheed in August 1945 to firm up postwar Constellation plans, they were shocked to be told that Lockheed had decided to cancel the "gold plated" Constellation that they'd pinned their hopes on. Instead, Lockheed planned to manufacture new, "plain vanilla" Model 049 Constellations with minimal changes from the wartime C-69, and to renovate surplus C-69s (some of which were never delivered to the Army) for airlines that wanted to buy them.

Frye and TWA management were frustrated by Lockheed's abrupt reversal but had no alternative because the airline was effectively committed to the Constellation. They reluctantly concluded that the advantages of waiting for the improved Constellation were outweighed by the imperative to put the available existing aircraft to work as soon as possible. In the end, TWA agreed to take 39 of the 049s and modified C-69s.[51]

Although Hughes was usually not part of these difficult negotiations, he had ways of making his wishes known. On one occasion he contacted Douglas, arranged for a demonstration of the prototype DC-6 at Burbank Airport, and made sure that it took place at noon in front of Lockheed's executive dining room, where Lockheed's top management would see it. Hughes arrived and treated the executives to an extended display of interest in the Douglas product outside their windows. Hughes and the TWA entourage then boarded the DC-6, which made a spectacular departure. Instead of a demonstration flight, however, the plane returned directly to the Douglas

Hughes in the cockpit of a Constellation, ca. 1946. From J. E. Frankum, Legacy of Leadership, *1971.*

Shown here around 1946, the postwar TWA hostess uniform featured the airline's logo on the lapel. From J. E. Frankum, Legacy of Leadership, *1971.*

plant at Santa Monica, where a waiting Hughes car whisked the group away to lunch at a local country club.[52]

The demonstration "enlivened" TWA's negotiations with Lockheed, and the company decided to proceed with the improved Constellation, known as the Model 649. It was intended to compete effectively with the DC-6, with more powerful engines, a new interior featuring improved heating and air conditioning, increased fuel capacity, and longer range. Negotiations proceeded smoothly, and TWA ordered 18 of the 649s.[53]

TWA inaugurated international Constellation service from New York to Paris on February 5, 1946, in the appropriately named *Paris Sky Chief*, one of the early Model 049s. The flight took 15 hours, with fuel stops at Gander, Newfoundland, and Shannon, Ireland. Five days later the *Star of Rome* departed New York for Rome, with Cardinal Francis J. Spellman among its passengers, on the first US air service to Italy.[54]

A couple weeks later Hughes took the controls of the *Star of California* to fly 35 of his Hollywood cronies and celebrities—including Cary Grant, Veronica Lake, Myrna Loy, William Powell, and Tyrone Power—nonstop from Los Angeles to New York in 8.5 hours—almost 5 hours less than it took American and United's DC-4s to make the same trip.[55] The event received nationwide press coverage, just as Hughes had intended. TWA began regular scheduled transcontinental domestic Constellation service in March 1946. But it was Trippe who managed to put the Constellation into airline service first, between New York and London, in January 1946.[56] The struggle between Hughes and Trippe was far from over.

The end of World War II brought great opportunities and challenges for the airlines, and none more so than TWA. At first TWA's postwar fortunes looked rosy. The CAB authorized TWA to extend its international routes from Bombay (Mumbai) to Calcutta, Mandalay, Hanoi, Canton (Guangzhou), and Shanghai (though it never served the latter three destinations owing to civil wars in Indochina and China). TWA was the only US airline with both domestic and international routes and a growing number of Constellations in service.

Hughes and the XF-11 Crash

As all these developments were taking place, Hughes was preparing to test-fly the first prototype XF-11. It was a large aircraft, with a 101-foot wingspan and twin 65-foot fuselage booms, powered by two 3,000 hp Pratt & Whitney engines. As with all of Hughes's airplanes, the XF-11 was sleek and graceful. But, like the flying boat, its protracted development had lasted beyond the war's end. Overtaken by jets, it was now obsolete.

Nonetheless, as soon the XF-11 was rolled out of Hughes's Culver City factory in the summer of 1946, he began making daily test runs up and down the runway, acting as his own test pilot. While skilled at flying, Hughes was neither an engineer nor a trained test pilot and was not qualified for the role. But thanks to his wealth and power he was accustomed to doing as he wished, indulging his whims and impulses, and disregarding established procedures and rules.

The first flight test of the XF-11 was set for July 7. Hughes invited 19-year-old starlet Jean Peters, the latest object of his affections, to see him fly the new plane. He made a series of test runs on the runway without taking off. After each one the right propeller required additional oil, but no leak was found, and Hughes elected to proceed. For no apparent reason he ordered the plane's tanks filled with 1,200 gallons of gasoline—twice the amount specified by the military flight test plan. He directed his chief engineer to follow him in an A-20 chase plane but failed to coordinate on the radio frequency to be used, making it impossible for them to communicate in the air.[57] It was typical of Hughes's undisciplined habits.

Hughes took off and immediately retracted the landing gear, another deviation from the flight plan and from standard military test procedure. But the position lights indicated that the landing gear was not fully retracted and locked in position. Fixating on the indicator lights, Hughes repeatedly cycled the landing gear control up and down. Eventually the offending lights went out, but Hughes was still uncertain if the gear had fully retracted. The A-20 chase plane joined up in formation, but because of the radio confusion, Hughes could not get a report on his landing gear. Instead of contacting Culver City control for assistance, Hughes inexplicably called the Los Angeles Municipal Airport tower, said that he was having landing gear trouble, and asked the tower to call Culver City and find out what frequency the A-20 was using. But the Los Angeles tower personnel were unaware of his flight and did not respond.[58]

Hughes continued flying in circles above the Culver City airfield, well beyond the 45-minute limit specified in the test flight plan. After 75 minutes, at an altitude of 5,000 feet and about 2 miles east of the field, the XF-11 suddenly yawed sharply to the right and began rapidly losing altitude. Instead of immediately returning to the field, Hughes continued flying while trying to analyze the problem. Then he lost control. The plane veered toward Beverly Hills and fell into a residential area, where it hit the second floor of one house, ricocheted into another, and came to rest between two homes on Whittier Drive, bursting into flames.[59]

A Marine sergeant walking in the area heard the impact and ran toward the crash site. Although badly burned with multiple severe injuries, Hughes managed to free himself from the wreckage and was stumbling around in shock when the Marine spotted him. The Marine picked up the nearly lifeless Hughes and hauled him to safety, aided by a fireman who was responding to the incident. Doctors found that Hughes had suffered a crushed chest and collapsed left lung, fractured left clavicle, numerous lacerations, and extensive second- and third-degree burns. He very nearly died. To relieve the terrible pain doctors administered large doses of morphine, thinking that he was unlikely to survive. Yet despite his injuries and condition, within days Hughes had accurately analyzed the cause of the accident. He asked one of his doctors to advise the military to inspect the right propeller, saying, "I don't want this to happen to anyone else."[60]

The Army Air Force investigated and found that the right propeller had reversed in flight, making it impossible for the plane to remain airborne. But it concluded that the underlying cause was Hughes's deviations from the flight test plan procedures and his failure to land immediately after the emergency when he could still have done so.[61]

Against all odds Hughes survived and was discharged from the hospital after 35 days. He seemingly recovered from his terrible injuries within months and returned to flying. But Hughes never recovered from the trauma of the violent crash or the official verdict that he had caused it. He again began behaving erratically and continued receiving morphine and codeine for his pain, which seemingly initiated a lasting addiction despite consistent denials from some who knew him.[62]

Finishing the Flying Boat

While Hughes recovered from the crash, the flying boat inched toward completion. Over the course of two days in June 1946, a convoy of house-moving equipment painstakingly transported the outsize hull, wings, and tail surfaces from Culver City to Long Beach Harbor. The procession took on a festive air: It received extensive media coverage and was witnessed by thousands of spectators who lined the route. Schools even closed so that children could see it. The parade of giant parts wended its way through city streets in Long Beach to Terminal Island, where a specially prepared site awaited to receive and assemble the wings and tail to the fuselage, install the eight 3,000 hp engines, and compete the complex control systems.[63]

The plane was assembled in the open, and as the pieces came together, its enormous dimensions came into focus. It was by far the largest aircraft in the world (and would remain so until 2017), with a wingspan of 320 feet—equal to a football field, plus end zones—and 219 feet long. Its massive tail rose 80 feet above the keel. It was twice the size of the Navy's Martin Mars, the largest operational American flying boat. Yet despite its mammoth size, it was, like all of Hughes's airplane designs, graceful and aesthetically pleasing. Characteristically, Hughes had involved himself in every detail of its design and construction. Big as it was, it was his baby.

Meanwhile, the Constellation's Wright engines proved as troublesome as they had on wartime B-29s. Just days after Hughes's XF-11 crash, a TWA Constellation on a training flight caught fire and crashed near Reading, Pennsylvania, killing five of the six crew on board. Immediately after the accident Frye voluntarily grounded TWA's Constellation fleet. The next day the CAB grounded all Constellations pending investigation and determination of the cause. The official grounding order triggered a spate of negative publicity that questioned TWA's maintenance and Lockheed's design. The investigation ultimately identified a "crudely deficient" wiring design that ignited hydraulic fluid, inadequate smoke detection, and poor fire extinguishing equipment, among other deficiencies. All of TWA's Constellations were inspected, and several were found to have similar conditions.[64]

Its Constellations grounded, TWA was forced to substitute slower, unpressurized planes on its routes. But after diligent efforts by TWA and Lockheed to fix the problems, the CAB lifted the grounding order, and Constellations returned to the air once again in September 1946.[65]

Labor and Financial Woes

TWA's pilots went on strike on October 21, 1946, demanding pay increases and work rule changes, which would establish precedents for other airlines. TWA and the Air Line Pilots Association (ALPA), the pilots' union, agreed to engage in binding arbitration. The pilots returned to work on November 15. A three-person arbitration board convened, consisting of Captain Bob Buck, representing the pilots; TWA attorney George Spater, representing the airline; and Frank Swacker, an elderly retired judge who knew little of aviation, as the neutral member. Buck and Spater largely negotiated terms they thought would be acceptable to both sides and then convinced Swacker to sign on. Their deliberations were complicated by the machinations of ALPA president David Behncke, who attempted unsuccessfully to involve himself in the arbitration, to the annoyance of all concerned.[66]

An agreement was reached after three months that increased the pilots' pay scales. But the settlement was costly for the struggling airline, and the dispute delayed delivery of new Constellations. Moreover, the strike and its timing caused bad blood and distrust between the airline and its pilots that would persist for years.[67]

The costs incurred to get the Constellations operational and integrated into service weighed heavily on the airline. In early 1945, TWA's finance committee recommended selling stock to raise additional capital, but the plan fell through because Hughes, who controlled the airline through Hughes Tool Company's 46 percent stock ownership, vetoed it. TWA was forced to secure a $30 million loan from the Equitable Life Assurance Society in November 1945 and borrow an additional $10 million from Equitable in May 1946.[68] Little did Hughes know that forcing TWA into this debt would pave the way for him losing control of the company 15 years later.

By the end of 1946 the airline had lost $14 million, and the board had approved Frye's proposal to borrow up to $40 million from the government's Reconstruction Finance Corporation (RFC).[69] Later that month Noah Dietrich offered a new proposal whereby Hughes Tool would loan TWA a total of $10 million by June 1, 1947, with the right to convert the loan into common stock at any time. In return, six directors would resign and be replaced by six chosen by Hughes Tool, giving it control of the board. Frye raised multiple objections, including that it did not provide enough cash to meet the airline's immediate needs, and that the proposed loan terms were unfairly biased against the airline and its other shareholders.[70] The alliance between Frye and Hughes was breaking down.

The board convened on January 8, 1947, with Howard Hughes in attendance along with Dietrich, Civil Aeronautics Board chairman James Landis, and the RFC's Chauncey Dodds. Dietrich presented the formal Hughes Tool financing proposal, which called for Hughes Tool to control the majority of the TWA board in return for the $10 million loan. The directors adjourned to consider it.[71]

The climax came the next day when a letter from the president of Equitable was read to the directors that stated no loan application was pending, "and if such an application were made, it would have to be declined." It added, "It seems to us that you are subjecting the interests of your stockholders and creditors to serious risk in continuing to preserve a situation which results in the Company's being unable to obtain the additional funds which it needs promptly in order to carry on operations." It concluded, "We intend to hold those responsible strictly accountable for any loss which may arise from this continued inaction."[72]

The directors were predictably outraged by the letter's arrogance—an act instigated by Hughes and Dietrich.[73] While the directors were reacting to this affront, "word was received that Mr. Hughes would like to enter the meeting for a discussion with the Directors not associated with the management of the corporation." With Frye and Richter out of the room, Hughes advised the board that he "did not seek the resignation of any present members of the Board at this time" but "merely desired to have representatives of Hughes Tool Company added to the Board." Hughes wanted Frye and Richter to remain until the annual shareholders meeting scheduled in April, and he proposed a severance pay arrangement "if they should leave the service of the Corporation by their own volition or at the request of the Corporation."[74]

Faced with Equitable's refusal to consider further financing and Hughes's demands, the board capitulated. It accepted the Hughes Tool loan proposal and amended the corporation's bylaws to more than double the number of directors, from 11 to 24, and then elected a Hughes-dictated slate of 13 additional directors, including Victor Leslie, who would become the corporate treasurer, and Hughes attorney Thomas Slack.[75]

With his days now numbered, Frye submitted his resignation on February 21, saying, "I am not in agreement with the controlling shareholder with respect to the financing of TWA."[76] Paul Richter followed

Paul Richter served as TWA executive vice president from 1935 to 1947. Richter was an able pilot and manager—as well as Frye's right-hand man—before Hughes removed him. From J. E. Frankum, Legacy of Leadership, 1971.

Frye out the door in April. The Hughes-controlled board elected Noah Dietrich a TWA director, subsequently placing him on the executive committee as well.[77]

The 13-year Frye-Richter era was over. Under their leadership TWA had led the industry in technical innovation, pioneered high-altitude flight, and created groundbreaking new aircraft. It had become the second US airline with international routes and the only one with a domestic network to feed them. But all of these efforts had strained TWA's finances to the breaking point and paved the way for Howard Hughes to emerge as its financial savior, giving him unfettered control over its fate. And Hughes was guided by Dietrich, whose only interest in TWA was holding down its costs.

After Frye's departure the Hughes-dominated board elected LaMotte Cohu to be TWA's president. Although Cohu had a long history in aviation, his tenure as TWA's president proved unsuccessful, for he never gained Hughes's confidence or respect. Hughes was now firmly in control of the airline.

Potomac Fever

Republicans regained control of both houses of Congress in the 1946 elections for the first time since 1932. The 80th Congress took office in January 1947, and the Republican majority promptly began making changes. Maine senator Owen Brewster became chairman of the Senate Committee Investigating the National Defense Program. (It was popularly known as the Truman Committee when Harry Truman had chaired it and investigated waste and mismanagement in the wartime defense industry.) Once in charge, Brewster turned his sights on Hughes. Brewster was a political ally of Pan American and Juan Trippe. Trippe saw the CAB's award of overseas routes to TWA as a serious threat to his hope of controlling this market. Before departing, Frye warned Hughes that Trippe believed Hughes had invaded his territory and would make Hughes's life miserable.[78]

In January 1947, Brewster announced that the committee would launch an inquiry into Hughes's defense contracts, and in particular, the incomplete flying boat, which he mocked as a "flying lumber yard." The fact that Hughes had received $60 million for two aircraft projects, neither of which had flown successfully, and had wined and dined the president's son, seemed a political goldmine.[79] Brewster also revived the former "Chosen Instrument" bill as the "Community Airline" bill.

Hughes, now recovered from the XF-11 crash six months earlier, testified before the committee in a closed executive session and agreed to an inspection of his books. He even flew Brewster in his personal airplane to an engagement in Columbus, Ohio, letting Brewster sit in the copilot's seat, and sent him back to Washington in a TWA plane. The charm offensive seemed to be working. The next day Brewster invited Hughes to lunch with him in the senator's suite at the Mayflower Hotel. What happened there became the subject of bitter controversy.

Over the summer a series of unflattering documents and information on Hughes's contacts with the military about the XF-11 and the flying boat were leaked to the press before open hearings began on August 5, 1947. Hughes appeared on the first day, charging that at the Mayflower Hotel meeting Brewster "in so many words told me that if I would agree to merge TWA with Pan American Airways and go along with his Community Airline bill, there would be no further hearing in this matter."[80]

Senator Homer Ferguson, who was chairing the hearing, asked Brewster if he wished to take the stand to respond. He did. Brewster gave an impassioned statement denying Hughes's charges. "It is inconceivable," he thundered, "that anyone who has been in public life as long as I have" could make "so bald a proposition as he describes. It sounds more like Hollywood than Washington."[81]

Ferguson then proceeded to read a series of questions written by Hughes to Brewster. "Are you going to ask the public to believe that having this unique position [as committee chairman] you did not use the whip that was in your hand to try and extract from Howard Hughes the things you wanted so badly?" read one. Brewster huffed that the question impugned his good faith and denied that he was "cracking a whip or making threats." Next question: "While occupying this unique position, did you or did you not lobby with Howard Hughes or attempt to sell him your Community Airline bill?" Brewster admitted that he had "discussed the matter with Hughes."[82] As Brewster continued responding to Hughes's written questions it became clear that, despite his denials, he had close relationships with Trippe and others who stood to gain if the Community Airline bill passed, to the detriment of Hughes and TWA.

Hughes returned to the stand and called Brewster a liar, pointing to his denials of any connection with Pan Am that were patently false. As for himself, he said, "I have been called a playboy, and I have been called an eccentric, but I do not believe that I have the reputation of being a liar. For 23 years nobody has questioned my word."[83] Hughes was asking the committee and the public to weigh Brewster's credibility against his own based on the record. And he offered to let Brewster have all day to defend himself, "if I can cross-examine him."

It was an extraordinary moment—a witness before a Senate committee putting its chairman on the defensive and demanding the right to question him as a witness. After sparring with Ferguson over his demand, Hughes declared, "I feel that Senator Brewster is not telling the truth. If I can cross-examine him, I think I can prove it. If I do not have that right, I would like to drop the matter at this point." Ferguson ruled the matter closed and ended the session. The next day Brewster left Washington and flew home to Maine.[84]

Hughes now had his revenge. He held a news conference, stared into the newsreel cameras, and mocked his vanquished adversary. "As soon as Senator Brewster saw he was fighting a losing battle against public opinion he folded his tent and took a run-out powder," he snarled in a hard, sarcastic voice, adding, "When Senator Brewster headed for the backwoods of Maine, that was the tipoff. Washington was getting too hot for him!"[85]

Despite avowals that the investigation would continue, Hughes was never called back. The Republican committee members eventually produced a report highly critical of Hughes, but the Democrats issued a minority report saying, "There is absolutely nothing in the evidence which discloses any fraud, corruption or wrongdoing on the part of Howard Hughes or his associates." The Community Airline bill failed to gain support and fizzled out. Hughes contributed to Owen Brewster's opponent in 1952, and Brewster lost, ending his political career.[86] Against all odds Hughes had come back from near death, humiliated a Senate committee chairman in his own hearing and procured his political demise, and rehabilitated his own standing in the public eye.

Flying the Flying Boat

With the Senate investigation now behind him, Hughes turned his attention back to his beloved flying boat. On November 2, 1947, he was at the controls for its only flight, a mile-long hop across Long Beach Harbor at a maximum altitude of 70 feet, accompanied by a flotilla of small craft filled with reporters

Howard Hughes's flying boat was a hive of activity when this picture was taken at Long Beach, California, in 1947. Gerald Balzer Collection, Greater St. Louis Air and Space Museum.

chasing and filming the giant airplane. Reporter Jim McNamara was allowed on board to provide live radio coverage of the event and interviewed Hughes on the flight deck after landing. One of the flight crew described Hughes's reaction "like a little kid," "grinning and talking a lot, almost jumping up and down in his elation." Hughes told reporters that he intended to make more test flights in the spring.[87]

He constructed a special humidity-controlled hangar at Long Beach to house the giant. Hughes maintained the craft and made modifications and improvements to it, but the flying boat never again emerged from its hangar during his lifetime. Some of the mechanics who worked on it claimed it suffered from structural weaknesses that made Hughes reluctant to attempt additional flights.[88]

In December 1947, Hughes hired Bill Gay, an earnest young Mormon, to manage his day-to-day business and personal activities from his nondescript headquarters at 7000 Romaine Street in Los Angeles. Gay took charge, hiring a group of other dedicated young Mormons to staff the operation. By catering totally and unquestioningly to Hughes's increasingly bizarre demands and ensuring that they were carried out to the letter, Gay and his underlings reinforced and exacerbated Hughes's withdrawal from the world and reality.[89] Never again would he appear in public. As he disappeared from view, Hughes increasingly became an object of mystery, manipulating TWA, Hughes Tool, and his other interests from behind the scenes like an invisible Wizard of Oz.

Hard Times at TWA

After the punishing 1946 loss, TWA was forced to cancel its order for the 18 postwar Model 649 Constellations and start borrowing against the $10 million Hughes Tool loan.[90] Facing stiff competition from the Douglas DC-6 now entering service with American and United Air Lines, Lockheed offered TWA the improved Model 749 Constellation, with increased range and payload for international operations. A contract was signed in October 1947 for 12 749s, with deliveries beginning in 1948. TWA immediately put them to work on international services, freeing up the earlier Model 049 Constellations for domestic use.[91] But 1947's turmoil and disruption had taken a toll; TWA lost more than $8 million for the year.

By March 1948, TWA faced a severe cash shortage and decided to delay paying $1 million worth of bills to conserve funds. Treasurer Victor Leslie warned that this was "the last line of defense in conservation of cash," and if unsuccessful, "the Company was in danger of receivership."[93]

Hughes now made his move. In June 1948, Dietrich presented an offer to convert the loan into TWA common stock at $5 per share. Although stacked with Hughes allies, the TWA board rejected the offer and made a

The reliable Model 749 Constellation is pictured in 1959. It outlasted all other versions of the Constellation in TWA's fleet. David Ostrowski Collection, Greater St. Louis Air and Space Museum.

counteroffer. Eventually an agreement was reached that TWA would issue an additional 1.3 million shares of stock—considerably more than the total number of then-outstanding shares—in exchange for the $10 million loan, plus accrued interest. Selling the additional shares to Hughes Tool increased its ownership stake to 73 percent.[94] TWA was now truly Howard Hughes's airline and would remain so for the next 12 years.

Shopping for New Planes

With the immediate financial crisis behind it and new Constellations in hand for its overseas routes, TWA now turned its attention to replacing the aging Stratoliners and DC-3s with modern equipment. Two contenders were the twin-engine Martin 202 and Convair 240. Both manufacturers had distinguished themselves during World War II, but neither Martin nor Convair had any experience building commercial airliners. The Convair 240 was more advanced, carrying 40 passengers on short routes in pressurized comfort comparable to the Constellation and DC-6. The unpressurized Martin 202 carried 36 passengers, and Martin promised the pressurized Model 303 for later delivery. Martin offered TWA favorable financial terms on 202s and 303s, and TWA executed a letter of intent for both. But the contract negotiations bogged down when Hughes became involved. LaMotte Cohu, reluctant to proceed without Hughes's blessing, refused to act, and the deal fell through.[95] Hughes insisted on controlling all important equipment decisions, but he often took far too long to make them or failed to make decisions altogether—even on issues that required prompt action. Frustrated by Hughes's lack of support, Cohu resigned as president in June 1948.[96]

Despite these headwinds, TWA grew its international division. It accounted for 40 percent of the airline's total revenue in 1948. As a result, TWA was able to reduce its 1948 net loss to $478,000, down from $8 million in 1947.[97] TWA's route network now stretched from the US West Coast to India, and its domestic flights fed passengers to its international service—something archrival Pan American lacked.

The International Scene

Before World War II, American Export, a transatlantic shipping firm, established an airline subsidiary known as American Export Airlines (AEA) to fly between the United States and Europe using flying boats. In 1940 the CAB granted AEA a certificate to operate to and from Lisbon in neutral Portugal. As the war moved toward a close AEA was authorized for transatlantic passenger service to Europe, along with Pan Am and TWA in June 1945, and it began carrying passengers before either of its rivals. But American Airlines had its eye on international operations too, and with CAB approval it acquired AEA in late 1945, rebranding it American Overseas Airlines (AOA).[98] With American's financial resources, AOA acquired a fleet of Constellations and Boeing Stratocruisers—a large, luxurious, double-deck airliner derived from the wartime B-29, which Pam Am had also ordered. AOA looked to be a formidable competitor for Pan Am and TWA, and it had access to American's extensive domestic structure to funnel passengers to its international gateway.

But international travel demand in the early postwar period was insufficient to support three carriers, and AOA suffered the most. Its parent company quickly tired of the losses and began looking for a buyer. Trippe jumped at the opportunity, for AOA's fleet and routes to the UK and Northern Europe were a perfect fit for Pan Am. Acquiring it would eliminate a competitor and solidify Pan Am's transatlantic dominance. Anxious to stop the bleeding, American quickly concluded a sweetheart deal in September 1950: $17.5 million for all of AOA's routes, fleet, contracts, and other assets. But the Pan Am–AOA deal brought TWA an unexpected dividend: a new president.

Damon Comes Aboard TWA

Ralph S. Damon, American Airlines' vice president and general manager, had crafted the AOA purchase. Damon was committed to making American an international player, and he resigned after AOA was sold over his objections.[100] Howard Hughes knew and respected Damon, and he quickly reached out to him. Damon became TWA's president in January 1949. He had an in-depth understanding of the technical and business sides of aviation, a wealth of experience in the industry, and an open, self-confident nature that

Ralph Damon served as TWA's president from 1949 until his death in 1956. He was a gifted leader who gained Hughes's respect and led the airline during its most successful years. From J. E. Frankum, Legacy of Leadership, *1971.*

made him a joy to work with. And, most important, he understood how to effectively collaborate with Hughes, retaining his confidence without falling prey to his eccentricities.[101]

In a letter to TWA stockholders and employees Damon wrote, "I have joined a very fine airline operating team and hope and believe that we may be able to go forward to future years of profit. . . . It will be my objective to serve your Company to the best of my ability in sound organization and constructive selling and operating policies in coordination with all other members of the TWA team."[102] His words expressed the sense of community and teamwork he brought to the airline. Although not a visionary in the mold of Frye, Damon was a capable businessman and a leader who restored the airline's morale.

In 1949, Damon's first year as president, TWA returned to profitability, earning $3.7 million. It also ordered 20 improved Model 749A Constellations for its international operations and converted older planes to high-density configuration for new low-fare domestic air coach operations.[103] Damon also fulfilled TWA's requirement for a new twin-engine short-haul plane. TWA agreed to lease 12 improved Martin 202As to its fill immediate needs and ordered 30 new pressurized Martin 404s for delivery in 1951, allowing it to finally retire the obsolete DC-3s and Stratoliners.[104] With a new president and the turmoil of war and the financial crises behind it, TWA could now confidently look toward the 1950s. Damon would serve as TWA's president for seven years, a period that would be one of TWA's most successful.

Chapter 4
TRANS WORLD: 1950–1959

Through sheer force of will Howard Hughes had managed to pull himself together in 1947 and resist Juan Trippe's effort to force a merger with Pan American. He put on a bravura performance before a Senate committee, shut down the investigation of his wartime activities, and made the hearing a laughingstock. He ended the threat to TWA's international routes. He completed the flying boat and flew it. Then, having triumphed over adversity and his adversaries, he withdrew from public life and began a descent into darkness. It continued for the rest of his life and affected all of his business interests, including TWA.

Hughes's Descent

Hughes apparently suffered from an extreme form of obsessive-compulsive disorder, which compelled him to control every aspect of his existence, from multimillion-dollar business deals to his most intimate bodily functions. He had phobias about cleanliness and health. Bill Gay and his staff at 7000 Romaine Street, known as "Operations," continued to manage Hughes's business and personal life, indulging and effectuating his compulsions and fears, carrying out his endless demands without question.[1]

Hughes retreated into a world of darkened rooms, isolating himself in a bungalow at the Beverly Hills Hotel. All his contact with the outside world went through Operations, which staffed a communications center around the clock. It received incoming calls and prepared messages for Hughes to review. Hughes returned calls he deemed important, dictated replies to some, and ignored others. At Hughes's behest, Operations created a classified information system said to be more elaborate than the government's.[2]

Having irregular sleeping and working habits, Hughes often returned calls in the middle of the night. He summoned TWA executives to Los Angeles for meetings, then kept them waiting for hours—or even days—before sometimes canceling the meetings altogether. Hughes weighed in on all business decisions, but his chronic indecisiveness, vacillation, and unavailability hamstrung efforts to get the results he demanded.

Despite Hughes's growing mental illness, TWA's fortunes improved during the 1950s, thanks to its president, Ralph Damon. He was one of the most respected aviation figures of the time and quickly set about putting TWA's house in order. He also managed to retain Hughes's confidence and was given a relatively free hand in running the airline.[3] Damon was not only a good businessman but also a capable engineer and a skilled administrator. He was a hands-on CEO who made a point of visiting every TWA location annually, talking to the employees and addressing them by name, which he often remembered from previous visits.[4] The Damon years were golden ones for TWA. Its traffic and revenues were rising, and the airline was consistently profitable.

Damon could not and did not try to prevent Hughes's interventions in TWA's operations on behalf of his Hollywood cronies, such as producer Darryl F. Zanuck: Hughes had reserved five berths on every Monday-night New York–to–Paris flight for him, even though they were rarely used.[5] Hedda Hopper insisted on and received private limousine service from TWA between her home and the airport. On one occasion Hughes canceled a scheduled flight and reassigned the plane to fly the relatives of a recently deceased film personage from New York to Los Angeles. The passengers on the canceled flight were booked into a hotel overnight and flown to their destinations the next morning.[6]

Ever on the lookout for media coverage, Hughes directed TWA to provide gossip columnist Louella Parsons free round-trip travel from Los Angeles to London. Parsons and her party were greeted at the Los Angeles airport by actor Robert Montgomery, TWA personnel, and Hughes's staff members. The group was entertained at the Ambassadors Club prior to departure, and upon their arrival in New York, limousines brought them to the Waldorf Astoria, where a three-room suite had been reserved. The next morning they were met by more TWA personnel and transported to the airport for departure to London. While there, Hughes required TWA to do everything possible for their convenience and pleasure, including furnishing a town car for Parsons and her companions' use during their four-week stay, and comparable amenities were furnished upon their return to the US.[7] All of this was part of a deliberate effort to raise TWA's profile among the rich and famous.

Trans World

TWA began putting "Trans World Airline" on its planes and promotional materials in 1945 to emphasize its new status as an international carrier, but its formal corporate name remained "Transcontinental & Western Air Inc.," as it had been since 1930. The board finally recommended changing the name to "Trans World Airlines Inc.," which was formally approved on April 27, 1950.[8] TWA would remain Trans World Airlines for the rest of its lifetime.

TWA's early international operations could be an adventure for passengers and flight crew alike. The Constellations and DC-4s didn't have the range to cross the North Atlantic nonstop and had to be refueled twice on the way from New York City to Paris. It was rare for all passenger seats to be occupied, so during these 20-plus-hour flights passengers and crew mingled in the galley, and friendships were formed. Some Constellation passengers enjoyed berths on overnight segments, but both cockpit and cabin crew shared a double lower and a single upper berth behind the cockpit. Hostesses usually claimed the upper berth, but occasionally a male crewmember would find himself sharing the lower with an exhausted hostess. Over the course of a lengthy international flight, the cockpit would reek of cigarettes, equipment, and bodies. Restful sleep was elusive.[9]

Local European hostesses were employed on flights east of Paris, lending a cosmopolitan atmosphere. The route to Cairo stopped at Geneva, Rome, and Athens. Each stop lasted about an hour and passengers could disembark, stretch their legs, and enjoy some local refreshments. Passengers and crew shared one another's company on the ground before boarding for the next leg, adding to the pleasant informality of international air travel.[10]

But TWA's presence in the Middle East would expose it to increasing dangers, including wars in 1956, 1967, and 1973. Israel's victories and growing strength led to terrorist acts. As the region's principal US carrier, TWA was a frequent target because of the country's support for Israel.

Flying in the region was also subject to all the operational hazards that came with the era's piston-engine airliners. Shortly before midnight on August 30, 1950, TWA Flight 903, a newly delivered Constellation, took off from Cairo bound for Rome. It reported its position 25 miles west of Cairo but failed to respond to repeated calls from air traffic control. Observers on the ground saw the plane erupt in flames. As it turned back toward Cairo, a flaming engine separated from the plane and fell. The plane was unable to maintain altitude and crashed into the desert, killing all 48 passengers and 7 crew on board. The CAB accident investigation determined that an engine suffered a massive failure that triggered the intense fire.[11] Despite the political and operational risks, TWA's international service was largely successful and helped boost the airline's revenue and profits during the 1950s.

TWA put its improved Model 749A Constellations to work on international routes in 1950. These efficient, reliable planes proved to be the best of the Constellation series. They outlasted later models and continued carrying passengers until 1967, becoming TWA's last and longest-serving piston-engine airliners. Hughes also claimed one of the 749As for Hughes Tool, but it was never moved from the Lockheed plant in Burbank. Hughes placed it under 24-hour armed guard and allowed no one to approach it, even though it was on Lockheed's premises and occupied needed ramp space. Eventually Hughes sold the plane at a profit, without ever having flown it.[12]

The Deluge

TWA suffered a major disruption in July 1951, when the Missouri River experienced record flooding at Kansas City. High water inundated both the Kansas City Municipal Airport on the Missouri side and Fairfax Municipal Airport in Kansas, forcing the airline to evacuate to Grandview Airport, 18 miles to the south. Fairfax was a former bomber plant that had become TWA's principal maintenance facility. It held 11 aircraft in various stages of disassembly as the waters rose.[13] The planes and precious spare parts and equipment had to be saved. On Friday, July 13, as the rising waters cut off traffic in and out of the base, 45 employees worked feverishly through the day and night moving supplies and equipment to upper floors as well as readying five aircraft to be flown out. By 8 a.m. Saturday water was 18 inches deep in the hangars, and the exhausted crew beat a hasty retreat to higher ground. The water level eventually reached 12 feet in the hangar before slowly receding.[14]

On Sunday the flood abated sufficiently to allow cleanup efforts to begin. The hangars were filled with mud and debris from the water. Tools, equipment, and parts that had not been moved were scattered everywhere, some damaged beyond repair. During the recovery effort TWA was forced to contract out vital maintenance functions. The base was able to resume limited activity by the end of August, and full-scale operations commenced one month later. The total cost exceeded $6 million (about $70 million in 2023).[15]

Even with this setback, TWA managed to increase sales and earnings in 1951, and it learned an important lesson. The city began purchasing farmland 18 miles to the north for a much larger commercial airport, called Mid-Continent International, to replace its cramped, flood-prone facility downtown. Moreover, TWA made plans to relocate its maintenance base there.

The Postwar Airline Boom

Before World War II, airline travel had been predominantly used by business travelers and the elite. Spurred on by newer planes, improved comfort and safety, and growing public acceptance, air travel surged postwar—as did demand for cheaper fares. A new group of cost-cutting airlines arose in response. After some initial resistance, the airlines embraced "air coach service," and by 1950, TWA and American both offered coast-to-coast coach service, with more seats per plane and fewer amenities, for $110 (about $1,400 in 2023). In 1952, $99 transcontinental and $32 New York–Chicago coach fares were approved by the CAB and adopted by the major airlines. Air coach traffic grew rapidly, and air travel was now directly competing with the railroads.[16]

In an effort to broaden its passenger base, TWA marketed itself to women. "Women are no longer tied down to their homes," said TWA public relations director Ed Broughton. "They have the money to fly, and they want to go places and see and do things." Believing that education was critical, the airline hired a group of female travel advisers (each of them given the fictitious name "Mary Gordon") and sent them to speak to women's groups across the country. They gave women advice on places to visit, and what they should wear and pack. TWA noted that housewives comprised the largest single group on flying vacation trips, usually accompanied by their families. The airline encouraged wives to go on business trips with their husbands and enjoy time together away from home and family responsibilities. Such marketing helped stimulate the rapid growth of air travel in the postwar period.[17]

The Super Constellation

To counter Lockheed's Model 749 Constellations, Douglas developed the DC-6B, a stretched version of the DC-6 that had increased passenger and cargo capacity. Lockheed responded with the Model 1049A Super Constellation—which featured a 19-foot fuselage stretch—and offered it to

Hughes's delay in ordering a modern postwar twin, the Martin 404 pictured here, put TWA at a competitive disadvantage. R. A. Burgess Collection, Greater St. Louis Air and Space Museum.

TWA. TWA's chief engineer, Robert Rummel, was interested and wanted to get involved early to tailor the design and specifications to the airline's needs. But Lockheed would make no commitments without Hughes's approval, and he remained out of touch—a longtime practice.[18] As Hughes stalled, Eastern Air Lines placed an order for the Super Constellations in early 1950. Then, after months of silence, Hughes demanded that a contract for 10 Super Constellations be negotiated immediately.[19]

TWA began receiving its Super Constellations in 1952, putting them into operation on its prime transcontinental routes. The Super Constellation seated 64 passengers—a valuable increase over the 749's 49 seats—and could fly coast to coast nonstop. But TWA initially resisted nonstop service, asserting that passengers actually preferred stopping in Chicago to stretch their legs.[20] TWA finally introduced nonstop transcontinental Super Constellation service in October 1953 with much fanfare. "The first nonstop transcontinental flight in scheduled airline history arrived at New York after an eight-hour 17-minute overnight flight from Los Angeles," proclaimed a TWA press release. California governor Goodwin Knight presided over pre-departure ceremonies for the inaugural flight, and celebrity passengers included Eva and Zsa Zsa Gabor, Paul Douglas, and Helen Wright Russell— the closest living relative of the Wright Brothers.[21]

But because of TWA's delays in deciding on a postwar twin, it did not begin receiving its Martin 202As until 1950, and its pressurized 404s didn't arrive until a year later. It was forced to continue operating its vintage Stratoliners until 1950 and did not retire its last DC-3s until January 1953.[22]

The Need for Speed

The Model 1049A Super Constellation was essentially a stretched, heavier 749A with slightly more powerful engines. Although this gave it good operating economics, it also made the plane somewhat underpowered and slow. Douglas responded by developing the DC-7, which also had transcontinental range and was powered by the Wright turbo-compound engine that had been originally designed for the military. This engine used three exhaust-driven turbines to boost its output to over 3,000 hp, giving the DC-7 a considerable speed advantage over the Super Constellation.

Speed mattered on nonstop transcontinental flights. The Super Constellation took nearly 10 hours to make the trip between Los Angeles or San Francisco and New York, while the DC-7 could do it in 8. But the added speed came at a price. The powerful turbo-compound engines were noisy and created vibration in the passenger cabin. And extracting so much power from the same basic engine design reduced its reliability. Nevertheless, shorter transcontinental flight times gave the DC-7 a major competitive advantage. American Airlines quickly ordered DC-7s and put them to work on nonstop, coast-to-coast flights in late November 1953, barely two months behind TWA's Super Constellations. United followed suit, putting its DC-7s into service in 1954.[23] Bookings on TWA's transcontinental flights declined significantly because of this competitive disadvantage.

The Model 1049A Super Constellation was no match for the speedy DC-7 and proved a commercial flop. Once again TWA was forced to play catch-up. Hughes devised the idea to add auxiliary jets to TWA's 1049s to dramatically boost their speed. He called this "Project Dynamite" and pressured Lockheed to explore it. Characteristically, Hughes insisted that it be kept absolutely secret.

In response Lockheed came up with a plan to install a pair of military J-34 jet engines at the wingtips of the Super Constellation. But it soon became apparent that the jets' high fuel consumption in cruising flight would severely limit its range in airline use, requiring fuel stops that would make nonstop transcontinental flights impossible, thereby nullifying the speed advantage. They would also create noise problems in the vicinity of civil airports. The project was soon dropped.[24]

But the Super Constellation could be competitive with the DC-7 by installing the same turbo-compound engines. Lockheed was already fitting turbo-compounds to a military version of the 1049 for the Navy and Air Force from which a civil airliner could readily be created. The resulting Model 1049C was faster than the 1049A, with longer range and higher payload. Eastern Air Lines quickly ordered 1049Cs, as did several international airlines. The 1049C would have fulfilled TWA's needs, but buying them would have strained TWA's finances. Hughes had previously made funds available from Hughes Tool to support new TWA equipment purchases, but now he balked at doing so and missed the opportunity for an early response to the DC-7 challenge.[25]

Marketing the Super-G

TWA's focus then shifted to the Model 1049E, a strengthened 1049C that promised higher gross weight and greater range. The original DC-7s lacked transatlantic range, an important consideration for TWA's international routes. But Lockheed, now enjoying a sales boom, was unwilling to modify the 1049E to meet TWA's requirements. Douglas responded by offering the DC-7B, which had increased range and even higher speed. Ralph Damon favored the DC-7B, but Hughes overruled him and ordered 20 1049Es in September 1953 to be delivered in 1955.[26]

Hughes then demanded an all-out effort from Lockheed to fully satisfy TWA's needs. The manufacturer finally relented and agreed to TWA's requested changes, increasing the plane's gross weight and adding 600-gallon wingtip tanks designed for military craft that would enable the coveted transatlantic range. This new version was the Model 1049G. Although the Model 1049G was still slightly slower than the DC-7, its transoceanic range was vital for TWA and more than made up for the small speed disadvantage. With Hughes's blessing, the order for 20 Model 1049Es was changed to 1049Gs.[27]

TWA quickly dubbed the new model the "Super-G." Equipping it with plush interiors and murals depicting TWA's international destinations, the airline mounted a vigorous marketing campaign to promote the Super-G as new, different, and exciting. TWA personnel were introduced to the Super-G through a series of "Connie Grams" (short for "Constellation"). "TWA's new Super-G Constellation is the newest and finest airplane in transcontinental service today," proclaimed the first Connie Gram. "You will be impressed with this newness as a passenger as you pass by the large galley of gleaming stainless steel and aluminum," it continued. "On either side of the galley the airplane is divided into compartments which break the long cabin into intimate room-like surroundings. The interior is entirely new in design, incorporating a décor which will exceed any transport airplane in beauty and restfulness. This interior with its rich colors and delicate fabrics and luxuriously soft rugs was designed by the Henry Dreyfuss Company which is foremost in the field of developing designs incorporating both the functional and the beautiful."

As part of a comprehensive publicity campaign TWA also redesigned its hostess uniforms to coordinate with the new planes' interior furnishings. "Designed by the women who will wear them and keyed to color harmony to the sumptuous interior decoration of Trans World Airlines' new Super-G

This postcard of the Model 1049G "Super-G" Constellation marketed the airplane as well as the airline, ca. 1955. Alan Hoffman Collection.

Constellation, a brand-new uniform will give TWA's corps of hostesses a 1955 high-fashion look," another press release reported. "Henry Dreyfuss, famed industrial designer who is responsible for the décor of the new Super-G Constellation, was called in to coordinate the color scheme of the new hostess uniforms with the shades of warm cocoa brown, soft green and gold-touched beige which set the color scheme for the Super-G interior."[28]

TWA inaugurated nonstop transcontinental Super-G service in April 1955, offering both first-class and coach fares on the same airplane—an industry first. A press release touted the plane's different compartments decorated with "deep pile carpets, rich colors with gold accents, indirect lighting, natural wood paneling, and wide comfortable seats [that] suggest the atmosphere of a fine hotel."[29] The Super-G reduced nonstop, transcontinental flight times to around 8 hours, making it competitive with American and United's DC-7s. By midsummer, with the full complement of 20 Super-Gs in service, nine daily flights were offered, including nonstop between San Francisco and New York, and service to Chicago, St. Louis, and Kansas City.[30] Long-range Super-Gs also served on international routes.

The Wonderful World of Disney

By the mid-1950s growing numbers of Americans had enough disposable income that leisure air travel became an important market, a trend TWA and other carriers expected to continue. Walt Disney launched a new form of family entertainment with Disneyland, a groundbreaking theme park in Anaheim, California. In the fall of 1954 he inaugurated the weekly *Disneyland* television series with episodes featuring Davy Crockett, "King of the Wild Frontier," to build public interest in Disney films and the new park. TWA saw an opportunity to enlist Disney in its marketing efforts. The airline negotiated a contract in October 1954, giving it exclusive identification rights for a period of five years at an annual cost of $45,000 in connection with "the Space Ship Theatre to be constructed and operated by Disneyland, Inc. in the 'Land of Tomorrow' area of Disneyland." Disney's Rocket to the Moon ride in Tomorrowland bore TWA markings, and TWA became the "Official Airline to Disneyland."

TWA used the Disney connection to promote vacation travel. "TWA takes you comfortably, swiftly to fabulous Disneyland. Enjoy all the wonders of Fantasyland, Frontierland, Adventureland and Tomorrowland . . . take a ride in TWA's 'Rocket to the Moon.' Fly TWA to Los Angeles," read

As depicted in this July 1955 timetable cover, the union of TWA and Disney was made in the heavens. Alan Hoffman Collection.

a promotional postcard. "Fly TWA to Walt Disney's Magic Kingdom. Disneyland—A Dream Come True." TWA also used Disney in its Super-G promotions. Noting that both Walt Disney and his wife had lived in Kansas City, TWA's public relations department organized a press flight from Kansas City to visit the Disney studios and view progress at the Disneyland construction site.[31] TWA made the Super-G its flagship and symbol in the mid-1950s, using the plane to sell air travel as a vital part of the vacation experience.

In the fall of 1955, Disney premiered the *Mickey Mouse Club* on network TV to entertain kids after school. It had an ensemble cast of child actors and serials—*The Hardy Boys*, *Spin and Marty*, *Corky and White Shadow*—to keep kids tuning in. Producer Stirling Silliphant created a series of episodes titled "What I Want to Be" and negotiated a deal with TWA for the first of the series: "Airline Pilot, Airline Hostess." Youngsters Duncan and Pat teamed up with adult actor Alvy Moore, who led Duncan through TWA pilot training and Pat through hostess training. Then they traveled on a TWA Super-G Constellation from Los Angeles to New York, where they shadowed their adult counterparts. The 10-part series ran for two weeks in October 1955 and was a hit.[32] It made air travel appealing to kids and adults—and helped sustain demand for recreational air travel in the 1960s.

The Coming of the Jet

Although the American aircraft industry dominated commercial aircraft manufacturing in the early postwar period, Britain had a head start in jet engine technology. Its aviation leaders hoped to leapfrog over American manufacturers and airlines by developing the first jet airliner. The jet engine was well suited to military aircraft. It offered much greater power than piston engines and functioned best at high altitudes, where the thin air made far greater speed possible. But early jet engines were inefficient. Their high fuel consumption limited the potential range and payload of jet-powered aircraft, a major drawback for commercial use.

The British government promoted the development of several new postwar airliners, and the de Havilland Company accepted the challenge of creating the first commercial jet. In 1949 it rolled out the Comet, a sleek, elegant craft that could cruise at 460 mph at altitudes above 30,000 feet—nearly 200 mph faster and 10,000 feet higher than the contemporary Constellation and DC-6—with a range of up to 2,000 miles. The Comet could carry only 36 passengers, but it provided them a high degree of luxury. It was smooth, quiet, and fast, and after three years of testing, the Comet was put into service in May 1952. Demand exceeded capacity, and flights were fully booked months in advance.

Howard Hughes was fascinated by the prospect of jet airliners and sent chief engineer Robert Rummel to visit England and evaluate buying Comets for TWA. After returning home Rummel advised against buying the Comet, and Hughes agreed. But the decision was unpopular at TWA after Pan American placed an order for six of them.[33]

Then, in January 1954, a BOAC Comet exploded in midair and fell into the Mediterranean after departing from Rome. Three months later another Comet exploded, also shortly after takeoff from Rome, and once again the wreckage fell into the sea. After the second disaster the entire Comet fleet was grounded, and an unprecedented investigative effort was launched. The investigation determined that the crashes were the result of explosive decompression caused by fatigue cracking of the Comet's fuselage structure. The original Comets were modified to eliminate this defect, but they never returned to airline service. By the time the improved Comet 4 appeared in 1958, it had been overtaken by American jets. Rummel's advice to pass on the Comet was vindicated.[34]

The Jet Age Arrives

In the early 1950s, Douglas and Lockheed were busy building DC-6s and Constellations, but they were reluctant to tackle the challenge of creating commercial jets, which had unknown reliability, economics, and market potential. Boeing, the other major aircraft manufacturer, was almost exclusively a military builder. Responding to Cold War military needs, Boeing concentrated on developing the swept wing B-47 and B-52 jet bombers. Creating these large military jets put Boeing at the forefront of aviation technology and gave it a head start in innovating a jet airliner. The Air Force also needed a jet tanker with similar performance, and in March 1952 Boeing's president, William Allen, convinced his board of directors to take the plunge and build a prototype jet transport for potential military and commercial use.[35] The decision would change the company—and the world.

Boeing's prototype jet transport, commonly known as the "Dash 80," made its first flight in July 1954. Designed to satisfy the Air Force's need for a jet transport and tanker, the Dash 80 was capable of speeds double those of current piston-powered airliners. In addition to generating a large contract for the military KC-135, it also became the prototype of the commercial Model 707—the airplane that truly launched the jet age and revolutionized air travel.

Meanwhile, Douglas announced the DC-8, its competing jetliner. It did not offer the plane to TWA—perhaps as a way to avoid dealing with Hughes—leaving Boeing's 707 the only alternative. But Hughes dithered. He even considered buying Comet 4s or Britannia turboprops as an interim measure. By the end of 1955, Pan American, United, and American all placed large orders for DC-8s and 707s while TWA had yet to act.[36] It was a time of great frustration for Damon, who was stymied as competitors moved swiftly ahead. Hughes's hand was finally forced. In late December 1955 he relented and allowed expedited negotiations with Boeing for a token, "stopgap" order of only eight domestic 707s.[37]

Then, on January 4, 1956, Ralph Damon died suddenly after a short illness, leaving TWA leaderless at a critical time. The TWA directors named John Collings, TWA's vice president of operations, as interim chief executive while the search for a new president began. Brusque and peremptory, Collings was not well liked by his colleagues or his subordinates, but he was subservient to Hughes, a quality that figured in his selection by the Hughes-controlled board.[38]

The Last Constellation

Although the days of piston-powered airliners were coming to an end, a gap remained to be filled before jets were available for long-range international routes. Douglas responded with the DC-7C. It not only had greater range than TWA's Super-G, but it also was faster. Pan American quickly ordered DC-7Cs for the highly competitive transatlantic routes to Europe. Douglas was willing to tailor the DC-7C to meet TWA's requirements, but once again Hughes procrastinated.

At this time Lockheed was developing a new Constellation, combining the Super-G's fuselage with a massive new wing and powered by four turboprop engines. Called the Model 1449, it promised to be 100 mph faster than the Super-G, making it nearly competitive with pure jet designs. But the new turboprop engine had no established track record, and it was expensive to operate. Nevertheless, Hughes was excited by the 1449's potential performance, and Hughes Tool ordered 25 of them. Hughes Tool offered to provide TWA an option to purchase all the planes at cost, plus interest on the purchase price. The Hughes-dominated TWA board accepted this proposal.[39]

Shortly after this deal was made, Lockheed informed TWA management that the new plane could not proceed owing to engine development problems. The only feasible alternative was to install the same piston engines used by the Super-G. The new wing's additional fuel capacity gave the Model 1649 a range of over 5,000 miles—greater than any other airliner—and Hughes eventually decided to buy it. Then, recognizing that the market for the 1649 was limited, Lockheed tried to cancel the plane. Instead of seizing the opportunity to extricate himself from a bad deal, Hughes demanded that Lockheed honor the Model 1649 contract.[40]

When this ultimate Constellation finally entered service, TWA called it "Jetstream" to downplay the reality that it was piston powered. Its great

Displaced by jets, "Jetstream" Model 1649A Super Constellations lasted only five years in TWA passenger service. A Model 1649A is shown here, its engines running, at Lambert Airport in 1962. David Ostrowski Collection, Greater St. Louis Air and Space Museum.

range allowed nonstop flights between the West Coast and Europe; the inaugural flight from Los Angeles to London took nearly 24 hours—the longest scheduled airline flight in history up to that time. But the allure of spending an entire day on a propeller-driven plane wasn't great, even with luxurious amenities. The 1649 was a money loser for the airline and the manufacturer—a bad deal for all concerned, thanks to Hughes's intransigence and inability to make timely decisions.

Hughes Orders Jets

In March 1956, Hughes finally authorized Hughes Tool to contract for eight domestic 707s—not nearly enough to compete effectively with American and United. A few days later Hughes Tool contracted for 18 larger international 707s. Hughes took nearly another year to increase the domestic order to 15 planes, for a total of 33 Boeing jets on order. But his delays lost valuable early delivery positions and put TWA at a competitive disadvantage in commencing jet service.[41] Although the 707s were ordered for TWA, Hughes emphasized that Hughes Tool owned them and that TWA had "no rights whatsoever" to the planes.[42]

With the ink barely dry on the 707 contracts, Hughes entered into negotiations with Convair for another new jetliner. Rather than develop one to compete with the 707 and DC-8, Convair opted for a smaller plane to serve US domestic routes. Originally called the Model 22 Skylark and later renamed the 880, it offered 80-passenger capacity and transcontinental range, potentially complementing TWA's larger 707s.[43]

Six months later Hughes Tool signed a contract for 30 Convair 880s. As with the Boeing 707s, Hughes took the position that TWA had no rights to the 880s—they were owned by Hughes Tool—leaving TWA in limbo while attempting to break into the jet age.[44] Hughes increased the original order for 8 domestic 707s to 15 in January 1957. With 15 domestic 707s, 18 intercontinental 707s, and 30 Convair 880s on order, Hughes Tool was now committed to buy 63 jets, plus spare engines and parts, at a cost exceeding $400 million.[45] The question was whether it could finance them.

Do It Yourself

While the jet purchases were being negotiated with Boeing and Convair, Hughes decided that the Hughes Aircraft division of Hughes Tool should manufacture its own jetliners. Called "Project Greenland," this venture envisioned building even larger, longer-range planes than Boeing's Intercontinental 707s. In addition to requiring financial resources beyond those of Hughes Tool, it presented serious legal obstacles. Since 1934 the government had outlawed common ownership of airlines and aircraft manufacturers, and it was questionable whether the project could be approved by a waiver from the Civil Aeronautics Board.[46] Undaunted, Hughes filed a motion with the CAB in May 1956 to permit the arrangement, saying, "During the past few years important new developments have occurred affecting jet performance which make it possible to design aircraft that are superior in performance, safety, and economy to the commercial aircraft now being constructed." With the 707 and DC-8 still on the drawing board, this filing was a bombshell. *Business Week* asked, "Does Hughes have a design that will render obsolete the Douglas and Boeing jets?"[47]

Hughes made plans for a massive complex in Florida where the as-yet-undesigned airliner would be built. He acquired options on thousands of acres of bare ground and began discussions with Florida governor LeRoy Collins, giving him a "tentative commitment" (whatever that meant) to proceed with the project. He opened an office in Miami and held a press conference announcing his intention to build the complex and employ more than 20,000 workers. By all indications, Hughes was serious about these plans.

While Hughes was sowing these great expectations in Florida, the CAB was less than enthusiastic. It commenced an investigation into Hughes's application, demanding detailed information on the proposed aircraft and the relationship between Hughes Tool and TWA. It also announced a public hearing on the application, where Hughes would be required to testify. At this point Hughes had not been seen in public for years, and the prospect of having to appear and give sworn testimony in a proceeding that would be a major media event chilled his interest in Project Greenland. The CAB application languished until it was finally withdrawn in 1958. Whether Hughes ever really intended to pursue such a far-fetched scheme, whether it was a negotiating ploy to strengthen his hand with the manufacturers, or whether it reflected a further loss of touch with reality, were all questions that went unanswered.

Tragedy at the Grand Canyon

On June 30, 1956, TWA Flight 2, a 1049A Super Constellation, departed from Los Angeles for Kansas City and began climbing to its assigned cruising altitude of 19,000 feet. Minutes later United Flight 718, a DC-7, also took off from Los Angeles, bound for Chicago, and was cleared to climb to 21,000 feet by air traffic control (ATC). Passing Needles, California, both planes entered uncontrolled airspace where ATC was not required to provide traffic separation under the regulations then in effect, even though both were operating on instrument flight plans. Each crew was responsible for seeing and avoiding the other aircraft.[50]

Prior to leaving controlled airspace, ATC cleared the TWA Super Constellation to fly at "1,000 feet on top" of the clouds, which also put it at 21,000 feet. Although ATC informed the pilots that the United DC-7 was flying at the same altitude, it failed to warn either flight that they were estimated to reach a checkpoint near the Grand Canyon at the same time. The two planes collided and fell into the canyon. All 128 passengers and crew on both planes died, making it the worst US air accident up to that time. How could such a disaster have happened?

More than a year later the CAB released its accident investigation report, but it ultimately assigned no responsibility and made no recommendations. It stated unequivocally that under visual flight conditions, it was the pilots' responsibility to maintain separation from other aircraft, but it found neither flight crew at fault for failing to see and avoid the other plane. It also noted that collision studies had "pointed out that seeing other aircraft in flight is difficult"—a statement no pilot would dispute. The controller who failed to warn either flight that it was on a collision course with the other was absolved by the CAB because he had no duty to do so under the current regulations. Both flights were operating under a confusing patchwork of instrument- and visual-flight rules.

The report noted that "the vast percentage of flying today is separated by the 'see and be seen' philosophy with little or no external traffic control assistance" and that "control is not presently available in the uncontrolled airspace because sufficient facilities and means for such control do not exist."[51] This was hardly reassuring to the flying public. The "see and be seen" concept, dating to the 1920s, was clearly incompatible with increasing numbers of commercial and military aircraft flying at high altitudes and high speeds.

Reform was badly needed. Congress held hearings to address the safety of flying in these crowded skies. It resolved to increase funding to modernize air traffic control, hire and train more air traffic controllers, and provide additional radar capability. But control of airspace remained split between the military and the Civil Aeronautics Administration, which lacked authority over military flights.

In April 1958 a United DC-7 and a US Air Force jet fighter collided near Las Vegas, killing all 49 on both aircraft. Following this tragedy Congress finally acted. It passed the Federal Aviation Act of 1958, which created the Federal Aviation Agency (later renamed the Federal Aviation Administration). The FAA was vested with authority over all American airspace, including military activity, and given responsibility for all aspects of air safety. Air traffic control facilities were modernized, and airlines were required to operate under instrument-flight rules (IFR)—rules that govern flight operations solely by reference to instruments as opposed to visual reference—at all times. Midair collisions and near misses declined, but they did not cease altogether. Four years later another TWA Super Constellation would collide with another United plane, with a similarly tragic outcome.

Another New President

TWA remained effectively leaderless for a year after Ralph Damon's death and, in 1956, lost money for the first time in eight years. Acting on Noah Dietrich's recommendation, Howard Hughes finally selected Carter Burgess as TWA's new president in January 1957. Burgess, who had served as the assistant secretary of defense, was as strong willed and aggressive as Hughes. Soon after taking over, Burgess requested a report on TWA's jet acquisition plans. He was surprised to learn that Hughes believed TWA had no right to any of the planes ordered by Hughes Tool. Burgess explored the possibility of purchasing 707s directly from the builder, but Boeing declined, recognizing that it was impossible without Hughes's consent.[52]

Now leading an airline that, in his view, had "a lousy reputation for on-time performance and a lousy record for service," Burgess promptly tried to turn things around. He fired the interim CEO and went on the road making military-like "white glove" inspections of TWA facilities.[53] While Burgess wanted to improve TWA's management and service, his bluntness and peremptory manner did not endear him to TWA personnel. He also clashed with Hughes, who largely ignored him, preferring to deal directly with subordinates on aircraft acquisitions and other critical decisions.[54]

For more than 30 years Noah Dietrich had tended the seemingly boundless flow of Hughes Tool money that Hughes relied upon to finance his activities. But the $400 million in jet orders placed between 1955 and 1957 exceeded the company's financial resources. Dietrich and other Hughes Tool executives became alarmed, insisting that the company should use debt to finance the orders. But borrowing was anathema to Hughes because he feared it would threaten his absolute control over Hughes Tool. Potential lenders were also reluctant to deal with him.[55]

Dietrich reportedly attempted to have Hughes declared incompetent. It has even been suggested that Hughes's January 1957 marriage to actress Jean Peters may have been in part intended to forestall such an effort. Whatever the cause, Dietrich's relationship with Hughes became increasingly strained as he continued to insist that Hughes allow outside financing efforts to proceed.[56]

Matters came to a head in May 1957, when Hughes pressed Dietrich to increase profits. Dietrich responded by making demands for an equity interest in Hughes Tool. That proved to be too much for Hughes, who drew the line at sharing ownership with anyone. When Dietrich arrived at 7000 Romaine Street the next day, he found the locks had been changed. He was not even allowed to clean out his desk.[57] As the financial crisis deepened, Hughes was now without his indispensable right-hand man.[58]

The Viscount Debacle

In late 1956, Hughes renewed an earlier interest in the British Vickers Viscount, a four-engine turboprop airliner that had successfully entered the American market the year before with an order for 60 from Capital Airlines. Capital operated in the east, its prime route between New York and Chicago. At that time Capital had a motley fleet of secondhand planes and was struggling financially. The Viscounts allowed Capital to compete effectively with piston-powered equipment, and it ordered 15 more of them. But the airline's shaky finances could not support such a large fleet, and it soon canceled the additional order, leaving the planes with no buyer.[59]

Vickers offered the planes to TWA at a substantial discount. Hughes decided that he needed a Viscount for flight testing, and Vickers, anxious to make the sale, sent a Viscount across the Atlantic to New York and placed it at his disposal. Reprising earlier incidents, Hughes put the airplane under armed guard and allowed no one near it—even though he had no legal right to do so—then left it sitting at LaGuardia Airport for months. Meanwhile, Burgess decided that TWA could use the Viscounts, only to later change his mind. Hughes accepted the decision but honored his verbal agreement with Vickers by helping it find buyers for the orphaned planes.[60] As he had said during the congressional investigation, Hughes was a man of his word, but Burgess had burned his bridges. Still at odds with Hughes, Burgess resigned in December 1957, leaving TWA leaderless on the eve of the jet age.

Hughes allowed TWA to sell additional stock in 1957, raising $43 million to help pay for its Jetstream Constellations. Hughes Tool also loaned TWA $5.8 million and guaranteed an additional $12 million in short-term bank financing. But there wasn't a firm plan for financing the jet fleet or any guarantee that Hughes would release the new planes to TWA. TWA's financial vice president acknowledged, "The general outlook for business is far less satisfactory than last year," as TWA posted a $3.9 million loss for 1957.[61]

Following Burgess's departure TWA's board formed a committee to identify candidates for a new president, and a "jet planning function" was established to get ready for the hoped-for arrival of jets. But without effective leadership in the meantime, the company hemorrhaged money and lost nearly $12 million in the first six months of 1958.[62] Hughes eventually chose Charles S. Thomas to be TWA's next president. Like Burgess, Thomas came from the US Department of Defense and had a reputation for effecting change. He was initially horrified by the prospect of working for Hughes, but Hughes put on a charm offensive and Thomas finally succumbed, lured by the challenge of trying to rescue TWA. He told Hughes that he would come aboard for two years, and if Hughes was not satisfied with his performance, he would leave. Hughes agreed. Thomas was duly elected president in July 1958 and immediately went to work trying to clean up the mess he had inherited.[63]

One of Thomas's first acts was to request a $9 million reduction in the $28 million budgeted by the jet-planning group for integrating the new planes into TWA's operations. Through herculean efforts the group succeeded in making more than $15 million in reductions. He worked with TWA management to review operations and found ways to streamline them, cutting 1958's first-half loss of $12 million down to $1.7 million for the full year. Like Damon, Thomas also rebuilt employee morale. He learned how to say no to Hughes without getting fired while accepting that Hughes controlled the airline and could do as he pleased.[64]

TWA Enters the Jet Age

Pan American began operating 707s on its transatlantic routes in October 1958, and American Airlines inaugurated the first US domestic 707 service three months later. In response, Hughes allowed TWA to lease a single 707 from Hughes Tool on a day-to-day basis to prepare for jet operations. On March 20, 1959, TWA became the second domestic jet carrier when it began flying its one and only 707 nonstop between San Francisco and New York. It managed to sustain daily transcontinental service for three weeks with this single plane, without a cancellation or delay—an extraordinary accomplishment by an airline beholden to Hughes's machinations.[65] In February, Hughes agreed to lease TWA five additional 707s.

EFFECTIVE APRIL 1, 1959

TWA

TRANS WORLD AIRLINES
U.S.A. · EUROPE · AFRICA · ASIA

FLY TWA JETS

TWA BOEING 707
(see back cover)

Fly the Finest... FLY **TWA**

This April 1959 timetable shows TWA's newly inaugurated Boeing 707 jet service. Schwantes-Greever-Nolan Collection.

Jet service was highly successful from the start, but TWA fell behind American Airlines and intercontinental rival Pan Am owing to its shortage of jet equipment. As additional domestic 707s became available they were quickly put to work. By the end of 1959, TWA was operating 15 domestic and 4 intercontinental 707s. The airline served 12 domestic cities with 30 daily jet flights and operated daily jet flights from New York to London, Frankfurt, Paris, and Rome. That year TWA earned a near-record $9.4 million profit.[67] But despite these positive developments, all was not well. With growing financial pressure on Hughes Tool, the Convair 880 order was cut from 30 to 20 planes. Hughes also assigned six intercontinental 707s on order to archrival Pan American, thereby putting TWA at a further competitive disadvantage internationally.[68] But Hughes still hadn't secured financing for the undelivered planes.

A Jet Age Terminal

As part of marketing the air travel experience, TWA endeavored to create a unique passenger terminal at its international gateway in New York. After New York's LaGuardia Airport was built, Mayor Fiorello LaGuardia anticipated the need for a larger air terminal to handle more passengers and bigger airliners. A site comprising nearly 5,000 acres—eight times the size of LaGuardia—was assembled 15 miles southeast of Manhattan in Jamaica Bay, and construction began in 1942.[69]

The original plan called for no fewer than 12 runways, some over 2 miles in length—double the requirements of contemporary airliners—arranged around a central terminal area and served by limited-access high-speed highways. Originally projected to cost $10 million, by 1945 the price tag had already risen to $60 million (about $1 billion in 2023) and was estimated to reach $200 million. A permanent six-story administration building was planned for completion in 1947, with no fewer than 102 boarding gates. "The greatest railroad terminals will pale in comparison with this gigantic structure," one account predicted.[70]

After many construction delays and cost overruns, the new airport, named Idlewild, finally opened in July 1948. Far from the "gigantic structure" envisioned by prewar planners, it began with only a small, temporary terminal that quickly became overcrowded. Airlines were hesitant to move to Idlewild, and TWA did not start using the airport until 1951.[71]

In an effort to make Idlewild more attractive, the Port Authority of New York and New Jersey, which operated the airport, devised a plan to allow individual airlines to create their own dedicated terminals, including incentives to compete for excellence in design. Known as "Terminal City," the plan called for six individual airline terminals, a seventh to be shared by three airlines, and an international terminal for overseas carriers. TWA received a site close to the original terminal, and after a careful search tapped famed modern architect Eero Saarinen in late 1955 to design a structure that "would provide TWA with advertising, publicity and attention." Saarinen devoted himself to that goal and devised a futuristic design known as the TWA Flight Center.[72]

Saarinen began design work on the Flight Center in March 1956, an effort that took 18 months to complete. While some at TWA were unhappy with the site's location, Saarinen realized that it was directly in line with the airport access road and would be the first thing visitors saw as they approached the terminal area. To Saarinen, it was an opportunity to showcase the terminal and make it a dramatic, commanding presence.[73] Saarinen's wife, Aline, an art historian and former *New York Times* journalist, was his public relations and communications director. She worked tirelessly to build interest in the project from its inception through its completion.[74]

Creating the Flight Center

Unveiled with much fanfare in November 1957, Saarinen's Flight Center design admirably fulfilled TWA's objectives, as well as his own. Supposedly inspired by a grapefruit rind that Saarinen flipped over and pressed down, the design featured sweeping, wing-like roof structures intended to be evocative of flight and the coming jet age. It was to be a "distinctive and memorable" building that would "express the drama and specialness and excitement of travel." "As the passenger walked through the sequence of the building," Saarinen said, "we wanted him to be in a total environment where each part was a consequence of another, and all belonged to the same form-world."[75]

But translating Saarinen's vision for the Flight Center into reality would prove a monumental task with costly engineering and construction challenges. The graceful but complex thin-shell concrete roof required an intricate web of steel rebar that weighed more than 1 million pounds, with an additional 10 million pounds of concrete poured over it into wood forms.

Ground was broken on June 9, 1959, and the difficult task of executing the elaborate design began. By the end of the year the foundations had been poured, and work had begun on constructing the formwork and its reinforcements. "Nothing like this has ever been attempted," the project manager said after construction commenced. "Engineers and architects all over the world are watching to see how this turns out."[76]

The project was originally approved by the TWA board in 1957 for a cost not to exceed $8.5 million (about $92 million in 2023). It included the main terminal building and two satellite structures for boarding areas; planes could park around them, and they'd be connected to the terminal by reinforced concrete tubes. Then major revisions were made, including the decision to use jetways for boarding, which necessitated redesigning the satellites to allow boarding from the second level. The estimated cost ballooned to over $13 million by early 1959. Extensive negotiations with the architect and the contractors resulted in changes that brought the cost back to the original estimate. The board gave its blessing to proceed in March 1959.[77]

TWA's marketing strategy had long been to sell air travel as modern, glamorous, and exciting. The Flight Center was an integral part of that strategy. TWA again turned to commercial designer Raymond Loewy to give the airline a refreshed look for the jet age. Loewy created a new TWA logo using the traditional slanted red block letters surrounded by interlocking golden hemispheres, symbolizing TWA's domestic and international reach— something no other US airline offered at the time. TWA used the twin-globe logo at ticket offices, airport gates, boarding stairs, and ground support equipment. Loewy also replaced the planes' conservative parallel red stripes with a dynamic, arrow-like red design that conveyed the speed and drama of the new jetliners. He helped design TWA hostess uniforms that coordinated with his theme. "One moves through miles by becoming somehow a slightly different person," said Loewy. "Instead of being just plain old Joe, here he is an interesting stranger bent on some unknown mission."[78]

As the 1960s began TWA looked expectantly toward the jet age. But behind the upbeat publicity, a crisis was looming for the airline and its owner.

Chapter 5
THE JET AGE: 1960–1969

TWA had 28 Boeing 707s in service by the start of 1960. The jets proved extremely popular with passengers, even though ticket prices were higher. TWA soon relegated its Constellations to second-level routes as jet service expanded. Along with its president's sound management reforms, these factors helped return TWA to profitability for the first time since Ralph Damon's death. But all was not well.

A New Decade

TWA's jet fleet was still too small to compete effectively with American, United, and Pan American, all of which were growing rapidly. Hughes had split his orders between Boeing 707s and the smaller Convair 880s. While he had managed to arrange financing for the Boeings, he had yet to solve the financial puzzle for the Convairs. Hughes Tool's finances were strained to the limit, and Hughes began resorting to increasingly desperate measures to buy time.

Convair had orders for 40 880s: 30 for Hughes Tool and 10 for Delta Airlines, with deliveries scheduled to begin in the fall of 1959. But Hughes Tool could not make the cash payments required for delivery. Hughes ordered the aircraft to be parked at the Convair factory under armed guard as they came off the production line and allowed no one near them—even though Hughes Tool did not own the planes, and Hughes had no right to do so. Convair could not complete the work needed for delivery, and TWA could not inspect them for acceptance. It was an extraordinary situation, but Convair acceded to Hughes's actions because its commercial aircraft business was suffering, and it wanted to keep him as a customer.[1]

Hughes tried to enlist Convair and Lockheed in arranging financing, but each manufacturer had its own problems and was unable to bail him out. Hughes could have solved his cash problem by using conventional commercial financing, but that would have limited his absolute control over Hughes Tool and TWA. Meanwhile, TWA's Thomas became increasingly frustrated trying to run the airline with an inadequate number of 707s leased on a day-to-day basis, as the 880s sat under armed guard at Convair.

As a financial crisis loomed in March 1960, Thomas revived a plan that had been drawn up by the financial house Dillion, Read & Company, which Hughes had previously rejected. The plan offered a $260 million financing package for TWA to purchase the jets outright, rather than lease them from Hughes Tool. It also called for Hughes to place his TWA stock, constituting 78 percent of the outstanding shares, in a voting trust if changes in TWA management occurred or other financial covenants were not met. Thomas submitted the Dillon Read plan to the TWA board, warning that if it were not accepted, the airline would fail. The directors approved the plan and threatened to resign if Hughes balked. Faced with this ultimatum, Hughes reluctantly acceded to the plan—or so it appeared.[2]

Thomas and Hughes were now on a collision course, with Hughes stating that Thomas had developed the plan without him and then turned TWA's board against him. "I assure you that if [the plan] is employed, it will be over my dead body," he said.[3] Thomas's patience finally ran out. He resigned in July 1960, accusing Hughes of damaging TWA by denying it the jets it needed. Seeking to stave off the inevitable, Hughes solicited Irving Trust to devise an alternate plan, including funding from Convair in return for orders for 880s and 990s, but it foundered because of Convair's own financial difficulties.[4]

In the wake of Thomas's resignation, TWA's executive committee voted to remain in continuous session "to administer the business and affairs of the Corporation, including those matters normally requiring action by the President."[5] Meanwhile, Convair continued to tender 880s for acceptance as they came off the production line, which Hughes refused to accept. With no prospect of early payment, Convair suspended production of the 880s for TWA in October 1960. Hughes then negotiated an agreement to reduce the Hughes Tool order from 30 planes to 24, hoping to find a way to finance and lease them to TWA on a long-term basis. This would allow Hughes Tool to deduct depreciation on them and substantially reduce its income taxes.[6]

Colonel Henry Crown, principal shareholder of Convair's corporate parent General Dynamics, put forth yet another rescue plan. It called for $150 million in bank loans, $150 million in new borrowing by TWA, and, not incidentally, additional jet purchases from Convair. Hughes welcomed the Crown plan as a possible escape from Dillon Read and the voting trust, but it went nowhere because of the financial markets' distaste for airline debt securities—particularly TWA's.

Howard's End

Hughes's financial woes deepened when a $12 million loan he had taken out years earlier from Irving Trust to buy RKO Studios came due in October 1960. Irving seized Hughes Tool and TWA's accounts, threatening to force

Hughes's inability to finance a fleet of these sleek Convair 880 jets led to his ouster in 1960. R. A. Burgess Collection, Greater St. Louis Air and Space Museum.

Hughes Tool into bankruptcy if the loan were not repaid. Then Convair, its patience exhausted, demanded that Hughes Tool accept the completed 880s and pay for them, which it could not do.[8] In November the Civil Aeronautics Board warned TWA that unless it provided definite assurance of financing within one week, it would commence an investigation of Hughes's fitness to control the airline.[9]

Adding to the chaos, Hughes fired Raymond Cook, the Houston attorney who had handled the negotiations with lenders and gained their confidence, and replaced him with Greg Bautzer, a Hollywood lawyer who had represented him in personal matters. Facing a revolt by the directors of both TWA and Hughes Tool, plus the possible loss of his wealth and empire, Hughes had no choice but to accept the Dillon Read plan and the despised voting trust.[10]

Hughes Tool and TWA both approved the Dillon Read plan on December 3, 1960, and four days later Hughes signed off on it.[11] Given two of the three seats on the voting trust, the lenders chose Ernest R. Breech, the recently retired chairman of the Ford Motor Company who had been associated with TWA in the 1930s, and Irving S. Olds, the former chairman of US Steel. Hughes picked Raymond Holliday, the financial vice president of Hughes Tool, who had represented Hughes on the TWA board since Noah Dietrich's 1957 departure. At 7:25 p.m. on Friday, December 30, the last business day of 1960, Holliday signed the last of the papers to close the Dillon Read agreement. The title to all of TWA's planes was immediately transferred to the lenders.[12]

In the end, Hughes's obsessive need for total control cost him TWA and very nearly cost him Hughes Tool. He still owned 78 percent of TWA's stock, but his shares would now be controlled by the voting trust. Hughes's tumultuous years in charge at TWA were over, but he began trying to regain control of the airline almost immediately—battles he would fight for the rest of his life.

Leaving on a Jet Plane

The coming of jet airliners revolutionized air travel. They were 200 mph faster than TWA's Constellations, without the noise and vibration of piston engines. Jetliners flew much higher, above most weather and turbulence, and finally achieved the benefits of high-altitude flight that TWA's pioneering 1930s research flights had anticipated. Jet engines were more reliable than complex, highly stressed piston engines. The speed and passenger capacity of jetliners made them more productive, allowing the airlines to lower fares and attract more passengers. Where TWA's Constellations carried 60 to 65 passengers at 300 mph, its domestic 707s carried 125 passengers from coast to coast in 5 hours at 500 mph. Intercontinental 707s took 140 passengers nonstop from New York to London in 6 hours.

Jets made the world more compact: Flying coast to coast would have taken 48 hours barely 30 years earlier, but now it was all in a day's work to board a jet in New York in the morning and have lunch in San Francisco, or to leave New York in the evening and attend a meeting or sightsee in Paris the next morning—albeit, perhaps, with a bit of jet lag.

All of these changes made air travel more appealing and more affordable than ever before, and leisure travel flourished. Families could now escape from the cold and snow of Chicago in March, reach Los Angeles in 4 hours to spend spring vacation in sunny Southern California, and take a ride on the TWA Rocket to the Moon at Disneyland. US domestic passenger air traffic grew from 56 million in 1959, the first year of jet service, to 92 million in 1965. It reached 153 million by 1970.[13]

Travelers' introduction to jets was exhilarating. Climbing the steps to a TWA 707 (jetways for boarding were not common until the late 1960s) and passing through the door was to enter an almost magical realm. Welcoming hostesses in their sharp new jet age uniforms were ready to greet passengers and help them to their seats. They provided pull-over socks so passengers could remove their shoes and rest or stroll comfortably about the cabin. In the early days, hostesses handed out paper sunglasses to protect passengers' eyes from the supposedly harmful rays of sub-stratospheric sunlight. (The practice was soon abandoned as needless, and it tended to make passengers feel less at ease, rather than more.)

Raymond Loewy designed the TWA hostess uniform depicted here, ca. 1960. The style of this uniform was the embodiment of the jet age. From J. E. Frankum, Legacy of Leadership, *1971.*

Meal service was of a higher caliber than standard airline fare, enjoyed on a drop-down table instead of on a metal tray attached to the passenger's seat or from a tray balanced precariously on the passenger's legs. TWA inaugurated a champagne brunch service for its Ambassador Class jet flights, consisting of hot lobster Newburg in a pastry shell and asparagus spears garnished with pimentos, French dessert and, of course, a glass of champagne. Passengers' tables were set with linen tablecloths, delicate Rosenthal china, crystal, and Reed & Barton flatware. Cocktails were followed by a large and varied menu, including caviar; hors d'oeuvres; soup; and a choice of chicken, steak, lobster, lamb, or duckling entrées. Chateaubriand was cooked to order and carved on a cart at the passenger's seat. Salad, cheese, fresh fruit, pastries, and ice cream desserts rounded out the dinner menu.[14]

But TWA's hostesses did not jump to bid for these early jet flights. The doubled passenger loads and shorter flight times brought new and unwelcome burdens. Hostesses had to fly 70 hours a month, with more trips and fewer days off. There were also new duties to be mastered, including administering emergency oxygen service and deploying escape slides. The first jet hostesses came from the lowest seniority ranks and were generally younger and more amenable to change.[15] By the time aviation writer Lou Davis took his first transcontinental flight on a TWA 707 in early 1960, more than 1 million people had already experienced jet travel. Those who had flown jets before shared their experiences with the newcomers. Davis wrote, "Passengers relaxed as if to say, 'Why didn't someone tell us it was like this?'"[16]

The Crowded Sky

Tragedy occurred on December 16, 1960. United Flight 826, a DC-8 jet from Chicago bound for New York's Idlewild, struck TWA Flight 266, a Super Constellation en route from Dayton, Ohio, to New York's LaGuardia. The collision occurred over Staten Island on a foggy, wintry day with low clouds and poor visibility. The right wing of the United jet sliced into the Super Constellation's fuselage just ahead of the wing, tearing the airplane apart. It crashed onto Staten Island, killing all 44 on board. The United aircraft, minus one engine and much of its right wing, staggered on as the crew fought unsuccessfully to remain airborne before falling into a densely populated Brooklyn neighborhood near Prospect Park. It crashed into an apartment building and continued into the street, coming to rest in the Methodist Pillar of Fire Church, which burst into flames along with the jet's wreckage. All 84 on board and 6 others on the ground perished. The toll could have been even worse, for the plane narrowly missed two schools holding 1,700 students and teachers.

The event was shocking, coming only four years after the 1956 Grand Canyon midair collision involving the same two airlines. The Federal Aviation Administration had been formed to prevent such disasters. Millions of dollars had been spent on improving the air traffic control system, and FAA administrator Elwood Quesada had confidently assured the public that airline traffic was being monitored by radar "from takeoff to touchdown."[17] What had gone so horribly wrong?

The Civil Aeronautics Board accident investigation found that the United jet approached the New York terminal area still flying at cruising speed and altitude. The captain had elected to remain at high altitude because of possible weather delays in the busy New York airspace. Air traffic control cleared the flight to the Preston intersection, a holding point near New York, but because one of the plane's navigational radios was out of service, the United crew could not use their avionics to locate it. Instead they had to resort to manual time and distance calculations.[18] A few minutes later ATC gave the United flight a revised clearance that shortened the distance to Preston, saying, "It'll be a little bit quicker." The fast-moving jet was now forced to make a high-speed descent, barreling into the area at over 400 mph while attempting to shed altitude and slow down, as its crew tried to determine its position literally on the fly. United erroneously reported that it was "approaching Preston" when it was already 11 miles past it.[19]

Meanwhile the TWA Super Constellation was proceeding in accordance with its clearance and controllers' instructions. LaGuardia Approach Control, following the plane on radar, advised the pilots that the United flight was 6 miles distant and directed them to turn. Seconds later LaGuardia advised the TWA pilots that the United DC-8 was now only 1 mile away but did not alert them to a possible conflict or warn them to take prompt evasive action. Moments later the jet hit the Super Constellation at over 350 mph.[20]

The CAB found that the United crew, trying to calculate their position manually and experiencing a high workload, failed to account for the difference between their original and revised clearances, concluding, "United Flight 826 proceeded beyond its clearance limit and the confines of the airspace allocated to the flight by Air Traffic Control" and that "a contributing factor was the high rate of speed of the United DC-8 as it approached the Preston intersection, coupled with the change of clearance which reduced the en route distance by approximately 11 miles."[21]

Even though LaGuardia had both planes on radar—and controllers watched the two blips merge—they gave no warning to TWA. Air traffic control, which was also following United on radar, didn't note that the jet was far beyond its clearance limit, nor did it direct the United flight to change course. Yet the CAB assigned no responsibility to the FAA for these breakdowns in communication. The boast that airliners were being monitored by radar "from takeoff to touchdown" rang hollow in the face of this systemic failure.

After this crash the FAA imposed speed limits for planes operating within airport terminal areas, required pilots to report in-flight equipment failures, and implemented improvements to radar control procedures to help prevent other such tragedies. Even though the TWA pilots bore no responsibility for the collision, TWA and its insurers paid 15 percent of the settlement of the ensuing litigation, while United paid 60 percent, and the US government 25 percent.[22]

Better Times Ahead

The turmoil of 1960 inevitably took its toll on TWA's financial performance: Net income fell to $6.4 million from $9.4 million in 1959. But with Hughes no longer in control, TWA wasted no time taking action to resolve the mess he had created. On New Year's Day 1961 the airline accepted delivery of its first operational Convair 880 and received five more before the end of January, finally breaking the Convair logjam. Scheduled 880 service began on January 12, seven months later than originally planned.[23] Even so, the 880 was a hit with passengers.

Although Hughes no longer had authority over his TWA stock, he continued making mischief. He told the TWA directors whom he still controlled to skip board meetings, preventing action through absence of a quorum. The voting trustees countered by calling a special stockholder meeting to replace the Hughes holdouts.[24] The reconstituted board then authorized hiring independent counsel to investigate and report to the directors on the possibility of legal action against Hughes and Hughes Tool for the damage inflicted on the airline, setting the stage for an unprecedented, decades-long legal battle.

The TWA board formed a search committee to recruit a new president. It recommended Charles C. Tillinghast Jr., a senior vice president of Bendix Corporation, a major manufacturer of aviation and industrial products. Tall and distinguished looking, Tillinghast was the Hollywood central casting image of a corporate president. An effective manager who was also trained as a lawyer, he earned the respect of subordinates by carefully weighing their views and then acting decisively. Tillinghast was elected TWA president in April 1961, ushering in a successful tenure that would last for 15 years.[25]

Less than two weeks after Tillinghast took office, the board accepted his proposal to purchase an additional 18 domestic and 5 international Boeing 707s powered by Pratt & Whitney's new JT-3D turbofan engines, which produced more thrust, had better fuel economy, and were quieter than pure jets. The board also authorized a short-term lease of four turbofan-powered Boeing 720Bs, a slightly smaller version of the domestic 707 optimized for shorter routes. These moves put TWA back on a favorable course to recover the competitive position it had lost during the 1960 crisis.[26]

As jets brought more people into the sky, passengers now needed diversions to pass the time. Historically, airlines had devoted much effort to reassuring passengers that flying was safe and enjoyable by filling seatback

Charles Tillinghast was TWA's president, CEO, and chairman from 1961 to 1976. He led the airline out of the chaos of the Hughes era and into the jet age. From J. E. Frankum, Legacy of Leadership, *1971.*

pockets with detailed information on how planes were maintained and how pilots were able to safely take off, fly, and land in all weather. Passengers were told where to look for interesting landmarks on the ground and were even allowed to visit the cockpit while in flight. Those traditions began to change during the jet age.

With six-abreast coach seating, passengers had little opportunity for sightseeing from jets' small windows. As air travel became more commonplace, fewer passengers were interested in doing so anyway. The airline supplemented seatback safety information with advertising and descriptions of enticing air travel destinations. TWA offered products such as flight bags and luggage tags with the TWA logo—popular amenities that doubled as marketing tools.

But passengers confined to a long aluminum tube yearned for more entertaining options. TWA, with its legacy of Hollywood and entertainment connections, was the first to offer in-flight movies in the summer of 1961. Its film debut for transcontinental domestic first-class passengers was *By Love Possessed*, starring Efrem Zimbalist Jr. and Lana Turner. The service proved a hit, increasing TWA passenger loads and forcing the competition to follow. TWA quickly added movies to international flights with equal success.[27]

Hughes Sued

Howard Hughes was not yet finished with TWA. His "burning ambition" was to undo the voting trust and recover control of the airline. Ironically, his detested deal not only revived TWA but also saved Hughes Tool by repaying

$158 million it had invested in the jet aircraft the airline now owned. Hughes was now well positioned to begin plotting a comeback.

Having previously ordered six Convair 990s as part of his effort to enlist the manufacturer in solving his financial crisis, Hughes now ordered seven more, which he intended to force upon TWA. He also asserted that TWA should acquire turboprop Lockheed Electras, despite the success TWA's 880s were enjoying. He further claimed that the trustees had acted improperly by ordering the additional Boeing jets—ignoring the fact that they were fully authorized to do so. To make his arguments Hughes relied on New York attorney Chester Davis, who had no expertise in aircraft design, operation, or procurement. TWA's directors patiently heard Davis out but summarily rejected his advocacy as "vague and general in character, and [not] backed up with documentation, studies, or other technical data or reports."[28]

After assessing the damage done during the Hughes era, TWA decided to take legal action to seek recovery. It hired John Sonnett, a former high-ranking attorney in the US Justice Department's Antitrust Division, to bring a case against Hughes and Hughes Tool. The suit was filed on June 30, 1961, in the United States District Court for the Southern District of New York, but the complaint was kept under seal while attempts were made to reach a settlement. TWA also requested an order compelling Hughes to appear for his deposition under oath to strengthen TWA's position. By now Hughes was a prisoner of physical and mental illness, a recluse who had not been seen in public for nearly 10 years and was unlikely to appear for a deposition. Undeterred, he continued trying to force the airline to cancel the Boeing 707 orders and instead acquire Convair 990s and Lockheed Electras through Hughes Tool. When TWA refused, the negotiations fell through.[29]

With the settlement off the table, the suit was unsealed in August. The theory of the case was novel, to say the least. TWA alleged that Hughes—its controlling shareholder—had conspired with Hughes Tool to force the airline to acquire planes from Hughes Tool, an arrangement that prevented TWA from getting the airliners it badly needed to remain competitive. TWA claimed $35 million in damages, asking to have this amount trebled under the antitrust statutes.

TWA also filed a second suit against Hughes and Hughes Tool in the Delaware Chancery Court, which had jurisdiction over Delaware corporations. The factual allegations against Hughes and Hughes Tool were similar to those in the federal case but without the antitrust and treble damages claims. Essentially a backup to the federal case, the Delaware suit would ultimately prove decisive.

Hughes Moves

Despite the deposition threat, Hughes was still capable of resisting and fighting back with all the resources at his command, just as he had in the 1947 Senate hearings. He now embarked upon a complicated strategy to regain control of TWA. After merging RKO Studios with Atlas Corporation in the mid-1950s, he had gained an interest in Northeast Airlines, a financially troubled carrier with an unprofitable network in New England but a lucrative route between New York and Miami. Despite leasing six Convair 880s relinquished by Hughes Tool for the Florida route, Northeast's financial situation remained precarious.[30]

Hughes first sought permission from the CAB to advance emergency funds to Northeast. Responsible for overseeing the health and vitality of the US airline industry, the CAB looked favorably upon any plan that could revive Northeast and avoid bankruptcy. It approved Hughes's emergency funding proposal with little inquiry in December 1961, which set the stage for Hughes to formally apply for CAB authorization and take over Northeast.[31]

The CAB held a public hearing on Hughes's application in April 1962. National Airlines and Eastern Air Lines both opposed it because Northeast competed with them in the valuable New York–Florida market. TWA did not participate in the proceedings, wishing to avoid any distraction from its pending suit against Hughes. The CAB examiner found that "the record will not support a finding that Hughes Tool engaged in improper or unlawful activities in regard to TWA or Northeast" and rejected the opponents' claims that Hughes had manipulated TWA for personal advantage. Because no other party was prepared to rescue Northeast and the CAB was eager to avoid a regulated airline failure, Hughes's application was approved in June 1962.[32] So far Hughes's strategy was working. Now he was poised to take back control of TWA—if he could pay off the Dillon Read loan and dissolve the voting trust.

Chester Davis entered his appearance for Hughes and Hughes Tool in both of TWA's suits and immediately began fighting back. He succeeded in thwarting TWA's efforts to call Hughes as the first deposition witness when Federal Judge Charles Metzner allowed him to begin questioning TWA witnesses, starting with Charles Tillinghast. Beginning in January 1962, Tillinghast's deposition lasted over 40 days. It generated 180 hours of testimony and more than 6,000 pages of transcript. A routine was established that had Tillinghast testifying from 9:30 a.m. to 3:30 p.m. on Tuesday through Thursday of each week, leaving him to run the airline when not in the witness chair. The proceedings were acrimonious; both sides had skilled, aggressive lawyers. Eventually Judge Metzner appointed a special master to oversee the deposition, handle objections, and maintain order. As the deposition progressed, Davis demonstrated that Tillinghast could not clearly explain or quantify how Hughes's actions had harmed TWA.[33]

Davis's legal defense was that Congress had given the CAB complete jurisdiction over the airline industry, which took precedence over the antitrust statutes, and that the CAB had authorized everything that Hughes had done. Then, while the Tillinghast deposition was in progress, Davis filed a counterclaim for Hughes and Hughes Tool that was, in effect, an independent suit against TWA and its lenders, naming Tillinghast and Breech as additional defendants. The counterclaim alleged that they, not Hughes, had damaged the airline, and they'd wrongfully deprived Hughes of control over his TWA stock. The counterclaim also alleged TWA and its lenders had violated antitrust laws by denying Hughes access to other lenders and forcing him to accept the voting trust. Moreover, the counterclaim alleged that TWA and its lenders had violated the Federal Aviation Act by gaining control of the airline without CAB approval.[34] This gambit was intended to put TWA's lenders and its new management on the defensive—and to buy time to keep Hughes from having to testify.

TWA's lead lawyer Sonnett continued demanding Hughes's deposition, knowing it was highly unlikely that he would comply. Sonnett finally obtained an order from Judge Metzner that required Hughes to appear for his deposition at the federal courthouse in Los Angeles in February 1963.[35] When Hughes failed to do so, Sonnett asked the judge to strike Hughes's pleadings and enter a default judgment in favor of TWA. He also increased TWA's damage claim by $10 million and secured another order requiring Hughes to produce tax records. In May 1963, Judge Metzner held Hughes in deliberate and willful violation of his order to appear, granted TWA a default judgment, and dismissed the counterclaim with prejudice, barring Davis from amending and re-filing it.[36] Chester Davis appealed Metzner's ruling to the United States Court of Appeals, which affirmed Metzner's rulings. It looked to be an unqualified victory for TWA.

The Flight Center

Meanwhile, construction of the TWA Flight Center at New York proceeded with drama of its own. All 11 million pounds of the elaborate concrete roof structure was supported on just four massive yet graceful Y-shaped concrete buttresses. The port authority insisted on making changes to the concrete reinforcing elements and required daily tests to prove that the building would not collapse.[37]

The complex and difficult process of forming the concrete structure had consumed most of 1960. The ceiling vaults, poured over a vast network of steel reinforcing rods, had to be cast in one continuous process that lasted

120 hours. The supports that held the concrete ceiling in place while it dried and cured then had to be removed in a carefully orchestrated way to ensure that excessive strains were not imposed anywhere on it.

The Flight Center's project manager said the job presented problems that would not be encountered in a lifetime of normal construction. Weeks or even months of advance planning preceded every major step, requiring lead times of up to 60 days before construction could begin on each separate component. To assist with identification, workmen were given shirts that had large numbers on them, visible from long distances, and they were addressed by those numbers.[38]

The building's walls were transparent, consisting of 8,500 square feet of glass. There were 236 separate panes, each one a different size and shape, cut at the site and trimmed to fit as it was installed. Teams of workers using rubber suction cup grips carefully fitted each pane into position and secured it to the steel framework, which was curved and sloped outward at a 15 degree angle.[39] The building's interior was just as unusual and spectacular as its exterior, more like the set of a futuristic movie than a facility for getting passengers to and from airplanes. Overcoming all of these challenges inevitably led to delays, and the scheduled completion date slipped from early 1961 into 1962. Saarinen died suddenly of a brain tumor in September 1961, before he could see his design realized.

On May 28, 1962, the Flight Center officially opened to great publicity and fanfare. Charles Tillinghast and a contingent of 400 distinguished guests attended a gala ceremony that was broadcast live on NBC. Aline Saarinen, the

The Flight Center opened to much acclaim in 1962. An architectural monument, it was an integral part of TWA's jet age marketing. From J. E. Frankum, Legacy of Leadership, *1971.*

architect's wife, collaborator, and publicist, choreographed the festivities and unveiled a plaque dedicated to her late husband. "He wanted the architecture of the Trans World Flight Center to express the drama and wonder of air travel," she said. "He wanted to provide a building in which the human being felt uplifted, important, and full of anticipation."[40]

Aline Saarinen also played a key role in TWA's marketing campaign for the new building. "Publicity-wise, the Flight Center has earned for TWA more favorable comment in magazines and newspapers, and on television and radio, than ever received by any other airline facility," said TWA's in-house newspaper. And it was surely correct. The media attention she helped coordinate attracted 1.5 million visitors—not all of them passengers—in its first year of operation, a quarter-million more than had been estimated.[41]

In keeping with its international theme, the Flight Center had no fewer than four dining areas: the Lisbon Lounge, the Paris Café, the London Club, and an Italian snack bar. "Most formal of the four is the Lisbon Lounge, a particularly elegant dining room," proclaimed TWA's PR department. "The London Club features hearty beef main dishes served from a buffet cart and has a decorative bar. The Paris Café, open 24 hours a day, provides a range of moderately priced dishes, sandwiches, fountain specialties, served at the 'sit down' counters or at tables."[42]

But making the Flight Center an architectural monument and PR darling had its downsides. The extended design process and construction delays put TWA two years behind its New York competitors that had built more straightforward terminals, forcing the airline to operate out of a temporary terminal during the interim that passengers disliked.[43] And once in operation, the Flight Center's design was poorly suited to its primary purpose of serving air travelers. This stemmed in part from a lack of data in the 1950s about the effect jet airliners would have in carrying twice as many passengers nearly twice as fast as piston-powered aircraft did. These difficulties were exacerbated by airline cost-cutting efforts as construction proceeded, such as eliminating moving walkways and requiring travelers to trek through the narrow, 310-foot windowless concrete tube that connected the terminal building with the satellite boarding facility. As part of the cost containment, construction of a second "flight wing" and its additional boarding gates was postponed, which only added to the congestion and further reduced the facility's operational efficiency.[44]

Better Times for TWA

As part of its efforts to recover from the crises of the Hughes era, TWA began exploring possible merger opportunities. Tillinghast put out feelers to Northwest, National, Continental, and Western, all to no avail. Discussions

Although the TWA Flight Center's exterior was stylish, its interior was not well suited for moving passengers and luggage. This was its information desk. Library of Congress, Prints and Photographs Division.

with Eastern went on for several months before Eastern announced a proposed merger with American Airlines in January 1962.[45] Tillinghast then shifted his attention to Pan American, TWA's international rival.

Juan Trippe still nurtured hopes of making Pan Am the sole US international carrier. Merging with TWA would not only accomplish this goal but would also provide Pan Am access to the US domestic market and a direct passenger pipeline to international flights. Tillinghast and Trippe devised a plan to prevent Hughes from trying to gain control over a merged airline, whereby Pan American would become a holding company owning all the airline's stock, with Hughes and the minority TWA shareholders getting no stock in the holding company. Trippe would be the CEO of the holding company and the merged airline.[46] On December 20, 1962, TWA and Pan Am signed a merger agreement, which was subsequently approved by the directors of both airlines and filed with the CAB. But it was not to be. In October 1963, Tillinghast told the board that there was "no reason to suppose that the proposed merger with Pan American World Airways, Inc. could be consummated within a reasonable period" and "circumstances had changed since the merger agreements were entered into." Acting on his recommendation, the board terminated the merger agreement.[47] As TWA's 1963 annual report put it, "TWA's economic recovery made the reasons for the merger considerably less compelling than when it was negotiated." The merger now off, the two longtime rivals would continue competing with renewed intensity.

TWA lost nearly $15 million in 1961, largely due to the turmoil of the financial crisis and the delay in adding the badly needed Convair 880s to its fleet. But things began to turn around in 1962 when TWA started receiving its new Boeing 707s and leased 720s. By the next year its jet fleet consisted of 27 Boeing 707s, 23 turbofan-powered 707Bs, and 20 Convair 880s.[48]

A cloud appeared on the horizon when Howard Hughes applied to the CAB for permission to pay off the Dillon Read loans, dissolve the voting trust, and regain control of TWA through his ownership of 78 percent of the airline's stock. Doing so would require Hughes to divest himself of his interest in Northeast Airlines, which he agreed to, and in July 1964 the CAB granted Hughes's application without holding a hearing or taking any evidence.[49] The ruling struck TWA like a thunderbolt. It threatened to undo the improvements to TWA's management and performance and risked a return to chaos. TWA appealed the CAB order to the court of appeals, which overturned the CAB decision and ordered the CAB to conduct a full evidentiary hearing. A hearing would likely mean that Hughes would have to appear and testify, which now he was even less able to do than when he failed to appear for his deposition nearly two years earlier. The Supreme Court declined to review this holding, thwarting Hughes's efforts to take back TWA.[50]

Its house finally in order, TWA returned to consistent profitability. It earned $19.8 million in 1963, $37 million in 1964, and more than $50 million in 1965. Tillinghast and the voting trust had succeeded in getting TWA back on its feet. In TWA's 1965 annual report Tillinghast summarized the effects the jet age had on air travel generally and on TWA's hard-earned financial success in particular. "There are growing indications that more and more people regard air travel as the safest and most reliable, convenient, and comfortable means of moving over appreciable distances. . . . The quiet comfort of jets, the attractiveness and convenience of modern terminal facilities, the increasing ability to fly smoothly and reliably even under adverse weather conditions, the increasing frequency of scheduled flights and the customer-orientation of airline personnel have all combined to make air travel a pleasant essential of the business and vacation plans of growing numbers of air travelers."

As TWA's fortunes rose so did its stock price, from $7.50 per share in 1962 to $62 in 1965. It soared to over $80 by the first quarter of 1966, prompting Hughes to cash out his TWA stock. In one of the most widely anticipated private securities sales of all time, Hughes sold his 6,584,937 shares on May 3, 1966, for $86 per share. The sale, which netted nearly $546 million (over $5 billion in 2023) after underwriting fees and expenses, was said to generate the largest check ever written up to that time. Yet such were TWA's prospects that the share price continued to rise even after the market had absorbed this huge influx, eventually peaking at over $100 per share.[51] For the first time since 1940, TWA was once again a completely publicly owned company. Its management was free to direct its own affairs, raise capital, and make decisions about its own future, without the lingering threat of intervention and manipulation by Howard Hughes—at least for the time being.

While TWA's financial picture was improving, the Hughes antitrust litigation dragged on. In an unrelated case, the United States Supreme Court held that Congress had empowered the CAB to exempt airlines and their owners from antitrust laws. This was essentially the position of Hughes and Hughes Tool, which did not bode well for TWA's antitrust case. Encouraged by this holding, Davis petitioned the United States Supreme Court for certiorari, asking it to hear the case and reverse the court of appeals ruling in favor of TWA. The Supreme Court accepted the case. After hearing oral arguments in March 1965, it sent the case back to Judge Metzner for further proceedings, without deciding the legal issue.

Judge Metzner then appointed Herbert Brownell, a former US attorney general, as a special master to conduct the hearing on TWA's damages. The hearing began on May 2, 1966—coincidentally, the day before Hughes sold his stock—and continued for over two years. In September 1968, Brownell awarded TWA treble damages of $137.6 million. The judge confirmed this award and later assessed costs and attorneys' fees, bringing the total judgment to $145.4 million.[52] The outcome seemed to vindicate the novel antitrust theory that TWA had pursued since 1961. But Hughes appealed, and the litigation continued into the next decade.

Still Crowded Skies

Five years after the tragic Staten Island midair collision, the unthinkable happened yet again. On December 4, 1965, Eastern Air Lines Flight 853, a Super Constellation operating the air shuttle service from Boston to Newark, collided with TWA Flight 42, a Boeing 707 inbound to New York's JFK near Carmel, New York. The Super Constellation crashed and broke apart; the captain and three passengers died. The 707, missing 20 feet of its left wing, managed to make a successful emergency landing at its destination with no fatalities or injuries.

Although air traffic control had separated the two planes by 1,000 feet of altitude, the CAB determined that when the jet suddenly emerged from a cloud an optical illusion caused the Eastern captain to believe that they were about to collide. He pulled back sharply on the controls, inadvertently putting the Super Constellation directly in the path of the TWA 707. The 707 captain's split-second attempt to avoid the impact only made the situation worse.[53] In this case the crew of each aircraft saw the other, and in trying to avoid a collision, caused one. The air traffic control improvements adopted since the 1956 Grand Canyon and 1960 New York collisions had still not completely eradicated the hazard of midair collisions.

Encounters between airliners and the rapidly growing general aviation fleet were also on the rise. On March 9, 1967, TWA Flight 553, a DC-9 approaching Dayton, Ohio, in clear weather struck a Beech Baron light twin. The jet was traveling at 323 knots (370 mph), far above the 250-knot speed limit imposed by the Federal Air Regulations within 30 miles of a terminal airport. The Baron was not using its radar transponder and was not in radio contact with air traffic control—and was not required to do so—but the Dayton controllers saw the Baron and warned the TWA pilots. Nonetheless, they failed to see and avoid it, and the aircraft crashed, killing all on board. The National Transportation Safety Board accident report bluntly stated that the US air traffic control system "was not designed or equipped to separate a mixture of controlled and uncontrolled aircraft."[54]

The FAA responded to this and a spate of other collisions between airliners and light aircraft with new measures. It mandated a 370-mph speed limit everywhere below 10,000 feet and established new radar control procedures in airspace surrounding major and secondary air terminals.

Marketing in the Jet Age

TWA succeeded in cultivating an image of glamour and sophistication, and in broadening its passenger base.[55] As it had done with the Super-G Constellation in the 1950s, TWA made its new planes a key part of the airline's identity, calling its turbofan-powered Boeing 707Bs "StarStream" jets and their engines "DynaFans." A 1962 promotional brochure proclaimed, "If you feel that today's jet aircraft have reached peaks of comfort, speed and efficiency, a delightful surprise awaits you on TWA. An entirely new airplane is going into service. It is called the StarStream, and it surpasses all your previous experience, setting new standards for tomorrow, improving on what previously was perfection."[56] The brochure's cover artwork depicted a StarStream 707 taxiing toward the Flight Center under a starry night sky, linking these two symbols of TWA in the jet age. Another flyer, "TWA Wings for the World," contained an explanation of the differences between the "conventional turbojet engine" and the "DynaFan Engine."[57] Similarly, TWA branded its Convair 880s "SuperJets" and called itself "TWA THE SUPERJET AIRLINE"—even registering it as a service mark. In reality TWA's 707s and 880s were identical to those of other airlines, but TWA depicted traveling on them as a one-of-a-kind experience.

TWA continued building Hollywood connections to sell air travel to the public. Movies and television shows were often shot at TWA's Los Angeles terminal, thanks to the airline's Special Services Department, which maintained close ties with the entertainment industry. Most filming was done at night to minimize operational disruption and distraction. Among the celebrities glimpsed at those nighttime hours were Steve Allen and his wife, Jayne Meadows, who regularly commuted from New York to LA on flights that arrived around 2:30 a.m. Going the other way, passengers riding TWA Flight 2, the 10:45 p.m. LA-to-JFK red-eye, might be treated to a Frank Sinatra or Danny Kaye sighting.[58]

The Jet Set

Serving VIP passengers, now popularly known as the "jet set," was a crucial element of TWA's jet age marketing. One high-profile assignment was flying the royal family of Monaco from Los Angeles to New York in 1967. "TWA has managed to steal the business from United and American to carry Prince Rainier and Princess Grace and the Royal Party from Los Angeles to New York, Sunday, August 20," bragged an internal company memo. "The Royal Party was very pleased with the treatment on their recent TWA arrival from San Francisco," it continued, "and graciously extended to us the opportunity of serving them again." The prince and princess stipulated that they did not wish the other passengers to get the impression that they were receiving preferential treatment and that "[TWA's] usual fine service will suffice." "As you all know we have received much in revenue, publicity and prestige from our previous effort," the memo concluded, "and we now have a chance to triple the results."[59]

Popularly attributed to fashion designer Igor Cassini, the term "jet set" was typically used to describe wealthy international travelers. TWA had catered to this cohort to sell air travel since its earliest days, but the advent of jets led to a democratization of the glamour and excitement their lifestyle conveyed. Author William Stadiem called the jet set "the shock troops of fantasy, the stuff of dreams—and of ticket sales," to be distinguished from the "real people in the back of the plane." "They might not have made the [gossip] columns," he said, "but they were having the time of their lives. And they fueled the big, big business of aviation."[60]

The speed, comfort, and economy of jets opened the world to these new air travelers. In the decade after jets appeared, the number of Americans visiting Europe quadrupled, from half a million to 2 million, creating a travel demand that led to the appearance of the Boeing 747 and other wide-body jets.[61]

The Flight Center was also a main component of TWA's carefully crafted public relations and marketing campaigns, used to distinguish the airline from its jet age competitors. "We want to project in a uniform, attractive manner our image around the world of a reliable, friendly airline offering good service everywhere," said TWA president Thomas.[62] But paradoxically the Flight Center's operational shortcomings were exacerbated by the growing demand for air travel. With only seven passenger gates, the single flight wing was an operational headache from the start. While the airline sought financing for a second, it built a temporary concourse with four additional gates. After protracted negotiations with the port authority and its lenders, the TWA board approved a plan to construct a second concourse (counterintuitively called Flight Wing One) at a cost of $19.2 million in May 1967.

PAPER UNIFORMS?

As part of its international marketing theme, TWA began coordinating its hostess uniforms with the airline's prime overseas destinations by adopting four uniforms for its international flights. One was inspired by dresses worn by English pub waitresses; the others included a stylized Roman toga, a French cocktail dress, and a black pantsuit dubbed the "Manhattan Penthouse." The English pub dress would appear on London flights featuring English-themed food service, the Roman toga on flights to Rome that served Italian food, the French cocktail dress on Paris flights with French cuisine, and the Manhattan Penthouse on flights from Europe to New York. The dresses were made from paper that had a high fiber content for strength and resilience.

The idea flopped completely. There was a greater supply of some styles than others, which made it impossible to match the dresses with their corresponding destinations. Then the supply of all styles fell short, forcing hasty substitution of dresses made of even lighter paper that did not hold up and sometimes only lasted a single flight. Above all, hostesses hated the dresses and the concept. Many found the material an uncomfortable fire hazard and thought the designs were ugly. The paper uniforms became the butt of jokes in the industry and the media, and TWA unceremoniously abandoned them after only a few months. One positive outcome for the hostesses: They secured a provision in their union contract guaranteeing they'd be asked for input about future designs for their uniforms.

The Space Age

In the 1960s the United States was still reacting to the shock of Sputnik and other Soviet space accomplishments. Interest in the space program rose as America sought to catch up and regain the lead in this realm of science and technology. President John F. Kennedy made it a national priority, calling for American astronauts to reach the moon before the end of the decade. Public attention turned toward Cape Canaveral and the Kennedy Space Center, where American spacecraft were launched.

In 1966, NASA rolled out public tours of the Space Center to help build support for the space program, and it selected TWA to run them. The business fit nicely with the airline's marketing, echoing its 1950s relationship with Disneyland. TWA initially operated secondhand Greyhound buses that suffered frequent mechanical failures, such as losing air-conditioning in the stifling Florida heat. Reel-to-reel tape players broadcast a narrative that began with the loud exclamation, "Welcome! You are on the threshold of space!" followed by excerpts from Aaron Copland's *Fanfare for the Common Man* and President Kennedy's famed moon speech. But when the recorders or public address systems failed, guides were left to ad-lib and entertain the passengers as best they could.[64]

After overcoming these early issues, the Space Center tours became an enduring and much-loved attraction. The tours took visitors to see historic relics of the space age, including the original Mercury mission control blockhouse and the rusting remnants of the launch pads for early flights, as well as the new Launch Complex 39 from which the Apollo moon missions (and, later, space shuttle flights) departed.

Retiring the Connie

As TWA's fleet of domestic jets grew, the airline began disposing of its propeller-driven planes. The last of the World War II–era DC-4s were sold in 1959, followed by the Martin 404 twins and the early Model 049 Constellations in 1961 and 1962. TWA disposed of its last Model 1049A Super Constellations in 1964 and its last 1049G Super-G Constellations in

1967. The long-range Model 1649As were sold or converted into freighters until they were replaced by jets in the late 1960s.

The longest-lived TWA Constellations proved to be the Model 749As, delivered in 1950 and 1951. TWA's last scheduled Constellation passenger flight was Flight 249 from New York to St. Louis, on April 6, 1967, with stops at Philadelphia, Pittsburgh, Columbus, and Louisville. At each stop ceremonies were held to mark the occasion, called the "passing of the props." Some passengers had booked the flight specifically to be part of the Constellation's retirement. Also on board were three TWA employees who had flown on the record-setting 1944 transcontinental Constellation flight piloted by Howard Hughes and Jack Frye—a fitting end to the airline service of this groundbreaking plane pioneered by TWA. When Flight 249 terminated at St. Louis, TWA became the first all-jet US domestic airline.[66] Despite being late to inaugurating jet service, it had made up for lost time.

The retirement of TWA's Constellations was aided by the arrival of smaller, short-range jetliners designed for high-traffic routes between metropolitan centers. The growing public acceptance of air travel sparked by first-generation jets brought more demand for jet service in less populated metropolitan areas with smaller airports and terminal facilities, which the airlines now scrambled to fill.

The first true short-haul jetliner tailored to US needs was the Boeing 727, a 100-seater powered by three rear-mounted turbofan engines. It also featured advanced high-lift wing flaps suited to shorter runways and smaller airports than the first-generation jets while providing similar performance. TWA ordered 10 727s in March 1962.[67] Additional orders included stretched 727-200s. This later model carried as many passengers as the early 707s but with only three engines, each of which was more fuel efficient than those of the 707s—a significant consideration when fuel prices soared in the 1970s.

Not to be outdone, Douglas offered the DC-9, a rear-engine twin jet capable of carrying 70 passengers. TWA ordered 20 DC-9s in 1964, putting them into service in March 1966.[68] Like the 727, the DC-9 came equipped with built-in air stairs and an onboard auxiliary power unit, which eliminated the costs of stationing boarding stairs and ground power equipment at outlying airports. The 727 and DC-9 allowed TWA customers in cities like Dayton, Ohio, to fly to New York in jet comfort and speed, and then on to Europe, the Middle East, or Asia, all on TWA.

Supersonic Airliners

Just as jets had doubled the performance and productivity of propeller planes in the 1950s, the 1960s held promise for doubling the speed of jetliners. The military was already operating jets capable of exceeding

The three-engine Boeing 727 was TWA's first short-haul jetliner. Shown here in 1972, it successfully served the airline for many years. Photo by George Hamlin.

Mach 2—twice the speed of sound, over 1,200 mph. The next logical step was developing supersonic airliners. But creating an airliner capable of traveling at supersonic speeds presented daunting engineering and design challenges: Military jets reached such speeds in short bursts, and only by using afterburners, which consumed prodigious amounts of fuel. Further, military jets could also be refueled in flight to extend their range. To achieve a significant reduction in flight times, airliners would have to travel at supersonic speed for extended periods. Accomplishing this would require advanced aerodynamic design to reduce high-speed drag, as well as new jet engines powerful and efficient enough to maintain supersonic speed without afterburning. Plus, supersonic airliners would greatly exceed noise limits around airports, and in flight they create startling sonic booms affecting millions on the ground.

American manufacturers and airlines adopted a cautious approach to supersonics. Seeing an opening, Britain and France announced the joint Anglo-French supersonic Concorde Supersonic Transport (SST) project in November 1962. In response, the United States initiated the National Supersonic Transport program, a far more ambitious project, in June 1963. While Concorde was to be a 100-passenger, 1,200-mph aircraft with 3,000-mile transatlantic range, the US program envisioned a 200-passenger airplane capable of 1,800 mph and a 2,400-mile range. To avoid possibly being left behind other airlines, in October 1963, TWA's board informed the FAA, which was administering the program, of its intent to order 6 SSTs (later increased to 12), with a $600,000 cash deposit.[69]

The board also approved an option to purchase four Concordes. The TWA board agreed to this arrangement solely "as a hedge against the possibility that a U.S. supersonic transport might not become available within a reasonable time for [TWA] to remain competitive."[70] Because of the uncertainty surrounding the technical and commercial viability of supersonic airliners, other airlines adopted a similarly conservative stance.

The ambitious US SST project progressed slowly. In January 1967, Boeing was selected to proceed with development of the 280-passenger Model 733-290, but technical hurdles forced a series of significant design changes and a reduction in size and capacity to 235 passengers. Re-designated the Model 2707, construction of a full-size mockup and two prototypes began in late 1969. Meanwhile, the Anglo-French Concorde had made its first flight in March 1969.

War and Peace

Although TWA had yet to gain approval for transpacific scheduled passenger service, it bid for and received a Military Airlift Command contract to fly military personnel between the United States and Vietnam following the escalation of the war. Flights began in July 1966. It took two weeks to transport troops across the vast Pacific Ocean by ship, but the military contract flights from Travis Air Force Base near Sacramento to Saigon via Honolulu and Okinawa took only 35 hours, including stops. By 1967, TWA was making 25 round-trip flights each month, which continued for the rest of the war.[71]

These flights to and from the combat zone made a deep impression on the crews who flew them—particularly on the hostesses who served young soldiers. Eunice Kost collected more than 200 military unit badges from returning servicemen, which she wore proudly on a sash. Marilyn Genz traveled to front line combat areas, where she became known as the "Sweetheart of the First Air Cavalry Division." And then there was Ida Staggers, TWA's most senior hostess, who had served since 1936. Known to the troops as "Aunt Ida," Staggers finished her flying career on military charters. During the holidays she decorated the cabin with wreaths and candy canes and posted a sign that read: "Merry Christmas from your TWA flight crew."[72] Her efforts were rewarded by a commendation from Military Airlift Command chief General Howell M. Estes Jr. in 1969.[73]

As the Vietnam War intensified, Pope Paul VI travelled to New York on a whirlwind peace mission in October 1965. After he had conferred with President Lyndon Johnson and celebrated Mass for 90,000 of the faithful at Yankee Stadium, TWA had the honor of returning the pontiff to Rome that evening. TWA president Tillinghast greeted him, and Captain George Duvall circled New York after departing to give the pope a nighttime view of the great metropolis.[74]

IDA STAGGERS

After 35 years of service hostess Ida Staggers retired in 1972. She was TWA's senior active airline flight attendant and the first to be grounded by a work rule that mandated hostesses retire at age 60.[75] Staggers joined TWA in 1936 and participated in some of the airline's first hostess classes. "They showed us the airplane and where to find things. We had to learn ticketing and all the names of the top people in the company," she recalled. "We had to know connections, our routes, and what towns we were flying over. And we had to know how to make out railroad tickets. If we came to a city and had to cancel, the hostess had to take her passengers to the train station, buy their tickets, get on the train with them no matter how long they had been on duty, and ride with them to the next city where they could board again." After completing her training, she was intimidated by the prospect of having to serve breakfast to 14 passengers in just over two hours.[76]

TWA brought Staggers into management in 1942, putting her in charge of all hostesses during the Second World War. After the war she returned to flight duty on TWA's early international flights. Twenty years later she moved to TWA's military charter flights to Southeast Asia, where she worked to reassure frightened GIs traveling to an uncertain fate in the war-torn region and comforted combat-weary veterans returning home.[77]

Upon her retirement the TWA directors adopted a resolution honoring her long service:

WHEREAS, the unique career of Miss Ida Staggers, most senior TWA hostess, has drawn to a close; and

WHEREAS, we the members of the Board of Directors wish, on behalf of the Board and all of the employees of Trans World Airlines, to make a lasting record of our deep regard and affection for Miss Ida Staggers, be it

RESOLVED, that the Board of Directors does hereby enter into the Minutes and permanent records of the Corporation this tribute to the very special qualities of charm, warmth and dignity which Miss Staggers brought to her profession and to the airline for which she worked for so many years with such great distinction.

It wasn't the end of Staggers's career at TWA, however; the airline assigned her to the hostess training school at Kansas City as a consultant.

The Hotel Business

The 1960s saw a growing trend of corporate diversification. Firms looked to expand beyond their core business as a way to protect corporate revenues and profits from the ups and downs of a single business line. When one industry was down, the reasoning went, others might be up. The airlines were particularly vulnerable to boom-and-bust swings. As TWA recovered from the downturn of the early 1960s, management became interested in acquiring a more stable business partner or partners. At this time Barron Hilton, son of hotelier Conrad Hilton, approached TWA about taking over the airline. Instead, TWA began preliminary discussions with Hilton International, operator of 42 Hilton Hotels in 28 countries. The TWA board formed a committee to explore the possibilities of a merger in December 1966.[79]

An agreement was reached two months later. TWA would acquire control of Hilton International for $17 million and merge with it. Hilton management and operations would continue unchanged. Among the factors considered were the growth of international air travel, the shortage of hotel accommodations in foreign countries, the desirability of having adequate accommodations to handle the growing volume of international travelers, the desirability of promoting international business and tourist travel, and the opinion of both companies' management that TWA and Hilton "together could do this more efficiently and economically."[80] TWA's board approved the merger, and its stockholders voted to accept it at the March 1967 annual meeting. TWA was now in the hotel business.

The Hilton International merger made sense, in theory, because TWA and Hilton could package international transportation with hotel accommodations and thereby stimulate both businesses. But TWA's diversification in 1967 put it on a path that ultimately led to its dismemberment and eventual downfall.

That same year TWA received authorization to open new routes to sub-Saharan Africa. Amid great anticipation, TWA began once-weekly passenger service from New York to cities in three newly independent nations: Nairobi, Kenya; Kampala, Uganda; and Dar es Salaam, Tanzania.[81] But sufficient demand for these services never materialized, and they were soon abandoned.

TWA had served the Middle East since 1946, a period beset by tension and conflict arising from the effort to create a Jewish state in Palestine and the resistance to it by the surrounding Arab states. War erupted upon the cessation of British colonial rule and Israel's declaration of independence in 1948. A second war was triggered by the nationalization of the Suez Canal by Egypt and a failed invasion by Britain and France in 1956. TWA's presence in the region put it directly in the firing line, and its service to Israel made it a consistent target of Palestinian nationalism.

TWA avoided major disruptions in 1948 and 1956, but the Six-Day War in June 1967 was another matter. The conflict forced TWA to suspend operations to its North African destinations, Saudi Arabia, and Israel, and to evacuate its US national employees. TWA continued its Asian service by rerouting flights around the area. Normal operations gradually resumed, but the turmoil that came from the war and Israeli occupation of Jerusalem, the West Bank region of Jordan, and the Golan Heights in Syria would continue to affect TWA for the next two decades.

The year ended with two fatal accidents only weeks apart. On November 6, 1967, TWA Flight 159 crashed while attempting to take off from Cincinnati/Northern Kentucky International Airport. Just before the accident, a Delta Airlines DC-9 had gone off the runway after landing and became stuck with its engines still running. Nonetheless, the tower cleared Flight 159 for takeoff. As the TWA flight passed the marooned DC-9 the captain heard a loud noise and, believing an impact had occurred, attempted to abort the takeoff at high speed. The TWA 707 overran the end of the runway, went over the edge of a hill, and slid down an embankment, sustaining major damage and a post-impact fire. All passengers and crew were successfully evacuated, but one passenger later died of injuries.[82]

A far worse incident happened just two weeks later at the same airport. TWA Flight 128, a Convair 880, crashed on a night approach at the Cincinnati airport, where part of the instrument landing system and the runway approach lights were out of service. The aircraft descended below the minimum safe approach altitude and crashed in a wooded area nearly 2 miles short of the runway, breaking up in the process. Of the 82 passengers and crew on board, 70 died. The NTSB found the accident was caused by pilot error in attempting to land under the prevailing conditions with the partially inoperative landing aids, and in failing to properly monitor the altitude during the approach.[83]

Around the World

Ever since Howard Hughes and Jack Frye filed TWA's first application for international routes in 1944, the airline had aspired to circle the globe. In 1958 it received authorization to extend its international routes east from Bombay (Mumbai), India; and Colombo, Ceylon (Sri Lanka); to Bangkok, Thailand; and Manila, Philippines; and onward to Hong Kong in 1966. TWA then applied to fly from Hong Kong to 17 US destinations. In April 1968 the CAB awarded TWA its coveted routes from Hong Kong and Tokyo to the United States via Hawaii. President Lyndon Johnson confirmed the award in December 1968 but denied TWA the right to serve Japan.

Weeks later newly elected President Richard Nixon rescinded all the route awards made under his predecessor. Then, in April 1969, Nixon relented, allowing TWA to serve the US West Coast from Hong Kong but only by the less desirable route via Okinawa, Guam, and Honolulu. Scheduled around-the-world service finally began on August 1, 1969.[84] After 25 years the dream of Howard Hughes and Jack Frye became a reality, and TWA was now truly "Trans World" in fact as well as in name.

After years of struggling to overcome the capacity deficit created by the Hughes turmoil, by the late 1960s, TWA had an all-jet fleet of Boeing 707s and 727s, Convair 880s, and Douglas DC-9s. In the aftermath of the abortive Pan American merger talks, the two airlines resumed their fierce competition on the lucrative transatlantic routes between the United States and Europe. Passengers increasingly expressed a preference for TWA based on its quality of service, and TWA finally surpassed its longtime rival in the summer of 1969. It would continue to best Pan Am for the next decade.[85]

The year also brought changes at the top. Ernest Breech announced his retirement. He had played a key role in TWA's early years and returned to serve as chairman of the board and a member of the voting trust that controlled the Hughes stock. Breech was succeeded as chairman by Charles Tillinghast, who retained the title of CEO but relinquished the role of president to executive vice president Forwood C. Wiser Jr., also known as "Bud."

Tillinghast's eight-year tenure as president outlasted Damon's and was equally successful. He steered TWA back from the chaos of the final Hughes years to an unbroken record of growth and profitability. On his watch TWA finally achieved its ambition to extend its overseas routes, and it displaced mighty Pan American as the dominant carrier on the profitable and prestigious North Atlantic routes to Europe.

Skyjacked

On August 29, 1969, TWA Flight 840 was hijacked shortly after departing from Rome bound for Tel Aviv. When a hostess opened the cockpit door, the hijackers, Leila Khaled and Salim Essawi, entered carrying guns and hand grenades. Khaled announced, "We are taking command, and we will blow up the aircraft unless you obey orders." She directed Captain Dean Carter to fly to Damascus, Syria, then commandeered the public address system and told the passengers that "the Che Guevara commando unit of the Popular Front for the Liberation of Palestine has taken command of TWA Flight 840."[86]

As the flight approached Syria, the Israeli Air Force scrambled jets to intercept the flight but were unable to intervene. The aircraft landed in Damascus, where hijackers allowed the passengers and crew to deplane. As soon as the aircraft had been evacuated, Essawi re-entered and tossed a grenade into the cockpit, escaping before it demolished the entire area. Though surprised by the unscheduled arrival, Syrian authorities disarmed the hijackers and took them into custody. Most of the passengers and crew returned to Rome two days later on an Italian airliner chartered by TWA, but six passengers—all Israeli citizens—were detained in Damascus.

Forwood Wiser, who had become TWA's president just three months earlier, and other TWA officials flew to Damascus to take part in securing the passengers' release. Syrian officials released the four female passengers two days later but continued to detain the two male passengers. Wiser returned to Rome, where he told the press that the release of the remaining two "is a matter that is being pursued at the highest diplomatic level. We are making approaches to all possible sources." In New York, Tillinghast and Wiser worked "for the purpose of bringing all possible force to bear to secure the release of all the TWA passengers," meeting with Secretary of State William Rogers and United Nations Secretary General U Thant. The UN General Assembly adopted a resolution condemning the hijacking. Secretary Rogers called it an act of international piracy and warned the Syrian government to "give due weight to the consequences which could flow from this situation and immediately take steps to release the detained passengers."[87]

Despite these diplomatic efforts, Syria continued to hold the two Israelis. The US didn't have diplomatic relations with Syria, so all contacts went through the Italian embassy. Finally, on December 5, the two remaining male passengers were let go. Wiser issued a statement saying, "Our next goal must be to put an end to hijacking and aerial piracy. Through world legislation, backed by public opinion, we must make the skies free for everyone."[88] But by then TWA had already suffered another international hijacking, albeit without a political motive.

Just two months later on October 31, 1969, Rafael Minichiello, a 20-year-old Marine Vietnam veteran absent without leave and armed with a folding stock carbine, forced a hostess to open the cockpit door of TWA Flight 85, which was on its way from Los Angeles to San Francisco. Once inside the cockpit, he ordered Captain Donald Cook to fly to New York, saying, "I mean business." Cook took to the plane's public address system to announce, "There's a man here who wants to go someplace, and he's just chartered himself a plane." The jet lacked fuel for a transcontinental flight, and Cook persuaded the hijacker to allow the plane to land at Denver to refuel and to release the passengers.

While on the ground at Denver the FBI unsuccessfully tried to talk Minichiello into surrendering. The 707 then departed for New York with the cockpit crew and one hostess, who volunteered to stay aboard and assist. While in flight, Minichiello demanded to fly on to Rome. After arriving at New York, the cockpit crew, who were not cleared for international operations, were replaced by Captain Richard Hastings and First Officer Billy Williams. The FBI surrounded the plane with sharpshooters and sent two agents disguised as mechanics to approach the plane. The hijacker, unnerved by this activity, fired a shot and demanded an immediate departure without refueling. The plane took off again, with Cook and the hostess remaining on board, followed closely by a small plane carrying FBI agents. It landed at Bangor, Maine, to take on fuel for the transatlantic crossing. The pilots insisted that no one but the refueling crew approach the plane at Bangor.

Once over the Atlantic, the hijacker talked with Cook and the hostess in the cabin, becoming increasingly nervous and agitated. "He claimed he was born in Rome and he wanted to come back again," Cook said afterward. "He wanted to fight someone and die." Approaching Rome, he demanded the city's police chief meet him at the airport, unarmed and coatless. The police chief complied. He led Minichiello to a waiting car and the two departed. After a few miles Minichiello ordered the chief out of the car and took off, soon abandoning it and proceeding on foot across the Italian countryside. Eventually he was captured in a small chapel amid parishioners celebrating All Saints' Day. "Why did I do it?" he said. "I don't know."[90]

The Italian authorities refused to extradite Minichiello to the United States to face air piracy charges. Instead, he was prosecuted in Italy only for crimes committed in Italian airspace and sentenced to seven years in prison, which was reduced on appeal. He was released in May 1971, after serving less than two years, seemingly regarded sympathetically as a victim of the unpopular Vietnam War. In 2009 he staged a bizarre reunion in the United States with members of his Vietnam Marine platoon and two members of the TWA crew he had hijacked 40 years earlier.[91]

The leniency Italy showed Minichiello did little to deter future hijackers. On December 21, 1969, another attempted TWA hijacking was foiled by alert employees in Athens. A young woman and two men carrying identical large briefcases boarded a 707 bound for New York. A TWA ground crewman became suspicious and called the police, who boarded the plane and searched their carry-ons. Police discovered pistols, hand grenades, and explosives. The three would-be hijackers intended to force the TWA crew to fly to Tunisia, where they would have destroyed the plane unless TWA acceded to their demand to cease serving Israel.

Chapter 6
UPHEAVAL: 1970–1984

On February 25, 1970, TWA Flight 100 departed Los Angeles for New York with 254 passengers on board. They were the first to fly within the United States on the massive Boeing 747.[1] The 747 and the jumbo jet era it ushered in arose from the loss of an important military contract. In 1964 the United States Air Force issued a requirement for a very large four-engine transport, with a cargo capacity of 180,000 pounds and an unrefueled range of over 5,000 miles. Several major manufacturers submitted proposals, and Boeing and Lockheed emerged as the prime contenders.

The Wide-Body Era

To power the large aircraft, Pratt & Whitney and General Electric offered new high-bypass turbofan engines that were more than twice as powerful as the most powerful commercial jet engines in service at the time. Lockheed won the Air Force contract, and its winning entry went into production as the C-5 Galaxy transport.[2]

In a move as bold as its decision to launch the 707 a decade earlier, Boeing used the technology it had developed for the military transport competition to create a new airliner twice the size of the 707—with two aisles and up to 10 seats across that could carry more than 400 passengers. Boeing launched the 747 with an order for 25 from Pan Am in April 1966. TWA followed with an order for 15 of the new jets in September 1966, scheduled for delivery three years later. Because its existing factory was too small to house the aircraft, Boeing constructed an enormous new facility in Everett, Washington. When completed in May 1967, it was the largest structure in the world by interior volume.[3]

Nearly everything about the giant 747 was unprecedented. It was 231 feet long with a wingspan of 196 feet. Its belly cargo compartment was as high as the passenger cabin of the 707. The 747's passenger deck was 16 feet above ground level, which would require new terminal facilities to accommodate it. But would the 747's costs overwhelm the airlines' financial capabilities? Would airports be able to cope with its demands? How would the traveling public react? And what about the consequences of a potential air disaster involving more than 400 people?

Nor was it clear whether the future belonged to wide-body jets, such as the 747, which could carry many passengers economically, or to supersonic jets, which could carry fewer passengers twice as fast at premium fares. TWA had already ordered the 100-passenger Concorde, able to fly at twice the speed of sound, as well as the US–built supersonic transport. Although still only a project, the US SST had a promising 200-passenger design capable of flying three times the speed of sound.

TWA initially decided to limit passenger capacity of its 747s to 357 people so that the cabin would be roomier. The first-class section had 58 seats on the main level with a 15-seat lounge on the upper level behind the elevated cockpit, accessed via a circular stairway. Three coach compartments on the main level held 284 seats. The main cabin ceiling was 8 feet high and had abundant overhead carry-on storage. There were 12 lavatories and seven galley units, plus an elevator to deliver food to the upper level. Passengers on the main level could choose from two movie selections.[4]

TWA also instituted a new system of in-flight customer service managers for the 747. These personnel offered specialized service: They arrived at Kennedy Airport three hours before each flight to ensure the meals were set up properly, then went back to the terminal where they assisted with the boarding process and briefed the cabin crews. At the end of the flight they helped passengers with their luggage.

Once the 747s entered service and overcame their growing pains, they were popular. The flying public loved their size and spaciousness, which lent a more open, welcoming atmosphere—especially on international flights. During their first year of service, TWA's 747s enjoyed a higher passenger load factor than the airline's other jets. But all of this came at a price. Each 747's $22 million acquisition cost (about $172 million in 2023) was twice that of a 707.[5]

Just in time to accommodate the 747, the TWA Flight Center's new Flight Wing One opened in March 1970. Designed to handle wide-body jets, it nearly doubled the Flight Center's capacity, and TWA's international passengers could avoid JFK's congested International Arrivals Building and "the ordeal of transferring from one JFK terminal to another."[6] It alleviated (but did not entirely overcome) the operational difficulties that had beset the Flight Center since its 1962 opening, a period when air travel grew beyond all expectations. But that trend was coming to an end.[7]

The Troubled Tristar

By early 1971, TWA possessed a fleet of 245 jets, including 14 747s. The cost of these new jets and their support infrastructure took a toll on TWA's finances. At the same time, the Vietnam War—along with its economic stimulus—was winding down, and inflation caused operational costs to rise. The arrival of wide-bodies brought excess capacity at a time of falling demand and revenues: TWA's domestic passenger traffic declined in 1970 as its capacity increased by 10 percent. The 1960s era of profitability turned into a punishing $72.5 million loss in 1970, a year in which the industry as a whole lost $175 million.[8] In an effort to boost traffic, TWA inaugurated its new "Ambassador Service" on transcontinental flights, with spruced-up furnishings and special TWA representatives at the gates and baggage claim areas. TWA extended the popular perk to domestic flights the next year.[9] Meanwhile, in contrast to TWA's struggles, the Hilton International hotel chain reported a record profit of $8.65 million in 1971 and was expanding rapidly.[10]

TWA and other airlines recognized the need for a more economical wide-body for US domestic routes. McDonnell Douglas and Lockheed responded by offering the DC-10 and L-1011 TriStar, both three-engine wide-body jets. TWA selected the TriStar, ordering 22 for delivery beginning in 1971, followed by an order for 11 more to be delivered in 1973.[11]

But the TriStar's new Rolls Royce RB 211 engines encountered difficulties so severe that they forced the historic firm into receivership, leaving it unable to supply the engines. The TriStar became a major source of concern for TWA. After traveling to England in May 1971, Tillinghast reported to the board that "satisfactory progress was being made on the RB-211 engine program," and that Lockheed was making steps toward satisfying TWA's concerns. However, only one month later Tillinghast recommended that "in view of the uncertainty of the Lockheed situation," discussions be initiated with McDonnell Douglas for the possible alternative purchase of up to 20 DC-10s.[12] Then, in September, TWA reaffirmed its commitment to purchase a total of 33 TriStars, with deliveries to commence in 1972.

Trouble in the Middle East

The aftermath of the 1967 Six-Day War—with Israel ruling the Palestinian populations of the occupied former West Bank of Jordan and the Gaza Strip—continued to roil the Middle East and led to the rise of the militant Popular Front for the Liberation of Palestine. The PFLP was dedicated to gaining attention for the Palestinian cause by committing terrorist acts and violence. Skyjacking became a favored tactic.

TWA continued to be the airline of choice for Middle East terrorists. TWA Flight 802 was seized on January 8, 1970, after leaving Paris for Rome. The hijacker originally demanded to go to Damascus, Syria, then changed his mind and ordered the captain to fly to Beirut, Lebanon. After landing he fired three shots inside the plane—fortunately no one was hit, and he surrendered to Beirut police without further incident. TWA president Forwood Wiser

The wide-body Lockheed L-1011 TriStar entered TWA service in 1972. It bankrupted Rolls Royce and caused headaches for TWA. Jon Proctor Collection.

expressed gratitude to the Lebanese government "for its swift and resolute action, which resulted in the apprehension of the hijacker and the subsequent safe arrival of our passengers at their destination." TWA's latest hijacking was not an auspicious start to the new decade—nor would it be its last incident.[13]

The PFLP's boldest and most dramatic effort to date began on September 6, 1970, when separate teams took over TWA Flight 741 after departing Frankfurt and Swissair Flight 100 out of Zurich, and forced both planes to fly to Dawson's Field, an abandoned airstrip in the Jordanian desert.

On the same day another team—led by the notorious Leila Khaled, one of the hijackers of TWA Flight 840 in September 1969 who had since been released by Syrian authorities—attempted to hijack an El Al flight from Amsterdam. Khaled had undergone plastic surgery to disguise her identity, but an alert Israeli crew managed to disarm the hijackers and killed Khaled's accomplice. The plane landed at London, where Khaled was swiftly taken into custody. Meanwhile, two more PFLP agents, who had been prevented from boarding the El Al flight, transferred to a Pan American 747 flight and took it over. After the crew convinced them that the jumbo jet could not land at the crude strip in the Jordanian desert, the hijackers directed them to land at Cairo, released the passengers and crew, and blew up the Pan Am 747.[14]

At Dawson's Field the TWA and Swissair passengers and crew suffered inside the sweltering airliners in 120 degree heat. The airlines flew in packaged meals for the hostages and arranged makeshift kitchens and portable toilets for them. On September 7 the hijackers released 127 female non-Jewish passengers, who were transported to Amman, Jordan, and repatriated. The rest remained held hostage in the desert, bargaining chips for the release of PFLP prisoners. The stakes got even higher when a different PFLP team hijacked another airliner and forced it to fly to Dawson's Field as well.[15]

The remote desert airstrip, renamed Revolution Airport, was now at the center of world attention as the media flocked to report on the events unfolding there. The International Red Cross unsuccessfully attempted to negotiate the release of the hostages. On September 11, Palestine Liberation Organization leader Yasser Arafat took over the negotiations from the PFLP. President Richard Nixon ordered Secretary of Defense Melvin Laird to bomb the PFLP in Jordan, but Laird refused, citing adverse weather. Britain's prime minister Edward Heath elected to negotiate over Nixon's objections.[16]

A deal was finally struck. All the hostages on board the stifling planes—except for 40 Israelis "with military capability"—were released in return for all Palestinian prisoners held by European nations. The next day the PFLP blew up the three jetliners. By now Jordan's King Hussein had had enough. He declared martial law and launched an all-out attack on the Palestinian militants. More than 20,000 people were killed. The Israeli hostages were exchanged for Leila Khaled and other PFLP prisoners, and the crisis finally came to an end. Richard Nixon met the hostages in Rome on September 28. The PLO and PFLP, having badly overplayed their hand, decamped to Lebanon.[17]

After the hijackings and the ensuing crisis, the United States initiated a new air travel security effort, which included creating the federal sky marshal program, and established the first mandated airport security passenger screening policies in 1972. It marked the beginning of increasingly rigorous measures that culminated in the formation of the Transportation Security Administration in the aftermath of 9/11.

Supersonic Demise

At the beginning of the 1970s the troubled US SST program was more than a year behind schedule. It had 122 aircraft on order, including 12 for TWA. In addition to technical obstacles, the idea of supersonic airline flights was met with growing resistance. NASA and Air Force test flights in the 1960s prompted public opposition to overland supersonic booms. And research showed that regular flights above 60,000 feet could potentially cause environmental harm in the form of water vapor, nitrogen oxides, and ozone depletion. Although the Nixon administration supported continuing government subsidies for the SST, political opposition was mounting. In March 1971 the Senate voted to eliminate further funding, and the House of Representatives followed suit in May.[18] The project was promptly terminated.

The demise of the American SST left TWA with options on six Concordes. The airline had little enthusiasm for the planes, and TWA's president Wiser advised the board that the Concordes' economics would be worse than initially projected. The airline would need to charge premium fares for its Concorde service, which would greatly reduce the passenger market.[19]

Charles Tillinghast proposed forming a consortium of major international airlines to operate the Concordes, but the idea went nowhere. In the end only British Airways and Air France bought 14 of the planes, both under pressure from their respective governments, which had subsidized the costly prestige project.

Recovery and Retrenchment

TWA management waged an aggressive campaign in 1971 to recover from the previous year's financial losses. It reduced its workforce by nearly 12 percent, explaining that the loss of trained, experienced employees was "unfortunate" but "absolutely necessary, in view of the economic conditions faced by TWA and the airline industry." Management also reduced flight frequencies, and 16 early Boeing 707s were grounded and sold. The CAB allowed TWA to suspend service to unprofitable overseas destinations (Algiers, Colombo, Dhahran, Tripoli, and Tunis), and it granted the airline a 6 percent fare increase, which reduced the company's loss to $5.3 million in 1971.[20]

By the end of the year TWA's fleet included 19 Boeing 747s, 104 Boeing 707s, 72 Boeing 727s, 25 Convair 880s, and 19 DC-9s, with the first TriStars scheduled for delivery in 1972. However, the 1971 annual report warned that TWA and the broader airline industry continued to face the serious problems of overcapacity, price weakness in international markets, and inflation.[21] On the positive side, the Hilton International hotel chain's profitability continued to support the airline's difficult situation. Hilton earned $8.8 million in 1971, which offset the airline's loss and gave TWA a net profit of $3.2 million for the year.

Encouraged by these figures, TWA's board approved a search for another merger partner that it hoped would provide a similar benefit. The effort came to fruition when Canteen Corporation, a nationwide operator of vending machines, became a wholly owned subsidiary in August 1973.[22] While owning hotels was arguably beneficial to TWA, there was no obvious synergy between vending machines and the airline business. The Canteen Corporation acquisition seemed to have been made solely to improve the corporate bottom line.

Better Times

In 1972 the airline earned a net profit of $33.8 million, and Hilton International added another $9.3 million. Nonetheless, Tillinghast and Wiser pointed out that the airline earned only a 5.4 percent return on investment, compared with the CAB's target of 12 percent. They also noted that the industry had reached that target just once in the last 20 years, adding, "There is a need for broadening awareness, on the part of shareholders as well as regulatory agencies, of the constraints under which U.S. airlines are required to operate."[23] Little did they know when those words were written that in a few years one stroke of the pen would sweep away all of those constraints, and the airlines would find themselves in a chaotic, totally deregulated industry.

TWA had the distinction of being the first US airline to land in post-revolutionary China when a Boeing 707 touched down at Beijing on February 1, 1972, carrying technicians and equipment to cover Richard Nixon's historic trip there. TWA used the occasion to ask the CAB for permission to extend its transpacific routes to China and exercise its long-dormant authority to serve Shanghai and Canton. However, TWA never obtained the necessary authorizations from the American and Chinese governments and abandoned the effort when it relinquished its transpacific routes a few years later.[24]

TWA also renewed its flirtation with Pan American Airlines in the early 1970s. Like TWA, Pan Am suffered from excess capacity, declining revenue, and rising fuel prices. And it too owned a hotel chain. Pan American president (and former FAA chief) Najeeb Halaby approached TWA in 1971, pointing out that both airlines faced heavy competition on the blue-chip North Atlantic routes to Europe. Combining their airlines and hotel chains could potentially bring many benefits. Talks continued for much of the year but eventually fell through because of the Nixon administration's hostility toward the deal.[25]

Nevertheless, in March 1975, TWA and Pan Am agreed to exchange several of their international routes to rationalize their services. TWA relinquished its transpacific routes to Taiwan and Guam from Honolulu, ending the globe-circling service it had inaugurated with great fanfare five years earlier but that ultimately proved unprofitable. It also turned over its Frankfurt, Hong Kong, and Bombay (Mumbai) destinations to Pan Am in return for Pan Am's Paris, Barcelona, Nice, Vienna, Casablanca, and London routes from Chicago, Los Angeles, and Philadelphia. The CAB approved the deal for a period of two years, after which TWA reclaimed Frankfurt. TWA also abandoned its unprofitable African routes to Kenya, Tanzania, and Uganda.

Still in Court

The 1970s marked the second decade of TWA's litigation with Howard Hughes and Hughes Tool Company. District Court Judge Metzner handed down a ruling that awarded TWA $145 million in treble damages, costs, and attorneys' fees, which both sides appealed. Hughes Tool asked to have the judgment overturned on the grounds that the Civil Aeronautics Board had exclusive jurisdiction over the airlines and had approved all of Hughes's actions, so TWA had no viable antitrust claims. For its part, TWA sought to increase the amount of the award. The court of appeals affirmed the decision for TWA in September 1971 and increased the rate of interest on the judgment, bringing the total award to $160 million.[27] It was an enormous victory for TWA.

Hughes Tool requested the United States Supreme Court to review the case, and the Supreme Court accepted. This came as a surprise because in 1965 the high court had declined to hear the case without considering the jurisdictional issue raised by Hughes. In oral arguments in October 1972, Hughes and Hughes Tool were represented by professor Charles Alan Wright of the University of Texas, author of a textbook on federal courts and an expert on federal jurisdiction, while Dudley Tenney represented TWA as corporate counsel. Ominously, the justices' questions now focused on the jurisdictional issue.[28]

On January 10, 1973, almost 12 years after TWA filed suit, the Supreme Court handed down its decision. It held, in a 7–2 opinion, that the CAB did indeed have exclusive jurisdiction and had approved all of Hughes's actions—leaving TWA with no claim under the antitrust laws—and vacated TWA's huge judgment.[29] The ruling was a devastating blow to TWA. It had prevailed at every prior stage of the proceedings, only to lose in the court from which there was no appeal. Further rubbing salt in the wound, Hughes and Hughes Tool now moved to recover their costs. After two more years of litigation, a judgment was entered against TWA that required it to pay more than $2 million.

In the aftermath of the Supreme Court decision, TWA's special litigation committee re-activated the Delaware State Court suit filed against Hughes and Hughes Tool, which had been put on hold while the antitrust case wended its way through the federal courts. The Delaware case was based solely on Delaware corporate law, with no antitrust issues involved. It alleged that Hughes's actions—such as failing to acquire an adequate jet fleet and preventing the timely delivery of the Convair 880s, all to promote his own interests—had violated his fiduciary obligations to TWA and the minority TWA shareholders, which led to the 1960 financial crisis and the imposition of the voting trust that finally ousted Hughes from control of the airline. Hughes and Hughes Tool argued that the case's dismissal precluded pursuing these claims in Delaware, but TWA countered that they had never been litigated in federal court because of Hughes's failure to appear and the resulting default judgment. The Delaware Supreme Court agreed and allowed the case to proceed in 1975.[30]

Howard Hughes had long since disappeared from public view, becoming an object of mystery and speculation. After selling his TWA stock in 1966, he successively moved to Las Vegas, the Bahamas, Nicaragua, Canada, London, and back to the Bahamas. He increasingly withdrew into a nightmare world of physical and mental illness, as well as addiction. The man who insisted on controlling everything was now controlled and manipulated by competing factions of his own entourage.

In February 1976, Hughes relocated from Freeport, Bahamas, to a penthouse in the Acapulco Princess Hotel. On April 5, 1976, his aides made a final desperate effort to transport him to Houston Methodist Hospital for medical care, but by the time the chartered jet reached Houston, its passenger was dead. Howard Hughes had come full circle, returning in death to his birthplace. The Hughes Tool Company oil drill business, his fountain of wealth, had been sold to the public in 1972. Its other enterprises were renamed Summa Corporation, and the TWA litigation continued against Summa and the Howard Hughes estate.

In June 1977 the Delaware court held Summa and the Hughes estate liable for Hughes's violations of his fiduciary duties to TWA. The wheels of justice would grind on in the litigation battle between Hughes, now deceased, and the airline he once owned.

They Who Served

When TWA introduced hostesses aboard its flights in 1935, they were required to be registered nurses who were unmarried and childless, and they had to take retirement at age 35. Their role was to make passengers feel welcome, comfortable, and safe at a time when few Americans had ever flown and flying was often less than comfortable. The nursing requirement was soon abandoned; for most hostesses, the job was a temporary interlude between school, marriage, and becoming a homemaker.

The hostess role became more glamorous in the postwar period, but the duties broadened as recreational travel increased and more families came aboard. Although the training—particularly related to safety—was more extensive and demanding, the rigid rules about children and age remained in place. But changing cultural values and expectations began to erode these arbitrary strictures by the 1960s. The 1970s marked major shifts in public attitudes toward many issues, including gender roles and stereotypes, as well as women's position and role in society. The airline industry, despite its extensive daily contact with the public, was slow to recognize and respond to these changes. For instance, even as TWA began to hire male flight attendants in the early 1970s, the airline continued to use the term "hostess."

The center of the TWA hostess universe was the Breech Training Academy, located on a 34-acre campus in Overland Park, Kansas, a suburb of Kansas City. Opened in 1969, the Breech complex was the largest flight attendant training center in the world. Its facilities included 32 octagon-shaped classrooms, plus 10 galley trainers and mockups of all aircraft cabins in the TWA fleet. Desks were arranged in a horseshoe, so every student had a front-row seat. The complex also featured grooming rooms where makeup application and poise were taught, and it had sets of training stairs so hostesses could practice how to walk up and down them properly. Breech also included a beauty salon, dining room, 300-seat auditorium, visitor lounge, offices, and other support facilities.[31]

As of 1970 the potential TWA hostess was at least 19.5 years old with a high school diploma at minimum. The candidate had to be 5 feet, 2 inches, to 5 feet, 9 inches tall, and weigh 100 to 140 pounds "in proportion to height." Prospective hostesses had to pass two interviews. Ninety percent of applicants were eliminated at the first interview, while 75 percent of those invited for the second interview were accepted. The company interviewed 50,000 applicants a year, only 1,200 of whom made it all the way to graduation.

Approximately 120 candidates arrived at the Overland Park campus every week to begin training. Divided into classes (or "wings"), each group was assigned an experienced hostess to oversee their progress and supervise their training. The trainees were quartered in 10 units around a sunken living room where they could relax or study, surrounded by motifs of TWA's overseas destinations. At full capacity Breech could accommodate 300 student hostesses. Notwithstanding the emphasis on grooming and service, most of the training involved the FAA-mandated performance of safety functions and emergency procedures, plus passing the written examination required for certification.[32]

After graduating from the academy, TWA assigned each new hostess to its domestic or international division. The international division had foreign bases open only to foreign nationals, who were subject to a different working agreement, but most of the international division hostesses were West Coast–based hostesses who flew military charters to Southeast Asia and commercial flights across the Pacific. The starting monthly salary was $376 (about $2,950 in 2023). A generous benefits package was also included. One of the most valued job perks was travel privileges on domestic routes—and, after three years of service, on international ones.[33] As a hostess explained in 1970, "The most important fringe benefit for any girl working for an airline is inexpensive travel when she's *not* working."[34]

Years later former hostess Ann Hood fondly recalled her experience. "TWA dazzled me, a 21-year-old girl from Rhode Island, with the lure of layovers everywhere from Cairo and Bombay to Paris and Rome. And in a time when other airlines had their flight attendants decked out in shades of screaming blue and pink, TWA's wore cool military-inspired uniforms designed by Ralph Lauren. Who could resist? At the Breech Training Academy in Kansas City—a *Jetsons*-style office complex complete with sunken living rooms and modular furniture—I learned the sophistication that had eluded me in my small-town upbringing," she said. "I tasted caviar, sipped nice wines, carved chateaubriand, dressed lamb chops in tiny gold foil booties. TWA flight attendants never chewed gum or smoked cigarettes in front of passengers. We could mix a perfect martini. In short, working at TWA was a ticket to a lifestyle."[35]

Like TWA's Flight Center at JFK, the Breech Training Academy was an embodiment of the airline's dedication to the travel experience, and it was lavished with high-end resources. Conceived and created at the pinnacle of TWA's success in the 1960s, Breech would see great changes in air travel and the role of cabin crews in the 1970s.

A group of hostesses filed a charge with the Equal Employment Opportunity Commission in 1970 challenging the "no motherhood rule," which TWA finally rescinded. The following year a class-action suit for employment discrimination and wrongful termination under Title VII of the 1964 Civil Rights Act was filed on behalf of all hostesses who were terminated under the rule, as male flight attendants were not grounded if they became parents. This suit brought years of litigation.

While the civil rights litigation was pending the union contract expired, and negotiations over a new agreement became protracted and contentious. The National Mediation Board intervened as the talks dragged on—primarily about wages and working hours—and reached a stalemate. On November 5, 1973, TWA's 5,000 attendants walked out on strike, shutting down all TWA domestic and outbound international flights. The work stoppage lasted 45 days, the longest in the airline's history, and ended with bad blood on both sides. Along with the pregnancy termination litigation, it reflected a "deterioration in company-attendant relations even though TWA had been one of the first carriers to let married women fly."[36] These disputes were a harbinger of things to come.

In 1979, TWA reached a settlement with the terminated hostesses who were to be retrained and rehired with full seniority as positions became open. The airline also agreed to pay $3 million in damages. But then the Independent Federation of Flight Attendants—now representing all working flight attendants, both men and women—filed suit challenging the settlement. The suit contended that rehiring flight attendants with up to 30 years' seniority would put current flight attendants at an unfair disadvantage with respect to layoffs and bidding on work schedules, transfers, and vacations. The case went all the way to the United States Supreme Court, which finally upheld the settlement in February 1982. [37]

Meanwhile, Back in the Middle East

On October 6, 1973, Egypt and Syria launched coordinated attacks on the Sinai Peninsula and the Golan Heights, both occupied by Israel as a result of the Six-Day War. The combined offensive began on Yom Kippur, the holiest day of the Jewish calendar, and caught Israeli defenses by surprise. Egyptian forces advanced virtually unopposed into the Sinai Peninsula, but Israel quickly mobilized and halted the Egyptian offensive. The Israelis then counterattacked the two Egyptian armies in Sinai, crossed the Suez Canal into Egypt, and began moving toward the city of Suez. By October 24 the Israelis had encircled the Egyptian forces, which were in danger of being wiped out, before US and Soviet pressure ended in a ceasefire and brought the war to a close. Once again TWA was affected by a Middle East war, and all service to Egypt and Israel ceased for the duration of the fighting.

But that was not the only repercussion. In October 1973 the Organization of the Petroleum Exporting Countries (OPEC), led by US ally Saudi Arabia, agreed to reduce oil production by 5 percent per month. Saudi Arabia and other Middle East oil-exporting nations also declared an embargo against the United States in response to American support for Israel during the war, which led to an energy crisis. The US Department of the Interior announced a mandatory fuel allocation program, and it fell heavily on the airlines. TWA president Wiser advised the board in December 1973 that the airline would receive 25 percent less fuel in 1974 than it had consumed in 1973, and costs were projected to rise from $200 million to nearly $350 million despite the reduced consumption. The CAB granted the airlines fare increases to cope with the burden, but Wiser said higher fares would not even cover half of the increased fuel costs.[38]

The 1973 oil crisis prompted TWA to ground its Convair 880 fleet, whose troubled acquisition had precipitated Hughes's downfall in 1960. Ordered in the late 1950s when jet fuel was cheap and abundantly available, an airliner with four engines—which burned more fuel than the three engines that powered TWA's Boeing 727s and carried more passengers—no longer made sense in a new era when efficiency was vital. TWA also began disposing of its small, less efficient DC-9s after fewer than 10 years in service.

A Greek Tragedy

On September 8, 1974, TWA Flight 841—a Boeing 707 en route from Israel to New York via Athens—went out of control shortly after takeoff from Athens and plunged into the Ionian Sea, killing all 79 passengers and 9 crew on board. The crew on an eastbound Pan American flight reported seeing a four-engine TWA aircraft pitch up into a steep climb, then roll over on its back and enter a spiral dive, making at least one full 360 degree rotation. About two hours later debris and bodies were found floating on the ocean surface near the reported site of the incident. Nearly a ton of debris was eventually collected.[39]

The water's depth prevented the 707's flight data recorder from being recovered. Based on examination of the wreckage, however, investigators concluded that a bomb had detonated in the rear cargo compartment. The explosion buckled the cabin floor and damaged the aircraft control cables running beneath it, causing violent movements that pitched the plane upward into a stall and then a dive.[40]

A malfunctioning explosive device in a suitcase had caused an aft cargo compartment fire on a similar flight a few weeks earlier. The passengers' baggage wasn't checked in either case. In the wake of these events the NTSB issued five safety recommendations, including that the aircraft security programs of US air carriers "contain provisions that are more responsive to high-risk situations in international as well as domestic operations."[41]

Who planted the bomb was never determined. What was clear, however, was that TWA faced continuing danger in the Middle East.

Disaster at Mount Weather

TWA Flight 514, a Boeing 727-200, was approaching the Washington, DC, area en route from Columbus, Ohio, on December 1, 1974. Strong crosswinds at Washington National Airport, the flight's scheduled destination, necessitated a diversion to Dulles International Airport. The crew contacted Dulles approach control, which cleared them for an instrument approach. The controller intended this only as a traffic advisory, but the crew interpreted it as clearance to commence the approach, and the captain believed he could descend to a minimum altitude of 1,800 feet above sea level.

The weather was miserable, with low ceilings, poor visibility, and winds of 40 mph. The pilots had difficulty controlling the aircraft. An altitude alert sounded at 1,800 feet, and two more warnings went off at 500 feet and 100 feet above the terrain. The pilots added power in an unsuccessful attempt to halt the descent, but seconds later the 727 smashed into Mount Weather, Virginia, at 250 mph, disintegrated, and burst into flames. All 85 passengers and 7 crew members died.

The accident's circumstances aroused controversy. The cockpit voice recorder transcript showed that the pilots were uncertain about the minimum safe altitude for their location, and the captain interpreted the controller's clearance as allowing a further descent. The FAA took the position that because the flight had not been vectored to a final approach course it was not a "radar arrival," and the crew was responsible for terrain avoidance—even though they were amid clouds and had been cleared for the approach.[42]

The National Transportation Safety Board concluded otherwise. It found that the flight was in a "radar environment," and terrain restrictions should have been included in the clearance. Three NTSB members found that the crew descended below the minimum altitude for the approach, which was reflected on the charts they were using.[43] But in a rare public disagreement, two other members dissented, concluding that the flight was definitely on a "radar arrival"—and that the controller was responsible for providing terrain clearance instructions—but still held that the pilots had "adequate information" on their approach chart to alert them that they should not have descended. Nevertheless, all members agreed that the air traffic control procedures in effect were inadequate and confusing for the pilots and controllers.[44]

The investigation revealed that pilots were not always aware of the nature and extent of the radar services air traffic control provided. The NTSB made no fewer than 14 recommendations to the Federal Aviation Administration for improvement and noted that by the time the report was issued, the FAA had already changed its air traffic control procedures to deal with such situations.[45] More important, the FAA required all US air carrier aircraft to be equipped with Ground Proximity Warning System (GPWS) equipment that would alert crews about their height over terrain, descent rate, glide slope deviations, and aircraft performance. Following the GPWS mandate, such "controlled flight into terrain" accidents sharply declined. Once again, it took a tragedy to improve air travel safety.

More Hard Times

Like the rest of the airlines, TWA was rocked by the 1973 oil crisis, rising fuel prices, supply shortages, rationing, and a sharp decline in traffic volume. After increasing by an average of more than 12 percent annually for 10 years, passenger traffic went up by only half that rate in 1973. The airline was also hard hit by the flight attendant strike and the disruption of its Middle East flights. But because most of these challenges came late in 1973, the airline still managed to post a respectable $39 million net profit before taxes.[46]

TWA fared much worse in 1974. The corporation's annual report characterized it as "one of the most difficult in TWA's history." Jet fuel costs rose by a staggering $204 million over 1973—an increase of 122 percent, even though the airline used less fuel than it did the year before owing to the supply shortage and reduced schedules. Fuel-related fare increases granted by the CAB recouped only $65 million of these costs. System-wide passenger traffic fell by 5 percent, and international traffic went down by nearly 12 percent, but because of rising inflation, costs did not fall proportionately. The airline sustained a $46 million pre-tax loss for the year.[47]

Hilton International and Canteen Corporation, which had helped mitigate the volatility of airline operations, also suffered in 1974, but both remained profitable. Tillinghast was steadfast in his belief that TWA's partners would achieve solid profits, but added, "I cannot say the same of our airline operations." He called for "a higher degree of sensitivity among our numerous governmental regulators as to the need for an improved economic environment for airlines."[48] In a few short years, however, governmental regulators would no longer be a factor.

"Significant benefits" were expected from the route swap with Pan American in March 1975 that relinquished the transpacific route and ended TWA's around-the-world service. "Our decision to suspend service to the Pacific was a sad and difficult one," TWA's annual report said. "When we inaugurated service in 1969, our long-term projections were for substantial traffic growth. However, the fuel crisis and an uncertain economic environment required a re-evaluation of our total international operations."[49] Globe-circling routes had been the jewel in the crown of TWA's 1944 international route application and fulfilled the grand postwar dream of Howard Hughes and Jack Frye. It had taken more than two decades for the service to become a reality, only to be abandoned just five years later. The airline's world had changed, and many more changes were coming.

TWA responded by curtailing its jumbo jet fleet. Because other airlines were also suffering, it looked overseas to the government of imperial Iran to dispose of six Boeing 747s at a substantial loss to raise needed cash in 1975. TWA also tried unsuccessfully to sell some of its TriStars to Iran and to defer deliveries of new TriStars on order, but instead it negotiated a deal to stretch out the payments for these large jetliners that were now surplus to its needs. Three additional 747s were later sold to Iran.[50]

President Wiser resigned amid this turbulence, in June 1975. Despite being a graduate of the US Naval Academy with impressive credentials in commercial aviation, his tenure had been less than auspicious. He had struggled to cope with the impact of the wide-body era and the financial difficulties that came from rising costs, excess capacity, and the 1973–1974 oil shock. Airline historian Robert Serling attributed Wiser's departure to a "nervous disorder." Tillinghast later recalled, "[Wiser] seemed to be doing a great job. Then something seemed to happen to him and I didn't find out until later the nature of his disability."[51] The *New York Times* reported that prior to his departure, Wiser had voiced "deep pessimism about the future of the airlines and had been predicting he would be out of the business by year's end."[52] Instead, six months later Pan American hired Wiser as its president, a position he held until 1978. Wiser died in 1987 at age 66 from Alzheimer's disease.

New Times and New Leadership

TWA's financial woes deepened in 1975. The cascade of adversity in 1973 and 1974 led to a crushing pre-tax loss of $121 million in 1975—the worst in its history. At the same time Hilton International and Canteen Corporation continued to be profitable, which prompted TWA's management to focus increasingly on non-airline businesses to improve TWA's profit-and-loss picture.

In January 1976 the TWA directors elected Charles E. Meyer president and "Airline Chief Executive"—a title that acknowledged TWA's drift from its core business. Meyer was a certified public accountant with an MBA who had been TWA's financial vice president. During the coming decade he would struggle to cope with controlling costs and other unprecedented issues, including the deregulation of the airline industry.

Meyer got off to a good start: TWA rebounded to a $32 million pre-tax profit in 1976, thanks to increased traffic, a healthier economy, stringent cost controls, deferral of new aircraft deliveries, higher load factors, and higher fares. The airline launched an aggressive marketing campaign that stressed it had the best on-time performance in the industry. TWA's non-airline subsidiaries also had a good year.[53]

Yet amid the positive news Meyer sounded a cautionary note, telling shareholders, "Much of TWA's fleet is growing old and will require replacement for reasons of obsolescence, technical and/or environmental reasons during the 1980s." He continued that in order to be attractive to potential lenders, the airline had to prove it could be consistently profitable, saying, "If we are unsuccessful, the result can only be a net reduction in the size of the airline."[54] His prediction was accurate. TWA would continue to contract during the coming years. Meyer also faced the challenge of complying with the FAA's new aircraft noise regulations. The cost to modify TWA's aging fleet was estimated at $200 million. Replacing the airlines' old planes with new, quieter ones would cost $3.5 billion.[55]

Another top management change occurred in 1976 when Charles Tillinghast stepped down as chairman and CEO, ending nearly 15 years at TWA's helm. He had presided over a dramatic reversal of TWA's fortunes, from the chaos of the Hughes era to prosperity. Tillinghast's success came in considerable part from the rapid growth in demand for air travel and a booming economy in the 1960s. But the 1970s brought a brand-new slate of challenges for TWA and for the industry. Tillinghast seemed to sense that the future did not look rosy. "I finally concluded," he would later say, "that airlines were a lousy business."[56]

Tillinghast handed over the chairmanship to L. Edwin Smart, his protégé and hand-picked successor. After graduating from Harvard Law School,

Smart had joined his mentor's Wall Street law firm and followed Tillinghast as he moved from law to corporate management. Tillinghast brought Smart to TWA in 1966 as vice president of external affairs, putting him in charge of the diversification efforts that led to the acquisition of Hilton International.[57] By the time Smart became TWA's chairman, his belief that diversification would remedy the uncertainties of the airline business was stronger than ever, a conviction he held throughout his tenure.

Old Planes and New

Struggling to cope with the airline's financial and operational needs, Meyer negotiated a complex deal in 1977 to reschedule the delivery of stretched Boeing 727-231s, now the backbone of TWA's domestic schedules, and Lockheed TriStars. Two TriStars were sold before delivery, and four more were leased out at rental rates above TWA's ownership costs. The remaining DC-9s were sold or reconfigured to increase passenger capacity.[58]

By the end of 1977, TWA had a fleet of 253 jets, including 10 Boeing 747s, 30 Lockheed TriStars, 88 passenger and 12 all-cargo Boeing 707s, 74 Boeing 727s, and 14 DC-9s, along with 24 Convair 880s that had been inactive for several years. In 1978, TWA modified four TriStars with increased fuel capacity for international service, and the airline reconfigured its remaining domestic models to allow for greater passenger capacity.[59] The last of the sleek Convair 880s—the cause of so much corporate turmoil in 1960—were finally disposed of in 1978 at fire-sale prices. And TWA grounded its 10 remaining early Boeing 707s, half of which were scrapped at the Kansas City maintenance base for lack of buyers.[60]

Meyer cautioned the company's board in the fall of 1978 that by the end of 1979, TWA's fleet would still be the oldest of any domestic air carrier—despite the recent retirements and new planes. He also warned of the competitive disadvantages that TWA would face and recommended purchasing additional Boeing 727-200s. TWA ultimately acquired 56 of them. Each of them was given an "unofficial" pig-themed name: Road Hog, Sty Stream, and Ozone Oinker among them. These unglamorous planes would serve TWA faithfully for many years, some of them into the 21st century.[61] At the same time, TWA disposed of its fuel-inefficient 707-131Bs, part of the StarStream fleet that had epitomized the elegance and luxury of jet travel in the early 1960s.

Amid its effort to acquire more fuel-efficient jets, TWA inexplicably bought planes that carried fewer passengers than its existing 747s but had the same fuel burn and operating costs. The airline acquired three ultra-long-range Boeing 747SP ("Special Performance") aircraft for $160 million, with deliveries in 1979–1980. The 747SP traded payload for additional fuel capacity and gave it the then-unprecedented range of 7,200 miles. Meyer also proposed buying six new standard 747s—three years after *selling* 747s to Iran.[62] He based these decisions on TWA's growing international business, which earned $50 million in both 1976 and 1977. International operations continued to see strong traffic growth in 1978. An average flight had 79 percent of its seats filled during the peak summer months, a 15 percent increase over 1977.[63]

Meyer assured the board that the 747SPs were the best option to meet TWA's international needs, as they could fly nonstop to the Middle East. Moreover, their reduced passenger capacity—100 fewer seats than the standard 747—would provide "the flexibility to better tailor capacity to market size." A financial analysis predicted that the SPs could earn an 18 percent return on investment valued at more than $32 million, but these estimates proved to be wildly optimistic.[64]

The 747SP was one of TWA's worst equipment decisions. Its operating economics, combined with limited revenue potential, made no business sense, and the forecasted travel boom to the Middle East never materialized. TWA quickly relegated its SPs to North Atlantic and domestic transcontinental routes and then sold them after only a few loss-making years.[65] This flawed equipment choice may have come from Meyer's lack of operational knowledge and experience. By contrast, his warnings about TWA's aging fleet and future competitive disadvantages would prove to be prescient.

Depicted here in 1981, the Boeing 747SP was an ill-considered acquisition. The model quickly disappeared from TWA's fleet. Photo by George Hamlin.

Meyer also ended TWA's unprofitable air cargo service. The airline had 12 Boeing 707 all-cargo aircraft that could not be used for passenger service and sold 4 of them in the spring of 1978, when the resale market for these planes was strong.[66] In September 1978, Meyer announced that TWA would dispose of its remaining all-cargo 707s and exit the dedicated air cargo business, while continuing to offer air cargo service in baggage holds on passenger flights.[67] Unfortunately, this pattern of vacillation, uncertainty, and inconsistency would continue to plague TWA and set up its decline in the 1970s.

In addition to its other difficulties, TWA faced an indictment from the justice department for allegedly conspiring with Pan American and Lufthansa to fix military excursion fares between Europe and the United States. In a gesture laden with irony, TWA moved to dismiss the indictment on the grounds that the CAB had exclusive jurisdiction over such issues, preempting the antitrust laws—the same defense used to defeat TWA's antitrust case against Howard Hughes and Hughes Tool. Reflecting the weakness of the government's claims, TWA and its "co-conspirators" soon negotiated a no-contest plea in which they paid nominal $50,000 fines and agreed not to confer over fares in the future.[68]

An Airline Business No Longer

Under Meyer's financial stewardship, "the Airline," as it was now known, managed to eke out another $32 million pre-tax net profit in 1977. Chairman Smart proudly announced, "Our corporation's net earnings for 1977 were the highest in the company's history—$64.8 million." He also pointed out that Hilton International and Canteen Corporation had performed much better than "the Airline." He added bluntly, "With pre-tax profits in 1977 of only $32.4 million on airline revenues of $2.4 billion—only about 1 and a half percent—even a small change in prospective revenues or costs could seriously impact the Airline's future."[69]

The reference to "the Airline" told the story. Under Smart's leadership, TWA was becoming a hospitality company that also happened to operate an airline. The pioneering air carrier whose birth was presided over by Charles Lindbergh, nurtured by the vision of Howard Hughes, and eventually spanned the globe, had been reduced to the status of an unloved stepchild in its own house.

In August 1978, Smart unveiled a plan to fundamentally change TWA's corporate structure. It called for the creation of a holding company known as Trans World Corporation (TWC), with TWA, Hilton International, and Canteen Corporation becoming wholly owned subsidiaries. The board unanimously approved the plan and set a special meeting on October 12, 1978, to submit it for shareholder approval.[70] Smart outlined the potential advantages of the holding company structure in a letter to stockholders, saying, "It will provide greater flexibility and strength in dealing with a wide range of future financial issues." Among these were "an expanded potential to invest in additional consumer-oriented businesses" and "a change in the favorable vote required for mergers and other holding company transactions."[71]

The stockholders duly approved the reorganization, becoming owners of TWC effective January 1, 1979. TWA thus became a mere subsidiary of an enterprise designed to engage in mergers and acquisitions, right as a historic change was about to take place that would put TWA on a course that led to its demise.

The Road to Deregulation

In the decades after 1938, when Congress created the Civil Aeronautics Board and empowered it to regulate the airlines, the CAB treated the airline industry as a public utility. Under its governance the airlines were prohibited from competing on fares or routes served, and those could only be changed through a laborious (and often fruitless) application process. As a result, the airlines competed for customer satisfaction and loyalty. During the 1950s and 1960s, US airlines' passenger traffic measured in passenger miles (one passenger carried 1 mile, the airline industry's basic yardstick) increased by an average of 15 percent annually, and the total doubled every five years.[72]

Much of this growth was generated by first-time air travelers who now had more discretionary income and could fly to their vacation destinations. TWA was a leader in marketing itself to this new traveling public, but such growth could not continue indefinitely, and it leveled off in the 1970s. At the same time an economic downturn and sharply rising fuel costs from the 1973–1974 energy crisis handed the airline industry $100 million in losses.[73]

The CAB responded cautiously to these changes. It attempted, unsuccessfully, to guarantee the airlines a 12 percent return on investment, keep fares relatively high, and discourage discounting. The airlines flew many empty seats and chafed at the regulatory constraints imposed on them. The CAB also restricted the entry of new, low-cost carriers, which brought increasing demand for lower fares and pressure to reconsider the premises of airline regulation.[74]

In the 1970s, Congress became alarmed by Penn Central Transportation Company's bankruptcy and the federal bailout that followed. Congress wanted to avoid "a Penn Central with wings."[75] In response the CAB created a Special Staff on Regulatory Reform. It issued a report in July 1975 that called for phasing out airline regulation.[76] The Ford administration began preparing legislation, and hearings were held by Senator Edward Kennedy, who was sympathetic to deregulation.[77]

While TWA was frustrated by the CAB's rigid control over fares and service, the airline also relied on it to limit competition. In October 1975, Tillinghast told the board, "In the past 15 years airline fares increased far less than the prices of any other major products or services." He asserted that the future of the airline industry hinged on the ability to pass through to customers "the vastly increased costs, beyond its control, which it likely would be facing for some years to come."[78]

TWA's management called deregulation "one of the more fashionable fads on the Washington scene." Reflecting its ambivalence on the subject, management told stockholders, "While we feel strongly that there should be much less stringent control over fares and rates, we believe that deregulation would be detrimental to the continuation of a private-enterprise air transportation system of the type we now enjoy" and "the inevitable result would be a reduction in service to smaller communities and the elimination of a number of carriers. Chaos rather than an improved regulatory system would result from the Administration's proposals, and more regulation rather than less likely would then occur."[79] Of these predictions only "more regulation, rather than less" would not come to pass.

In January 1977, Alfred E. Kahn was appointed chairman of the CAB. Kahn, a Cornell University economist and well-known champion of free markets, became the most visible advocate for doing away with the CAB and its regulatory powers. Kahn asserted that the airline industry was well suited for effective competition and urged a return to free enterprise.[80] TWA disagreed. In March 1977, Meyer testified before the Senate in opposition to deregulation. "The airlines have long suffered from the unfortunate effects of being highly regulated, and at the same time, highly competitive," he said. "The proposed legislation simply worsens that situation." He predicted that deregulation "would, following an initial burst of competition and eventual financial weakening of both new and existing carriers, eventually lead to an oligopolistic situation that will call for more regulation, not less." He concluded, "I believe change is inevitable, but it should be undertaken with due, deliberate speed and with a clear understanding of the consequences."[81] Meyer's prediction would prove accurate, except that the oligopoly and loss of competition would be wholly unregulated.

The political momentum for deregulation was irresistible. Introduced in 1978 with bipartisan support, legislation passed the House and Senate with large majorities. The Airline Deregulation Act, signed into law by President Carter on October 24, 1978, was intended "to encourage, develop, and attain an air transportation system which relies on competitive market forces to determine the quality, variety, and price of air services." Kahn called it "a dramatic event in the history of economic policy" and the first thorough dismantling of a comprehensive system of government control since the 1930s, as the rules imposed by the CAB were swept aside.[82] It was also one of the most poorly conceived and executed reversals of public policy in American history. Instead of phasing regulation out gradually and with appropriate safeguards, the act abruptly ended the entire process with the stroke of a pen. Chaos ensued, and the industry would not recover for nearly 30 years.

Brave New World

With the coming of deregulation, the airlines plunged into "an orgy of fierce competition." Even before the act took effect, airline representatives lined up outside the CAB's Washington, DC, offices seeking to claim new routes. By the end of 1978 more than 150 aspiring new airlines had been formed, few of which survived.[83] TWA quickly added service to Miami, Fort Lauderdale, West Palm Beach, Orlando, Fort Meyers, and Tampa in an effort to reduce the seasonality of its predominantly east-west route structure by filling previously empty seats in the winter months.[84] In 1978, its final year of operation under regulation, TWA posted a $35 million pre-tax profit—the last it would earn for many years to come. Yet Ed Smart commented disparagingly on TWA's "disappointing traffic growth and unfavorable yield trends during the final months of the year."[85]

A spike in jet fuel prices added to TWA's difficulties. An Islamic republic replaced the Iranian monarchy in 1978 and ushered in yet another Middle East oil shock. TWA's 1979 fuel bill increased by nearly $250 million over the previous year, compelling the airline to abandon plans for nonstop service between its new St. Louis hub and Honolulu, and ending long-established international services to Geneva, Shannon, Dublin, Casablanca, and Nice, while adding new domestic service to destinations in the Sun Belt and the Southwest.[86]

In addition to unbridled competition among airlines, deregulation also unleashed a wave of airline mergers and acquisitions. TWA's struggles attracted the attention of brash airline entrepreneur Frank Lorenzo, who had parlayed control of struggling local service airline Trans-Texas Airways—renamed Texas International—into a cash-rich powerhouse through innovative management and aggressive cost cutting, largely at the expense of the airline's union workforce. Lorenzo began buying TWC stock in September 1979, fueling speculation that he would attempt a hostile takeover. TWC engaged Wall Street law firm Wachtell Lipton as counsel, and the directors "unanimously reaffirmed that Trans World [Corporation] has no desire to sell TWA to Texas International or anyone else and that in the Board's view the interests of Trans World's shareholders, TWA employees and the public are best served by Trans World's remaining an independent company with TWA continuing as a wholly owned subsidiary of Trans World."[87] TWC proved too big for Lorenzo to swallow. After accumulating 4 percent of TWC's stock, Lorenzo sold his shares and turned his attention elsewhere. But it was not the end of his interest in the airline. He would surface again when it was far more vulnerable.

Meanwhile, Ed Smart's appetite for new acquisitions remained unabated. In July 1979, TWC acquired Spartan Food Services, a restaurant chain. Months later shareholders approved the acquisition of Century 21 Real Estate, a national realty chain, despite stockholder opposition.[88] Smart bragged about the profitability of the non-airline subsidiaries and pointed out TWA's $50 million pre-tax loss: "While TWA and the entire airline industry suffered a major reversal, Trans World's non-airline businesses successfully provided offsetting sources of earnings."[89]

Glenn Zander, who later served as TWA's CEO, observed that management had become focused "on selling hamburgers and Coke" rather than carrying passengers. Charles Meyer agreed, recalling, "In retrospect, I would say the diversification did distract from the main objective of running an airline."[90] And with each new acquisition, TWA became more isolated and more vulnerable to corporate raiders.

New Planes for Old

While these corporate machinations proceeded, Meyer continued his efforts to balance TWA's fleet requirements with its available financial resources. In late 1979 he proposed acquiring two additional TriStars for delivery in late 1981 and agreed to purchase 10 767 wide-body jets from Boeing.[91] It was a good choice. The 767 was smaller than the 747 and TriStar but still offered twin-aisle comfort for passengers. It also featured a "glass cockpit" with digital video displays that replaced most of the analog dials and gauges of prior cockpit architecture. TWA took delivery of its first 767-231s in November 1982 and inaugurated 767 service between Los Angeles and Washington, DC, a month later.[92]

While the first 767s suited TWA's domestic routes well, Boeing soon offered an extended-range version called the 767ER, which was capable of flying up to 6,000 miles nonstop. The 767 became the first airliner authorized to operate under new Federal Aviation Administration extended-range, twin-engine operational performance standards (ETOPS), which allowed transoceanic flights with only two engines. The FAA granted the first ETOPS approvals to 767 operators in 1985, and TWA became the first US airline to fly the 767 in scheduled transatlantic passenger operations under the new rules. Airline historian R. E. G. Davies called ETOPS "one of the most important developments in the history of air transport."[93]

Shown here in 1987, the Boeing 767 was the first transoceanic twinjet. TWA pioneered transatlantic twin-engine service with the 767 in 1985. R. A. Burgess Collection, Greater St. Louis Air and Space Museum.

At the same time, Meyer was hard at work disposing of aging airliners with operating costs that made them unprofitable in the new world of expensive fuel and all-out fare competition.[94] But despite these efforts, 1979—TWA's first full year of operation under deregulation and as a subsidiary of TWC—produced a $50 million pre-tax loss. This was $85 million worse than 1978 and more than $100 million below forecast.[95] But one bright spot remained: TWA's international routes, which were not yet affected by deregulation, continued to perform well.

The airline was once again selected to provide transportation for the pope on his 1979 visit to the United States. A TWA 727 transported Pope John Paul II between Boston, New York, Philadelphia, Chicago, Des Moines, and Washington, DC, from October 2 to 6. On October 7, TWA flew the pontiff from Washington to Rome on a specially outfitted Boeing 747, its entire upper level transformed into a papal apartment.[96]

A Troubling Incident

On the night of April 4, 1979, TWA Flight 841, a Boeing 727 en route from New York to Minneapolis at 39,000 feet near Detroit, suddenly went out of control. It dove steeply, completing two full 360 degree rolls while the pilot, Captain Harvey Gibson, desperately tried to steady the craft. The 727 fell 30,000 feet in 1 minute, reaching a speed of Mach 0.96, close to the speed of sound and far greater than the aircraft's maximum design speed. Gibson finally regained control and leveled out at 8,000 feet, in the process subjecting the plane and its passengers to six times the force of gravity. The flight turned back toward Detroit and made a safe landing there without further incident. Remarkably, given the violence of the maneuvers, only eight passengers sustained minor injuries.[97]

The National Transportation Safety Board investigation found that a leading-edge flap on the right wing detached and fell to the ground during the incident, and that an inflight extension of this surface could result in a similar loss of control. But no evidence of a malfunction was uncovered, so the NTSB turned its attention to the flight crew.

The NTSB concluded that the crew extended and then attempted to retract the leading-edge flaps, and slat No. 7 had remained extended. The pilots and flight engineer all unequivocally denied any such action under oath. The NTSB also found that the 727 could have remained under control with a prompt, proper control input, and Gibson's failure to do so led to the wild ride.[98]

These conclusions were controversial, and one of the three participating NTSB members dissented. "I am troubled by the fact that the Board has categorically rejected the crew's sworn testimony without the crew having had the opportunity to be confronted with all of the evidence upon which the Board was basing its findings," he wrote. And he disagreed that Gibson's "untimely flight control inputs" were a causal factor, saying, "In my opinion, the captain acted expeditiously and reasonably in attempting to correct for the severe right roll condition."[99]

The dissent was justified. The majority was wrong to dismiss the sworn testimony of the crew and blame them based on nothing but speculation. Regardless of what caused the upset and loss of control, through skill and determination Gibson recovered the plane and saved all on board from certain death. Recognizing this, TWA took no action against any of the crew, and all returned to flying the line. But for the rest of his career Gibson was haunted by the cloud unfairly placed over him. He was ostracized and shunned by other pilots, and a bleeding ulcer forced him to take medical leave. He eventually opted for early retirement.[100]

Out with the Old, In with the New

Meyer continued trying to match TWA's fleet with the airline's needs. In December 1980 the board approved acquiring three new TriStars and two used Boeing 747s, only four years after having sold half a dozen of its original 747 fleet to Iran. At the same time, Meyer recommended disposing of one of the three newly acquired 747SPs after less than a year in service.[101] Because Boeing now offered advanced 747s with long-range and full-passenger capacity, the uneconomical SPs were now unwanted white elephants. Two eventually went to American Airlines and one to the government of the United Arab Emirates.[102]

Meyer also turned his attention to TWA's aging StarStream 707 fleet. Numbering nearly 80 aircraft—now 15 to 20 years old with four engines and high fuel burn—they were no longer viable in an age of high fuel prices and extreme cost pressures. These veterans of TWA's glamour days were all gone by the end of 1984. TWA also began selling its early Boeing 727s. These dispositions reduced the airline's fleet count from 220 to 184.[103]

On a more positive note, TWA announced an agreement with McDonnell Douglas to lease 15 new MD-80s in 1982.[104] Originally known as the DC-9-80, the MD-80 was the ultimate stretched version of the DC-9 design dating from the mid-1960s. The MD-80 featured an extended wing and a fuselage 50 feet longer than the original version, plus a pair of powerful, fuel-efficient engines. With its 150-passenger capacity now exceeding TWA's Boeing 727-231 trijets and aging four-engine 707s, the new twin was economical, flexible, and well suited to TWA's domestic needs. It didn't require a flight engineer—a cockpit crew member who managed the engines and systems of more complex airplanes—so the airline could now begin phasing out this job position and greatly reduce labor costs. The MD-80 was so successful that TWA eventually acquired more than 100 of them, taking delivery of the last in 1999.[105]

THE WORKHORSE

TWA operated more Boeing 707 jetliners—126 of them—than any other airline. The beloved four-engine craft ushered in the jet age in the late 1950s and proved to be a workhorse on both international and domestic routes. As TWA said goodbye to its last 707s in the fall of 1984, one of the airline's employees did some quick calculations regarding the productivity of a single 707 during its tenure with TWA. Bearing the Boeing manufacturer's No. 8778, the 707-331B entered the TWA fleet on February 21, 1963, and flew its last trip on October 30, 1984. During its 21 years of service, No. 8778 logged 68,340 flying hours (21,791 landing cycles)—the equivalent of 7 years and 10 months in the air. Assuming a conservative average speed of 508 mph, No. 8778 flew 34,716,720 miles. Multiplied by its 148 seats, this single Boeing 707 operated more than 5 billion available passenger seat miles. Stated another way: One Boeing 707 jetliner's potential productivity during its 21 years at TWA equaled the productivity of all the piston airliners TWA operated during its first 28 years of service. Moreover, the Boeing 707 had substantial belly cargo capacity excluded from these calculations.[106] A workhorse, indeed, but it was replaced by even more efficient and productive jetliners made necessary by the demands of deregulation.

Depicted here on a 1960 TWA brochure, the Boeing 707 revolutionized air travel. With its speed and comparatively high passenger capacity, the 707 was significantly more productive than its piston-engine predecessors. Schwantes-Greever-Nolan Collection.

New Challenges and Challengers

TWA and the other legacy carriers faced growing competition from the new companies spawned by deregulation, such as People Express Airlines. Organized by several former executives of Frank Lorenzo's burgeoning Texas International Airlines, People Express began operations in April 1981, with a handful of twin-engine Boeing 737s. The upstart carrier saw explosive growth, primarily in the eastern United States. Within two years it was offering transatlantic service to London on its Boeing 747s. The airline only had economy-class seating, and all tickets were sold at the same rock-bottom price. Anticipating trends that would become standard 30 years later, People Express charged passengers for checked baggage and for food and beverage service. Without unions or work rules, People Express enjoyed labor costs far below those of legacy carriers.

These new competitors posed a dilemma for high-cost airlines such as TWA: Either attempt to meet their fares and incur ruinous losses, or abandon routes and market share to the cost cutters. The outcome was usually a compromise that brought the worst of both worlds. TWA tried to meet the low-cost carriers' fares on its key transcontinental routes while simultaneously seeking to differentiate itself by inaugurating a new "Ambassador Class" service that offered "superior comfort at a modest premium over coach, yet well below first-class fares."[107] But such amenities did little to overcome the harsh financial realities the airline was facing.

Meet Me in St. Louis

In response to deregulation, nearly all carriers adopted "hub-and-spoke" route systems. Airlines concentrated their operations at selected hub cities and served other cities primarily (if not exclusively) from these hubs. Hub-and-spoke route networks enabled increased passenger load while establishing regional market dominance and lower operating costs. The development of "fortress hubs" at airports dominated by a single airline became a key element of post-deregulation airline operations.[108]

Following this trend, TWA scaled back its presence in Chicago (dominated by American and United) and moved most of its O'Hare flights to St. Louis's Lambert Airport.[109] Lambert Airport was a sensible alternative because it did not suffer from O'Hare's intense congestion and competition. By mid-1979 it had become TWA's busiest airport, with more than 100 flights a day. Three years later TWA made St. Louis its principal domestic hub, and New York's John F. Kennedy Airport served as its international hub.

The decision to make St. Louis its domestic hub put TWA on a collision course with Ozark Air Lines, nicknamed "St. Louis's Hometown Airline." One of the local service airlines created to feed passenger traffic from outlying points to airports served by the major airlines, Ozark had experienced cautious and steady growth since 1950. Under deregulation it rapidly expanded its routes, competing directly and effectively with TWA in St. Louis by stressing customer service and amenities.

A TWA spokesperson said, "The 1980s will be a battle of the airline hubs, and we will make it more attractive for people to move through St. Louis than through any other hub."[110] The growing rivalry between Ozark and TWA overwhelmed Lambert's capacity. Traffic increased by more than 30 percent in the first half of 1983, making Lambert the sixth-busiest airport in the country. Its passenger terminal was unprepared for such growth, and its runways lacked adequate separation to accommodate simultaneous landings in bad weather. An FAA study found Lambert to have the third highest rate of delayed flights of all US airports in 1983, exceeded only by New York's JFK and LaGuardia.[111]

Lambert struggled to cope with these demands. In July 1983 it opened an extension to the concourse occupied by TWA, including 12 additional gates, snack bars and lounges, and 400 feet of moving sidewalks. It also began construction of a new southeast concourse with 15 additional gates for Ozark.[112]

The Rise of Commuter Lines

Alliances between major airlines and independent regional carriers operating small aircraft with non-union crews through code-sharing agreements became a much more common strategy in the deregulated era. Under code-sharing, the major airlines booked passengers from outlying cities onto regional carriers to their hubs and then onward to destinations in their own networks. These arrangements allowed the majors to increase their dominance at fortress hubs at minimal cost.[113]

Following this pattern, TWA established a network of regional airlines called Trans World Express to deliver passengers from smaller cities to its burgeoning St. Louis hub. TWA's principal regional partner was Trans States Airlines. Formed in St. Louis in 1982 as Resort Air, it connected destinations such as the Lake of the Ozarks, Springfield, and Joplin, Missouri, as well as Carbondale, Illinois, with St. Louis using 19-seat Fairchild Metroliners and 21-passenger British Aerospace Jetstreams, plus 48-seat ATR 42s for higher-volume routes. Eventually, Trans States expanded its TWA code-sharing operations from St. Louis as far as Madison, Wisconsin; Grand Rapids, Michigan; and Memphis, Tennessee.[114]

Trans States Airlines operated regional aircraft, such as the ATR 42, as Trans World Express. R. A. Burgess Collection, Greater St. Louis Air and Space Museum.

The Controllers Strike

Even as deregulation's effects were unfolding, the Professional Air Traffic Controllers Organization (PATCO)—which represented the majority of the FAA's air traffic controllers—called a strike that threatened to cripple air travel nationwide in August 1981. Although the controllers were forbidden to strike by federal law, PATCO believed that the government wouldn't risk a shutdown and would bow to their demands. It was a fatal miscalculation.

Anticipating the strike, the US Department of Transportation and the FAA worked for months to develop contingency plans to operate air traffic control with supervisory personnel, non-striking employees, and military controllers, which it immediately implemented when PATCO controllers walked out. President Ronald Reagan ordered the controllers to return to work within 48 hours and threatened to terminate the employment of anyone who failed to do so. More than 12,000 controllers ignored the order and were dismissed. The air traffic control system continued operating, albeit with limited resources, greatly restricting operations at major airports.

The strike disrupted flights at TWA's St. Louis hub. Fifteen military controllers were temporarily transferred to St. Louis to work under the direction of FAA supervisors, and flight operations continued at 65 to 75 percent of normal levels.[115] But the sudden loss of most of its professional cadre strained the air traffic control system. Air travel suffered when the FAA ordered a reduction in air traffic to 75 percent of pre-strike levels until April 1982.[116] The restrictions gradually eased but were not completely phased out in St. Louis until the next year. Other TWA airports were similarly affected, and the loss of peak-season revenues—combined with aggressive price cutting within the industry—destroyed TWA's plans for improved profitability in 1981.[118]

Relentless price competition caused TWA to view all of its costs, but particularly labor costs, with "intense concern." The furloughs and layoffs that followed undermined morale and esprit de corps. The airline sustained a net loss of $28 million in 1981; little had changed from 1980.[119]

TWA was able to negotiate concessions from its pilots in 1982, but similar efforts with its mechanics and flight attendants failed. Despite these measures and the continued profitability of its international routes, the turmoil in US domestic markets caused by deregulation cost TWA dearly, ending in a $30 million loss in 1982.[120] Others fared even worse. In 1982, Braniff Airways, a pioneer airline that fell victim to mismanagement in the 1960s and 1970s, became the first legacy carrier to succumb to deregulation when it failed to find a merger partner. It ceased operations and was liquidated.

Going Public Again

As the unprofitable subsidiary of a conglomerate whose profitable sister corporations were unaffected by the ravages of deregulation, TWA became increasingly isolated and vulnerable. The company explored the possibility of raising capital by floating a $66 million debt issue, which was shelved in favor of selling 6.6 million shares of $2.25 preferred stock in December 1982.[121] For the first time since 1978, the public could buy TWA stock. It was the start of a process that would make TWA an independent, publicly held corporation once again.

In January 1983 the board authorized management to begin preparations for a public offering of TWA common stock, two-thirds of which would be newly issued shares by TWA and one-third shares owned by TWC, its corporate parent.[122] The sale was completed in March, reducing TWC's ownership stake to 81 percent and providing TWA with a much-needed $54 million cash infusion.[123] The handwriting was now clearly on the wall.

TWC announced in October 1983 that it would seek shareholder approval to spin off its remaining 81 percent interest in TWA. When this restructuring went into effect on February 1, 1984, TWA was once again a wholly publicly owned corporation, completely separate from TWC and its non-airline businesses. "Perhaps the most immediate effect," TWC's president Meyer told the new stockholders, "is to heighten the organization's awareness that its ability to compete in a more demanding free market environment now rests wholly upon its own resources and responses to the new challenges it faces."[124]

While acknowledging that TWA had benefited from access to capital as part of the otherwise profitable TWC family, Meyer tried to put an optimistic face on the situation for shareholders, saying, "With its new structural accountability and entrepreneurial mandate, an independent TWA is positioned to continue providing a fully competitive level of service while seeking a more competitive cost structure and improved earnings performance."[125] But this amounted to whistling in the dark. TWA had been cast adrift on troubled waters without a chart or a compass—and the sharks were waiting.

More Hard Times

Despite Meyer's efforts TWA lost $35 million in 1983. The airline returned to public ownership with an operational fleet of only 156 airplanes. The last Boeing 707s had been withdrawn from service and were either sold or awaiting disposal. Half of its planes were 727s. The rest were a mix of 747s and TriStars, along with the efficient new 767s and MD-80s. But there was no escaping the difficulties the airline faced. Meyer warned shareholders,

"TWA's major current problem is the high employment cost structure it inherits from the regulatory era in which the government set fare levels on the basis of industry average costs." He continued, "Mature carriers are at a severe disadvantage vis-à-vis newer organizations having entry-level, usually non-unionized work forces. The new entrants' far lower seat-mile costs allow them to invade selected markets offering substantially lower fares than the incumbents."[126]

Attempting to respond to deregulation challenges, TWA management tried to reduce costs by seeking concessions from its unionized labor force. The pilots agreed to a 10 percent salary cut worth about $65 million. But the machinists, representing mechanics and several other trades, dug in their heels. After a one-day strike the company agreed to a 28 percent wage increase with no change in work rules.

That left the flight attendants, represented by the Independent Federation of Flight Attendants. Flight attendants were essential to airline operations—Federal Air Regulations mandated them. But unlike pilots and aircraft mechanics, flight attendants did not require extensive training and experience. TWA vice president of operations Ed Frankum decided to hold the line, replacing union flight attendants with management personnel and "contingent" flight attendants trained to step in if a strike occurred. The strike deadline came and went in March 1984 with no agreement. Picket lines went up. Then, despite the contingency plan, management accepted a 30 percent wage increase with no work rule changes. It had bought labor peace, but another and far more damaging confrontation loomed.

Surprisingly, TWA's first year as an independent entity since 1978 was profitable; it ended 1984 $30 million in the black. Total revenue increased by $300 million over 1983, boosted by a strong economic recovery from the 1982–1983 recession. Operations at TWA's St. Louis hub stabilized and improved during 1984, which helped reduce TWA's domestic operating loss to $85 million from $226 million the year before. Continuing profits from TWA's international operations, as yet unaffected by deregulation, also contributed to the profitable year.[127]

But the airline's future remained uncertain as the effects of deregulation continued to ravage the industry. The company cautioned investors, "Many of the adverse factors which underlay TWA's poor financial performance in prior years are continuing, are not subject to TWA's control, and constitute important constraints on its ability to operate profitably. TWA's domestic system, measured by revenue passenger miles flown in the US, ranked fifth among domestic carriers for the last three years, and its relative share of revenue passenger miles in scheduled service among domestic air carriers had steadily decreased over the last decade."[128]

TWA considered scaling back domestic operations in favor of its historically profitable international services but concluded that domestic service was "inseparable from and indispensable to successful international operations." Accordingly, the airline continued expanding its St. Louis domestic hub and began offering transatlantic service from this medium-size inland metropolis with the goal of transforming it into a major international gateway.[129] The stage was set for a confrontation with Ozark Air Lines—its St. Louis neighbor, erstwhile partner, and now rival.

Chapter 7
OZARK INTERLUDE: 1950–1985

Even as the Second World War raged, the Civil Aeronautics Board anticipated a postwar era that would see rapidly increasing demand for air travel and set about promoting its vision of the future. In 1944 the CAB established a new classification of airlines designated "feeder airlines" (later dubbed "local service airlines"), based upon the premise that the public would benefit from scheduled airline service to small cities that didn't have enough potential passenger traffic to make it economically viable for the major airlines to serve them. Providing such service would therefore require direct government subsidies. The local service airlines would link these outlying points by air to metropolitan-area airports, where passengers could connect with larger carriers.[1] The concept had political support, and these new carriers could convert large numbers of cheaply available surplus military C-47s into DC-3 airliners at relatively little cost.

The Birth of Ozark Air Lines

Homer "Laddie" Hamilton, a bus operator and private pilot in Missouri, started Ozark Air Lines in 1943. Hamilton began intrastate operations between Springfield, Rolla, St. Louis, Columbia, Kansas City, and Clinton, Missouri, in January 1945, using four-passenger, single-engine Beech and twin-engine Cessna aircraft. Because it operated strictly within Missouri, the fledgling carrier did not need CAB approval. Using such small planes proved unprofitable, and operations ceased in late 1945.[2] However, Hamilton and his backers did not give up, viewing this as a first step and a learning experience. They turned their attention to re-creating Ozark as a local service airline.

Meanwhile, Oliver Parks, the founder of the respected Parks Air College near St. Louis, was also interested in the local service opportunity. He formed Parks Air Lines hoping to operate a route system from St. Louis south to Tulsa, Oklahoma, and north to Chicago, serving a network of small cities with DC-3s. Parks received CAB approval in November 1946. Although Parks College had built a reputation for excellence, Parks himself had great difficulty securing financing for the new airline, and several years passed without operations commencing. The CAB opened an investigation that led to the revocation of Parks's certificate in July 1950. The CAB then issued a three-year experimental certificate for the same route system to Hamilton and his Ozark backers.[3]

Ozark Air Lines began operations as a local service airline on September 26, 1950, with four former Parks Air Lines DC-3s and a cadre of former Parks employees.[4] Although Ozark's founders hailed from southwest Missouri, they based their operations in St. Louis. The new airline began operations between St. Louis and Chicago with intermediate stops at Springfield, Decatur, and Champaign–Urbana, Illinois. Its first flight departed with a single passenger—a modest start for a carrier with a bright future.[5] In 1952 the City of St. Louis built and leased to Ozark a hangar and offices at Lambert Airport.

Growth and Maturity

Ozark and other local service airlines in the early 1950s looked a lot like the major airlines did 20 years earlier. Most of the airports they served lacked control towers and modern navigational facilities. Pilots often had to "fly the beam" in instrument weather conditions using vintage low-frequency radio ranges rather than more modern navigational aids. In visual conditions they looked out the window and followed familiar landmarks and surface features. Pilots joked that IFR stood for "I follow roads, rivers, and railroads."

The small-town atmosphere and values of the Midwest region it served became part of the culture at Ozark Air Lines. Ozark flight crews were often invited to barbecues and Sunday dinners during their overnight stays. From the company's humble beginnings, Ozark employees gained a reputation for outstanding customer care. In the days before in-flight food service, crew members sometimes got off the plane at stops to buy doughnuts and hamburgers for their passengers. Stewardesses played cards with them. In May 1959 the CAB reported that Ozark ranked first in on-time performance among all US airlines, with 85.8 percent of its flights arriving and departing within 15 minutes of their scheduled times.[6]

Ozark's leadership stressed financial prudence and operational efficiency. They developed a strong tradition of excellence in training, and they emphasized safety to meet the needs of equipment and facilities. Ozark leaders recognized the significant challenges of aircraft maintenance and repair at smaller airports, so they established a team of mechanics equipped with a specially outfitted truck to reach and repair DC-3s stranded in remote locations.

Throughout the early 1950s, Ozark steadily increased its fleet and service. In 1955, when Congress enacted legislation authorizing permanent certification for the local service airlines, Ozark employed 535 people, served

36 cities, and carried almost a quarter million passengers with a fleet of 16 DC-3s.[7] By then Ozark's green and white airplanes had become a common sight throughout the heartland.

In accordance with the local service concept, Ozark funneled passengers from outlying regions to connect with the major airlines at St. Louis and Chicago. Its principal connector was TWA at St. Louis, and the two airlines enjoyed a symbiotic relationship for many years. TWA gave Ozark a birthday salute in its October 1958 issue of *TWA Skyliner News*: "Ozark Airlines, which is celebrating its eighth birthday this fall, is the youngest of the nation's scheduled airlines," the article declared. "But it is one of the most thriving, being the second-highest producer and receiver of interline passengers and dollars in the local service airline industry," adding that, "Ozark and TWA have worked closely together on many joint interline promotions." It even made a tongue-in-cheek reference to a "fifth column" of TWA "loyal alumni and alumnae who are now working for Ozark."[8] Years later, however, this friendly relationship would dissolve into a bitter rivalry.

Ozark experienced slow but steady growth during the 1950s. Like other local service airlines, it still depended upon federal subsidies to stay in business.

Ozark in the Jet Age

Throughout the 1950s the local service airlines flew surplus military C-47s and DC-3s retired by the major carriers. But the widening gap between their service and that of the large airlines limited their passenger appeal and potential for growth and survival. By 1959 the major airlines were flying jet and turboprop aircraft, and local service airlines urgently needed more modern equipment.

In November 1958, Ozark placed an order for three Fairchild F-27s, a 40-passenger, pressurized turboprop airliner designed to provide modern service on short routes. Many other local service airlines did likewise. The acquisition and operating costs of these planes strained their financial resources, but the CAB assisted by providing loan guarantees for up to 90 percent of the costs of acquiring new equipment.[9] Ozark took delivery of its F-27s in July 1959 and put them into operation on routes between St. Louis and Chicago—and between St. Louis and Minneapolis later that year—even before some large airlines offered turbine-powered flights.

By the end of 1959, Ozark served 52 cities in Missouri, Illinois, Wisconsin, Minnesota, Iowa, Nebraska, Kansas, Tennessee, Kentucky, and Indiana. Its fleet had grown to 24 DC-3s and 3 F-27s, and its work force expanded to more than 1,000 employees.[10] While the F-27s greatly improved Ozark's service quality, they were far more expensive to operate than the DC-3s. Moreover, most of Ozark's routes did not generate enough traffic to make F-27s financially viable. Seeking to improve passenger appeal but keep costs low, Ozark bought four piston-engine, pressurized Convair 240s secondhand in 1962.

During the 1960s the local service airlines began seeking CAB approval to compete directly with the major airlines in large urban markets, while they continued to satisfy their government-mandated service to small cities. Ozark wanted to offer nonstop service on the heavily traveled route between St. Louis and Chicago to compete with American and Delta. The majors resisted such efforts, but the CAB was supportive. In 1959 the CAB instituted a "use it or lose it" policy allowing cancellation of certificates for routes that failed to average five passengers per day—unless the airlines were able to increase usage or if "special circumstances" existed. This effectively allowed local service airlines to abandon their most unprofitable destinations and begin competing head-to-head with the major airlines in more lucrative markets by flying nonstop between urban centers, thereby helping to reduce subsidies.[11] Ozark gained approval to fly nonstop between St. Louis and Chicago as well as between St. Louis and Kansas City—eliminating unprofitable and time-consuming intermediate stops.

Changing of the Guard

Owing to his declining health, Hamilton resigned as Ozark's president and chairman of the board in August 1959. Under his leadership Ozark had progressed from operating light aircraft within Missouri to serving 52 cities in 10 states, carrying a half million passengers each year. His partner, Ozark treasurer Floyd Jones, became board chairman, and executive vice president Joseph H. Fitzgerald was promoted to president.

Fitzgerald, a lawyer by training, had joined Ozark in 1958 after a career in government service that culminated as director of the CAB's bureau of operations. Even though Fitzgerald was the first person outside of Ozark's original founders to assume an important management role, he was cut from the same careful, conservative mold and continued the airline's trajectory of steady, prudent growth. Meanwhile, St. Louis supported Ozark by constructing a new 130,000-square-foot maintenance facility and office building west of the passenger terminal at Lambert in late 1964.[12]

Fitzgerald resigned in July 1963. After Jones briefly served as acting president, Ozark hired Thomas L. Grace to lead the company. A pilot since the 1920s and a veteran of the wartime Hump airlift between India and China where he rose to become director of operations in India, Grace had been vice president of operations and maintenance at Northeast Airlines when Jones lured him away to head Ozark in early 1964. A dynamic, take-charge personality, Grace immediately made his presence felt and wasted no time expanding and improving Ozark's fleet, ordering three additional F-27s and exchanging the Convairs with Mohawk Air Lines for Mohawk Martin 404s, plus cash. But the piston-powered Martins were only a bridge between Ozark's veteran DC-3s and the new turbine equipment—including jets—that would soon join the fleet.

Entering the Jet Age

By the mid-1960s aircraft manufacturers offered a new generation of smaller planes with jet speed and comfort that required very little ground support. Ozark ultimately chose the Douglas DC-9 twinjet. At the dedication ceremony for Ozark's new hangar and office facility in January 1965, Grace announced an order for three 80-passenger DC-9s, supplemented six months later with an order for three more. At the 1965 annual meeting stockholders gave Ozark management a standing ovation for the airline's "spectacular success."[13]

The DC-9s were a giant step for an airline that still predominantly served small cities separated by short distances. DC-9 service began on July 15, 1966, when Ozark Flight 960 departed St. Louis for Chicago. Aboard was Arthur Skinner of Kirkwood, Missouri, the sole passenger on Ozark's first flight 16 years earlier.[14]

Ozark also ordered 21 Fairchild FH-227s in 1965 to complement its jets. A stretched F-27 with 48-passenger capacity, the FH-227 entered service in December 1966, replacing the Martins and F-27s. The new plane was more economical and well suited to Ozark's changing mix of routes and markets.

Ozark's DC-9s served alongside vintage DC-3s in the late 1960s. Greater St. Louis Air and Space Museum.

They were equipped with modern avionics, plus an onboard auxiliary power unit to operate aircraft systems during ground stops, which eliminated the need for costly ground power units at outlying airfields.

Ozark became an all-turbine airline after it flew its last scheduled DC-3 passenger flight from Lambert to Kansas City in October 1968. Ozark's FH-227 fleet now connected smaller cities to St. Louis and Chicago, while its DC-9s flew between major markets.

Ozark's trajectory was reflected in the slogan it adopted in 1971: "Up There with the Biggest." Its success arose in large part from superior customer service and its food, promoted as "unique among airline cuisine." The airline instituted an in-flight wine-tasting program in 1974, with baskets of domestic and imported wines, as well as hot hors d'oeuvres and cold cheese trays. For the main courses Ozark's FLAIR service offered international cuisine and food from popular restaurants in cities it served, including the American in Kansas City, Ports O'Call in Dallas, Chez Paul in Chicago, and Le Vert Galant in New York. FLAIR meals featured special menu covers that passengers could keep as souvenirs and, hopefully, encourage them to book another flight on Ozark. Full meal service was even offered on 50-minute nonstop flights between St. Louis and Chicago and Kansas City, which kept flight attendants busy from takeoff to landing.[16]

When Tom Grace died unexpectedly after a short illness in 1971, vice president of finance and treasurer Edward Crane became president, a position he would hold for the next 15 years. Under his leadership the airline successfully coped with the challenges of the 1973 fuel crisis and continued to expand.

Ozark's only fatal accident happened on July 23, 1973, when Flight 809 crashed on approach to Lambert in a severe thunderstorm, killing 38 of 44 on board. Although the tower warned of heavy rain, it cleared the flight to land. The aircraft disappeared from radar, then crashed about 2 miles from the airport, near the University of Missouri–St. Louis campus. Flight 809 was the first in a series of accidents later attributed to microbursts, a form of severe wind shear that occasionally occurs beneath thunderstorms.

By 1976 Ozark had displaced American as the No. 2 airline in St. Louis and presented a growing competitive threat to TWA. Its passenger count rose from 2.7 million in 1971 to more than 4 million in 1977.[17] Ozark even gained CAB authorization to serve Philadelphia in 1978, the last time it would need such permission.

In October 1978, Crane announced an $85 million aircraft acquisition program, including eight DC-9-30s and two 149-passenger Boeing 727-200s, noting that it was "the most extensive equipment purchase for Ozark in its 28-year history." The two new Boeings, scheduled for delivery in late 1979, were intended for new routes to the Caribbean, the Bahamas, and the West Coast, as well as for existing high-density domestic routes. But the airline never took delivery of them and instead bought more DC-9s. It was a sound move, for the 727s were too large for Ozark's needs, too costly to operate with three engines, and required flight engineers (a position Ozark had never needed to fill). It sold the Boeings to Pan American at a profit of over $3 million—making them, it was said, the most profitable aircraft the airline ever owned.[18]

Ozark's success in the 1970s came from perfecting the business model that had served it well throughout the era of airline regulation: competing for market share and customer loyalty based on outstanding passenger service. But that model was about to be completely upended. Recognizing that a historic change was on the horizon, Crane confidently declared, "We are positioning Ozark to be competitive in a deregulated industry."[19]

During the first two years of deregulation US airlines lost $200 million, and passenger traffic declined by 5 percent. While TWA struggled, laying off employees and cutting service elsewhere, it continued expanding in St. Louis to meet Ozark's threat to its dominant position.

Ozark versus TWA

Advocates anticipated that deregulation would bring increased competition and lower fares. However, as the major airlines cut prices to combat discounters, legacy carriers offset losses by increasing fares at their fortress hubs. That trend also played out in St. Louis. As airfares spiked by more than 100 percent in Kansas City, New York, and Los Angeles between 1978 and 1981, Ozark's competition constrained TWA's ability to raise fares in St. Louis. Ozark took full advantage of the freedom to add new routes, abandon unprofitable ones, and engage in price competition. Deregulation allowed Ozark to transform itself into a national carrier competing effectively with TWA. By June 1982, TWA was operating 110 daily flights from St. Louis, and Ozark operated 93, adding Atlanta, Miami, Orlando, Tampa, Fort Lauderdale, Las Vegas, and San Diego to its network.[20] Three years later Ozark increased its daily St. Louis schedule to 137 flights.[21] TWA also continued upping its flights to more than 200 daily, while seeking concessions from its machinist and flight attendant unions.[22]

Ozark gained an international connection when British Caledonian began nonstop service between London and St. Louis. In 1983 the two airlines entered into an agreement to coordinate their schedules, so Ozark passengers could conveniently connect with London flights. However, this arrangement ended when British Caledonian ceased its St. Louis flights in the fall of 1984.[23]

As Ozark became a national carrier, it abandoned its traditional short-haul routes, such as Chicago to Peoria and Springfield, Illinois. It also disposed of its FH-227s and became an all-jet airline in 1980 with a fleet of

39 DC-9s. It introduced hourly nonstop Executive Express service between St. Louis and Chicago, and it eliminated nonstop service between Chicago and other cities. To accommodate its burgeoning passenger volumes, Ozark ordered four new 152-passenger MD-80s in 1983. Following another deregulation trend, in 1985 the airline forged a code-sharing agreement with regional airline Air Midwest, operating as Ozark Midwest, to act as a feeder between its St. Louis hub and outlying traditional Ozark destinations. For all practical purposes, by 1985 Ozark had transformed itself into a major airline—and a successful one at that.

All of these changes put Ozark in ever-increasing competition with TWA as both airlines added flights to build market share in St. Louis, further stressing the airport's facilities. The struggle damaged both airlines. TWA lost $193 million in 1985, and Ozark went from a profit of $12.7 million in 1984 to only $636,000 in 1985. Ozark's president attributed the decline to increased competition, fare discounting, and increased costs of doing business—a situation all too familiar to industry observers.[24]

Changing Times

By the mid-1980s, Ozark had created a business model and a corporate culture similar to Southwest Airlines, the only airline to successfully weather the challenges and seize the opportunities presented by deregulation. Over the course of 35 years Ozark had grown from a local service airline that served a handful of midwestern destinations with 4 DC-3s to a transcontinental airline serving 65 cities from coast to coast with 50 DC-9 jets. It became one of the best managed and most successful of the local service airlines conceived by the CAB during the Second World War. Ozark's success arose from a combination of solid management, midwestern work ethic, a spirit of cooperation between its employees and management, and devotion to customer service. Many Ozark employees likened it to a family.

Ozark underwent a corporate reorganization in 1984. Ozark Holdings Inc. was created to serve as the vehicle for expansion by acquiring other airlines and entities, and Ozark Air Lines became its subsidiary. Ozark Holdings began exploring merger opportunities and entered into discussions with TWA in 1984. Because Ozark was in a better financial position, it was thought that Ozark would survive, and TWA would merge into it. But Ozark didn't have the financial resources to take over its larger rival, and the negotiations ended.[25]

Deregulation had put Ozark on a collision course with TWA, pitting the two airlines against each other in a desperate struggle for survival. Ironically, Ozark's success ultimately sealed its fate.

Chapter 8
THE RAIDER: 1985–1993

TWA continued increasing service at its St. Louis hub, and by 1985 more than 200 flights were taking off every day.[1] Even still, losses mounted. The unionized major airlines that existed before deregulation had labor agreements with work rules that required large union workforces, and there was little emphasis on efficiency. When TWA bought labor peace with its unions in 1984, it assumed that other airlines would be compelled to follow—but that never happened. Turning a profit in 1984 was a fortuitous fluke for TWA, largely thanks to economic recovery and its international routes.

Welcome to the Jungle

Throughout his tenure as TWA's chairman, Ed Smart was committed to acquiring businesses that produced reliable profits and burnished the bottom line. He saw running an airline as a distraction to achieving that goal, which led to his 1984 decision to spin off TWA from the other businesses.

TWA's strategy of expanding its dominance at the St. Louis hub also met headwinds. By 1985, Ozark Air Lines had become a serious rival, serving 65 cities coast to coast with 137 daily flights at St. Louis. Cost-cutting upstart Southwest Airlines entered the St. Louis market that same year, increasing pressure on both airlines.

Now publicly held, TWA found itself at the mercy of the stock market. Its share price fell below $10 in early 1985, making it an inviting target for corporate raiders. Carl Icahn, who had a well-deserved reputation for preying on undervalued corporations and selling their assets or being bought off, quietly began buying TWA stock. By May 1985, Icahn had acquired more than 20 percent of it. Frank Lorenzo—the aggressive airline entrepreneur who had made an unsuccessful effort to acquire TWA in 1979 and was building an airline empire based on his Texas Air Corporation—also became interested in TWA and began acquiring his own stake.

Icahn inspired fear, and TWA's unions joined management in opposing him. They filed suit in federal court to block the effort, alleging that Icahn lacked the competence to manage the airline, that he would loot TWA for his own benefit, and that an Icahn takeover would result in "economic dislocation, unemployment and impaired productivity." The City of St. Louis also joined in: TWA's presence in St. Louis, including its hub operation at Lambert Airport, was worth billions to the region. But the court denied a preliminary injunction. Icahn responded with a hostile tender offer at $18 per share and wanted to replace TWA's existing board.[2] TWA reviewed the offer and found it inadequate. The board then voted to "actively pursue alternatives superior to that of Mr. Icahn and at the same time being in the best interests of TWA's employees, communities served, and the traveling public."[3]

Next, TWA asked the US Department of Transportation to block the takeover effort, and Congress held hearings to evaluate Icahn's fitness to control TWA. Missouri senators Thomas Eagleton and John Danforth introduced legislation intended to block the sale of TWA's valuable international routes. TWA's president Meyer sought St. Louis–area congressman Richard Gephardt's assistance, urging him to support a companion bill in the House, writing, "We continue to believe that Carl Icahn would not operate TWA in the best interest of the communities we serve, the 28,000 TWA employees and the stockholders." Meyer's letter included a lengthy exposition of Icahn's unfitness and TWA's efforts to resist: "[Icahn's] initial plan was to dismember TWA, shutting down domestic services and liquidating planes. Despite his assurances, Icahn's investment objectives and operating history have made him one of the country's notorious 'greenmail' and liquidation artists."[4]

Not to be outdone, Icahn fired off his own letter to Congressman Gephardt, saying, "If TWA's shareholders accept my offer, I am committed to the long-term interests of TWA, its employees and the traveling public. I personally believe that the airline will continue to grow and with proper leadership a well-managed TWA could become a leader in this deregulated environment."[5]

The State of Missouri passed legislation requiring two-thirds of TWA's other stockholders to approve an Icahn takeover, and the St. Louis County Circuit Court issued a restraining order that blocked Icahn from acquiring more TWA stock. But all of these efforts came to naught. A federal judge held the Missouri law unconstitutional.[6] The St. Louis County judge vacated his own restraining order against Icahn.[7] And the Reagan administration's Department of Transportation declined to get involved, saying there was "no credible evidence" that Icahn lacked managerial expertise or that he would sell off TWA's assets.[8]

On June 7, Icahn testified before Congress. With him were Meyer and Harry Hoglander, chairman of TWA's master executive council (MEC) of the Air Line Pilots Association (ALPA), the TWA pilots' union representative. Hoglander found Icahn to be "a very shrewd and forceful individual." During a break in the hearing Hoglander introduced himself to Icahn and said they ought to talk. Icahn readily agreed.[9] The proverbial chickens were about to invite the fox into the henhouse.

Lorenzo now emerged as a potential white knight to save TWA from Icahn. On June 12 his Texas Air Corporation offered to acquire TWA for $23 per share, including $19 in cash and $4 in new Texas Air preferred stock. Under Lorenzo's plan TWA would become a subsidiary of Texas Air, along with Texas International, Continental Airlines, and New York Air. Texas Air was prepared to close the deal immediately, and TWA's board met the next day to consider Lorenzo's offer. After investment bank Salomon Brothers opined that the proposal was fair from a financial point of view, Icahn announced that he "did not presently intend to make a counterbid or to purchase additional shares," but reserved the right to do so. While the board was meeting, casino operator Resorts International Inc. presented another offer at $24 per share.[10] TWA and its future were on the auction block.

TWA's directors were told there was a "substantial risk" that if they did not act promptly to accept Lorenzo's offer, they would not be able to later. The Resorts International offer didn't appear to be serious, and Icahn would likely oppose it anyway. Meyer pointed to Texas Air's "familiarity with the industry and that the combined fleet would exceed 300 aircraft." The board voted unanimously to reject Resorts's offer and accept Lorenzo's.[11] It was a done deal—or so it seemed.

The Unions Intervene

ALPA and the TWA pilots detested Lorenzo for his union-busting tactics. "Frank Lorenzo was being toasted as the darling of the 'Yuppie' right," said Hoglander. "He was praised for being able to beat down the labor guys and knock labor on its ass. I had a fear of Lorenzo coming on and wanted to beat him."[12] With Lorenzo emerging as TWA's savior, Icahn and his advisers went into overdrive. In a marathon bargaining session they negotiated a deal to sell Icahn's stock to Lorenzo for $16 million, giving Icahn a handsome profit on his investment and clearing the way for Lorenzo's Texas Air to acquire TWA. But Lorenzo repudiated the deal, countering at $9 million, which Icahn summarily rejected. Icahn was secretly delighted that it had fallen through, having given "a billion-dollar gift to Lorenzo and I'd given it away too cheap." He called Lorenzo's rejection "a bad blunder," and he was right.[13]

Two days after the TWA-Lorenzo deal was announced, the pilots formed an alliance with TWA's flight attendant and machinist unions to resist Lorenzo. The unions engaged investment bankers Lazard Frères & Co. and Brian Freeman, the machinists' financial representative, to assist them. They reached out to the other major airline unions and encouraged Eastern Air Lines to make a competing bid for TWA, but to no avail. Icahn was the only alternative to Lorenzo, and the unions hated Lorenzo more than they feared Icahn.

The Ordeal of Flight 847

As the battle raged between Lorenzo and Icahn, TWA suffered yet another Middle East hijacking. On the morning of June 14, 1985, TWA Flight 847, a Boeing 727 commanded by Captain John Testrake, departed Athens for Rome. Shortly after takeoff two Arabic-speaking passengers armed with a pistol and hand grenades took control and ordered Testrake to fly to Beirut, Lebanon, a city gripped by a brutal sectarian civil war. As the flight approached Beirut, air traffic controllers refused permission to land. Testrake argued with the controllers, saying, "He has pulled a hand-grenade pin, and he is ready to blow up the aircraft if he has to. We must, I repeat, we must land at Beirut. We must land at Beirut. No alternative."[14]

The plane took on fuel while on the ground at Beirut. The hijackers spoke little English, but one could speak German. Flight attendant Uli Derickson, a native German speaker, was able to communicate with him and became the point of contact. Through her efforts the hijackers released 19 passengers. The hijackers then ordered Testrake to depart for Algiers, at the other end of the Mediterranean Sea. Because there was no airline service and no airway between Beirut and Algiers, the crew used a map of the Mediterranean and improvised a direct route. The flight was also unwelcome at Algiers, and the tower declared the airport closed. The crew replied that they were landing anyway because they were low on fuel, and the hijackers were threatening to blow up the plane.[15]

Once on the ground at Algiers the hijackers released 20 more passengers and the cabin crew, but the ground-service workers refused to refuel the aircraft without payment. Once again Derickson interceded, paying the $6,000 bill with her personal credit card. The hijackers then ordered a return to Beirut. En route, they demanded and examined passengers' passports. The hijackers identified several US military personnel and began beating them as the other passengers looked on helplessly. Derickson unsuccessfully attempted to intervene.

The flight reached Beirut at 2:30 a.m., its crew exhausted from the ordeal. Once again the Beirut tower declared the airport closed, saying that barricades had been set up on the runway. Testrake responded that he was landing, barricades or no barricades. The tower then asked them to circle while the barricades were removed, and a routine landing followed. Once on the ground, the hijackers shot Robert Stethem, a US Navy diver, opened a cabin door, and dumped his body onto the ground.

After refueling, five Shia militiamen boarded, and shortly before dawn they ordered the plane back to Algiers. The flight was allowed to land without incident. The hijackers released three more passengers and permitted a doctor to come aboard. The hijackers used the aircraft's radio to announce their demands, including the release of more than 700 Lebanese prisoners held by Israel. After negotiating with Algerian officials, the hijackers released 50 more passengers and the five-member cabin crew, leaving only the pilots and a group of American male passengers on board.

By now one of the militiamen who spoke fluent English and called himself "Jihad" had taken over from the original hijackers. Testrake, First Officer Philip Maresca, and Flight Engineer Christian Zimmerman were able to catch some sleep overnight in the passenger cabin, now strewn with trash and passenger belongings ransacked by the hijackers. The next morning "Jihad" informed the crew that they were now to fly on to Aden, South Yemen, at the end of the Arabian Peninsula. Advised that it was beyond the range of the 727, "Jihad" ordered a return to Beirut to refuel. By now the crisis had dragged on for over 48 hours. President Ronald Reagan issued a warning to the terrorists that "for their own safety they had better turn these people loose." It was reported that the elite US Army Delta force was deployed from Fort Bragg, North Carolina, to the Middle East.[16]

While in flight Testrake received a request from the TWA Athens station to land in Cyprus instead of Beirut. He refused. He later learned that the Army's Delta Force anti-terrorist unit had been deployed there to attempt to storm the plane while on the ground—a venture that likely would have ended in more deaths. Realizing that "Jihad" had no game plan and that they had to take action to end their aerial odyssey, the pilots decided to fake engine failure when they reached Beirut. As they turned off the runway Flight Engineer Zimmerman surreptitiously shut off the fuel to two engines. As the engines wound down Testrake told "Jihad" that they had failed due to lack of maintenance, and replacing them would take two to three weeks. The ruse worked. More armed militia came on board, and for the next 16 days the crew were held hostage on the plane.

Negotiations began for release of the crew and the hostages. The group in control on the plane were members of Hezbollah, an Iranian-supported Shia militia, while the hostages in the city were held by Amal, a less extreme Shia faction. Lebanese justice minister Nabih Berri acted as an intermediary in negotiating with the militia groups, representatives of the International Red

Cross, the United Nations, the Lebanese interior minister, and the French British and Spanish ambassadors to Lebanon for the hostages' freedom. The crew and passengers were finally released on June 30. Members of International Red Cross met them in a local schoolyard and drove them to Syria. Israel denied making any deal, but over the next several weeks it released more than 700 prisoners. The standoff was finally over. However, it was a stark reminder of the hazards inherent in TWA's Middle East presence amid civil war and ongoing violence.

Playing the Unions

TWA's pilots and machinists had made substantial concessions by the end of June, including 20 percent across-the-board pay cuts, if Icahn gained control of the airline.[17] Sensing his strength, Icahn raised the stakes, demanding first 30 percent and then 38 percent pay reductions from the unions. The pilots and machinists finally agreed to 22 percent wage cuts, plus work-rule concessions. Icahn signed the deal on August 5, and the unions sent it to their members for ratification.[18] But the flight attendants, led by Vicki Frankovich, held out.

Frankovich, the first woman president of the woman-dominated union in a decade, was under pressure from her membership to hold the line. Frankovich's predecessor, Art Teolis—who had been forced to resign over allegations of misusing union funds—had gotten a 30 percent wage increase only a year earlier, and Frankovich needed to show that she was just as powerful. She disliked Icahn and thought remaining aloof would increase her leverage. While the Flight 847 crisis was still playing out, she held a vote; 95 percent of the flight attendants' union members favored a strike if no new contract was negotiated.[19]

Icahn wanted all three major unions on board before proceeding. He summoned the leaders to a weekend meeting at his Westchester County mansion to discuss a takeover plan, which Frankovich refused to attend. Incensed, Icahn decided to go forward with the concessions by the pilots and the machinists, then deal with the flight attendants later. Icahn raised his offer to $19.50 per share on August 5 and increased his TWA stake to 45 percent. Lorenzo countered at $26 on August 13. TWA's board responded that it was "pleased" with Lorenzo's latest offer but said it was "mindful of Mr. Icahn's large stock position and the difficulty it poses to consummating a merger with Texas Air." It set another meeting on August 20 to consider the competing bids. Icahn raised his offer to $24 per share. He told TWA that the unions were supporting him and promised to indemnify it for any termination fees if it failed to close the Lorenzo deal.[21]

The pilots placed an "Open Letter to the Board of Directors of TWA" in the *Wall Street Journal*, signed by Harry Hoglander, that touted the claimed benefits for the airline and its stockholders from the Icahn offer. It also included an exceptionally naked threat: "We believe that if Texas Air ever takes control of TWA *immediate* labor unrest will result, with serious consequences to TWA's shareholders and employees, the traveling public and the communities served by TWA."[22] At midnight on August 19 the pilots' union announced that 82 percent of its members had voted to ratify the deal with Icahn. Armed with this vote, Hoglander sent a letter to the directors saying the deal "obligates Mr. Icahn to preserve the integrity of TWA's assets and obligations, ensures labor peace at TWA and protects the communities where TWA plays an important role."[23]

Showdown

The stage was set for a confrontation at the next day's board meeting. Salomon Brothers advised the board that both offers were "fair from a financial point," and that in evaluating them, "one should look at more than the arithmetic numbers," including "the value of the Icahn labor concessions and the short- and longer-term prospects for TWA under each offer."[24]

Frank Lorenzo appeared and outlined the benefits that would come from combining TWA with his other airlines, his vision for TWA, his views of Icahn's labor concessions, and his plans to support TWA in the event of strikes. Lorenzo then left the meeting. Icahn entered, accompanied by Harry Hoglander and Brian Freeman.

Following Icahn's presentation Hoglander told the directors, "The TWA pilots do not care to work for Lorenzo. We don't like a man like Frank Lorenzo, who uses phony bankruptcy to break his labor contracts and his labor unions, and who then robs his employees of dignity. We don't want to work for a man who puts a fast buck ahead of safety." He concluded, "If the board of directors takes action to lock us into Lorenzo, the Air Line Pilots Association will call an authorized strike, and I will lead it against you."[25] Speaking for the machinists, Freeman warned the directors that if Lorenzo acquired TWA, the rank and file might "take matters into their own hands," including "nighttime trashing of airplanes and other real trouble around TWA"—an extraordinary message for an investment banker to deliver.[26]

Faced with these threats the directors had little choice but to reject Lorenzo's offer. TWA issued a press release saying, "The Board considers it very important to TWA stockholders that, in light of Mr. Icahn's presumptive ability to block the Texas Air [Lorenzo] merger, TWA should have available to it Mr. Icahn's $24 merger proposal. We think $24 per share, which is 33 percent above Mr. Icahn's initial offer of $18 per share, is an excellent price for our shareholders." It also pointed to the "very significant concessions" made by the pilots and the machinists, "which would be major factors in making TWA a more competitive and profitable airline," adding, "[We] could not help but be concerned over possible disruptions that might have ensued" as threatened by the unions. It offered to allow TWA stockowners to vote on Lorenzo's $26 per share offer.[27] But because Icahn could vote his 45 percent stake against it, Lorenzo had no interest in this empty gesture.

With Icahn now in the driver's seat, Lorenzo agreed to relinquish his TWA stock for a total payment by TWA of $57 million, including the termination fee for abandoning the Texas Air merger. Charles Meyer retired as TWA's president and CEO and was replaced by senior vice president Richard D. Pearson. All but three directors resigned. The remainder voted to elect Icahn; Alfred Kingsley, Icahn's self-described "right-hand man"; and Icahn's uncle and business partner, Elliot Schnall, to the board.[29]

The pilots' and the machinists' unions thus delivered TWA into the hands of Carl Icahn. But not all TWA pilots were pleased. Some thought that Lorenzo was the lesser of two evils and viewed Continental's route structure and equipment as a good fit with TWA's. They believed that Lorenzo, unlike Icahn, wanted to operate the airline and would be able to do so. But the majority wanted and got Icahn—a choice they would soon bitterly regret.

All About Icahn

Carl Icahn was 50 years old when he took over control of TWA. He grew up in Queens, New York, reared by his father, a lawyer and occasional cantor at the family's synagogue, and his mother, a schoolteacher, who described Carl as an excellent student who rarely studied hard. He attended Princeton University on a scholarship, where he was sociable but not particularly driven unless a subject interested him—then he'd put everything he had into it. As a pre-med student he became fascinated by organic chemistry and stayed up all night solving problems. He later said that complex takeovers gave him satisfaction much like solving those chemistry problems had.[30]

After graduating from Princeton in 1957, Icahn briefly attended New York University School of Medicine before dropping out and spending two years in the US Army. He then became a stockbroker trainee with the Dreyfus & Co. investment house in 1961. His mother was so distressed by the prospect of her son entering the financial world that she enlisted a family friend who was a Wall Street analyst to warn him of the business's pitfalls. The effort failed. "See how wrong a Jewish mother can be," she later lamented.[31] Her son would spend the rest of his life in the world of high finance, founding his own firm with his uncle as the major investor.

Although Icahn readily acknowledged that he liked making money, his biggest motive was simply to succeed at playing the game. His first takeover target was appliance maker Tappan. In 1977 he acquired 8 percent of the shares of the undervalued stock, clashed with Tappan's management, and won a seat on the board. Within a year the company sold out to Electrolux for more than double the share price Icahn had paid. His next prey was Baird & Warner, a money-losing real estate investment trust, and Saxon Industries, which went bankrupt after spending $9 million on a buyback—Icahn and his partners netted a $1.9 million profit. But those early coups were only a warm-up. In 1981, Icahn went after Marshall Field, Chicago's premier department store. After battling the company for six months, he walked away with a gain of $17 million.[32]

Even when his takeover bids failed, Icahn still managed to profit handsomely. In 1980 he acquired a large holding in Hammermill Paper Company and tried to force his way onto its board. Eventually Hammermill paid him greenmail, a premium over market value, to buy him off. Icahn made $9.6 million, even as the company absorbed more than $30 million in costs connected with the buyout. The company recovered after warding off Icahn, and its stock reached a record high under the same management Icahn had tried to remove.[33]

By 1985, Icahn had become notorious for his raids on well-known corporations, including American Can Company, Gulf and Western, Phillips Petroleum, and Uniroyal Inc. He took control of ACF Industries in St. Louis, using it as a platform for further acquisitions and raids. Icahn epitomized the "greed is good" ethos made infamous by the character Gordon Gekko in the 1987 film *Wall Street*, claiming that he was standing up for stockholders by preying on companies whose stock was depressed by poor management.

Much of Icahn's success was based on intimidation. At 6 feet, 4 inches tall, he was an imposing figure in personal confrontations, unafraid to raise his voice and use profanity to assert dominance. One TWA pilot said Icahn had "an almost bionic ability" to know when his adversary was vulnerable. "I admire someone with strength who stands by his guns," Icahn told *St. Louis Post-Dispatch* reporter Paul Wagman. "You learn in this business that if you want a friend, get a dog."[34]

Yet Icahn was also skilled at manipulating the press for favorable coverage, taking reporters' calls and giving them memorable quotes. "Icahn was his own best PR man," recalled Wagman. "He was superb at it, and part of the reason was that he was accessible. Almost every time I called his office I got him on the phone, and he would just talk away without restraint, say whatever he thought. Furthermore, he was funny. He was a pleasure to talk to. He answered the questions, and he was entertaining while he did it."[35]

In person, Icahn came across as unpretentious. "I had dinner with him once, and I was struck by how unpolished he was," Wagman said. "He was very down-to-earth, he kind of bent over his food, and his table manners were considerably less than they should have been considering that he circulated at the top level of society. As one person who knew him said, 'Carl's not fancy.' He was for sure not a fancy guy."[36] Icahn resembled Howard Hughes in this regard.

Icahn used his media skills to promote his image as a champion of the underdog, the small stockholders who were investing in the newly created individual retirement accounts (IRAs) and employer 401(k) plans in the 1980s. But the unions would learn that TWA management's predictions about what he would do to the airline were all too accurate.

Icahn Takes Over

Having paved the way for Icahn, the TWA pilots now faced his well-practiced intimidation and hardball negotiating tactics while trying to reach an agreement on the specifics of their August 5 deal with him. The talks dragged on for months, dogged by breakdowns and false starts. As negotiations stalled, TWA's operating results fell below forecasts. Lorenzo again stepped forward, making a new offer of $22 per share in cash and causing speculation that Icahn would be "happy as a clam" to be bought out.[37] But the unions' diehard objections remained an insurmountable obstacle to any deal with Lorenzo. An "emotional meeting" ensued between TWA management and leaders of the pilots and machinists when the latter again threatened violence and disruption if TWA was sold to Lorenzo, while also threatening to sue Icahn for breaking the agreements he had made with them in August.[38] All the while Icahn skillfully pitted the various parties against one another and strengthened his own hand.

On January 3, 1986, the unions finally came to terms with Icahn, signing a package of agreements that positioned him to take control of TWA.[39] One of these was a so-called "wraparound agreement" among ALPA, Icahn, and TWA. It provided that if Icahn or TWA acquired control of another airline, there would be no full merger of TWA's pilot seniority list with that of the other airline without prior consent of ALPA.[40] Although the agreement was intended to keep Icahn from merging TWA with a non-union carrier, it would have a much different result.

On the same day TWA and Icahn entered into a "standstill agreement." It terminated the merger agreement and reduced the board to four members, three of whom were designated by Icahn, and one—Richard Pearson, the airline's president—by TWA. The two remaining directors resigned and were designated a "special committee" to represent the interests of the airline's public stockholders, and Icahn was elected chairman of TWA's board.[41] Thanks to the pilots and the machinists, Icahn finally had his airline, which had lost a staggering $217 million in 1985 due in no small part to the turmoil caused by the struggle for control. But TWA was now the crown jewel of

Icahn's financial empire. It was rumored that he pranced around his office in a TWA pilot uniform to celebrate the victory.[42]

The Flight Attendants Strike

With TWA in Icahn's hands the stage was set for his revenge on Vicki Frankovich and the flight attendants' union. In his mind flight attendants were little more than waitresses in the sky. Once when talking about them, he went over to his office window, pointed to the street far below, and said, "See those people down there? That's a flight attendant, that's a flight attendant, that's a flight attendant—anybody could be a flight attendant!"[43]

The union rebuffed Icahn's demands for pay, benefits, and work-rule concessions. Predictably, negotiations broke down. A strike deadline of March 7, 1986, was set. Unbeknownst to the flight attendants, the airline was prepared and spoiling for a fight. TWA leadership dusted off and updated a two-phase strike contingency plan that had been developed during the 1984–1985 negotiations. As part of Phase 1, non-union personnel (including secretaries, administrative, and management employees) had already been trained to fly as temporary replacements on a portion of TWA's schedule. From the moment the strike began the airline would be able to keep its airplanes staffed and flying.

Phase 2 involved hiring and training permanent replacements. The airline started recruiting new flight attendants in the fall of 1985—not a difficult task, as it was a desirable job. After successfully completing training,

On March 7, 1986, Carl Icahn announced that TWA would continue to fly, using replacements for striking flight attendants. Bettmann/Getty Images.

the replacements were released but had to be ready to report for duty on short notice, even in the middle of a strike. Although fully qualified, these new flight attendants would not be offered employment until they were called and reported for work. TWA now had 1,600 permanent replacements on hand.

Nearly all of TWA's 6,600 union flight attendants walked out on strike. Management immediately sent their replacements to the airline's domiciles at Boston, Chicago, San Francisco, Los Angeles, and St. Louis. More than half went to New York for a reception and orientation at the JFK Hilton Hotel. The union established its strike headquarters at a neighboring hotel. Union members solicited the new hires to join the union—and the strike—after being offered employment as flight attendants. There were few takers.

Because the replacements had to have operating experience before they could fly independently, most of the airline's in-flight services management and training personnel were assigned to fly with them on their first flight. The FAA was sympathetic to the union and would not have hesitated to shut TWA down for deficiencies. If an FAA inspector boarded a flight the replacements had to be able to answer questions correctly and perform all of their duties. Anyone who failed to measure up would be removed and replaced, but that rarely happened, thanks to the intensive training.

Things grew heated as picket lines went up. The airline took a hard stance on incidents of violence or property damage and ensured that perpetrators would face arrest and charges. The port authority police, who were responsible for maintaining order on airport property, were also union members and sympathetic to the strikers. But the private security personnel who supplemented TWA's in-house security staff were well acquainted with the police's hierarchy and were able to encourage the officers to act. Strikers who engaged in illegal activity on the picket line were sent to the port authority jail, identified, and fired; termination letters were often hand delivered while strikers were still in lockup. Management aimed to immediately start "behavior modification" as a way for management to maintain control over strikers' behavior.

The strategy worked: TWA continued flying while the strike dragged on without results. Over time strikers started drifting back, and eventually 1,300 union flight attendants crossed the picket lines to return to work. Meanwhile the airline unilaterally imposed pay cuts, benefit reductions, and work-rule changes. With the strike faltering, Frankovich capitulated on May 21, ordering her members back on the job without an agreement. By then there were only 200 positions left for the thousands who had not previously returned to work, and many of them gave up. It would take five years for the rest to be reinstated.

The TWA flight attendants' union leader, Vicki Frankovich, frequently clashed with Carl Icahn. Alan Hoffman Collection.

The airline broke the strike, but the wounds were deep and long lasting. The bitter divisions among strikers, replacements, and returners festered for years. Like the 1981 controllers' strike, it demonstrated the declining power and influence of organized labor and the enhanced position of management, all of which only strengthened Icahn's position.

More Terror in the Air

While the strike was underway another tragedy struck. On April 1, 1986, a bomb exploded on TWA Flight 840, a Boeing 727 en route from Rome to Athens. The device, placed under a seat in the passenger cabin, tore a 6-foot-by-3-foot hole in the right side of the fuselage ahead of the right wing. Four passengers, including an 8-month-old baby, were blown out of the aircraft; seven others were injured by flying debris. The pilot, Captain Richard Petersen, made a safe emergency landing at Athens. A group calling itself the "Ezzedine Kassam Unit of the Arab Revolutionary Cells" claimed responsibility, saying it had acted in retaliation for a US air attack on Libya the previous month.[44]

The perpetrator was identified as Mai Elias Mansur, a Palestinian woman associated with the Abu Nidal Organization. She had occupied the seat under which the bomb was placed on an earlier flight and presumably thought the evidence would be destroyed in the blast. She was never charged with the crime.[45] This incident further reinforced TWA's image as the airline of choice for Middle Eastern terrorists.

Ozark in the Crosshairs

Icahn wasted no time in replacing TWA's prior management with his own entourage, most of whom had no airline experience, background, or interest. He forced out Richard Pearson as president and replaced him with ACF Industries president Joseph Corr, who boasted that his modus operandi was management by intimidation. Icahn served as his own CEO and created the "Office of Chief Executive," composed of himself and hand-picked loyalists, to ensure that his wishes were fully and faithfully implemented.

Icahn quickly turned his sights on Ozark Air Lines, TWA's principal competitor at St. Louis. Together the two carriers accounted for 82 percent of St. Louis's commercial airline traffic, and their routes overlapped in 31 cities. On February 27, 1986, Icahn announced that TWA would acquire Ozark Holdings Inc., Ozark's corporate parent, for $224 million in a deal approved by both corporations' boards. By "combining two losers," he said, "we hope to create one profitable carrier." An all-too-effective rival, Ozark was no loser, but from TWA's perspective, it had to be removed.

The merger agreement provided that Ozark, with 50 DC-9s and 4,100 employees, would initially continue to operate separately as a wholly owned subsidiary of TWA, with its 165 planes and 28,000 employees. Ozark president Edward Crane received a golden parachute, remaining president and CEO of Ozark Holdings and becoming vice chairman of TWA, while Ozark chairman Lester Cox became a TWA director. In reality, these positions were mere sinecures that ensured their support for the deal. The *Los Angeles Times* called the merger "the latest in a trend toward consolidation in the airline industry," including Lorenzo's efforts to buy Eastern Air Lines and Northwest's acquisition of Republic Airlines.[46] While acquiring Ozark's fleet and eliminating it as a competitor made good business sense for Icahn, it led to labor strife and turmoil with Ozark's pilots and flight attendants.

The Pilots' Struggle

TWA's pilots had been battered by hard times as the airline's fortunes declined. Many had endured years of furlough time; some served as flight engineers to continue flying. By contrast, Ozark had been profitable. It had young captains with 10 years of seniority and no furlough time, while TWA had copilots with 20 or more years of seniority who had spent years on furlough. The Ozark merger was a gift for the TWA pilots, complete with 50 new airplanes they were eager to fly, but now there was the fraught issue of merging seniority lists. Seniority governs the routes pilots can fly, their vacation, and other benefits, and whether (or when) they are furloughed or laid off. For Ozark pilots the worst-case scenario would be getting "stapled to the bottom" of TWA's seniority list, with senior Ozark captains ranking below the newest TWA hires.

While ALPA recognized that "seniority list integration has always been the most contentious and troublesome of issues in the merging of airlines," it represented both TWA and Ozark pilots—a direct conflict of interest. To address this dilemma, which was becoming increasingly common amid the wave of airline mergers that occurred during deregulation, ALPA had adopted a merger policy with the stated purpose of handling seniority integration in an ostensibly fair and unbiased manner. It called for the two pilot groups to seek agreement on seniority integration during a negotiation period. Lack of agreement within 155 days would automatically send the dispute to binding arbitration.[47] The policy further emphasized that "voluntary agreement is preferable to enforced agreement,"[48] but "voluntary agreement" was unlikely; pilots of the surviving carrier usually held the upper hand and were loath to relinquish it, so a neutral arbiter would be needed.

Following the announcement of the Ozark merger, Mike O'Toole, chairman of the Ozark pilots' master executive council, called on ALPA president Henry Duffy to initiate proceedings under the merger policy. The Ozark pilots met with their TWA opposite numbers in early March 1986 and were informed of the wraparound agreement. Duffy told the Ozark pilots that the agreement was designed to deal with a possible merger between TWA and a non-ALPA carrier, such as those Lorenzo controlled, and that it would not be used against them. "ALPA will not let the Ozark pilots be lopped off," he assured them. "ALPA merger policy will prevail."[49]

Meanwhile, TWA leadership told their pilots that the wraparound agreement prevented TWA from merging the seniority lists without ALPA's express approval, which "would not be given unless such a merger would be in the permanent best interest of the TWA pilot group." The TWA pilots contended that their wraparound agreement with Icahn trumped ALPA's merger policy and gave them the power to dictate the terms of how seniority integration would occur.[50]

When Duffy asked Angelo Marchione, the TWA pilots' chairman, to begin proceedings under the merger policy, Marchione responded that it didn't apply to the TWA/Ozark merger. He insisted the TWA pilots would not accept arbitration under the merger policy and demanded that seniority lists be integrated "through negotiation." He also threatened that the TWA pilots would leave ALPA and join a newly formed Allied Pilots Union (APU) if ALPA insisted on applying its merger policy.[51] Icahn quickly took advantage of the growing dispute to demand a three-year extension of the concessions extracted from the TWA pilots and threatened to liquidate the airline if they didn't agree.[52] Facing reelection as ALPA president in 1986, the last thing Duffy needed was a major defection. Whether or not the APU threat was credible, he believed that the TWA pilots would pull out if he tried to enforce the policy. Repeated requests by the Ozark pilots to implement ALPA's policy were ignored, and Duffy told them to "work something out."[53]

The ALPA executive committee appointed a veteran labor mediator to conduct discussions, but the TWA pilots refused to budge. The talks went nowhere, and Icahn intervened.[54] On October 10 he announced that Ozark's MD-80s would be flown exclusively by TWA crews, and TWA's pay rates and work rules would now apply to the Ozark pilots. Then, on December 2, Icahn announced the indefinite furlough of 86 Ozark pilots—nearly 20 percent of them—and told the remaining Ozark pilots that he would begin furloughing them too unless they ratified the seniority list agreement dictated by the TWA pilots. Lacking support from ALPA and facing Icahn's dire threats, the Ozark pilots had no bargaining power and were forced into an agreement consigning them to second-class citizenship at TWA. One labor authority commented, "ALPA, faced with an explicit threat by the TWA pilots that they would leave ALPA if efforts were made to enforce the arbitration provisions of ALPA merger policy, found itself unable to do more than exercise moral suasion on the TWA group to act responsibly, to little or no avail."[55]

The deal done, TWA had to call on Ozark captains to train its pilots on Ozark's DC-9s, an aircraft TWA didn't have. TWA pilots could then displace the very Ozark pilots who had trained them to fly the Ozark planes. The arrangement was not conducive to warm relations within the merged pilot cohort, but most of the former Ozark pilots made the best of the situation. Over time, some were even able to take advantage of opportunities at TWA they never had at Ozark.

The Flight Attendants' Struggle

While the struggle continued with the Ozark and TWA pilots, another was playing out among the flight attendants. TWA flight attendants went on strike shortly after the merger was announced, a move the Ozark flight attendants initially supported. They even walked TWA picket lines, hoping that the TWA attendants would treat them fairly. But Vicki Frankovich claimed the Ozark flight attendant jobs for TWA and refused to agree to seniority integration.

As the strike dragged on, both TWA strikers and returnees began asking about joining Allied Flight Attendants (AFA), the Ozark attendants' union. Linda Kunz, head of the Ozark council of AFA, filed for a representation election to substitute AFA as the TWA flight attendants' union representative. She collected 3,000 signatures in support of AFA, just short of the number needed to take over. Frankovich called Kunz and said, "You don't have the cards." Kunz replied, "That's a risk you are going to have to take because we are filing."

Just 30 minutes later Frankovich called Kunz back, wanting to know what it would take for her to pull the cards. Kunz said, "I want the Ozark flight attendants to have their seniority. I want our vacation to transfer over, and our sick leave, and we want to be treated as if we were on the TWA seniority list."[56] The TWA flight attendants were in a precarious position, and Frankovich ultimately agreed to all the Ozark flight attendants' demands. When the striking TWA flight attendants returned to work, they did not displace the former Ozark flight attendants.

The Icahn Era Begins

TWA and Ozark officially merged on September 26, 1986. Icahn quickly sold 35 of Ozark's DC-9s for $217 million to a company he controlled, essentially recouping the money he spent to buy the airline. He then leased the jets back to TWA, saddling it with $50 million in annual lease obligations and putting more money in his own pocket. He terminated Ozark's fully funded retirement plans, which netted an additional $35 million in cash, and put the Ozark employees into TWA's underfunded plans.[57] Icahn also began monetizing other TWA assets, including arranging a sale and leaseback of TWA's ground-service equipment for $50 million, which forced the airline to pay $5 million annually to use assets it owned.[58]

Icahn's business model consisted of selling assets, cutting fares, slashing costs, and squeezing unions for concessions. International traffic, historically TWA's strongest segment, fell by almost 15 percent in the wake of high-profile terrorist incidents and greater competition. The turmoil caused by the takeover fight, the flight attendants' strike, and the Ozark merger further battered TWA's financial performance and brought a $106 million loss in 1986—half of what it was in 1985, though hardly cause for celebration.

Icahn also used TWA as a platform for other financial ventures. In October 1986 the Icahn-controlled board authorized the formation of TWA Investment Plan Inc. This wholly owned subsidiary of TWA participated with a wholly owned subsidiary of ACF in a limited partnership named Ferris Wheel Associates as a means to pursue Icahn's interests in other corporations. By the end of 1986, TWA Investment Plan had paid Ferris Wheel nearly $100 million to acquire 10 percent of USX Corporation, another Icahn target.[59] Not content owning an airline beset by financial woes, Icahn caused TWA to acquire a 15 percent stake in USAir for the purpose of making a hostile takeover offer in March 1987. USAir quickly rejected the offer and announced that it would acquire Piedmont Airlines, thwarting Icahn's bid.[60]

Once the integration of Ozark was complete, Icahn made moves to take TWA private by buying out the other shareholders, which spurred a wave of anxiety among the pilots and machinists who had engineered Icahn's takeover of TWA two years earlier. The pilots even considered buying the airline themselves. Yet Marchione told them in September 1987, "We remain confident that Mr. Icahn will act in the best interest of TWA, and when the opportunity exists, take actions that will result in the growth and expansion of the airline."[61] Unfortunately, his confidence would prove unfounded.

Icahn owned three-fourths of TWA's common stock by late 1987. His privatization proposal called for borrowing $800 million to exchange each share of TWA stock—including his own—for $20 cash and a $20 subordinated debenture, commonly known as a "junk bond." Under this plan Icahn would not only own the airline but would also reap a $440 million payday. However, the privatization proposal quickly ran into opposition from the airline's creditors. TWA's machinists filed suit to block the deal, contending that it would require TWA to shoulder $600 million of debt in addition to its existing $2 billion indebtedness. The airline's two independent directors, responsible for protecting the interests of TWA's minority shareholders, also opposed the deal.[62]

Then, on October 19, 1987—"Black Monday"—the stock market collapsed, losing 20 percent of its value in one day. Icahn immediately withdrew his offer after causing the airline to borrow $800 million to finance the deal. TWA's stock price plummeted from $26 to $14 per share, and trading was suspended. TWA's $100 million stake in USX stock, which Icahn had forced upon it, was also savaged by the market meltdown.[63] But it was only a temporary setback. In November 1987, Icahn used some of the cash he borrowed to finance the buyout to acquire 12 million shares of Texaco, the third-largest oil company in the United States, for $348 million. He promptly began interfering with Texaco's efforts to settle a $10 billion judgment obtained against it by Pennzoil.[64]

Largely due to the Ozark merger and the labor concessions Icahn had extracted, TWA managed to book a $107 million pre-tax profit for 1987. However, since taking control of TWA, he had more than doubled its debt burden, even as the airline badly needed to modernize its fleet, one of the oldest in the industry.

Do You Still Love Me?

The romance between Icahn and the TWA pilots faded rapidly. In December 1986 the pilots agreed to extend their collective-bargaining agreement until 1992, locking in the concessions they had given. Chairman Marchione said they did so thinking it would "help ensure the long-term profitability of TWA and the continuation of TWA as a leading world-class airline."[65] That dream vanished within a year.

In December 1987 the pilots' negotiating committee told the membership that hopes of a beneficial "special relationship" with Icahn "have been dashed by a careful review of the facts." Citing Icahn's Texaco acquisition, the committee said, "He is greatly increasing the debt on TWA to buy securities in other non-airline industries," putting TWA in a delicate financial position and undermining the pilots' profit sharing and employee stock option plans. "All of the recent deals," it concluded, "indicate a totally selfish, personal style."[66] By placing their faith in Icahn and their fate in his hands, the pilots left themselves with no leverage. In a futile gesture of disapproval, the pilots stopped turning on the lights that illuminated the TWA logo on the planes' tails at night.[67] Icahn's love affair with the machinists had also broken down, and bitterness lingered from breaking the flight attendants' strike.

Icahn advised the board in January 1988 that TWA and ACF had acquired 1 million additional shares of Texaco stock. After some questions about this purchase and the effect that fluctuations in the market value of the Texaco stock would have on TWA's liquidity, the directors approved it. The Icahn-controlled board failed to discuss why TWA's resources were being used to further Icahn's investment interests rather than supporting the airline's needs.[68] A few days later Mark Buckstein, Icahn's handpicked general counsel, advised the board that TWA owned 8 percent of Texaco's common stock. He also advised the directors that they had been joined as defendants in litigation arising from the sale of Texaco and Pennzoil stock to ACF. Nevertheless, the directors authorized Icahn to continue his Texaco investment activities and endorsed all the actions he had taken.[69]

Going Private

While pursuing his machinations with Texaco and Pennzoil, Icahn renewed his efforts to take TWA private. In April 1988 he announced a new bid to acquire the remaining 23 percent of the airline's stock for $20 cash and $29 face-value junk bonds at 12 percent interest. The board thereupon established an "independent committee," consisting of former Ozark president Edward Crane and former Ozark chairman Lester Cox, to review Icahn's proposal. The directors, including the ostensibly "independent" Crane and Cox, proceeded to unanimously approve payments of $1 million to president Joe Corr, and $700,000 each to Mark Buckstein and executive vice president Morton Erlich "upon the effectiveness of the going private proposal," authorizing Icahn to make the payments before the closing.[70]

On May 6 the board met to consider the privatization proposal. In the interim, the Dillon Read financial house negotiated a slight increase in the value of the bonds, along with $20 cash for each TWA share. Dillon Read opined that the proposal was "fair to and in the best interests of the Public Stockholders" and recommended the board's approval. President Corr, who had already received a $925,000 bonus "for his efforts in facilitating the going private transaction," advised the directors that he was "confident the Corporation would have sufficient working capital to carry on its business" if the deal were done. He added, TWA "will be able to service its debt and also to expand as necessary in the future." Although the board unanimously approved the proposal, these rosy predictions would prove utterly groundless.[71]

At a special shareholders' meeting on September 7, 1988, the minority owners accepted Icahn's offer of $20 cash plus a $30 face-value 12 percent note for each share of TWA stock. Following this transaction, 90 percent of the outstanding shares of TWA common stock were held by a new corporation wholly controlled by Icahn, known as TWA Airlines Inc., with the remaining 10 percent held in an employee stock option plan.[72] After putting half a billion dollars of TWA's cash in his own pocket and adding a billion dollars to its debt, Icahn was now free to do as he pleased.

Going Downhill

After acquiring Ozark, TWA dominated the St. Louis hub, making over 300 daily departures. Despite this, and despite the addition of the Ozark planes to its fleet, TWA's share of the domestic market fell after Icahn took over. While TWA's minority shareholders were delighted at having been bought out, employee morale was at an all-time low. TWA's machinists filed suit alleging that under their 1985 agreement with Icahn they were entitled to 20 percent of TWA's stock if he took the airline private. As the flight attendants' Frankovich aptly put it, "TWA is being managed as an unsupervised mutual fund to fuel Mr. Icahn's stock speculation."[73] The pilots too had become disenchanted with Angelo Marchione. They forced him to step down from his post over his support of Icahn, then sued Icahn to "prevent him from looting TWA."[74] Their new leader, Tom Ashwood, personally served the suit papers at the shareholders' meeting where the privatization deal was approved. Ashwood said in a statement, "We won't stand idly by while Carl Icahn strips our airline of assets and keeps it from buying airplanes and improving service to our passengers because of heavy debt."[75] The pilots alleged that privatization violated the agreements made with Icahn at the time of his takeover, and that Icahn intended to force TWA to borrow massive funds and distribute $665 million to himself. "If Icahn is allowed to continue his pattern of using borrowings to loot TWA," they asserted, "the dissolution of TWA is inevitable."[76]

Icahn was unperturbed. "When they needed me," he fired back, "I left my $440 million in and turned down a $170 million profit to do it." Under his agreements with the pilots, he contended, "I could take the airline private whenever I wanted to, and they couldn't tell me what to do."[77] Ashwood replied that he now understood how Poland must have felt after the Russians saved them from the Nazis.[78]

The pilots' allegations were accurate. The huge debt TWA shouldered to finance the buyout exacerbated the airline's financial struggles, made profitability impossible, and brought no benefit to the airline or its employees. But Icahn was correct too: TWA's pilots, in their zeal to avoid Frank Lorenzo, had given him unfettered control over TWA.

"What Icahn has really done," business reporter Thomas G. Donlan wrote in *Barron's*, "is to restructure the airline into a hollow shell filled with debt and assured that much of the cash and stocks bought with the proceeds of the debt will end up in his hands."[79] Donlan also detailed how Icahn had manipulated TWA's books to make its financial picture look better.

The consummation of privatization also signaled the departure of several members of the management team whom Icahn had put in place in 1986, including TWA's president and Icahn loyalist Joe Corr and executive vice president Morton Ehrlich. They and others concluded that Icahn was far more interested in pursuing his investment schemes than in operating TWA, took advantage of the buyout to sell their stock, and left. Icahn responded by creating for himself the "Office of Chairman." Twenty-five corporate and staff vice presidents reported directly to him, which ensured his complete control over every aspect of TWA's management.

Icahn also moved its corporate headquarters from its longtime location at 605 3rd Avenue in Manhattan to a commercial office building he owned in Mount Kisco, New York—a suburb conveniently close his home—thereby allowing him to collect rent from the airline.

In contrast to the relatively austere airline offices, Icahn's opulent, tiered Mount Kisco office was decorated with tapestries and pictures of his racehorses, plus a balcony, a garden, and a gazebo. His office also featured a thick, clear Lucite wall, said to be bulletproof to protect Icahn from assassination attempts. Employees seeking access to Icahn's office had to first be cleared by his assistant (and future wife) Gail Golden, while the public had to enter via an elevator to his second-floor reception area where two "designer" receptionists (whose primary contribution, Icahn acknowledged, was their dazzling appearance) greeted visitors.

See You in Court No More

TWA's litigation against Howard Hughes and Hughes Tool finally came to an end as Carl Icahn took the company private. After the Supreme Court overturned TWA's $145 million default judgment in 1973, TWA revived its Delaware state court case. It made the same factual allegations but asserted claims under Delaware's corporation laws, none of which had been litigated in the federal case. The Delaware pretrial proceedings consumed another decade. While they dragged on, Hughes Tool was sold to the public. Summa Corporation took over Hughes Tool's non-oil-drilling business and was substituted as the defendant in the case.

The Delaware case finally went to trial in spring 1985. In a non-jury chancery court proceeding, the judge awarded TWA $17 million for injuries Hughes had inflicted upon it 25 years earlier. More legal wrangling over the award's interest rate followed and ultimately resulted in a final judgment in TWA's favor totaling $48.3 million in January 1987. The United States Supreme Court denied Summa's petition for review in October 1988. After more than 27 years the Hughes litigation was finally over. Ironically, the damage award benefited Carl Icahn who, like Hughes decades earlier, now had complete control over TWA's fortunes and was steering it toward another crisis.

Putting on a Happy Face

TWA posted a $250 million profit for 1988, thanks to the funds realized from the Hughes suit, the sale of the Texaco stock to ACF, and a change in the depreciation rate applied to TWA's planes. Icahn and his allies trumpeted this as a great success, but absent the settlement and the paper gains, TWA lost more than $20 million for the year.[80] Moreover, Icahn continued using TWA's funds to buy additional Texaco stock. The TWA flight attendants called for an investigation of Icahn by the US Department of Transportation, saying, "He has no intention of using the cash assets of TWA for the furtherance of the airline."[81]

In fact, those cash assets had already dissipated. The payouts to Icahn and the minority shareholders reduced TWA's working capital from nearly $700 million at the end of 1987 to a mere $27 million a year later.[82] Icahn also briefly explored acquiring Eastern Air Lines from Lorenzo's Texas Air but pulled out after learning he couldn't extract concessions from Eastern's unions as he had from TWA's.[82]

Promises, Promises

TWA had the oldest fleet of any US carrier in the late 1980s. Icahn promised to acquire additional fuel-efficient twin-engine MD-80s and announced a memorandum of understanding with Airbus in March 1989 to purchase 20 A330 wide-body twinjets for delivery in 1994–1995, with an option on

20 more in 1997–1998. The announcement had the desired effect. *Aviation Week* said the order "signifies optimism at an airline that was struggling since the mid-1980s" and that "performance has improved since TWA was taken over by Carl Icahn."[84]

In fact, the memorandum of understanding committed neither TWA nor Airbus to anything, but it demonstrated Icahn's skill at manipulating the media. It was mere window dressing that allowed Airbus to show airline interest in the A330 (still three years away from the model's first flight) and let Icahn claim he was ordering new planes. But TWA didn't need any more wide-bodies; it needed to modernize its aging narrow-body fleet. It never happened on Icahn's watch.

Icahn could not conceal the fact that TWA was suffering under his stewardship. Although it had increased its revenue over 1988, the airline lost $87 million in the first half of 1989.[85] Nevertheless, Icahn continued borrowing, floating a $300 million junk bond and offering spare parts and airport landing rights as collateral. With debt totaling $2.5 billion, TWA's annual interest costs of $375 million consumed nearly all of its operating revenue. The debt burden, in the words of an industry analyst, was "crushing earnings." Icahn responded, "Great opportunities come to him who has cash."[86] But those opportunities did not include modernizing TWA's fleet or investing in its future. Meanwhile, the liquidation of TWA's assets continued. Icahn even sold its showcase Breech Training Academy facility in suburban Kansas City for $11 million.[87]

Contract talks with the machinists' union were abruptly suspended in August 1989 because of a potential "corporate change." Rumors swirled of a possible buyout of Icahn or merger with another airline, such as Pan American, America West, or Midway Airlines. The machinists and the pilots both actively sought potential purchasers to acquire control from Icahn. Meanwhile, dissension arose within the pilots' ranks. A deeply divided master executive council removed chairman Tom Ashford over his sharp criticism of Icahn, barely a year after his predecessor had been forced out for being too close to Icahn. Half of the council walked out in protest.[89]

Despite the red ink flowing at TWA, Icahn's attention remained focused on his investment in USX and a possible takeover bid for the company. Bill Compton, chairman of the pilots' negotiating committee, said, "I personally don't see the airline surviving in its current state beyond 1991." The pilots considered possible avenues to save the airline, including finding another buyer or a possible employee buyout.[90] They coordinated strategies with the machinists and the flight attendants, agreeing not to grant additional concessions to Icahn or an outside buyer, and to oppose liquidation or sale to an arbitrageur.[91] But nothing came of these efforts.

Then Icahn dealt TWA the hardest blow yet, announcing the sale of its Chicago-London route to American Airlines for $195 million in December 1989. In a letter addressed to employees he claimed, in all caps, that "TWA IS IN NO WAY WHATSOEVER IN ANY FINANCIAL DIFFICULTY," while also saying "it is doing extremely poorly operationally." He added, "There are unprofitable assets at TWA which have been untouched purely because of 'tradition.'"[92]

All of TWA's unions objected to the sale. "There is no possible way that TWA can get stronger if it gets smaller," said Kent Scott, the pilots' new leader. Flight attendants and machinists voiced their concerns, and industry analyst Paul Turk agreed: "Any diminution of TWA's overseas operation is probably not a good sign—not for the long-term health of the airline."[93]

Historically, TWA's international operations had been its most lucrative business and made up for the relative weakness of its domestic network. As the gateway to the rest of Europe from the United States, London's Heathrow was the airline's most important overseas destination. Selling one of TWA's premier Heathrow routes to a competitor demonstrated that Icahn had no interest in the airline, only in its assets and how much cash he could realize from selling them.

"In agreeing to sell the carrier's Chicago-to-London operation to American Airlines for $195 million, Icahn has forced TWA's unions to confront the possibility that he will dismantle the company," wrote a *St. Louis Post-Dispatch* business columnist. "Icahn appears to be saying that employees should accept further concessions or prepare for the sale of additional assets."[94] TWA lost a staggering $300 million in 1989, exceeding its quarter-billion-dollar loss in 1985.

Icahn versus the Pilots

In January 1990, Icahn invited Kent Scott to his Mount Kisco headquarters to discuss the airline's future. Despite his recent claim that TWA was in no financial difficulty, Icahn now told Scott that the airline was going to sustain another substantial loss in 1990, and he demanded $100 million in new concessions from the pilots. It would amount to a 40 percent pay cut for TWA's pilots, who were already among the lowest-paid unionized pilots. Icahn coupled this with a threat to liquidate TWA's domestic operations and reduce it to a "boutique international airline" if the pilots failed to comply.

"There is only one word that accurately describes the tactics that are at work here: extortion," Scott reported to his members. "You and I are being asked to pay protection money to keep our airline intact and prevent it from being scattered to the winds."[95] Icahn made good on his threats. He sold and leased back eight TriStars and three 747s, generating $210 million in cash.[96]

But none of that cash was used to buy new equipment or improve TWA's operations.

Ironically, in their zeal to thwart Lorenzo in 1985, the pilots had given Icahn broad discretion to sell TWA's assets. Icahn's 1985 agreement with the union included a provision—Section 7(d)—that gave him the unlimited right to sell assets if TWA failed to earn "adjusted gross income," as defined in the agreement. That definition, the union believed, would never be satisfied. Yet by 1986, TWA was already in a loss position. Its annual interest payments, primarily on the massive debt incurred to privatize the company, reached $500 million by 1990, which allowed Icahn to invoke Section 7(d) and liquidate the airline if he chose. Icahn now threatened to do just that to extract further concessions.[97] The stage was set for a confrontation.

Icahn made his demands known in interviews with the *New York Times*, the *St. Louis Post-Dispatch*, and the *St. Louis Sun*, calling on TWA's pilots to accept a 10 percent wage cut, give up vacation days, and make concessions in their retirement benefits, collectively worth $80 million. He renewed his unfulfilled promises to add new planes to TWA's obsolescent fleet without explaining how he would do so. "The fate of the airline, whether it grows or shrinks, is in the pilots' hands," he said. "We can shrink the airline or shrink the costs." But the pilots weren't buying it. "We've given up concessions twice, and both times he's promised to grow the airline," said negotiating committee chairman Bill Compton. "He didn't live up to his promise in 1986, so we have a hard time believing he's going to keep his promise this time."[98]

Icahn also turned the screws on the machinists, who had been working without a contract, and whose wages had "snapped back" to pre-Icahn levels until a new contract was negotiated. But he didn't have the same leverage over them that he had with the pilots, and the machinists were now attempting to increase their clout by adding customer service agents and reservationists to their ranks. So Icahn orchestrated a media blitz against the pilots. In an interview with the short-lived *St. Louis Sun,* which had become his favored mouthpiece and cheerleader, he promised to commit to a timetable for buying new planes— but only if the pilots agreed in advance to his demands. "If we can't get the concessions, we'll have to continue with the [liquidation] program," he said, adding that concessions from the pilots would enable him to extract up to $150 million from the machinists and the rest of the workforce. "At the pace Icahn is selling TWA assets, the airline could reach a point by this summer where it would no longer be viable as an independent carrier," wrote the paper's editor.[100]

But the pilots held firm. "In effect, he's asking us to buy airplanes for him," said chairman Scott. "If we subsidize his business decisions, where does it stop?"[101] With the pilots resisting Icahn's demands, the airline appeared headed for liquidation.

As the confrontation between Icahn and the unions intensified, Missouri's political leaders became alarmed over the effects that a possible shutdown and liquidation would have on St. Louis and Kansas City. Spearheading efforts to expand Lambert Airport to accommodate TWA's hub traffic, St. Louis mayor Vincent Schoemehl said the airline's debt and financial weakness had frustrated efforts to find a buyer willing to operate the airline. Governor John Ashcroft and St. Louis–area congressman Jack Buechner met with *Sun* publisher Ralph Ingersoll, who had editorially urged the pilots to accede to Icahn's demands, in an unsuccessful effort to devise a rescue plan. Ingersoll reported back to the politicians that Icahn was "not interested in owning an airline much longer."[102] Meanwhile, Senator John Danforth, the ranking member of the US Senate Committee on Commerce, urged Transportation Secretary Samuel Skinner to deny Icahn's application to sell TWA's Chicago-London routes, a plea that fell on deaf ears.[103]

Second Thoughts about Deregulation

Deregulation had enabled Icahn's hostile takeover, privatization, and manipulation of TWA for his personal benefit, and had sewn chaos throughout the industry. By 1990 some analysts were questioning the premises of deregulation and its supposed benefits to the public. Advocates claimed that deregulation would lead to lower fares and wider access to air travel, and in some cases it did. However, a March 1990 report by the Economic Policy Institute found that airline ticket prices were, on average, 2.6 percent *higher* than they would have been without deregulation, stating, "In addition to more circuitous flights, deregulation appears to have brought us a roller coaster ride of high and low fares, which can change on an hourly basis and include a labyrinth of restrictions."[104]

The report also found that consumers suffered when weaker carriers merged or disappeared altogether. Travelers who lived near concentrated hubs like St. Louis, where TWA controlled 82 percent of the traffic, enjoyed nonstop flights to many destinations. But these flights also tended to be the most expensive. The report's author noted that it'd be cheaper to take a taxi to Kansas City than it would be to fly there.[105] He might have added that the cab ride was probably quicker, more comfortable, and less stressful, too.

Nosedive

The pilots published a chart showing that since Icahn's takeover of TWA, the airline's net worth had fallen from $550 million to negative $160 million. In response Icahn announced the sale of two more 747s and a sale and leaseback of six 767s for another $342 million, forcing the airline to prepay more than $100 million of debt.[106] The pilots refused to be intimidated. "We're not interested in concessions," said chairman Scott. "We have a very concessionary contract already, with huge competitive advantages [for Icahn]."[107] A *St. Louis Sun* survey found that one-third of TWA's pilots would be willing to consider additional concessions if the airline were sold to a different owner.[108] Icahn never explained how extracting another $80 million from the pilots would save TWA, which was paying nearly $500 million in interest annually for the debt he had imposed upon it. Icahn's action appeared to be purely an attempt to bend the pilots to his will and assert his power over them.

Icahn now tried a new gambit, announcing a "tentative" agreement to lease 12 Airbus A320 jets originally destined for bankrupt Braniff Airways, provided that the pilots accepted his concession demands. Chairman Scott quickly rejected this, saying, "We're not changing our attitude about concessions for this development because we aren't going to finance [Icahn's] business decisions."[109] Meanwhile, Icahn again flirted with buying bankrupt Eastern Air Lines while attempting to sell TWA to equally troubled Pan American. He even threatened to turn over TWA's domestic routes to non-union carrier America West Airlines.[110]

In May 1990 the TWA machinists staged a work slowdown at the airline's Kansas City maintenance base in response to a disciplinary action taken against one of their members for "low productivity." The action delayed work on 747 and TriStar wide-bodies and threatened the airline's lucrative European schedules. With negotiations over a new contract stalled, the machinists' union leadership held out hope that the airline could be purchased by employees or unidentified third parties. But pilots' union chairman Scott cited the airline's nearly $3 billion debt burden as a major obstacle to any such deal, and the pilots' financial consultant called TWA "hopelessly over-leveraged."[111]

That same month the *St. Louis Post-Dispatch* published a detailed analysis of TWA's fortunes under Icahn's control. It found that Icahn's net worth had grown tenfold, to $1.2 billion, while TWA's debt had doubled, to $2.67 billion. Icahn admitted he had acquired TWA to make money, bragging, "I've been doing this for years; I've never had a losing year." He continued to liquidate TWA's assets and pocket the proceeds, even as he refused to use any of the airline's $1.2 billion in cash to directly benefit the airline. "Instead of modernizing TWA," the newspaper reported, "Icahn has poured more than $1 billion of its money into the stock market, turning the airline into little more than an investment fund with wings."[113]

Undeterred, the machinists unveiled a plan that called for Icahn to transfer his stock to TWA's employees via a stock ownership plan, with Icahn retaining the airline's cash and its debt. Such a plan, they contended, would allow Icahn to "exit gracefully." Icahn responded by demanding assurances that the employees would agree in advance to the concessions he wanted. Giving up control of TWA's assets in return for $1.2 billion in cash and assuming nearly $3 billion in debt without operating income to pay the $400 million annual interest bill held no appeal for Icahn.

He continued disposing of airplanes and routes throughout 1990 with no break in the impasse with the unions.[114] By selling airplanes, airport facilities, and other assets, he was able to raise $160 million and post a paper profit of $100 million (in reality, a $60 million loss) for the second quarter. Matters came to a head in the fall. Three senior vice presidents abruptly resigned in September. The next month brought layoffs of non-union administrative personnel and newly hired pilots.[115]

On October 10 executive vice president and chief operating officer William Hoar announced that TWA would shrink its schedule and eliminate more routes to cut capacity by 10 percent system wide. The airline had already cut 20 daily flights from its St. Louis hub at the start of the year, its first reduction since the hub was established.[116] TWA announced layoffs of union ramp-service workers, ticket agents, and mechanics in November.[117] Inevitably, this downward spiral affected TWA's operations. In the fall of 1990, it had the third-lowest on-time percentage, the third-highest percentage of mishandled luggage, and the highest percentage of consumer complaints of any US airline.[118]

Selling the Crown Jewels

Amid the carnage Icahn made a bid for bankrupt Pan American Airlines for $450 million, contingent on unwinding Pan Am's recently announced sale of most of its US-to-London routes to United Air Lines. Indeed, some saw Icahn's bid as a Machiavellian ploy to boost the market value of TWA's remaining London routes for a possible sale.[119] It was not long in coming.

On December 16, 1990, Icahn announced an agreement to sell the rest of TWA's remaining London-Heathrow routes and facilities to American Airlines for $445 million. The deal greatly expanded American's European presence and provided Icahn with additional cash to pursue his efforts to purchase all or part of Pan Am, plus pieces of Eastern.[120] It was a deadly blow to TWA's international operations. Giving up service between New York, the prime gateway for European destinations, and Heathrow, the principal European hub, ended TWA's status as a major international carrier, leaving it a bit player in the lucrative European markets.

Missouri senator John Danforth demanded an immediate investigation by Attorney General Richard Thornburgh, saying the sale "inevitably will lead to a dramatic reduction in domestic airline competition." In addition to US Department of Justice antitrust scrutiny, the deal also required approval from the US Department of Transportation, neither of which was expected to be a major obstacle given the *laissez-faire* attitude of the Bush administration.[121] There was no realistic prospect that the airline could survive in the brutally competitive deregulated environment without a robust international presence.

Meanwhile, Icahn continued relying on financial legerdemain to obscure TWA's true condition. Contrary to industry practice, the airline treated its accounts receivable and its securities holdings (subject to market swings) as "cash." The airline's actual hard cash on hand totaled $350 million at the end of 1990, even as TWA spent $100 million a month during the slow winter season.[122] Despite the accounting gimmicks, TWA ended 1990 with a $237 million loss for the year and a $700 million negative net worth.[123]

Tenuous Times

After the London sale TWA cut services to Europe by half, furloughed 2,500 employees in January 1991, defaulted on $75 million in debt obligations, and began withholding payments on leased aircraft. With some justification, the airline blamed these setbacks on rising fuel prices, tensions in the Middle East, and the outbreak of the Gulf War. But TWA's fundamental weakness remained its massive debt burden. The airline's annual interest payments exceeded its operating income, a situation that was unsustainable. Creditors began suing to protect their interests, and TWA stopped paying preferred stock dividends to conserve cash.[124] In February 1991, Icahn acknowledged that TWA's true cash position, including the $110 million received from American Airlines for the earlier sale of the Chicago-London route, was down to $200 million.[125] With the handwriting on the wall, Icahn began maneuvering to extricate himself. He started quietly negotiating with creditors to reduce the airline's debt burden, and he directed his lawyers to begin working on a "prepackaged" Chapter 11 reorganization plan to present to TWA's creditors and unions.

Selling TWA's remaining London routes to American to generate additional cash was a key element of Icahn's exit strategy. The UK authorized the transfer of routes in March, but the sale still required approval from the US Department of Transportation. Senator Danforth brought pressure on Transportation Secretary Skinner to deny the application but to no avail. On March 15, Skinner rejected the sale of the St. Louis, Baltimore, and Philadelphia to London routes, but he allowed the sale of the New York, Boston, and Los Angeles routes, which were by far the most important.

This decision triggered an attempt by Missouri politicians to find another buyer. They focused on billionaire Beverly Hills investor Kirk Kerkorian, who promised to invest $250 million, but negotiations foundered on his demands for more concessions from TWA's union employees. The pilots and the machinists reached an agreement with Kerkorian, only to be rebuffed by the airline.[126] American Airlines also opposed the Kerkorian deal because it was contingent on unwinding the sale of the London routes.[127]

No fewer than 27 senators and House members jumped into the fray, urging Skinner to reject the sale outright, hold an evidentiary hearing, or delay acting for another 60 days to give Kerkorian time to negotiate a deal to buy the airline from Icahn. Meanwhile, Icahn threatened that TWA would file for bankruptcy if the sale were not approved, and American insisted that the Kerkorian machinations were merely an irrelevant distraction.[128]

Sealing the Deal

On April 25, 1991, Skinner affirmed his earlier approval of selling TWA's London routes to American. It came as no surprise: The administration was fully committed to deregulating domestic and international air travel, blessing route sales to United and Delta, too. The decision was a huge victory for Icahn, who announced that he would insist on the full $445 million sale price from American, notwithstanding loss of the three routes it had bargained for. It was also a huge blow to the TWA pilots and their congressional allies, as Kerkorian had no interest in the airline without its most valuable international destinations. Making Icahn's victory complete, American agreed to pay the full price for only the three routes whose sale Skinner had approved.[129] Once again Icahn had outmaneuvered his adversaries.

Fortified with the proceeds of the American sale, Icahn went ahead with his restructuring program. He offered to buy back $1.2 billion in junk bond debt for $490 million, warning that the sum "may exceed the amount holders of the securities would realize by the end of a bankruptcy proceeding."[130] Meanwhile, secured creditors filed suit to foreclose on their collateral, even as Icahn joined with American in offering to buy parts of bankrupt Pan American.[131]

In July 1991, Icahn unveiled his "prepackaged" restructuring plan. It called for TWA's existing common stock to be extinguished and new, post-bankruptcy stock to be issued to creditors, including Icahn. He agreed to put $35 million into the reorganized corporation, leaving it with $1 billion, less debt; $400 million in cash; and himself still in control, with 45 percent ownership of the new TWA. One difficulty, however, was TWA's unfunded pension obligations, estimated variously at $150 million to $900 million. Because Icahn owned 90 percent of TWA, putting it through bankruptcy would allow the federal Pension Benefit Guaranty Corporation (PBGC) to terminate the pension plan and look to Icahn and ACF Corporation to recover the shortfall.[132] Icahn hoped to avoid this scenario by reducing his ownership to less than 80 percent. In devising the plan Icahn consulted with his friend Donald Trump, a veteran of bankruptcy proceedings owing to his multiple casino failures. He wanted to have everything in place for filing by January 1992.

Kent Scott announced in August 1991 that he would take early retirement, telling his fellow pilots, "It has become very evident over the last several years that TWA is a very poorly managed company. Our problems start with a disastrously weak balance sheet, thanks primarily to the Icahn privatization of the company in 1988, when irreparable damage was done to the financial health of the airline." In his 23 years with TWA, he added, "this airline has never come close to providing a rewarding career, much less even steady work. There isn't another airline in the country which has deadened and demoralized the talented professional pilots they've hired in the manner that TWA has."[133]

Scott's replacement was Bill Compton. Like Scott, Compton was still a copilot after 23 years with TWA. "I recently contacted Carl Icahn," he told the pilots, "and reiterated the Association's position that we will not give him any additional concessions." He assured them that the union and its financial and legal advisers would oversee the planned reorganization, but cautioned, "Whether Icahn can surmount the many obstacles that may lie in the path to a successful restructuring remains to be seen."[134]

A November Surprise

Fed up with Icahn's intransigence, Senator Danforth took action. In November 1991 he attached an amendment to a banking bill that locked in Icahn's pension liability, even if he reduced his stake in TWA below 80 percent. "The federal taxpayer should not have to assume liability for TWA's unfunded pension obligations so long as Mr. Icahn has assets available and either owns [TWA] or controls its destiny," said Danforth. Richard Gephardt, now the House majority leader, shepherded a similar provision through the House of Representatives, and the bill became law despite Icahn's personal intervention.[135] It was an unexpected setback for a man accustomed to holding the winning cards and getting his way. And it spelled defeat for Icahn's "prepackaged" bankruptcy plan. Now he would have to negotiate with creditors and the unions over his own exposure and TWA's fate. In the end this legislation would lead to his removal—and a new lease on life for the struggling airline.

In December 1991, Icahn acquired Pan Am Express, a commuter line linking New York's John F. Kennedy Airport with East Coast cities. Icahn planned to create a domestic hub at JFK, a move that made little sense, as most domestic passengers preferred the more convenient LaGuardia Airport. Yet he failed to bid on Pan Am's more significant operations in an auction of the bankrupt carrier's assets, and he agreed to sell TWA's routes to London-Heathrow from Philadelphia and Baltimore to USAir for $50 million, thus completing the liquidation of TWA's most valuable international assets.[136]

The Beginning of the End

For 1991, TWA showed a book profit of $34 million—a meaningless figure as it included $682 million in extraordinary gains from the sale of the London routes and other assets. Overall, the airline sustained a $353 million operating loss and paid $333 million in interest on its $2 billion debt.[137] Icahn had liquidated TWA's assets and pocketed the proceeds before placing the gutted airline into bankruptcy court. It was stunning but perfectly legal. Nevertheless, Icahn's days of unfettered control over TWA were coming to an end.

TWA filed for Chapter 11 reorganization on January 31, 1992. But the Danforth-Gephardt pension legislation upset Icahn's carefully crafted plan to escape liability while retaining control of the airline. The PBGC now announced that it would take "all necessary steps" to protect TWA's pension plans, which were estimated to be underfunded by more than $900 million. Diane Burkley, the PBGC's deputy executive director and a tough negotiator, announced that the agency would require TWA to meet its pension obligations, and Icahn and his companies would be held liable for any shortfalls.[138] Burkley made it clear that the PBGC would be a major player in TWA's restructuring effort.

Complex and often contentious negotiations ensued among the PBGC, TWA's creditors and unions, and Icahn. The bankruptcy court approved the sale of two of TWA's three remaining London routes to USAir. Icahn inaugurated a new route to Moscow via Brussels—a service for which there was little demand—at bargain-basement fares. Having sold off TWA's premier international routes, Icahn now claimed that Moscow was a "major market" and serving it would add to its "global reach."[139] In another ill-considered move, Icahn announced that TWA would establish a "mini-hub" at Atlanta—a fortress hub already dominated by Delta. As TWA's revenues plummeted, Icahn continued to make more fare cuts that were promptly matched or ignored by other airlines.[140]

TWA posted a loss of nearly $90 million for the first quarter of 1992. The loss would have been closer to $200 million but for the sale of the London routes. Icahn continued liquidating TWA's assets, including gates and landing slots at Chicago's O'Hare Airport, and disposing of aging aircraft without replacing them. Industry analysts questioned TWA's viability, even after restructuring. "It's like burning the furniture to keep warm on a cold winter night," said one.[141]

Uncle Sam Turns the Screws

The PBGC took an increasingly hard line as the bankruptcy negotiations dragged on. "So far there is only a plan to save Carl Icahn, not TWA," said an agency spokesperson. "We will not let him walk away from that $1.2 billion in underfunding."[142] By the fall of 1992, TWA was losing $2 million daily and was on the verge of shutting down. Then, a breakthrough: The creditors agreed to give the unions 45 percent ownership in a reorganized TWA and to relinquish $1 billion in debt in return for 55 percent ownership. The unions agreed to 15 percent wage and benefit concessions, and both the creditors and the unions agreed that Icahn would have no place in a reorganized TWA. The agreement set an October 31 deadline for Icahn and the PBGC to resolve the pension issues; failing that, the unions could rescind the agreement and recover their concessions.[143]

The focus then shifted to Icahn and the PBGC. In November 1992 the PBGC negotiated an agreement with TWA to pledge $300 million to the PBGC, secured by the airline's international routes and maintenance facilities. The agency would terminate the pension plans and hold Icahn liable for up to $1 billion. "The deal was intended to bring Icahn to the table," said one of the negotiators.[144]

Getting Icahn to the table was one thing—getting him to contribute was another. Icahn doubted that TWA could come up with $300 million, and he once more skillfully pitted his adversaries against one another. Acting as his own representative, he spent long hours on the phone with PBGC's Burkley. The PBGC did not believe TWA could survive and was focused on making Icahn pay.

Burkley was as tough as Icahn, threatening to go after his financial empire to make sure taxpayers would not be stuck with the bill. Negotiations were often acrimonious and laced with profanity on both sides. Icahn was not used to being vulnerable in a negotiation. "Indeed," Burkley told Icahn, "we are prepared to bankrupt your companies." "OK," he replied sarcastically, "but are you at least going to leave me my house on the beach?"[145] The PBGC did not want to let a billionaire off the hook, but the unions were equally determined to save the airline and its 25,000 jobs. Compton was angry that the PBGC seemed more interested in protecting the pensions and taxpayers than the pensioners.[146]

When the PBGC threatened to pull out of the negotiations, the unions went back to Capitol Hill to apply pressure on the agency. Missouri senators Danforth and Kit Bond intervened directly with Labor Secretary Lynn Martin, who chaired the PBGC, warning that the Bush administration would be responsible for putting a major airline out of business and 25,000 employees out of work if the agency refused to compromise. "Because of

TWA's cash position only a short time remains to reach a solution that protects jobs, pensions, air service, and the federal taxpayer," they wrote on October 8. "We ask that you contact the parties involved to facilitate negotiations that will allow a transfer plan to proceed."[147] Senator Bond exclaimed, "I don't believe that in my lifetime I've ever seen a group of people who believe so strongly in a company and have been hurt so much" as TWA's employees. Kansas senator Bob Dole urged Treasury Secretary Nicholas Brady, another PBGC board member, to press for compromise. In the courtroom, the bankruptcy judge also put heat on the agency.[148]

Finally, after hours of fraught negotiations, an agreement was reached on December 6, 1992. In response to direct intervention by Secretary Martin, Icahn agreed to lend TWA $200 million, to contribute $20 million yearly to TWA's pension funds, and to pay up to $240 million. TWA agreed to contribute $300 million to the PBGC if the airline failed and the pension funds were terminated. The unions agreed to 15 percent wage and benefit concessions totaling $660 million over a three-year period.[149] Even before the deal was done, however, Congressman Gephardt was pitching the airline to move its headquarters to St. Louis, writing that "St. Louis recognizes the importance of a revitalized TWA and the thousands of jobs its success means. You will find a friendly home in St. Louis."[150]

Missouri congressman Richard Gephardt, ca. 1990s. He was a key TWA ally and advocate. Missouri Historical Society Collections.

A new management team was recruited, headed by Glenn Zander, TWA's chief financial officer, and Robin H. H. Wilson, former senior vice president of flight operations. They vowed that no more TWA assets would be sold and that they would endeavor to restore the airline's financial and operational integrity and rebuild public confidence. They had their work cut out for them.

The End of the Icahn Era

After seven tumultuous years, on January 4, 1993, Carl Icahn resigned as an officer and director of TWA and all of its subsidiaries. Over his tenure Icahn added more than a billion dollars of debt, sold hundreds of millions worth of assets, and put hundreds of millions into his own pocket. Yet he failed to order a single new aircraft for TWA.

Icahn was a shrewd investor and financial manipulator. Why he wanted to involve himself in TWA's day-to-day management was never clear. His forte was making deals and enriching himself, not managing businesses. But he clearly relished the power and prestige that owning TWA gave him. When he put TWA into Chapter 11, he still expected to remain in control post-reorganization, a goal foiled only by legislation. The promises and representations Icahn made in 1985 were less than candid, while predictions about what he would do to the airline proved all too accurate. It took the combined forces of Congress, the PBGC, and the US Department of Labor—as well as TWA's creditors and unions—to remove him.

Despite the havoc he wreaked on the airline and its workforce, Icahn could also be charming and personable when it suited him. He attended events where he mingled with TWA employees and was funny and entertaining. At one such function a 50-50 club was set up that had $400 to divide, most of it contributed by Icahn. He held up a big wad of tickets and said, "I have a controlling interest in the 50-50 club." The master of ceremonies replied, "If you want to change your position, I can get you 13 cents on the dollar for your 50-50 tickets." The audience howled. After attending a meeting of the Conquistadores del Cielo, the exclusive airline executives' club, he regaled employees with anecdotes about Bob Crandall of American and Herb Kelleher of Southwest. But a few such lighthearted moments could not heal the deep wounds he had inflicted.

With Icahn and his entourage now gone, TWA would operate under bankruptcy court supervision. Fifty-five percent of the stock of the reorganized airline was owned by its creditors and 45 percent by its employees. Both now had an interest in making it succeed, but the question remained whether that was possible. Icahn would continue to harm the struggling airline long after he left it.

Chapter 9
THE LAST AVIATOR: 1994–2001

Euphoria swept through TWA's ranks when Icahn departed in January 1993. Designated "co-chief executives," Glenn Zander and Robin Wilson also served as "responsible persons" appointed by the bankruptcy court to manage TWA's affairs. In effect, Zander and Wilson constituted both TWA's senior management and its board of directors while the corporation was in bankruptcy.

Trying to Recover

Zander was a 28-year veteran of TWA who had served as comptroller and, most recently, senior vice president and chief financial officer under Icahn. Respected for his business acumen and collegial management style, he was well acquainted with TWA's financial circumstances and challenges. Wilson, a native of Dublin, Ireland, first joined TWA in 1964. Over the years he held numerous titles in all of the company's major departments. He became senior vice president of operations in 1978, a position responsible for flight operations, in-flight service, engineering, maintenance, and purchasing. Wilson left in 1981 to become president of the Long Island Rail Road before serving as president and CEO of Western Airlines, where he presided over a major turnaround in the company's fortunes. After leaving Western he engaged in a variety of commercial and academic activities, including a stint as a professor of international business at the University of Limerick, before returning to TWA.

Zander and Wilson took the reins of a troubled company. It had a traumatized, demoralized workforce; a depleted and inefficient fleet of only 172 planes; and an unprofitable route structure. The airline had lost more than $300 million in 1992, Icahn's last year at its helm.[1] TWA's reputation for superior service had declined sharply even before it fell into Icahn's clutches. Service reductions made for unhappy passengers, and TWA's union employees were still recovering from their battles with management. Icahn had attempted to attract passengers by offering frequent sales, a tactic that only worked if a price advantage could be sustained. But the airline industry's computers were capable of instant price matching, so any airfare sales were self-defeating. As a result, TWA had both low fares and a low percentage of seats filled per flight.[2]

Selling Comfort

Zander and Wilson wanted to differentiate TWA from the competition. Fortuitously, the FAA had issued an order to add more seat spacing around exit rows, a change that would require moving every seat on every plane, along with overhead lighting and air vents. Employees suggested that TWA take advantage of the mandate to increase its seat pitch—the spacing between seat rows—without cutting fares. The result was "Comfort Class." Although each flight's seat capacity would diminish, little revenue would be lost as load factors were low anyway. And because competitors had already incurred the cost of moving seats to meet the FAA requirement, they would be reluctant to change them again to compete with TWA.

In one year, Comfort Class took TWA from ranking at the bottom in customer satisfaction to near the top. Besides restoring pride in TWA employees and confidence in its management, it set TWA apart at a time when air travel was an increasingly fungible commodity. Comfort Class was now the centerpiece of a new nationwide multimedia marketing campaign that rolled out in early 1993, touting TWA as "the most comfortable way to fly." "Comfort for our passengers means many things: comfortable seats, comfortable fares, comfortable check-ins, comfortable, friendly service," it added. "In summary, customers will expect the entire experience with TWA to be one of comfort."[3] Less explicit was the purpose of shedding the Icahn-era image of low fares and poor service. Competitors scoffed, saying TWA was taking seats out of its planes because it didn't have passengers to sit in them. There was some truth to this: On average, only 55 percent of TWA's seats were occupied on any given flight.[4] The goal of filling more seats with better-paying passengers remained elusive.

A New Plan

In February 1993, TWA filed its five-year reorganization plan with the bankruptcy court. Wilson and Zander went on the road to explain the plan to the workforce. The plan called for increasing service at the St. Louis hub, improving operating revenue and profitability, and expanding and modernizing TWA's aging fleet by replacing its three-engine Boeing 727s (which required flight engineers) with new and more efficient twin-engine, two-pilot MD-80s. Internationally, Boeing 747s and Lockheed TriStars would be phased out in favor of more Boeing 767s, along with the Airbus A330s Icahn had "ordered" four years before. The plan specified increasing TWA's fleet from 172 to 228 jets, a welcome improvement after the drought of new planes.[5]

The plan projected greater revenue per passenger mile, based on assumed industry-wide fare increases, more high-fare business passengers, and less dependence on low-fare leisure travelers. The plan predicted a rise in operating profits from less than $100 million in 1993 to $423 million, and a net income of $168 million in 1997.[6] But these figures were overly optimistic. TWA still needed an infusion of fresh capital, an unlikely development given the airline's continuing financial and operational weaknesses.

One area that saw dramatic improvement was TWA's on-time performance, which went from near the bottom in 1991 to first in January 1993. TWA also had the second-best baggage-handling record. Improved employee morale led to better customer service overall, and passengers noticed. One St. Louis lawyer who flew TWA regularly remarked that it almost seemed like a different airline. "TWA's personnel are much more enthusiastic and accommodating. They're going out of their way," he said. The additional legroom was also popular. "We've heard more positive comments from our customers in the last two months than in the past year," a regional sales vice president said in February 1993.[7]

Another positive change came with the announcement of a firm agreement with McDonnell Douglas Corporation to lease six new MD-83s and a dozen used DC-9-50s between May and December 1993, with plans to retire 14 older Boeing 727s. TWA also recalled two TriStars and a 767 that Icahn had returned to lessors.[8]

Despite these strides, TWA's consumer complaint record remained the worst in the industry.[9] The airline's "employee-owners" still had a long way to go to turn things around.

A New Home

TWA could also now move its headquarters away from Icahn's lair in Mount Kisco. Company leadership considered relocating to New York City, Kansas City, or St. Louis—all three had strong historical connections to the airline. Kansas City, located at the center of TWA's first transcontinental route, had been the airline's original home and remained the site of its major overhaul base and administration center. From the post–World War II period until 1988, TWA had called New York City home. It was the financial capital of the United States, where many of the largest American corporations were located. John F. Kennedy Airport was TWA's international hub and the jumping-off point for its European and Middle East routes.

The site of TWA's major hub, St. Louis was an important domicile for TWA flight crews and the heart of TWA's domestic operations. Leveraging the assistance he provided during the bankruptcy proceedings, Congressman Gephardt made a strong pitch for his hometown, even as negotiations with creditors continued. The airline sought concessions from each candidate city because it could not afford to build a stand-alone headquarters.[10]

Emerging from Bankruptcy

With eight directors named by the creditors, four by the unions, and three by TWA management, a new 15-person board of directors was established in July 1993. William Howard, the former head of Piedmont Airlines, was named chairman and CEO. He became the third "responsible person" in July 1993, with Zander and Wilson serving as vice chairmen. Howard had retired after selling Piedmont to USAir. His success in guiding Piedmont through the turmoil of deregulation was seen as an asset in the highly competitive deregulated airline market. Howard, Zander, and Wilson filled the three management seats on TWA's post-bankruptcy board. Many observers perceived Howard's selection as chairman and CEO (rather than Zander) as a political move: The unions could not stomach Zander in that role, which implied control by the company's creditors. Zander rejected a long-term contract in favor of an arrangement that allowed him to resign at any time with $500,000 in severance pay.[11]

The bankruptcy court approved TWA's reorganization plan on August 11, 1993. The next day Howard announced that TWA's new headquarters would be in downtown St. Louis. It was part of a deal that involved TWA selling its gates, jetways, and baggage systems to the city, thereby generating $70 million in cash and a waiver of unpaid lease obligations.[12] At the time it was typical for airlines to provide and own much of the equipment used for their operations, but St. Louis agreed to buy and lease back TWA's fixed operational equipment and to renegotiate its gate leases. This arrangement ensured that those assets belonged to the City of St. Louis and would not become part of a bankruptcy estate if TWA eventually failed and was liquidated. The fiscally challenged city's willingness to make such a deal showed a distinct lack of confidence in TWA's long-term prospects.

TWA could now prepare to emerge from Chapter 11. Judge Helen Balick set a hearing on November 3, 1993, to consider TWA's application, a process that was much more stressful than had been anticipated. All the principal creditors were represented, and all but one was prepared to consent. The Port Authority of New York and New Jersey was the lone holdout. It remained recalcitrant over payment of back rents at John F. Kennedy Airport. A recess requested by the other creditors and granted by the judge ended in an agreement with the port authority. The reorganization plan was confirmed, and TWA emerged from Chapter 11.

TWA's newly constituted board of directors met for the first time that same day. Its members included pilots' union chairman Bill Compton, flight attendants' president Vicki Frankovich, William O'Driscoll of the TWA machinists, and the machinists' international president William Winpisinger. This team reflected the greater role that labor now had in overseeing the airline. In one of its first acts the board canceled 10 of the Airbus A330s "ordered" by Carl Icahn in 1989. There was little need for the wide-body jetliners after Icahn had stripped the airline of its most valuable international routes, and TWA eventually canceled its entire A330 order.[13]

TWA's post-bankruptcy outlook was far from rosy. Despite shedding $1 billion in debt, the company still owed $1.8 billion, and it continued to lose money. It lost $61 million in the third quarter of 1993, traditionally its most profitable period, and its net loss for the year's first nine months was a staggering $417 million. The airline had only $200 million in cash reserves to get through the slow winter months, and it desperately needed additional capital. "There's not much room for error," said an industry analyst. "It will be a close scrape getting through the winter."[14] Similarly, TWA's 1993 annual report pulled no punches: "TWA's future viability will depend on its ability to increase revenues and improve its results of operations. No assurance can be given that the Company will be successful in generating the operating revenues required for future viability."[15]

Presenting a United Front

After seven years of erratic one-man rule, TWA was now controlled by the new board of directors. But the allocation of seats among creditors, labor, and management led to factionalism. The senior management team that Zander and Wilson had recruited lined up behind their champions, while Howard had no such constituency and clashed with other executives over the airline's future. "Howard was one member of a troika who could not agree on what needed to be done, so very little got done," said an industry analyst.[16] One observer described Howard as a relic of the regulatory era who was not well equipped to deal with powerful unions and a company struggling to survive. The board replaced him in early 1994 with Donald Craib, one of the directors selected by TWA's creditors. Howard's brief tenure proved lucrative, as he received nearly $1 million in severance pay.[17] Craib had joined the board after retiring as CEO of Allstate Insurance group and had no experience in the airline industry. Passed over once again for TWA's top job, Zander resigned.

All involved tried to put on a happy face. The board "unanimously expressed the view that Howard's leadership has been in large part responsible for the renewed enthusiasm and dedication of TWA's employees, and the resultant turnaround in the public's perception of the much-improved quality of the airline." Howard remarked that his primary goal had been to lead the airline out of bankruptcy and "with that task now accomplished, I have no doubt that the company will continue to grow and prosper."[18] Nonetheless, this early management shakeup did not bode well for the future.

Employee-ownership was not all sweetness and light either. After years of battling Icahn and trying to recover from the failed 1986 strike, many flight attendants had become disillusioned when dramatic improvements failed to materialize after Icahn's ouster. They blamed union president Vicki Frankovich, who asked in a letter to her fellow union members, "Where is the recognition of what we accomplished? We finally got rid of our nemesis—Carl Icahn. We played a central role in saving TWA and our 5,000 jobs. After all this we are perceived as having accomplished nothing?" Acknowledging "anger, stress and betrayal," she said, "We've all been victimized. We continue to suffer as a result of those forces, now gone, that drove our airline to bankruptcy." But, she added, "It's time to work together and make the changes that we can make today."[19]

Painful Realities

Excluding a $1.1 billion extraordinary credit for cancellation of debt in bankruptcy, TWA lost $450 million in 1993—far more than during Icahn's final year.[20] Upon taking over, Craib found the airline in imminent danger of running out of cash. TWA remained saddled with nearly $2 billion in long-term debt, and it continued losing money. Servicing this debt made it impossible for TWA to accumulate needed cash or to turn a profit.

Recruited from Reno Air, an airline one-tenth the size of TWA, Jeffrey Erickson became president and CEO of the airline. Robin Wilson survived the management turmoil and tried to put the company on a better path. He announced agreements to acquire additional aircraft that would increase TWA's fleet to 192 jets. The St. Louis domestic hub expanded to 300 daily flights, and JFK's international hub increased to 77 daily international departures. TWA dramatically scaled back its "mini-hub" in Atlanta, where the airline competed with Delta's mega-hub.[21]

Pilots' union chairman Bill Compton characterized TWA's status bluntly, saying, "TWA has a $50 million financial 'hole' that the airline must fill by year's end. In large part it is up to us, the employee/owners, to fill that hole with innovative productivity initiatives. Otherwise, TWA may have serious difficulty navigating the winter of '94–'95." He continued, "Now, for the first time in my 26-year career, I sense a real opportunity to change the culture at our airline, to redesign TWA from the inside out." He pointed to TWA's Productivity Task Force, the Change Teams, and the Leadership 2000 management training program as "the vehicles for revolutionary change."[22] The Reengineering Team, made up of TWA's labor leaders, was tasked with creating a new business plan, reaching new terms with creditors, and "modifying labor contracts and streamlining the management structure in a manner more conducive to productivity and success."[23] These leaders would now be responsible for administering some harsh medicine to their own memberships.

But fixing TWA's problems required more than corporate re-engineering. Rumors soon swirled that after agreeing to $660 million in concessions, some of the airline's "employee-owners" now faced layoffs. Turmoil continued in the executive suite at the new St. Louis headquarters: TWA's senior vice president of marketing resigned in April, the CFO left in June, and vice chairman Wilson followed in July. Wilson was the last of the trio who had guided the airline out of bankruptcy, and his departure concluded a complete overhaul of top management in less than six months.

Even though the 1993 reorganization had removed Icahn, it had not made TWA financially viable. The airline still carried a heavy debt burden with its attendant $200 million in annual interest payments. And Icahn continued to haunt the airline as his $200 million loan, which had been made as part of the reorganization, would mature in January 1995.

Uncomfortable Facts

Comfort Class proved a mixed blessing. While to some extent it succeeded in differentiating TWA from its competitors, it reduced badly needed revenue and made some flights unprofitable—even when nearly every seat was filled. Experience showed that low fares, rather than extra space, was the biggest factor in attracting passengers. The losses TWA incurred through adopting Comfort Class wiped out the savings realized through employee concessions, in effect making the employee-owners subsidize a failed marketing effort. After removing seats from its planes, TWA was forced to begin putting them back in.[24]

In a letter to TWA's pilots, Compton addressed other uncomfortable facts. "TWA's survival is in jeopardy," he wrote. "Fortunately, its destiny is still in our control." He pointed out that even though TWA had the lowest labor costs of all unionized air carriers, its labor costs as a percent of revenue were among the highest. Moreover, its revenue per employee was well below the industry average, and its employees per aircraft were higher than its peers.[25] Despite all the hardship and sacrifices, TWA still had too many employees and not enough revenue.

Layoffs followed. They began with 260 employees at the Kansas City maintenance base and continued with 500 domestic and 300 overseas employees. Occupying four seats on the board, the union leaders were tasked with exploring work-rule changes and other contract modifications to reduce costs and increase productivity. The hardest part was selling these measures to their rank and file. "We have said there will be radical changes at TWA," Erickson said, "and these are among the first."[26]

Although the layoffs constituted only 4 percent of TWA's 25,000 workers, they prompted new concerns about the airline's prospects. Analysts noted that these layoffs were just one part of a systemic restructuring, but what the company needed most was capital. A TWA spokesman acknowledged that the airline would not have enough cash to meet its obligations in 1995 "unless major cost cutting begins now."[27]

Putting union representatives on the board did not guarantee labor harmony. Friction arose when labor and management interests failed to overlap. The focus turned to contract negotiations with the three major labor unions, whose leaders were also TWA directors. In a video, Erickson called the negotiations critical to the longevity of the airline, saying, "All must be willing to manage change, or they will not be around." The messages to the employee-owners from their leaders were equally blunt. Compton told his members that studies showed TWA's workforce to be the least productive in the industry. The machinists' representative added, "We can't charge more than our competitors for a ticket, so we must cut our costs and increase our revenues." The flight attendants' Frankovich said, "We have to take a good look at ourselves and ask, 'Is there a better way to do this?'"[28]

The rank and file responded. In September the machinists approved a new contract, including cost reductions through work-rule changes and cuts in staff, overtime, and vacation that were valued at $85 million. The pilots agreed to modify work rules, pay, and schedules, which would save another $35 million annually.[29] As one pilots' union representative put it to his membership: "Gentlemen, you're buying your jobs." The flight attendants, still feeling the bitterness of the 1986 strike, reluctantly accepted $10 million in new concessions, in addition to those made only two years earlier. The total savings obtained from the union employees was estimated at $120 million to $130 million—significant, but still less than the $150 million the airline had hoped for.[30]

While the unions were agreeing to these savings, TWA's workforce demonstrated its commitment to the airline by making $233,000 monthly lease payments on a new MD-80 named *Wings of Pride*. Painted in a unique reverse color scheme—red with white trim and white TWA logos—the plane was emblazoned with large letters proclaiming it was "Sponsored by the Employee-Owners of TWA." The airline unveiled the aircraft and christened it at a gala held in St. Louis on September 10, 1994. More than 1,000 employees took part in the festivities, which included airliners that had served TWA since its earliest days, from the Ford trimotor and DC-2 to the Martin 404 and Super-G Constellation.

Four days later 150 flight attendants were laid off.[31]

Dubbed Wings of Pride, *this McDonnell Douglas MD-80 was sponsored by TWA's "Employee-Owners," many of whom posed with the aircraft for this 1994 photo. David Ostrowski Collection, Greater St. Louis Air and Space Museum.*

Restructuring, Again

With the unions now on board, attention shifted to reducing TWA's $1.8 billion indebtedness. The plan called for creditors to accept stock as full or partial repayment of TWA's obligations. For that to be palatable, creditors had to believe that TWA's stock would be worth more over time. On October 11, TWA filed its proposed reorganization plan with the Securities and Exchange Commission, which called for issuing new stock in return for extinguishing "a substantial portion" of the outstanding debt and a moratorium on aircraft lease payments. Creditor stock ownership would increase to 70 percent, and employees' stake would decline to 30 percent. The market responded poorly. TWA shares lost 40 percent of their value after the airline disclosed that it might be forced into bankruptcy again if stockholders failed to approve issuance of the additional stock.[32]

At the shareholders' annual meeting on November 1, 1994, TWA president Erickson announced a quarterly operating profit for the first time in four years. The airline also had a much lower net loss: $8 million, down from $61 million for the same quarter a year earlier. Erickson blamed the loss on TWA's heavy interest expenses—$50 million for the quarter and $146 million for the year to date—but said, "We are confident that our cost-cutting efforts to date and a successful restructuring of this burdensome debt will provide the solid groundwork for a profitable TWA."[33]

The market was not impressed. The American Stock Exchange suspended trading in the company's stock the next day after unfavorable reports surfaced in trade publications.[34] A week later, with trading still suspended, Erickson remained upbeat in talks with creditors and predicted that the restructuring plan would be in place by the end of the year. If not, he said, TWA might resort to a "narrowly focused" prepackaged bankruptcy plan.[35]

But creditors dismissed the proposed equity-for-debt deal as inadequate. Carl Icahn resurfaced to haunt TWA, which was due to repay him $190 million in January 1995, but had only $114 million in cash going into the historically slow winter season. However, if the airline shut down, Icahn was still potentially liable for TWA's underfunded pension plan, giving TWA some leverage. "We are hopeful that a prepackage bankruptcy will not be necessary," Compton said, "but if the necessary consents are not forthcoming it must be used as a forcing mechanism. In the end, all constituents will be advantaged by a successful financial reorganization."[36]

Not all the creditors agreed. The holders of notes secured by liens on spare parts and other assets balked at the stock-for-debt deals they were offered, asserting that they would be better off in a straight liquidation, and urged other creditors to reject the plan. The normally calm and diplomatic Compton blew his top. "We consider these noteholders' public statements an attempt at outright sabotage," he fumed, and TWA pilots began picketing their offices.[37] But the creditors' skepticism was certainly understandable: The airline posted a $435 million loss for 1994.[38]

Amid these financial problems the airline narrowly avoided a major disaster. On the night of November 22, 1994, a TWA MD-80 departing St. Louis bound for Denver was accelerating for takeoff when a private Cessna twin turboprop appeared out of the darkness in the middle of the runway. The TWA captain swerved violently, attempting to avoid a collision, but the airliner's right wing struck the Cessna, cutting it in half and killing its pilot and sole passenger. The TWA flight crew managed to retain control and bring the airliner to a stop on the runway as jet fuel poured from its damaged wing. All passengers were evacuated with only minor injuries.[39] The National Transportation Safety Board found that the Cessna pilot had misinterpreted his instructions from the tower and mistakenly taxied onto the runway in front of the departing jet.[40] Had the TWA pilots not reacted so quickly, the accident could have been catastrophic.

Enter Cahill

Struggles over debt restructuring continued as 1995 began. While TWA's management negotiated with trade creditors and those who owned the company's junk bonds, it became apparent that TWA was once again headed toward bankruptcy. Surprisingly, negotiations with Carl Icahn proceeded relatively smoothly. He offered to accept repayment of his $190 million loan through an arrangement known as the "Karabu Ticket Program Agreement" that allowed him to buy TWA tickets and resell them at a profit. The airline had little hope of otherwise refinancing Icahn's loan—and it believed the Karabu agreement would not harm its sales, as the seats Icahn would be selling might go unsold anyway—so TWA accepted.[41] It proved to be a grave miscalculation.

Donald Craib resigned as TWA's chairman in February 1995. His lack of experience in the airline industry had made him an ill-suited leader for the troubled carrier. John Cahill, another director who represented creditor interests, replaced him. Cahill had spent 37 years at British Tyre & Rubber before becoming chairman of British Aerospace in 1992 and joining TWA's board in the fall of 1994.

In addition to its other challenges, TWA also attempted to reorganize Trans World Express (TWE), the regional subsidiary Icahn had acquired from Pan American that was intended to collect international passengers from East Coast cities and bring them to the international hub at JFK. But in practice TWE served too many locations with too many types of planes and too many employees. TWA initiated efforts to eliminate unprofitable routes; reduce employee head count; and consolidate the fleet into a single airplane type, the ATR 42 turboprop. But these efforts floundered when the ATR fleet was grounded worldwide in the aftermath of a fatal accident and had to be cleared by the FAA before the planes could fly again.

TWE now needed to fill the gap that was left by the grounding of the ATRs. It had previously defaulted on the lease for some of the smaller, unprofitable types it had operated. The lessor had terminated the lease and was now threatening to repossess the aircraft. After assessing the benefits and burdens of continuing to operate TWE, TWA's board ultimately decided to turn the service over to its Trans States Airlines regional partner and closed TWE in late 1995.[42]

Perfidious Albion

As part of its efforts to recover from the damage inflicted by Icahn, TWA attempted to regain access to London's Heathrow airport and to London-Gatwick from New York. Airline service between the US and Britain was governed by the so-called "Bermuda II" treaty. Unless the treaty was modified, TWA could never regain what had historically been its most valuable overseas routes.

In the spring of 1995, US and British trade representatives began negotiating over liberalizing Bermuda II. Congressman Richard Gephardt took the lead in championing TWA's cause. He wrote Transportation Secretary Federico Peña, urging him to press the British for comprehensive liberalization of the agreement, but the talks failed.[43]

The 1997 arrival of a new British government under Prime Minister Tony Blair gave TWA and its allies hope for a more sympathetic reception. Gephardt even met with Blair personally.[44] But the new regime was no more amenable than its predecessor. TWA would never again serve London from New York or gain access to Heathrow—another legacy of the Icahn era.

Going Broke Again

TWA made its second trip to bankruptcy court with a true prepackaged Chapter 11 filing on June 30, 1995. All major parties were in agreement, and it was well received by the court. Despite being the largest prepackaged bankruptcy ever attempted, it breezed through with only token creditor opposition, and the court approved the reorganization plan on August 4. The plan secured $130 million in annual concessions by the unions, whose ownership stake was reduced from 45 percent to 30 percent. Creditors relinquished $500 million in debt in exchange for an increase in their equity interest from 55 to 70 percent. TWA also gained a deferral of equipment leases and conditional finance obligations worth $91 million and secured an extension of the Icahn loan to 2003.[45] Still, fundamental problems remained, including a weak route structure, inadequate revenue, and an aging fleet.

The new plan also had two serious flaws. First, it reduced long-term debt by only $500 million, far short of the original goal, leaving more than $1 billion of debt obligations in place. Second, in return for extending the Icahn loan, TWA agreed to the Karabu ticket program, which allowed Icahn-controlled Karabu Corporation to purchase an unlimited number of TWA tickets at a 45 percent discount from TWA's published fares. It also authorized Karabu to purchase up to $70 million worth of domestic TWA tickets annually, at bulk fare rates. Icahn then created an entity known as lowestfare.com to sell the TWA tickets to the public, in direct competition with TWA. Moreover, Global Discount Travel Services—another Icahn creation—sold TWA tickets as a travel agent.

Evidently no one at TWA really understood the Karabu agreement when it was created. TWA asserted that, under the agreement, tickets could only be sold to business travelers, while Icahn contended that his companies were free to sell to anyone. The airline filed suit alleging that Icahn and Karabu were violating the agreement by selling to the general public. Icahn and Karabu responded by filing a separate suit seeking a declaratory judgment in favor of their interpretation and monetary damages from TWA. TWA eventually succeeded in getting the Icahn/Karabu suit dismissed, only to have Icahn file another suit alleging violations of a separate agreement extending the term of his $190 million loan. These proceedings continued for years. Meanwhile, Icahn's companies flooded the market with deeply discounted TWA tickets, which undercut the airline's own ticket sales. The Karabu agreement cost the airline an estimated $100 million a year.[46]

The presence of TWA's union leaders on its board created internal tensions as the company sought to align all the interested parties on the restructuring plan. The union directors felt pressure to support the other directors and management in the interest of saving the company, while their rank-and-file members accused them of selling out to management and betraying those who had elected them. At one meeting Vicki Frankovich, confronted with assertions that the flight attendants were jeopardizing prospects for a successful restructuring, told her fellow directors that she could not negotiate on behalf of her union at a board meeting. On another occasion she opposed merit-based raises for management personnel, calling them "unacceptable" to her members, who she said were among the company's lowest-paid employees.[47] Statements like these highlighted the conflicts born of "employee-ownership" and eventually led to Frankovich's resignation as a director in January 1996.

Flight 800

TWA finished 1995 with a combined pre- and post-reorganization loss of $227 million—better than 1994's $435 million in red ink but hardly a promising start. TWA moved to improve its operational performance in the first half of 1996 by positioning itself as a high-value airline for budget-conscious business travelers and a no-frills carrier for leisure travelers headed to Mexico and the Caribbean. The airline recognized it needed to overcome "excessive flight cancellations, poor on-time performance and a general deterioration in product quality."[48] TWA was starting to make inroads after emerging from its second Chapter 11 reorganization when its fortunes took a tragic turn.

Shortly after 8 p.m. on July 17, 1996, a Boeing 747 operating as TWA Flight 800 pushed back at JFK and began taxiing to take off for Paris with 212 passengers and 12 crew aboard. The jetliner had been in almost continuous service since in 1971 and had accumulated more than 90,000 flight hours. Despite their age, TWA's Boeing 747s still provided elegant, first-class service and plenty of room for passengers to get out of their seats, walk around, and stretch their legs—even in coach. Like all TWA 747 flights, the crew included

The Boeing 747 was TWA's flagship for nearly 30 years. R. A. Burgess Collection, Greater St. Louis Air and Space Museum.

a management-level customer service representative on board to oversee the cabin service and ensure a superior transatlantic flight. Following the tradition set in the 1950s and 1960s, Flight 800 epitomized the best travel experience TWA could offer its passengers.

At 8:18 p.m. the JFK tower cleared the flight for takeoff. The 747 headed northwest and then made a sweeping left turn that brought its flight path about 10 miles off the south shore of Long Island. Twelve minutes after takeoff air traffic control cleared the flight to climb to 15,000 feet. Then the plane disappeared from radar. The crew of a Boeing 737 in the area reported seeing an explosion, saying, "it just went down into the water." Other aircraft radioed similar reports. Numerous witnesses saw an explosion, a large fireball or fireballs, and flaming debris falling into the sea. Wreckage was scattered across the ocean surface and over a 4-square-mile area of the ocean floor. Because the water was shallow, more than 95 percent of the wreckage was eventually recovered and meticulously reconstructed in a hangar as the investigation progressed.[49]

Many TWA employees lost friends and co-workers in the crash, a terrible blow to morale at a critical point in TWA's recovery efforts. The airline once again had to cope with tragedy as it was fighting to survive. Because the crash happened in New York City, "the media capital of the world," it was covered extensively, and TWA passenger bookings fell sharply.[50]

Many people on the ground claimed they saw a "streak of light" that some described as ascending and moving to the point where the fireball appeared. These reports ignited intense interest and speculation that somehow a missile had brought down the 747. The FBI began a criminal investigation alongside the National Transportation Safety Board's official accident investigation, causing a bureaucratic interagency struggle that impeded the proceedings. The FBI excluded the NTSB from its witness interviews and refused to allow the NTSB to conduct its own. The FBI never disclosed any verbatim records of its interviews, instead writing "summaries" for public consumption. The FBI finally closed its criminal investigation in December 1997 and turned its investigative materials over to the NTSB. But because it had been nearly a year and a half since the crash, the NTSB decided against trying to re-interview witnesses and instead used the FBI's summaries, which sparked accusations of a cover-up.

The NTSB formed a "sequencing group" tasked with examining individual pieces of the recovered aircraft and reconstructing both two- and three-dimensional layouts of sections of the airplane. The sequencing group concluded that the first event was a fracture in the wing center section, caused by an overpressure in the center wing fuel tank (CWT) under the cabin floor. Based on detailed analysis of the breakup sequence; witness information; wreckage damage characteristics; scientific tests; and research on fuels, fuel-tank explosions, and conditions in the CWT at the time of the accident, the NTSB concluded that "the TWA flight 800 in-flight breakup was initiated by a fuel/air explosion in the CWT."

After an exhaustive four-year investigation, in August 2000 the NTSB issued its final report. It determined that the accident was likely caused by "an explosion of the center wing fuel tank (CWT), resulting from ignition of the flammable fuel/air mixture in the tank." The NTSB was unable to definitively identify the source of ignition, but it concluded that a short circuit in aging electrical wiring most likely caused a spark that ignited fuel vapors. Contributing factors were design and certification assumptions that fuel-tank explosions "could be prevented solely by precluding all ignition sources"—i.e., a design flaw in the aircraft.[51] The NTSB found no shortcomings on TWA's part.[52]

Myth versus Reality

Flight 800 attracted widespread interest and notoriety. Former White House press secretary Pierre Salinger called a press conference in Cannes, France, on November 7, 1996, to announce "proof" that Flight 800 had been shot down, and the government was covering it up. He claimed to have been shown documentary evidence by French intelligence sources but refused to identify them or the alleged documents.[53] In fact, Salinger's sources proved to be no more than internet chatter and were quickly debunked. The NTSB's vice chairman said Salinger "didn't know what he was talking about, and he was totally irresponsible."[54] But the damage was done.

While the official investigation continued, conspiracy theories proliferated online and in print. A Gallup poll conducted in 1997 found that less than half of Americans accepted mechanical failure as the cause of the crash, while a substantial number of respondents were either unsure or believed it was caused by a US Navy missile. Fully 27 percent of respondents believed the missile theory, 8 percent believed it was a terrorist attack, and 6 percent thought it was "something else." As the Gallup researchers pointed out:

"Disbelief in government investigations is not something new for the American public. As recently as 1993, 75% of Americans felt that more than one man was responsible for the assassination of President John Kennedy, in direct contradiction of the official Warren Commission report. And last year a Gallup poll found that 71% of Americans think that the U.S. government knows more about UFOs than it is saying."[55]

A major proponent of the missile theory was William S. Donaldson, a retired Navy officer who submitted a report to the US House of Representatives two years after the incident.[56] Donaldson claimed that two missiles struck Flight 800 and called it (without factual support) a "terrorist attack." He also alleged that the FBI and NTSB were under political pressure from the Clinton administration to cover it up—a narrative that gained widespread currency among right-wing circles.

More fanciful theories offered by writers with no scientific or technical credentials included a strike by a meteorite known as a "bolide" and electromagnetic interference from a "high intensity radiated field."[57] The TWA machinists' union even jumped in, submitting a report to the NTSB stating that "a major event may have occurred on the left side of the aircraft" which "could have contributed to or been the cause of the destruction of Flight 800."[58] However, the union did not identify or explain what the "major event" might have been.

The NTSB carefully considered and rejected each of these theories. The persistent missile strike claims were based on witness reports of a flaming streak or streaks ascending into the night sky. But radar data showed nothing in the vicinity at the time of the accident that could have intersected with Flight 800's position, and there was no data consistent with a missile or other projectile traveling toward the aircraft.[59] Nor were any military surface vessels within 17 nautical miles of the flight when it exploded.[60] The Navy reported that the nearest warship, the USS *Normandy*, was 185 miles to the south, and its antiaircraft missiles had a maximum range of just 90 miles.[61]

The FBI asked the Central Intelligence Agency to join its investigation and share witness information. The CIA reviewed other data to determine if the reported "streak of light" might have been a missile. The CIA produced a video analysis that concluded eyewitnesses only saw the fire trail and downward cascade of flames following the explosion before the aircraft hit the water, and "there is no evidence that anyone saw a missile shoot down TWA flight 800."[62]

At the NTSB's request, the Naval Air Warfare Center at China Lake, California, conducted detailed examinations of the recovered wreckage and analyzed other data to evaluate the possibility that a shoulder-launched missile destroyed the airplane. But according to a Navy warhead testing expert, if a missile with a live warhead had impacted the airplane and detonated, the wreckage likely would have exhibited extensive damage to the impact area from the initial penetration of the missile and high-velocity fragments. The Flight 800 wreckage showed no such damage.[63]

Trace amounts of explosive residue were found on three samples of material recovered from the wreckage, which bolstered claims of a terrorist incident. However, forensic examination of the aircraft's structure, seats, and other interior components found no proof that a high-energy explosion of a bomb or missile caused the damage. The NTSB also considered, analyzed, and ruled out other possible causes, including a meteorite and electromagnetic interference.[65]

The board's meticulous forensic examination and analysis did nothing to dissuade skeptics, however. The FBI's involvement created the perception that Flight 800 was the victim of a criminal act. Conspiracy theories and government cover-up allegations became ingrained in popular culture, and science and technology could not dislodge them—even among many former TWA employees. Decades later Flight 800 remained fodder for conspiracy theorists. A television program titled *TWA Flight 800* was released in 2013 and rehashed the myths of a missile strike and cover-up. That same year a group calling itself "The TWA 800 Project" petitioned the NTSB to reconsider its conclusions, claiming that a "detonation or high-velocity explosion" caused the crash. NTSB staff met with the petitioners' representatives and listened to an eyewitness describe what he saw on the night of the accident. Ultimately the NTSB did not reopen the case, concluding that "the evidence and analysis presented did not show the original findings were incorrect."[66] By then TWA had been gone for years. Sadly, the melodramatic, politically driven conspiracy theories proved more prevalent in the public consciousness than the facts.

The loss and trauma of Flight 800 in 1996 shook TWA's management and shattered company morale. Thanks to the ensuing media circus, bookings fell, and the airline again resorted to offering low-fare travel in an effort to fill seats, with no more success than when Icahn had tried a similar strategy years earlier. TWA's directors became increasingly concerned that the management team had lost its way. Dissatisfied with the lack of progress, the directors expressed concern that there was no plan to effectively address the company's needs. And the airline was again running out of cash.

New Leadership

Jeffrey Erickson departed as president and CEO in December 1996, reportedly because of friction with the board's labor members and criticism over the way he handled Flight 800's aftermath. The board chose Gerald Gitner, one of the directors elected by TWA's creditors, to replace him. Described as "one of the true prodigies of commercial aviation," Gitner had originally joined TWA straight out of business school in 1968 as an associate analyst working at the company's headquarters in New York City.[67] By 1972, at the age of 27, he was the vice president of TWA's scheduling department, responsible for managing all of the airline's revenue-producing activity.

In 1974, Gitner moved to Frank Lorenzo's Texas International Airlines, where he eventually became the senior vice president of marketing—and a staunch believer in deregulation. He left in 1980 to help found People Express Airlines, a low-cost carrier that briefly flourished during deregulation's early days. In 1982 he moved to struggling Pan American World Airways, then left in 1985 to head Lorenzo's Texas Air Corporation soon after Lorenzo made his run at TWA—and wisely declined an offer from

Gerry Gitner, TWA's last chairman, took over the demoralized airline in the aftermath of Flight 800. Gerald Gitner Collection.

Carl Icahn to become TWA's president after Icahn bested Lorenzo. A year later Gitner left the airline industry but returned to join TWA's new post-Icahn board in 1993. His background gave him a unique perspective on the challenges and opportunities that deregulation posed.

As TWA's vice chairman and acting CEO, Gitner moved into TWA's St. Louis corporate headquarters and recruited directors David Kennedy and Bill Compton to try and turn things around. Kennedy had been the CEO of Aer Lingus, the Irish flag carrier, and Gitner recognized Compton's abilities from serving alongside him on the board. Compton stepped down as the pilots' union chairman to join management, and the three of them functioned as a triumvirate: Kennedy focused on marketing, Compton on operations, and Gitner on everything else. Kennedy relinquished his management role and returned to the board when Donald Casey was hired as executive vice president for marketing in May 1997.

Trying to Survive

Upon arriving in St. Louis, Gitner was greeted with a recommendation that TWA pay all the taxes that were owed but not yet due and essentially shut down the company. But Gitner hadn't agreed to become CEO only to close the doors. TWA lost $284 million in 1996 and was in danger of running out of money again. The new leaders had to devise a survival strategy—and do it quickly.

The three leaders had no illusions that TWA could continue indefinitely as an independent carrier. The airline had to service too much debt, and the Karabu ticket agreement undermined efforts to increase TWA's revenue. Their main objective was to improve the airline as much as they could while searching for a merger partner. Accomplishing that required streamlining operations and replacing aging planes with new ones that would be more appealing to potential buyers. The triumvirate concluded that TWA would pay the employees and pay for fuel, but nothing else. They believed that if they survived the difficult 1996–1997 winter months, they could begin paying creditors again. The trio also had to convince the public that the airline wasn't going to fold.

In addition to its St. Louis hub, TWA still carried on substantial operations at New York's JFK during the late 1990s. It had the Flight Center for international flights, a separate domestic terminal, and an East Coast maintenance base. Domestic operations moved to the Flight Center as international activity declined, and most gates in the domestic terminal were subleased to other carriers. TWA's 1996 operating losses of $131 million in New York more than wiped out a $100 million profit at St. Louis.[68] Accordingly, TWA reduced activity at JFK in favor of St. Louis, where it faced less competition. TWA's daily departures from St. Louis increased to 350 in

1996, and TWA representatives talked about adding new international flights from St. Louis to Rome, Madrid, and Tel Aviv.[69]

Out with the Old, Again

A decade after the Ozark merger TWA was still operating the 50 former Ozark DC-9s, but these planes were now too small and uneconomical. They also required expensive modifications to comply with new noise regulations, as did its 39 Boeing 727 trijets. The 727s—along with 14 four-engine Boeing 747s and 11 Lockheed TriStars—all required flight engineers, averaged over 20 years in age, and were far from fuel efficient. Two of TWA's early 747s were the high time leaders for the type, having accumulated more than 100,000 flight hours each.

The Gitner team began replacing the aging wide-body fleet with additional Boeing 767s and ordered 27 new narrow-body Boeing 757s configured to carry 178 domestic passengers coast to coast via smaller airports such as New York–LaGuardia; Washington-Reagan; and John Wayne Airport in Santa Ana, California, allowing passengers to sidestep the congestion and delays at JFK, Dulles, and LAX. The modern aircraft in TWA's fleet now consisted of MD-80s, the backbone of domestic operations; Boeing 757s, which joined the MD-80s on domestic flights; and stretched Boeing 767-300s, used primarily on international routes.[70]

The team also moved to rationalize and streamline TWA's international operations. Money-losing routes from New York to Frankfurt plus Athens, and Boston to Paris, were discontinued in early 1997. TWA leadership placed greater emphasis on the St. Louis hub for its international and domestic operations. The airline added new service to vacation destinations Cancun and Puerto Vallarta, Mexico. Daily St. Louis departures were up to 365 by the end of the year.[71]

Improving its dismal operational performance would be crucial to turning TWA around. Gitner and Compton stressed the importance of getting the airplanes out on schedule and keeping them clean. TWA leaders insisted that flights leave on time—not 5 minutes, or even 1 minute later—and it worked. TWA had previously been in last place among the 10 major airlines in operating performance, but three months later it was almost in first.

Trying to Work Together

Building a good relationship between management and the union workforce—which still owned 30 percent of the airline—was another important part of the turnaround effort. Unlike Eastern under Frank Lorenzo, where management and labor were bitter adversaries, TWA's management wanted to work collaboratively with the unions. As a former union leader, Compton was tasked with motivating employees to come up with ways to make the airline more efficient and cost effective, but doing so would not be easy within the established union work rules. In the deregulated world of the late 1990s, practices from the 1970s and 1980s were no longer conducive to a successful operation. Union leaders and rank and file recognized that they had a stake in the airline and its success—and that their jobs were on the line. At the same time, they also wanted to see some benefits after their years of sacrifice.

TWA's machinists, fearing a possible shutdown of the JFK hub, called for Gitner's ouster in early 1997, but the flight attendants resisted. "The IAM does not alone represent the voice of labor at TWA," said a spokesperson for the flight attendants.[72] This was the first crack in the labor harmony that had prevailed since Icahn's departure. TWA's flight attendants had been represented by the Independent Federation of Flight Attendants since the late 1970s, but the machinists were now making a determined effort to replace IFFA—an organization they contended had been ineffective. IFFA president Sherry Cooper secretly negotiated a merger with the machinists only to have it rejected by her board, which triggered her resignation.

A representation election ensued. The machinists argued that TWA's 5,400 flight attendants would be better off as part of their 700,000-strong international union than with IFFA, which only represented TWA personnel. The Association of Flight Attendants also got into the act with an eleventh-hour write-in campaign. But the safety-in-numbers argument carried the day, with 62 percent of the flight attendants voting to be represented by the machinists.[73]

The board elevated Bill Compton to president and COO in December 1997, giving TWA the distinction of being the only airline led by an active commercial pilot. Compton had started his TWA career in 1968 as a Boeing 707 copilot, and like many of his TWA colleagues, he had endured lengthy furloughs. Now a captain, he remained on flight status and continued to fly the line periodically, renewing the tradition of pilot leaders such as Charles Lindbergh, Jack Frye, Paul Richter, and Howard Hughes.

Meanwhile litigation over the Karabu ticket agreement continued without resolution. Icahn thrived on using the legal system to harass his adversaries, so battling him was not a productive use of corporate time and resources. TWA management recognized that the courts might sustain Icahn's position and allow him to sell tickets through travel agents or directly to the public, in which case the company could "suffer significant loss of revenue that could reduce overall passenger yields on a continuing basis."[74] In reality, that had been occurring ever since the agreement was signed. TWA eventually lost in both the trial court and on appeal, and Karabu continued to deprive the airline of desperately needed revenue, even after the underlying debt to Icahn had been satisfied.

Hopeful Signs

Despite these many obstacles the new team cut TWA's 1997 losses by over 50 percent to $110 million. Efforts to improve employee spirit and motivation paid off when TWA won the J. D. Power Award for customer satisfaction in 1998—an impressive achievement from the low ebb in the aftermath of Flight 800 just two years earlier. TWA now had 21,000 employees, one-third fewer than in the pre-deregulation 1970s. In response to the growing popularity of personal computers and the internet, TWA started a website where passengers could book flights directly, and e-tickets began to replace traditional paper tickets.

Even with these steps in the right direction, TWA badly needed to replace the legacy DC-9s it had inherited from Ozark. Some of the planes were 30 years old, and there was much interest and speculation over whether TWA would buy from Boeing or Airbus. In December 1998, Gitner and Compton gave the answer. They announced that TWA had ordered 50 Boeing 717s for delivery beginning in 2000. The 717 was a modernized and greatly upgraded version of the DC-9, which Boeing had acquired through its merger with McDonnell Douglas a year earlier. TWA also announced an order for 50 Airbus A318s, a smaller version of the highly successful A320 series, and for 25 A320s. Deliveries were to begin in 2003 and 2005, respectively.

Placing these orders was a bold move for the struggling airline. Neither manufacturer was informed of the parallel negotiations with its competitor. Gitner and Compton succeeded in persuading both Boeing and Airbus that replacing TWA's 1970s-vintage short-haul planes with efficient new ones would have a major impact on its bottom line. But in the interim the airline did not have the cash to make progress payments. In a major coup, Gitner and Compton succeeded in getting both manufacturers to agree to finance the progress payments by adding them to the lease payments after the planes were delivered. As 1999 dawned, TWA had 125 new airplanes on order, all fully financed by the manufacturers.

TWA closed out 1998 with a net loss of $120 million, 10 percent more than 1997. Despite the progress they had made, Gitner and Compton could not cure TWA's underlying financial weakness or manage to achieve profitability. While outwardly continuing their efforts to recover from Flight 800 and improve TWA's operational and financial picture, they began quietly talking to other airlines about a merger or acquisition.

Union Tension

After more than a decade of trauma and concessions, TWA's unions were eager to regain some lost ground. The concessionary contracts during the airline's second bankruptcy were subject to revision in 1997, and negotiations began with the pilots, flight attendants, and ground workers. The pilots agreed to a new four-year contract in 1998, calling for wages to reach 90 percent of industry average by 2002. It would be their first pay raise since before the Icahn era. Yet they voted out their chairman, Joe Chronic, believing that he should have held out for higher pay raises and more favorable work rules in negotiating the 1998 contract. "I wish we had a militant union," said one pilot. "We gave up too much." Ironically, Chronic had been elected only 18 months earlier as a tougher-talking leader than his predecessor.[75]

Negotiations with the machinists proved more difficult. After taking over representation of the flight attendants, they controlled two-thirds of TWA's union employees and three of the four board seats reserved for TWA's unions. Their leaders were now ready to flex their muscles. They not only demanded more pay and more favorable work rules but also insisted on participating in management decisions affecting their members. In early 1999, Sherry Cooper, the flight attendants' representative and now a machinists' officer and TWA director, asserted that TWA could have generated $300 million in additional revenue in 1998 by adopting a more sophisticated yield and capacity management system. She contended that instead of concentrating on cost-cutting, TWA should focus on growing its business—precisely what management was attempting to do.[76]

Armed with a growing sense of power and militancy, the union leaders decided to play hardball in the contract negotiations. In May 1999 management advised the board that the impasse with the machinists was impacting future bookings as passengers switched to other airlines to avoid a possible strike and shutdown. In response the directors adopted a resolution authorizing TWA management to take "any and all actions deemed . . . to be necessary and proper to safeguard the Company's operation and to preserve the Company's assets." The general counsel denied that this was "an authorization to file bankruptcy," calling it "the delineation of the Company's authority to protect the Company's assets in the event and to the extent such action might be necessary."[77] It appeared that the machinists might be prepared to reprise their role in the 1991 demise of Eastern Air Lines.

TWA made its final offer on May 28. Union leaders recommended that the rank and file reject it. It was a dramatic reversal from the Icahn era: The union now held the upper hand because the airline could not withstand a strike. Compton managed to restart negotiations in an effort to formulate a proposal that union leadership would support. Once again Congressman Gephardt and St. Louis civic leaders intervened to keep the parties talking. Management agreed to wage increases and work-rule concessions, and on June 13 a tentative agreement was reached on a new 18-month contract, which the membership subsequently ratified. For flight attendants and union ground personnel, management approved a wage increase between 86 to 91 percent of industry average by 2003, depending on job classification, and the company agreed to continue operating its New York maintenance base.[78]

Thomas Buffenbarger, president of the International Association of Machinists and Aerospace Workers, credited Gephardt with the breakthrough, writing in a letter to the *St. Louis Post-Dispatch* that the congressman "was always there, checking on progress and offering ideas of his own. His interest was sincere and real, and his assistance was a major force in the final agreement that the union is recommending to its members."[79] But the uncertainty caused by labor tension contributed to a nearly 7 percent loss in revenue at a time when TWA desperately needed every dollar.

St. Louis Blues

The St. Louis hub played an ever-larger role in TWA's operations as domestic activity displaced international business. International travel had historically been TWA's forte, but by 1998 domestic flights made up nearly 90 percent of its passenger revenue. "TWA believes one of its greatest opportunities for improved operational results will continue to come from focusing resources on its St. Louis hub in order to leverage its strong market position," TWA told its owners and creditors. "Because St. Louis is located in the center of the

TWA jets crowded the ramp at St. Louis's Lambert Airport in 1994. TWA's burgeoning traffic volumes at its St. Louis hub prompted efforts to expand the airport. Photo by George Hamlin.

country, it is well-suited to serve as an omni-directional hub for both north-south and east-west transcontinental traffic." TWA's 360 daily departures from St. Louis constituted 76 percent of all its traffic.[80]

St. Louis had been an important part of TWA's route structure since the airline's inception, and TWA had always been Lambert Airport's most important carrier. Lambert had undergone significant expansion in the 1950s and was one of the first airports to host jets when TWA inaugurated its Boeing 707 service in 1959. However, the city failed to acquire land for expansion when it was still available, and the airport was now landlocked, surrounded by suburbs, highways, and industrial development, including the McDonnell Douglas manufacturing complex. More than 20 million passengers were using Lambert by 1987—double the total in 1980—and more than the highest estimates made in the 1970s, thanks to the TWA hub.

Although Lambert's two parallel main runways were long enough to accommodate the planes using the airport, they were too close together to allow simultaneous instrument landings in bad weather. Consequently, 20 percent of the time Lambert was effectively a one-runway airport, and delays were becoming a serious problem. The airport sorely needed another runway, but acquiring the needed land would inevitably lead to major disruptions and cost—as well as bitter opposition from those who would be affected.

Efforts to expand Lambert began in 1989, when city officials announced a master plan involving four proposals, each of which involved taking substantial portions of the adjoining suburban city of Bridgeton. Detractors formed an organization called Bridgeton Air Defense—known as "BAD" by friend and foe alike—that would be the public face of the opposition for the next decade. Bridgeton also enlisted the support of local politicians. This opposition, combined with shortcomings in the expansion proposals, thwarted the airport's initial expansion efforts. But the battle was far from over.[81]

Traffic grew to more than 23 million passengers and 480,000 landings and takeoffs by 1994, which only intensified the pressure to expand. In April 1995, Lambert officials unveiled six new alternative plans that could handle the predicted future growth to 42 million passengers and 630,000 landings and takeoffs by 2015. Three months later St. Louis officials announced the selection of a plan known as W-1W, which called for buying and removing 1,500 homes and 70 businesses, displacing approximately 5,000 Bridgeton residents.[82]

Bridgeton city officials promptly swung into action, vowing to fight the new plan and proclaiming that they would "drag it through the courts in the hope of killing it." They also hired a major Washington, DC, law firm to fight the expansion. After three years of contentious proceedings the FAA approved W-1W in September 1998, finding it the least disruptive and most economical of the feasible alternatives. TWA welcomed the decision.[84]

Undaunted, Bridgeton filed suit in the United States Court of Appeals seeking to block the FAA approval. It also sued in Missouri state court, claiming that the new runway could not be built without complying with Bridgeton's zoning codes. Meanwhile, passenger traffic at Lambert continued to grow, reaching 30 million in 1999.[85] On April 7, 2000, the United States Court of Appeals affirmed the FAA's decision. It held that the FAA had properly weighed and reasonably selected W-1W over the other plans, saying that it would not "second-guess the substantive merits of the FAA's decision."[86] Four days later the Missouri Court of Appeals ruled against Bridgeton on its zoning claim.[87] After 10 years Lambert could at last proceed with expansion. But the question was whether it was too late to help save TWA.

THE HIGH AND THE MIGHTY

Even as its struggles continued, TWA had the distinction of carrying Pope John Paul II on two papal visits to the United States in the late 1990s. In October 1995 the pope made a five-day trip to the US, which included addressing the United Nations General Assembly and celebrating Mass in Yankee Stadium and Central Park. He flew to Baltimore for more events, then back to Rome on TWA. The airline tailored the interior of a Boeing 767 to accommodate the pope and his entourage. A papal suite was installed at the front of the passenger compartment, complete with a bed and furnishings befitting their high-profile occupant. Some of the furniture and decorations were the same that had been used during the 1987 papal visit; they were loaned back to TWA by a Kansas City museum.

Three years later, on January 26, 1999, the pope arrived in St. Louis for a whirlwind 31-hour visit, wherein the 78-year-old pontiff "managed to take part in a lively youth rally, celebrate Mass with 104,000 people, lead an ecumenical service at the New Cathedral, and persuade [Governor Mel Carnahan] to spare a condemned man."[88] Once again the Vatican selected TWA to fly him back to Rome from St. Louis on a specially outfitted Boeing 767.

The Last Aviator

In March 1999, Gitner advised TWA's board that he was stepping down as CEO, having accomplished his objective of pulling TWA out of its post–Flight 800 nadir. Effective May 25 he became the non-executive chairman of the board, chairman of the executive committee, and a consultant. Bill Compton was elected president and CEO on the same day, and once again an active pilot held the airline's top position. Although he feared it might harm the airline financially, Compton approved pay increases for both TWA's union and non-union employees for the first time in 15 years. TWA also managed to improve its on-time record from worst in the industry to the best in 1999, and it took home the J. D. Power Award once more.

Compton was a believer in employee-ownership. In a deregulated world, he thought customer service would set apart the successful carriers—and that employee-ownership directly contributed to better service. "When employees become shareholders," he said, "they also become interested in the financial returns of the company. They begin to understand that everything comes from the customer." He also saw it as a means to reduce the historically adverse relationship between labor and management in the industry. Still, he acknowledged that employee-ownership had not been entirely successful. Stock was typically put into stock ownership plans or retirement programs, and "employees cannot buy new refrigerators, new cars or pay the rent with that stock until they've retired or left the company."[89]

The history of employee-ownership at TWA reflected this reality. Following Icahn's removal, workforce morale and dedication soared. Union workers accepted concessions to help the airline through its second bankruptcy and reorganization while ceding one-third of their ownership stake. But even their achievements and sacrifices could not cure TWA's financial woes. By the late 1990s union leaders were questioning management's ability to solve the company's problems and again adopted a more adversarial posture.

With airport expansion finally moving ahead in St. Louis, TWA's prospects appeared to be improving. But the airline's financial condition remained precarious; it was still burdened by debt and the Karabu ticket deal. Despite all the progress made, TWA lost $352 million in 1999—more than double the losses of the two prior years combined.

Entering the New Century

TWA began the 21st century in much the same condition it had been in for the last decade of the 20th—struggling to survive. It now faced a new challenge in the growing importance of regional jets, a trend that began in the mid-1990s. Under code-sharing agreements, major airlines contracted with regionals to carry passengers to and from outlying destinations, with reservations and ticket pricing done through the major lines. TWA had contracted with regional airline partners to feed passengers into its St. Louis and New York hubs since the 1980s under the Trans World Express banner. Previously the regional carriers had operated small turboprop planes with a distinctly lower level of service than the major airlines, but that began to change when the first regional jets appeared. Carrying 50 passengers with jet speed and comfort, the Bombardier CRJ and Embraer 145 had the potential to take over some of the majors' own routes, and the industry quickly embraced the new opportunity. Small regional jets could offer better service to cities that otherwise received limited flights or none at all. But the unions resisted outsourcing their work to small, often non-union operators, and they imposed limits on the number and size of regional jets that could be used through collective-bargaining agreements.[90]

The regional jet trend presented a significant competitive challenge to TWA, which was characteristically late to adopt it. It started offering a few regional jet flights in the Midwest through its Trans States partner in March 2000 but took a more significant leap when it entered into a new agreement with Indianapolis-based Chautauqua Airlines. Operating as Trans World Express, in August 2000 Chautauqua began flying Embraer 145s on routes between St. Louis and Shreveport, Louisiana; Cincinnati, Ohio; Jackson, Mississippi; Knoxville, Tennessee; and other destinations previously served by TWA with DC-9s or MD-80s.

TWA's unions reacted cautiously to the potential job losses to non-union regional affiliates but recognized that regional jets could help develop new markets and increase revenues. The pilots and machinists agreed to allow TWA to expand regional jet service as long as its core system crew continued to fly a specified ratio of flights. Gary Poos, the machinists' chairman who represented 16,000 of TWA's 20,500 employees, expressed a preference for the airline to own a regional carrier, but financial realities ruled out that option.[91]

Meanwhile, TWA continued modernizing its own fleet. In December 1999 it took delivery of its last MD-80—the final MD-80 to roll off the production line—and its last Boeing 757s. In February 2000 it began receiving the Boeing 717s, the final version of the venerable DC-9 series. And in late 2000 it retired the last of its legacy DC-9s and Boeing 727s, ending decades of service by these reliable but now outdated and uneconomical jetliners. In just two years TWA had gone from having the oldest fleet in the industry to one of the newest. Gitner and Compton had accomplished all the goals they had set for themselves, except finding a merger partner.

In the first half of 2000 the airline lost $80 million with no sign of improvement on the horizon. The Karabu ticket agreement continued to deprive it of desperately needed revenue, and fuel prices sharply increased. Struggling to meet its obligations, TWA failed to make payments owed to employee retirement funds in October, causing the machinists—whose contract was up for renegotiation in January 2001—to threaten legal action against the company.[92] The real ticking time bomb, however, was a $100 million loan coming due on January 15, 2001. TWA lacked both the cash to pay it off and the credibility to successfully refinance it. Icahn delivered yet another blow to TWA employees in December when he announced he would terminate the two pension funds he'd agreed to support in the 1992 bankruptcy, turning them over to the Pension Benefit Guaranty Corporation. Retired TWA pilots—who had paved the way for Icahn's takeover 15 years earlier—were among those who saw their pension benefits reduced.[93]

Trying to Get Married

Throughout 2000, Compton struggled to find a willing merger partner. He met with the CEOs of all the major airlines, and some of the smaller ones, to pitch the possibility of making a deal. His goal was to protect as many employee jobs as possible, which was a hard sell to other airlines. Some showed interest, but none were willing to take more than 10 percent of TWA's workforce. In reality, most competitors would have preferred to liquidate TWA and feast on the carcass, as had happened to Braniff, Eastern, and Pan American—a fate Compton badly wanted to avoid.

American Airlines emerged as the only prospect interested in merging with TWA. It was cramped for space at its Dallas and O'Hare hubs, and TWA and American both had large MD-80 fleets—and some of TWA's were newer. The question was whether Compton could get American to the altar before TWA's money ran out. The $100 million debt was coming due, and TWA had nothing left to sell or mortgage. Unable to secure additional financing, it appeared that TWA would be forced to shut down and liquidate as 2000 drew to a close.

Chapter 10
THE NEW MILLENNIUM: 2001 AND BEYOND

The new year 2001 brought more troubling news when the Standard & Poor's credit rating service put TWA on its watch list. The agency noted that as of September 30, 2000, the airline had only $157 million in available cash reserves, "modest for a carrier of TWA's size and for the seasonally slow [winter] period it is entering." The agency added that TWA was vulnerable because of its "limited route structure, weak financial profile, and lack of significant alliances with other airlines." It also pointed to the uncertainty surrounding the imminent renegotiation of the machinists' union contract.[1]

The End of the Line for "The Lindbergh Line"

With time running out, Bill Compton and American Airlines chairman and CEO Donald J. Carty announced on January 10, 2001—just five days before the $100 million loan was due to mature—that American would purchase TWA. "TWA is one way or another going to disappear as a corporate entity," said Carty. "So what we are doing by acquiring TWA is simply preserving 21,000 jobs and a very important and vital hub operation."[2] Airline analysts agreed that Compton did everything possible to save TWA, but the company simply ran out of options.

"Like you, I am saddened by the knowledge that this process will culminate in the retirement of the oldest and proudest name in the airline industry," Compton told TWA employees. "On the other hand, I am heartened by the knowledge that our agreement with American includes provisions to keep TWA flying and preserve the jobs of TWA employees during the transition period." He pointed with pride to the achievements of the past four years. "We used to run a poor operation," he said. "We had little cash in the bank and almost no ability to access the capital markets. Our fleet was too old and inefficient, and our route system was out of step with our customers' needs. Working together, we made great strides. Today, we are in many ways the industry leader, with billions of dollars' worth of new, customer-pleasing aircraft. We lead the industry in operational reliability and on-time performance."[3] But even these achievements could not surmount TWA's financial burdens.

The agreement with American provided $200 million in short-term financing to forestall a shutdown and allow TWA to continue operating during the transition. American would pay $300 million for TWA's assets, including all of its aircraft and supporting facilities, and assume $3 billion worth of equipment leases for TWA's planes and other assets. For this to happen, however, TWA would have to make one final trip to bankruptcy court. The proceedings would allow American to shed unwanted obligations, including the Karabu ticket deal, and the lease agreements for the new Boeing 717s and Airbus planes, none of which had a place in American's fleet.

Most important, American agreed to retain all of TWA's current employees, fulfilling Compton's primary objective. And Carty extolled the benefits of the deal for the St. Louis area. "St. Louis is going to take its rightful place as one of the country's major hubs," he told the local media. The jobs of St. Louis workers would be protected, and most would earn more money with American than they had with TWA. The sale, he predicted, would be completed by April, but the details were not spelled out.[4] "Seniority issues raised over the merger of the American and TWA pilot lists—on down the line for all flying personnel—could mean a bloody battle," said a Washington University labor law expert.[5] It was an accurate prediction.

No sooner was the agreement announced than Carl Icahn tried to disrupt it. Claiming he had a plan that would have kept TWA independent and avoided bankruptcy, he threatened to sue American for dumping the Karabu agreement two years before it expired and vowed to oppose the American deal in the bankruptcy proceedings. This gambit came from an attempt by TWA's machinists to launch their own rescue effort, and it was denounced by TWA spokesman Mark Abels as "basically false."[6] Having already inflicted mortal damage on TWA, Icahn now characteristically sought to undermine its rescue by American.

Going Broke, Again

The downside of putting TWA into Chapter 11 was that it allowed others (including Icahn, Continental Airlines, and Northwest Airlines) to file objections and criticize various aspects of the plan.[7] Continental claimed that American was trying to "steal" TWA's assets and said it would buy some of them for $400 million—and somehow make a deal with TWA to keep it operating independently. Northwest offered to buy TWA's share of the Worldspan reservation system, while Icahn said he would support "others who would reorganize TWA as an independent carrier" to preserve the Karabu agreement.[8]

Cadres of lawyers descended on the bankruptcy court in Wilmington, Delaware, for the initial hearing. Icahn's lawyers attacked the plan, particularly a program designed to retain key managers during the transition period. They pointed out that one-third of the $4.7 million allocated to the program would go to TWA's top three executives, including Compton. Afterward Compton was trapped in a courthouse elevator with a dozen others for more than an hour before a fire rescue team led them up ladders to the escape route. While waiting to be rescued, a TWA pilot caught in the elevator cracked, "I guess we're all getting paid back for the times we told people on the PA system it would just be a few minutes."[9] Following the hearing, American's general counsel said the airline would not proceed with the deal if the court did not reject the Karabu ticket agreement, emphasizing, "We are not prepared to purchase any liability of Karabu."[10]

Compton went from the courtroom to a congressional hearing room where senators weighed in on the merger. Missouri governor Bob Holden, plus Missouri senators Christopher "Kit" Bond and Jean Carnahan, testified in favor, while John McCain, chairman of the US Senate Committee on Commerce, and ranking member Fritz Hollings grilled witnesses and voiced concerns about preserving competition in the airline industry. The key witnesses were Compton and American's president Don Carty. "Time is of the essence with respect to TWA" Carty told the senators. It had "run out of money, time, and options" and had already consumed more than three-quarters of the short-term financing American had provided. "We at American cannot commit our shareholders' money to keep TWA afloat indefinitely," Carty said.[11]

Compton spoke about the commitment and sacrifices TWA's employees had made in trying to save the airline that had been thwarted by harsh economic realities. "In fact," he told the senators, "by January 10, 2001, TWA had cash on hand of only $20 million and needed significantly more just to make it through the next day." He dismissed the claims of other carriers that TWA could somehow continue to operate independently, calling them "disingenuous and self-serving" and pointing out that American's offer was the only one actually on the table.[12]

Another hearing before the Senate Judiciary Committee followed, primarily about the effect airline mergers would have on competition. The notion that merging TWA with American would somehow further reduce competition in an industry where consolidation had been happening for more than 20 years was absurd. TWA was unable to continue operating independently, so it couldn't compete with any other airline. Either it would go out of business and be liquidated with the loss of 20,000 jobs, or the airline and its employees would become part of American. Senator Patrick Leahy said the country was headed toward "an oligopoly of three major carriers," but the TWA merger did not present serious competition issues and was needed to protect jobs. While calling for a nine-month freeze on all proposed airline mergers, Senator Charles Schumer said, "This acquisition would not lower competition; it would increase it."[13]

Getting to the Altar

The focus shifted from Congress back to the bankruptcy court proceedings, where parties with dubious motives sought to intervene. The first to do so was an unknown startup entity calling itself Jet Acquisitions Group Inc. Its backers included a financier who falsely claimed to be a faculty member at Ohio University, a Sri Lankan investor who was under investigation for operating an unlicensed bank, an Arizona lawyer, and an aviation consultant who falsely claimed to have been a Pan American Airlines pilot. This group said it would bid $889 million and take over TWA's debts. "If we didn't have any money, we could bid more, too," Carty joked.[14] Another would-be bidder, Galileo International, offered $220 million for TWA's remaining interest in the Worldspan reservation system.[15]

After the deadline for bids had passed, Icahn surfaced yet again, bankrolling another newly formed entity called TWA Acquisitions Group, which offered $650 million for TWA. Although it was promoted by Brian Freeman, the same investment banker who had represented the TWA machinists in supporting Icahn's 1985 takeover, the union was quick to disassociate itself from this ploy. The machinists objected that it would require them to relinquish their contractual protections, pending incorporation into American's labor contracts. TWA agreed to extend the deadline and consider the bid.[16] American responded by sweetening its offer from $500 million to $742 million at TWA's request, allowing for secured creditors to be paid in full. TWA's board promptly accepted, informing the other bidders that their offers were rejected.

Final approval of the American deal was now up to the court. A contentious hearing ensued when the Icahn-backed TWA Acquisitions Group purported to up its offer to $1.1 billion. American took depositions of Icahn and Freeman, in which Freeman admitted that the purpose of their proposal was to force a settlement of the Karabu agreement, and Icahn said it required "labor savings" of $40 million from the pilots and $60 million from the machinists. In effect, Icahn wanted to turn back the clock to 1991 and resume his labor warfare. Judge Peter Walsh dismissed Icahn's offer as "a joke" and refused to allow his lawyers to call any witnesses.[17]

Meanwhile, TWA was again running out of money. It spent $3 million in cash every day and had only $38 million on hand. Moreover, TWA required additional interim financing from American to avoid shutting down.[18] On March 12, 2001, Judge Walsh approved the sale of TWA to American, finding that otherwise there would be "an immediate and precipitous decline" in TWA's financial status and a high probability of liquidation. The final price for TWA was $4.2 billion, including an additional $130 million to keep TWA operating, $742 million in cash, and American's assumption of $3.2 billion worth of TWA lease obligations. TWA pilots' union chairman Robert Pastore expressed confidence that his members would get "fair and equitable seniority integration" with the American pilots, but it was not to be.[19]

Getting Married

The merger agreement was consummated on April 9, 2001. Hundreds of TWA employees and their families attended a ceremony at TWA's St. Louis operations center to mark the occasion. Positioned nose to nose, an American Boeing 777 and a TWA 757 provided the backdrop for speeches from Missouri political figures and leaders of both airlines. Some flight attendants showed up in vintage TWA hostess uniforms. Many attendees were former Ozark personnel who had survived the Ozark-TWA merger 15 years earlier. All were now employees of TWA LLC, the entity created to carry on TWA's operations, pending its integration into American. The two jets then took off, made a low pass over downtown St. Louis and the Gateway Arch, then headed west to Kansas City for another celebration at the TWA maintenance facility. The Kansas City festivities were marred when the tug assigned to position the American 777 in front of the hangar broke down and delayed the event by more than an hour, symbolizing the difficulties in uniting the two airlines.[20]

With the celebrations over, the hard work of incorporating TWA's physical, financial, and human resources could begin. Bill Compton agreed to stay on as president of TWA LLC while that process took place. During this period the TWA planes were repainted in a combination of American's colors and TWA's logo with the words "An American Airlines Company."

Integrating the fleets would prove much easier than combining the union workforces. As a condition of the purchase agreement, American hired almost all of TWA's unionized employees, contingent on eliminating certain labor protective provisions in their contracts. The TWA pilots' right to have seniority integration issues arbitrated in the event of a purchase or merger was one of them, and American would not proceed with the deal unless it was eliminated. The TWA pilots, represented by the Air Line Pilots Association (ALPA), refused. The American pilots were represented by the Allied Pilots Association (APA) under a collective-bargaining agreement providing that, in the event of a merger, pilots from the merged airline would be "stapled to the bottom" of the seniority list as if they were new hires. The stage was set for another battle over seniority, much like the struggle between the Ozark and TWA pilots 15 years earlier. TWA filed a motion in bankruptcy court to abrogate the protective provisions in the ALPA collective-bargaining agreement, and the TWA pilots agreed to waive

As many ex-TWA jetliners entered service with American Airlines, they were marked with hybrid TWA-American logos such as this Boeing 757 in 2001. Alan Hoffman Collection.

their seniority protection in exchange for American's promise to "use its reasonable best efforts" with APA to "secure a fair and equitable process for the integration of seniority."[21]

The day the merger was consummated, ALPA and the TWA pilots entered into a transition agreement with TWA LLC stating that the existing collective-bargaining agreement between ALPA and TWA would remain in effect until the National Mediation Board determined that the two airlines had become a single carrier. The transition agreement also incorporated American's promise to "use its reasonable best efforts" to ensure a fair seniority integration process. ALPA would remain the exclusive representative of the TWA LLC pilots until the mediation board made the single-carrier determination. One day later TWA LLC began operations, and the TWA pilots became employees of TWA LLC.[22]

Inevitably the TWA and American pilots failed to agree on seniority integration. American entered into an agreement with its pilots known as "Supplement CC," which provided limited protections for some TWA pilots, effective once the National Mediation Board declared American and TWA LLC to be a single carrier. Supplement CC called for TWA pilots to be added to the seniority list after 2,500 American pilots, at a 1 to 8 ratio. More than half of the TWA pilots would be stapled to the bottom of the seniority list, behind all American pilots hired before the merger date. Not surprisingly, the TWA pilots refused to accept Supplement CC.

The American pilots asked the mediation board to declare the airlines a single carrier effective December 2001. A spokesman for the TWA pilots said they were angry: "American purchased valuable assets with TWA, and part of those assets are the employees—and we're being treated unfairly."[23] For the former Ozark pilots who had gone to work for TWA, the scenario was painfully reminiscent of their 1986 seniority battle.

Expanding Lambert

Back in St. Louis, construction of Lambert's controversial new runway began on July 30, 2001. St. Louis mayor Francis Slay declared, "Today we embark on a long-awaited project that will provide a tremendous boost to our economy. Expanding and modernizing Lambert International Airport is one of the most important things we can do to ensure our economic future." Don Carty called the Lambert expansion "the crown jewel" of the merger. The new runway, he said, would allow the airline to "follow through on our commitment to grow and develop our new hub for many, many years to come." Moreover, he added, a new terminal with additional gates would be needed to allow St. Louis to supplement American's busy hubs at Chicago and Dallas–Ft. Worth.[24]

The integration of TWA into American continued throughout 2001. While heading TWA LLC, Bill Compton continued to fly the line as an active airline captain, which gave him the opportunity to talk with TWA employees on the job and observe the process firsthand. By September he concluded that the transition was on track and announced he would retire on October 1. Then, in a single day, everything changed.

9/11

At 8:46 a.m. on September 11, 2001, American Flight 11 struck the World Trade Center's North Tower. Seventeen minutes later United Flight 175 struck the South Tower. At 9:37 a.m. American Flight 77 hit the Pentagon, and at 10:03 a.m. United Flight 93 crashed near Shanksville, Pennsylvania. The FAA immediately grounded all airline and non-emergency civilian aircraft and closed US airspace to international flights.

These terror attacks changed American history and traumatized the nation. No industry suffered more than the US airlines as travelers shunned flying and businesses froze non-essential travel. Moreover, the heightened security requirements that followed made air travel increasingly time consuming, burdensome, and unpleasant.[25] Congress created the Transportation Security Administration to take over airport security from private contractors hired by the airlines. Passengers now had to endure lengthy lines to undergo rigorous and intrusive screening—and they were charged a "September 11 Security Fee" for doing so.[26]

Air travel demand in the United States fell by more than 30 percent in the aftermath of 9/11, and the number of passengers traveling by air did not rebound to pre–9/11 levels for three years.[27] The airline industry began drastically cutting flights and capacity, then slowly added seats as passengers returned, which made for crowded planes. Legacy airlines slashed employment and flights to reduce expenses. Meanwhile, Southwest Airlines and other low-cost carriers expanded their capacity and market share.[28]

The 9/11 attacks dashed all underlying assumptions about TWA's merger with American. American Airlines' traffic declined by 11 percent, and revenue fell by 17 percent. The newly combined airline sustained a record loss of $414 million for the third quarter of 2001, even after receiving $508 million in government aid. The airline reduced flights by 20 percent, cut 20,000 jobs, and deferred delivery of 29 new airplanes. American was not alone; seven of the nine largest US carriers booked third-quarter losses, and the industry was on track to lose more than $5 billion for the full year.[29]

American sustained another blow on November 12, 2001, when American Flight 587, an Airbus A300 bound for the Dominican Republic, crashed after takeoff from New York's JFK. All 260 passengers and crew and five people on the ground perished. The public immediately feared another terrorist attack, but no such evidence emerged, and pilot error was determined to be the cause. It was one more setback in American's efforts to recover from 9/11 and absorb TWA into its operations.

The Last Aviator

Bill Compton was at the controls of Flight 220—TWA's commemorative last passenger flight—from Kansas City to St. Louis on December 1, 2001. TWA employees and family members vied with the media for seats. Passengers received a certificate signed by Compton bearing the flight number and the names of the cockpit and cabin crew, plus a box lunch including a bottle of merlot and a souvenir wine glass. The flight received a water cannon salute from the airport fire department at Kansas City, prompting the tower controller to ask if someone was retiring. Compton replied, "Yes, TWA is retiring." A cheering crowd of "teary-eyed employees, retirees and sentimental customers" greeted the flight at St. Louis.[30] "Time and again the people of TWA have done the seemingly impossible to keep the airline afloat," Compton wrote afterward. "I congratulate each and every employee of TWA on a job well done. This is not the end of TWA; it is a new beginning. American is lucky to have us."[31]

Bill Compton, TWA's last pilot leader, was the captain of the airline's final passenger flight on December 1, 2001. James A. Finley/AP/Shutterstock.

There was a remarkable symmetry in this ending. Charles Lindbergh had helped create Transcontinental Air Transport, piloted its first eastbound flight in 1929, and later served as TWA's technical adviser. Jack Frye led TWA in the 1930s and 1940s, and he helped make it an international airline. Aviator Howard Hughes owned and controlled the company for 20 years, spearheaded the Constellation's development, and guided TWA to postwar success. After saving TWA from liquidation, Bill Compton, TWA's last president, piloted its final scheduled flight.

Labor Pains

In January 2002, American announced it would cease operating TWA's new Boeing 717s. American also revealed it would furlough 229 TWA pilots and 834 flight attendants the next month.[32] Meanwhile, the struggle over seniority grew increasingly bitter. ALPA filed a grievance on behalf of the TWA pilots contending that American had failed to use its "reasonable best efforts" to obtain a fair and equitable seniority agreement and requested arbitration to block the American–APA agreement. After hundreds of pilots had already been furloughed in the aftermath of 9/11, more TWA pilots followed, but American pilots were recalled. It was not what TWA employees had expected when the merger was hailed as their salvation the year before.[33]

In September 2002 a group of former TWA pilots filed a class action suit alleging that ALPA had breached its duty of fair representation by failing to adequately represent the combined TWA-American pilot group and failing to challenge certification of APA as the collective-bargaining agent for the combined pilot group. It further charged that ALPA had a conflict of interest because it was simultaneously attempting to recruit the American pilots to join ALPA and curry favor with them—a scenario much like the conflict of interest the Ozark pilots faced in 1986.

American Slips

Don Carty joined other airline executives in seeking federal assistance for the struggling post–9/11 airline industry in September 2002, telling the House Subcommittee on Aviation that the new security expenses were reaching up to $4 billion annually. After losing a record $7.3 billion in 2001, the industry was on track to lose another $6 to $7 billion in 2002 and asked Congress for a combination of cash and tax relief. "Without relief, our efforts to control our own costs will likely prove futile," Carty said. "More painful new cutbacks, employee furloughs, labor concessions, and bankruptcies will be unavoidable." He predicted deep service cuts in the event of a war with Iraq.[34] "Our industry's viability is seriously in question," said Delta Air Lines chairman Leo Mullin. Congress was not particularly sympathetic to their pleas and expressed an unwillingness to "be preoccupied with short-term fixes while fundamental flaws in this industry are allowed to exist and fester."[35]

One month later American announced plans to ground 42 planes, including 28 MD-80s received from TWA. It furloughed 695 pilots, 406 of them former TWA pilots who were based in St. Louis. In the year since 9/11, American had laid off 1,728 flight attendants, nearly half of whom were former TWA personnel, and more furloughs were expected to come. Carty attributed the company's "terrible financial results" to "a sluggish economy, continued weakness in the revenue environment, high fuel prices, the cost of enhanced security and the uncertainty of events in the Middle East."[36]

By early 2003, American, which had brought TWA out of bankruptcy less than two years earlier, was itself at risk of landing in bankruptcy court. It lost a record $3.5 billion in 2002. "American wouldn't be in this mess today if it hadn't bought TWA," one analyst said. "It would still be a mess, just not as big a mess." The $3 billion in assumed TWA liabilities weighed heavily on American, as did TWA's continuing revenue problems. American also faced difficult contract negotiations with its unions.[37]

Concessions and Contracts

American disclosed its concession demands in February 2003. It sought $1.8 billion in savings, of which $1.6 billion was to come from its union workforce. The former TWA reservations office in Norfolk, Virginia, would be closed, and an additional 750 flight attendants would be laid off—most of them ex-TWA employees based in St. Louis.[38] Carty told an audience of St. Louis business leaders that the airline was losing $5 million a day and that changes were needed soon. He acknowledged that what the airline was asking of its employees was "far from trivial," but United Air Lines and US Airways were already operating under bankruptcy protection. Without employee concessions, American might have to do the same.[39]

Because the former TWA pilots and flight attendants were stapled to the bottom of the seniority lists, they took the brunt of the furloughs. The flight attendants' contract did not even provide severance pay for those laid off, and many blamed the union for failing to represent their interests.[40] Management and non-union employees were also affected. Carty took a 33 percent pay cut and received no bonus for a third straight year.[41]

The flight attendants voted down the new contract negotiated by their leaders, only to reverse themselves in a second vote two days later. The ex-TWA flight attendants sued American and their union over their lost seniority rights and attempted to block the second vote as invalid. The mechanics and ground workers, represented at American by the Transport Workers Union, narrowly approved their new contract. The airline had lawyers standing by to file for bankruptcy if any of these contract votes failed.[42]

Immediately after the unions voted to accept their new contracts, American released its 2002 financial report. It disclosed that management had created a pension trust for 45 of its top executives to protect their retirement income in the event of a bankruptcy filing. Moreover, management had offered six top executives "cash retention bonuses" equal to double their base salary if they remained on board through January. Despite a cut to his base salary, Carty benefited from these perks.[43] It was an extraordinary error in judgment.

Withholding such information until after the unions had voted predictably infuriated the airline's rank and file. "Our members have been duped," said an officer of the Transport Workers Union. "If they had known this information before they voted, it could have made a significant difference in the outcome."[44] The *St. Louis Post-Dispatch* agreed. "To John Q. Public, the shenanigans at American Airlines are outrageous." The newspaper asked, "Why should a bunch of executives who have flown the company to the brink of bankruptcy get bonuses and pension sweeteners at the same time that employees are being laid off?"[45] There was no good answer.

American's management quickly rescinded the executive bonuses in response to the tidal wave of negative publicity, but the irrevocable pension protection trust remained in place. It proved to be Carty's undoing; he stepped down as chairman on April 24, 2003. Carty's replacement as American's CEO was 44-year-old Gerald Arpey, whose father had been a member of the TWA finance team in the pre-Icahn era. Arpey had been hired by American as a financial analyst in 1982, and within a month he was participating in strategy sessions with the airline's CEO. Praised by Wall Street as "brutally analytical,"[46] Arpey wasted no time in justifying this description.

Only days after Arpey took office, layoff notices began going out to 2,200 pilots, 2,400 flight attendants, 1,300 maintenance workers, and 1,200 ground-service employees, including nearly all the former TWA employees now at the bottom of the seniority lists.[47] Once again, Missouri's congressional delegation went to bat for them. Senator Bond called a hearing of the Senate Health, Education, Labor, and Pension Committee to consider whether "promises were made and promises were broken" in the merger process. Ex-TWA employees accused American of doing just that. "American Airlines has broken its commitment to all former TWA employees when it promised a fair and equitable process to determine seniority integration," said a former flight attendant with a special needs child who was facing a furlough that would eliminate her healthcare coverage. An American vice president for employee relations countered that the TWA employees "knew exactly what they were doing" when they waived their rights to seniority arbitration, which American had made a precondition of the merger agreement.[48]

A group of former TWA flight attendants filed suit against the Association of Professional Flight Attendants, which represented American's attendants, alleging that the union had discriminated against them when it negotiated concessions that gave the airline the right to change work rules and lay them off. The former TWA attendants asked the court to block the impending furloughs, but the court held that the flight attendants had not demonstrated improper action by the union or irreparable harm if the layoffs proceeded, and that American, its other employees, and the traveling public would be harmed if an injunction was granted and American was forced into bankruptcy.[49] The former TWA pilots fared little better; their suit against ALPA and the airline was dismissed, as the court found no breach of duty to the pilots by ALPA or wrongdoing by American.[50]

Emotions ran so high that the University of Missouri–St. Louis dropped plans to confer honorary degrees upon Carty and Compton, even though Compton had retired from TWA and had no responsibility for American's actions. A university spokesperson said the institution feared "people would lose sight of why the university would honor Mr. Compton," who had facilitated the donation of TWA's corporate records to the St. Louis Mercantile Library housed on the campus.[51]

The TWA employees had no alternative when they agreed to waive their seniority rights to facilitate the American merger in 2001. If they had refused, the merger would not have happened, TWA would have shut down and liquidated, and they all would have been out of work. They played the weak hand they'd been dealt and kept working for two more years. If not for 9/11 and the blows sustained by the entire airline industry in its aftermath, things might have worked out differently. Their seniority losses were similar to those sustained by the Ozark pilots at the hands of their TWA co-workers in 1986, who were now experiencing a second traumatic merger.

A Hub No Longer

As the pink slips were going out to former TWA employees, Gerald Arpey made an announcement that sent more shivers down St. Louis's spine: "The reality is we will not be able to fly every nonstop route we fly today, nor will we be able to provide the same level of service in markets that cannot profitably support our current flight schedule." Translation: The former TWA hub in St. Louis was expendable. American had been shedding planes ever since the service reductions in the wake of 9/11 and was cutting its daily departures from St. Louis.[52] Missouri governor Bob Holden and St. Louis mayor Francis Slay flew to Dallas to plead with Arpey. They offered incentives and encouraged him to maintain the hub operation but returned empty-handed, telling reporters, "We think we have done everything we can, but in the end [we] expect that American will announce cutbacks in St. Louis."[53]

Arpey viewed the Lambert hub as part of American's problems rather than part of a solution, saying that American was already doing everything in Dallas–Ft. Worth it could do in St. Louis. "While it made us bigger, it really didn't give us anything more to offer except in the local St. Louis market," he said. Congestion at those airports had eased in the wake of 9/11, making the Lambert hub unnecessary.[54] "Over the course of time, the negative margin in St. Louis is greater than the negative margin elsewhere," said an American marketing executive.[55]

A few days later the proverbial axe fell. In July 2003, Arpey announced deep service cuts in St. Louis. Daily departures would be reduced by more than half, from 417 to 207, and American would lay off another 2,000 employees in the St. Louis area. Arpey called this "more palatable" than reducing St. Louis to an outlying point served only through the major hubs. "Our current plan allows us to provide key services for the local community while strengthening our hubs at Chicago and Dallas–Ft. Worth," he told analysts.[56]

Although American did not immediately close the St. Louis domicile for pilots and flight attendants, for all practical purposes the city would become just another destination in American's massive hub-and-spoke operations anchored in Dallas and Chicago. An American spokesman attributed the reduction directly to 9/11. "No one can predict what would have happened otherwise, but it's specifically because of September 11 and other factors related to that, that led to what we had to do in St. Louis," he said.[57]

The painful effort to expand and improve Lambert Airport was now moot. The St. Louis Airport Authority immediately froze spending on $39 million in terminal upgrades and warned of further reductions. Senator Bond called the move "extremely disappointing," saying, "In two short years a promising acquisition has turned into a string of broken promises." Airport director Leonard Griggs pledged that work on the new runway—for which the city had borrowed over $1 billion—would continue, asserting that it would help attract new airlines to Lambert.[58]

The cutback's effect was profound. The total number of passengers using Lambert Airport fell from 26 million in 2001 to 13 million in 2004. Total landings and takeoffs dropped from 474,000 to 283,000—levels not seen since the 1970s.[59] Meanwhile, work progressed on the new runway with an expected completion date of June 2006.[60] Once operational, the $1.1 billion runway would increase Lambert's capacity by 34 percent in good weather and 63 percent during instrument landings in bad weather.[61] But the reduction in traffic since 2001 made the additional capacity unnecessary. Fewer passengers tanked the airport's revenues, and questions were raised about how the improvements would be paid for.[62]

The new runway formally opened on April 13, 2006, and many of the public officials and leaders who had worked to make it possible were on hand. Even the *St. Louis Post-Dispatch*—a consistent champion of the project—now said, "If we had it to do over again, we wouldn't."[63] It was a classic case of 20-20 hindsight.

Reviving the Flight Center

With no place in American's operations, TWA's JFK hub met a similar fate. The Flight Center, once the epitome of jet age glamour, was now old, inefficient, and sorely in need of repair. American ceased operations there in October 2001. American also abandoned JFK Hangar 12, which had been TWA's former East Coast maintenance base and the headquarters of its international operations since the 1950s.

Yet the Flight Center continued to occupy a unique place at JFK, surviving even as more conventional terminals were torn down and replaced. When the Flight Center was designated a city landmark in 1994, *New York Times* architecture critic Herbert Muschamp said, "Sharing JFK's general state of dilapidation, the TWA terminal is in dire need of design modifications." He said it sat "aloof amid the architectural hodgepodge of

JFK's Terminal City, like a bird that has lost its flock." Although Muschamp did not care for the Flight Center's exterior and criticized the "ungainly contours of the building's massive roof," he found its interior "the most dynamically modeled space of its era." He pronounced its design "as tightly controlled as a Beaux-Arts monument, though here the motif is not the classical one of gravity but rather the modern triumph over it."[64]

Dormant and vacant, the Flight Center's future became the subject of widespread interest. Its owner, the Port Authority of New York and New Jersey, said it was committed to protecting the structure "and enhancing its role as an airport centerpiece," but insisted that the building was "inadequate to meet passenger, baggage and security standards required for contemporary aviation operations." The port authority proposed transforming it into a restaurant or conference center, and perhaps combining it with a new terminal that would be used by several airlines to generate more revenue. Subsequently it devised a plan for an enormous new C-shaped terminal that would envelop the Saarinen building and be used by several airlines, including JetBlue Airways, which occupied the adjacent terminal.

Although cut off physically and separated visually from the airport, the Flight Center would be saved under this plan. Flight Wings One and Two would be demolished, but their connector tubes were retained to link the new terminal to the Flight Center structure. The Municipal Art Society of New York vigorously opposed the plan, as did noted architects Phillip Johnson and Robert Stern. The art society proposed adding new concourses and gates to the landmark Saarinen structure—but that would have meant demolishing the nearby former National Airlines terminal designed by I. M. Pei.[65]

The Flight Center hosted an art exhibition in 2004 that showed the work of 19 artists from 10 countries and featured compositions, lectures, and temporary installations inspired by the terminal's architecture. JetBlue Airways, one of the show's biggest sponsors, donated more than $100,000. But the Port Authority of New York and New Jersey shuttered the exhibition after "a raucous opening-night party that left broken glass on the floor, graffiti on the walls and further destruction in its wake." A spokesman for the port authority said officials pulled the permit because the show's organizer failed to control the guests' unlawful behavior. It was a far cry from the Flight Center's gala 1962 opening.[66]

The Municipal Art Society of New York succeeded in getting the Flight Center included on the National Register of Historic Places in September 2005. Meanwhile the Port Authority of New York and New Jersey pushed ahead with its development plan. Construction of the new passenger terminal enveloping the Flight Center began in December 2005. The combined structures, collectively known as Terminal 5, opened on October 22, 2008, to serve JetBlue. But the Flight Center itself remained empty, awaiting redevelopment.

JetBlue announced in spring 2015 that it was negotiating to convert the Flight Center into part of a new on-site hotel for airport passengers. On December 14, 2016, New York governor Andrew Cuomo gathered with other public officials, representatives from the developer, and former TWA employees for groundbreaking ceremonies.[67] The TWA Hotel opened on May 15, 2019. Two adjoining wings with 512 guestrooms overlooked JFK's runways and the Flight Center. Although replicas have replaced many of the Flight Center's original furnishings, its futuristic-looking departure board was restored and reinstalled. The Flight Center now includes a museum with more than 2,000 TWA artifacts, most of them donated by former TWA employees and their families. Guests can enjoy cocktails in a fully restored Jetstream Constellation, one that made 20-plus-hour flights in the late 1950s. Collectively these features appeal to a sense of nostalgia for the glamour of air travel that the Flight Center and TWA once represented in a modern era when air travel is typically anything but glamorous.

But even today the TWA Flight Center is an enduring example of midcentury modern architecture and the hope it embodied. Suzanne Stephens of *Architectural Record* called it a "singular temple of flight," and Stephanie Stubbs, managing editor of *AIArchitect*, observed that "the great, swooping concrete bird captured the essence of flight poised on the threshold of the Jet Age."[68]

Going Broke—and Growing

Meanwhile the litigation between the former TWA pilots and ALPA continued. In 2004 the court of appeals overturned the lower court's dismissal of the pilots' class action suit, holding that if they could prove ALPA had failed to act on their behalf for an improper purpose or in bad faith, they could obtain relief for the breach of its duty of fair representation and allow the case to proceed.[69] After seven more years of discovery and pretrial proceedings, a six-week jury trial in 2011 found that ALPA had violated its duty to fairly represent the TWA pilots. The case then turned to determining the damages the pilots would receive. In January 2014— 12 years after the suit was filed—ALPA settled with the pilots on the eve of the damages trial for $53 million.[70]

American Airlines had narrowly avoided bankruptcy in the wake of 9/11, even as its competitors went through Chapter 11 reorganizations. Industry consolidation continued as US Airways merged with America West Airlines in 2005, Delta merged with Northwest Airlines in 2008, United merged with Continental in 2010, and Southwest Airlines absorbed AirTran Airways in

2011. American closed the St. Louis pilot and flight attendant domiciles in 2010, eliminating the last vestiges of the former St. Louis hub. After losing more than $10 billion since the TWA merger, American sought Chapter 11 protection in November 2011.[71]

Amid reorganization, American announced in February 2013 that it would merge with US Airways. The plan called for American to be the surviving corporation, managed by the former US Airways team, with American's shareholders, creditors, unions, and employees receiving 72 percent of the merged airline's stock. US Airways's stockholders would receive the remaining 28 percent. American had already taken advantage of Chapter 11 to make labor cost reductions, institute managerial efficiencies, and commence fleet reconfiguration. But the US Justice Department, which had taken no steps to oppose the Delta-Northwest and United-Continental mergers, now filed suit to block the American–US Airways deal on antitrust grounds. It contended that, in addition to eliminating competition among the merged airlines, the merger would result in less competition in the industry, increased ticket prices and ancillary fees, lower capacity, and reduced levels of service.[72]

The antitrust suit was settled within a few months, after American and US Airways entered into an agreement described by one analyst as "basically a face-saver" for the government. The airlines agreed to sell takeoff and landing slots at Washington, DC's Reagan National Airport and at New York's LaGuardia, as well as some gate assignments and related facilities at five other airports. "The justice department was in an indefensible position," said a commentator. "Once you created a super-Delta and a super-United, you had to create a super-American. So the outcome was inevitable."[73] The merger was consummated on December 9, 2013. American exited Chapter 11 and began integrating its operations with US Airways, creating the world's largest airline. In 2014, its first year of post-bankruptcy operation, American Airlines reported a net income of $4.2 billion.[74]

Air Travel in the 21st Century

The American–US Airways merger was the last step in a process that deregulation had set in motion 35 years earlier. It transformed the industry from a regulated oligopoly dominated by four major carriers whose routes, fares, and terms of service were rigidly controlled by the government, to an unregulated oligopoly dominated by four mega-carriers—American, United, Delta, and Southwest—whose fares and service were set by the carriers.

A 2015 Federal Aviation Administration study concluded that the restructuring and consolidation of the airline industry that began in the aftermath of 9/11 resulted in less seating capacity, higher fares, and more ancillary fees. Additionally, passenger activity at the top 30 US airports had declined by 11 percent from 2005 levels. For example, passenger traffic dropped precipitously at Memphis and Detroit (both former Northwest Airlines hubs), Cleveland (a former Continental Airlines hub), Pittsburgh (a former US Airways hub), as well as at St. Louis in the aftermath of American's absorption of TWA.[75] "Since its deregulation in 1978, the US commercial air carrier industry has been characterized by boom-to-bust cycles," the FAA reported. "Looking ahead there is optimism that the industry has been transformed from that of a boom-to-bust cycle to one of sustained profitability."[76]

Airlines discovered new ways to cut costs and increase revenue by eliminating in-flight services that passengers had formerly taken for granted. Airlines first removed meal service on domestic coach flights, along with pillows and blankets for passengers. Then they began charging separate fees for services that were historically included in the basic fare. The first case of "unbundling" was the checked baggage fee pioneered by American Airlines in 2008. All other major airlines quickly followed (with the exception of Southwest). Ticket-change fees came next. By 2010 revenue from these two sources alone reached $6 billion, most of which went straight to the bottom line as profit.[77] Airlines went on to charge for seat assignments, food and beverage sales, entertainment, and carry-on bags. They also learned the benefits of "capacity discipline"—a euphemism for cutting flights and increasing load factors. As airlines tailored their schedules to match the number of available seats with the demand for them, empty seats became increasingly rare.

Cramming more seats into their airplanes, the airlines made flying uncomfortable. Seat widths, pitch, and even cushion thickness shrank. Every inch of legroom cost the airlines money; reducing seat pitch by just 1 inch over 30 rows allowed for an extra row of seats. The available passenger "living space" became a diminishing commodity—and a major source of air travel complaints. Indeed, "coach misery" was itself a revenue generator for the airlines: It created demand for amenities that could be sold to make air travel more tolerable.[78] The added revenue came at the cost of friction and altercations among passengers, as well as between passengers and cabin crew. Such "air rage" incidents increased every year after airlines began tracking them in 2007.

US airlines reported after-tax profits totaling $14.8 billion in 2019, up from $11.8 billion in 2018. It was the seventh consecutive year of growing industry profitability.[79] Many airlines funded stock buybacks and enhanced executive compensation instead of building cash reserves for the inevitable rainy day in their cyclical business. That rainy day arrived with the onset of the global COVID-19 pandemic in early 2020. As the pandemic's effects materialized, the airlines rushed to Congress for assistance. Industry lobbying group Airlines for America reported that the airlines had idled more than 2,000 airliners, and passenger volume was down by 90 percent compared to the year before. Bankruptcies were predicted.[80]

Congress responded by providing $25 billion in payroll support and another $25 billion in loans. In return the airlines were required to forego major staffing and pay cuts through September 2020, to refrain from stock buybacks and dividend payouts, and to accept limits on executive pay until March 2022.[81] US domestic airline travel fell dramatically in 2020, and the airlines responded by drastically reducing staffing. Then, when demand for air travel rebounded, the short-handed airlines struggled to cope. Thousands of flight cancellations left stranded passengers fuming. Resistance to pandemic-induced mask mandates and restrictions, congested airports and airplanes, and delays and cancellations combined to spark an unprecedented surge of air-rage incidents and demands for criminal prosecution of unruly passengers as the relationship between airlines and their customers became increasingly hostile and toxic.

Whatever else might be said about air travel in the 21st century, it stands in stark contrast to an era when airlines pampered their passengers and competed to offer the best customer experience—at which TWA excelled.

The Legacy of TWA

Over its 75-year existence TWA became part of American history and culture. Although other airlines were better managed and more efficient, none was more colorful or symbolic of America's love affair with air travel.

Its earliest ancestor, Western Air Express, carried its first passengers sitting on mailbags in open-cockpit biplanes. New York businessmen seeking to create reliable transcontinental air-rail passenger service founded TWA's other ancestor, Transcontinental Air Transport. TAT hired Charles Lindbergh as its technical director, kicking off a long tradition of pilot leadership that continued with TWA's Jack Frye and Paul Richter. Next came Howard Hughes, who turned TWA into a truly international airline that emphasized glamour, Hollywood, and entertainment. TWA survived the Airline Deregulation Act of 1978 and Carl Icahn before Bill Compton revived the tradition of pilot leadership and flew TWA's last flight in 2001.

TWA led the way in making commercial aviation safe and commercially viable, as well as appealing and enjoyable. Many airlines have come and gone, but no other became so firmly established in American culture as TWA.

ACKNOWLEDGMENTS

Every book is the product of many contributions from individuals and organizations. This one is no exception.

Dan O'Hara of the Missouri Aviation Historical Society was instrumental in introducing us to retired TWA pilots, who in turn led us to other pilots, flight attendants, and staff. Their interest and support for the project, including sitting for interviews, was of great value. All contributed generously from their personal collections of photographs, documents, and memorabilia. Working with them has been a great privilege and joy.

We are particularly indebted to Gerry Gitner and Bill Compton, who led TWA during its final years and saved it from extinction, and to Don Fleming, who held key positions before and after Carl Icahn gained control of the airline. They provided hours of invaluable knowledge and experience that helped advance the narrative of those critical years.

We were privileged to have the support and assistance of our late friend and colleague Jon Proctor for this project. Jon was a nationally recognized authority on airlines, air travel, and TWA. He wrote extensively on these subjects and amassed a treasure trove of written materials, artifacts, and photographs, which he made available for use in this book.

Mark Nankivil, president of the Greater St. Louis Air and Space Museum, made photographs available to us from the museum's extensive archives. He was a constant source of support and encouragement, as was the late Fred Roos, another renowned aviation historian, photographer, colleague, and friend.

We are indebted to the late TWA captain Allan Lynn Washburn and his family for making his personal collection of newspaper and periodical clippings, as well as internal TWA communications, available to us. Captain Washburn's collection was of great assistance in reconstructing the events of the Icahn years. The late TWA captain Mike O'Toole, who headed the Ozark pilots at the time of the TWA merger, contributed information and materials from his personal files on the struggle between the TWA and Ozark pilots. Retired TWA captain Keith Houghton contributed his personal collection of litigation filings and discovery materials from the Hammond labor case, which arose from the seniority struggle between the TWA and Ozark pilots.

Besides serving as a mentor and source of inspiration, we thank Dr. Carlos A. Schwantes for generously providing access to his extensive Schwantes-Greever-Nolan Collection of Travel and Transportation Ephemera. We also thank George Hamlin for allowing us to use in this book several of the photographs he took during his years at TWA. Moreover, we are especially appreciative to the Lexington Group for Transportation History for financially supporting the research for this book through the organization's Overton Fellowship program. A note of thanks as well to the University of Wisconsin–Superior, including the faculty and students in the university's School of Business and Economics.

We are grateful to the staff of the St. Louis Mercantile Library at the University of Missouri–St. Louis for their assistance in making TWA's archives and corporate and financial records available to us. We also appreciate the support and assistance of the Missouri Historical Society's Library & Research Center in accessing the collected papers of Representative Richard A. Gephardt and archival imagery. And we were fortunate to have the use of archival images and photographs from *Legacy of Leadership*: *A Pictorial History of Trans World Airlines*, published by Walsworth Publishing Company.

Lauren Mitchell, the Missouri Historical Society's director of publications, collaborated closely with us to transform our project into a published work. Kristie Lein, our editor, spent countless hours refining our manuscript into the finished form that appears on these pages. It was a joy working with both Lauren and Kristie. We, of course, are responsible for the work and for any shortcomings it may have.

Finally, we express our deepest appreciation for the encouragement, support, and patience of our families, without which this book would never have been possible.

—Daniel L. Rust and *Alan B. Hoffman*

SOURCE NOTES

Primary Sources

The primary documentary sources for this book were the Trans World Airlines Collection archives (M-234) and TWA's corporate records in the TWA Estate Collection (M-352) of the St. Louis Mercantile Library at the University of Missouri–St. Louis. The Trans World Airlines Collection contains a wide variety of historical materials, ranging from internal communications and memoranda to newspaper and periodical clippings and imagery concerning TWA and its predecessors. The corporate records comprise board of directors and executive committee minutes; annual reports; proxy statements; Securities and Exchange Commission filings and other financial records of TWA, Trans World Corporation, and TWA Airlines Inc.; as well as some Ozark Air Lines corporate records and annual reports. Collectively these documents establish a detailed record of the company's history, from before its formation in 1930 until its merger with American Airlines in 2001. This book is the first about Trans World Airlines to fully benefit from this archival treasure trove.

Clippings from the *St. Louis Globe-Democrat* housed at the St. Louis Mercantile Library provided valuable contemporary news accounts up to the time the paper ceased publication in 1988.

The collected papers of Representative Richard A. Gephardt housed at the Missouri Historical Society's Library & Research Center illuminated the role he played in the history of TWA in the 1990s, including the struggle to oust Icahn and the subsequent efforts to save the airline.

The late Allan Washburn, an Ozark and TWA captain, maintained a lively interest in TWA even after he retired in 1988. He amassed an extensive collection of internal TWA documents, newspaper clippings, and periodical stories that were used in reconstructing the history of the Icahn era.

Interviews

The authors interviewed the former TWA pilots, flight attendants, ground staff, and management personnel identified below. Their knowledge and experience greatly contributed to the narrative of the airline's history from the 1970s through 2001. Because most people preferred not to be directly quoted or cited, interview citations are absent from this book. Retired *St. Louis Post-Dispatch* reporter Paul Wagman, who covered TWA during the Icahn years, also agreed to be interviewed about that period.

Paul Booe	January 9, 2019
Bill Bowman	June 2, 2022
Catherine Bowman	June 2, 2022
Tom Brown	April 26, 2018
Jerry Castellano	August 30, 2018
Salvador Christifulli	August 30, 2018
Bill Compton	April 18, 2020
Don Dunn	June 21, 2018; January 9, 2019
George Fauser	August 5, 2018
Don Fleming	April 30–May 1, 2020
Dick French	April 12, 2018
Richard Fuchs	August 2, 2018
John Fuhermeyer	March 12, 2018
Gerry Gitner	April 28–30, 2020
Keith Houghton	April 5, 2018
Linda Kunz	August 16, 2018
Arvid Linke	January 9, 2019
Laura Linke	January 9, 2019
Mary McAlee	July 25, 2018
Don Morrison	October 12, 2020
Mike O'Toole	March 29, 2018
Greg Pochapsky	March 2, 2018; April 29, 2018
John Schwab	April 29, 2018
Peter Sherwin	May 24, 2018
Don Tate	February 18, 2018
Greg Tyler	July 23, 2018
David Venz	September 15, 2020
Paul Wagman	May 16, 2022
Allan Washburn	April 19, 2018; April 29, 2018
Malvin Yarke	March 1, 2018

Efforts to interview Carl Icahn and Victoria Gray (née Vicki Frankovich) were unsuccessful.

Secondary Sources

There is a wealth of published material on TWA, Western Air Express, and Transcontinental Air Transport; without it, it would be impossible to properly recount TWA's history. The sources used in this book are identified in the chapter notes and the selected bibliography.

Secondary sources particularly useful concerning the airline's history prior to the Icahn era include *Legacy of Leadership*, by TWA captain and executive J. E. Frankum and the TWA Flight Operations Department; *TWA: The Making of an Airline*, by TWA captain Edward Betts and the TWA Master Executive Council; and *TWA Cabin Attendants Wings of Pride: A Pictorial History, 1935–1985*, by Donna Steele.

Robert Serling's *Howard Hughes' Airline: An Informal History of TWA*, based on Serling's extensive knowledge of the airline industry and interviews with TWA personnel, provided crucial material about TWA and its predecessors from the 1920s to the late 1970s.

Bob Buck's *North Star Over My Shoulder: A Flying Life*, his account of flying for TWA from the DC-2 to the 747, was a valuable source of material about TWA at the operational level.

R. E. G. Davies is the unquestioned authority on commercial airlines, both foreign and domestic. His published works are essential sources on airline history and development. *TWA: An Airline and Its Aircraft*, *Airlines of the United States Since 1914*, and *Charles Lindbergh: An Airman, His Aircraft, and His Great Flights* were of particular value to this book.

Charles Lindbergh's *The Spirit of St. Louis*, published in 1953, is an autobiographical account of his life up to the time of the 1927 Paris flight and of the flight itself. His *Wartime Journals* covers his activities from 1938 to 1945. Anne Morrow Lindbergh's multivolume *Diaries and Letters* describe the Lindberghs' lives before and after their 1929 marriage. These firsthand accounts were important sources detailing their involvement with TWA.

A large volume of published work exists concerning all aspects of Howard Hughes's life. *Howard Hughes: His Life and Madness*, by Donald Barlett and James Steele; *Hughes: The Private Diaries, Memos and Letters*, by Richard Hack; and *Howard Hughes and His Flying Boat*, by Charles Barton, were used in fleshing out the Hughes era at TWA. Robert Rummel's *Howard Hughes and TWA*, an inside view of the Hughes years at TWA by an executive who worked closely with him, was a vital source concerning Hughes's control of the airline and the resulting litigation.

There is also a wealth of relevant published periodical and newspaper articles far too voluminous to catalog here. Those used in this work are identified in the chapter notes.

NOTES

CHAPTER 1

[1] Edward A. Keogh, "A Brief History of the Airmail Service of the U.S. Post Office Department, May 15, 1918–August 31, 1927," http://www.airmailpioneers.org/content/Sagahistory.htm.

[2] R. E. G. Davies, *Airlines of the United States Since 1914* (Washington, DC: Smithsonian Institution Scholarly Press, 1998), 19.

[3] Davies, *Airlines*, 25.

[4] James J. Horgan, *City of Flight: The History of Aviation in St. Louis* (Gerald, MO: Patrice Press, 1984), 306.

[5] Western Air Express Articles of Incorporation.

[6] Robert J. Serling, *Howard Hughes' Airline: An Informal History of TWA* (New York: St. Martin's/Marek, 1983), 13.

[7] Harris M. Hanshue, "The Los Angeles–Salt Lake City Airmail Line," *Aviation*, April 5, 1926, 493–494.

[8] R. E. G. Davies, *TWA: An Airline and Its Aircraft* (McLean, VA: Paladwr Press, 2000), 10–11.

[9] Davies, *TWA*, 6–9.

[10] Daniel L. Rust, *Flying Across America: The Airline Passenger Experience* (Norman: University of Oklahoma Press, 2009), 26.

[11] Col. Thurman H. Bane, "A Trip over the Western Air Express," *Aviation*, October 25, 1926, 711–714.

[12] "Harris Hanshue Addresses Aeronautical Conference," *Aviation*, May 23, 1927, 1094.

[13] Davies, *TWA*, 14.

[14] Davies, *TWA*, 12; U. S. Centennial of Flight Commission, "Daniel and Harry Guggenheim—Supporters of Aviation Technology," http://www.centennialofflight.net/essay/Evolution_of_Technology/guggenheim/Tech3.htm.

[15] Davies, *TWA*, 18.

[16] Edward Betts, *TWA: The Making of an Airline* (TWA Master Executive Council, 1981), 48–49; Davies, *TWA*, 18.

[17] Anne Morrow Lindbergh, *Hour of Gold, Hour of Lead: Diaries and Letters, 1929–1932* (New York: Signet New American Library, 1974), 53.

[18] Davies, *TWA*, 26–27.

[19] Betts, 26–27.

[20] Davies, *TWA*, 26–27.

[21] R. E. G. Davies, *Charles Lindbergh: An Airman, His Aircraft, and His Great Flights* (McLean, VA: Paladwr Press, 1997), 10.

[22] Charles A. Lindbergh, *The Spirit of St. Louis* (New York: Charles Scribner's Sons, 1953), 247.

[23] Lindbergh, *Spirit*, 214–216.

[24] Davies, *Charles Lindbergh*, 14; Lindbergh, *Spirit*, 287.

[25] Lindbergh, *Spirit*, 13–14.

[26] Davies, *Charles Lindbergh*, 18.

[27] Davies, *Charles Lindbergh*, 23.

[28] Davies, *TWA*, 16–17.

[29] Davies, *TWA*, 19.

[30] Ibid., 18–19; *Airlines*, 68–69.

[31] Ibid., 64–67; 20–21: Davies, *TWA*, 20–21; J. E. Frankum, *Legacy of Leadership: A Pictorial History of Trans World Airlines* (Marceline, MO: Walsworth Publishing Company, 1971), 47–49.

[32] Davies, *Airlines*, 50.

[33] A. Scott Berg, *Lindbergh* (New York: G. P. Putnam's Sons, 1998), 188–189.

[34] Transcontinental Air Transport, Inc., *TAT Plane Talk* 1, no. 1, January 1929.

[35] *Coast-to-Coast By Plane and Train: A History of the Conception-Organization-Development-Operation of Transcontinental Air Transport, Inc.*, 3.

[36] *Coast-to-Coast* 2, "Preliminary Survey," 2–3.

[37] Rust, 44.

[38] George H. Burgess and Miles C. Kennedy, *Centennial History of the Pennsylvania Railroad Company* (Pennsylvania Railroad Company, 1949), 599–604.

[39] Robert F. Kirk, *Flying the Lindbergh Line: Then and Now* (Bloomington, IN: AuthorHouse, 2013), 4.

[40] "TAT Weather Services," *TAT Plane Talk* 1, no. 4, April 1929.

[41] *Coast-to-Coast* 2, 4–5.

[42] Kirk, 223–224.

[43] Kirk, 225–235.

[44] TWA Museum Guides Blog, *Coast-to-Coast* 2, http://twamuseumguides.blogspot.com.

[45] Ibid.

[46] Ibid.

[47] Ibid.

[48] Davies, *Airlines*, 80–81.

[49] "Radio and Tele-Type Services," *TAT Plane Talk* 1, no. 3, March 1929.

[50] Ibid., "Night Operations"; *Coast-to-Coast* 4, "Lighting and Extraordinary Equipment," 1–2.

[51] Davies, *Airlines*, 83.

[52] *Coast-to-Coast* 6, "Personal," 2–3; "Pilot Personnel," *TAT Plane Talk* 1, no. 6, June 1929.

[53] Kirk, 27.

[54] Frankum, 36; Jon Proctor, "TWA 1925–2001," *Airways Classics* no. 6, 2012, 6.

[55] Davies, *Airlines*, 85; Kirk, 28.

[56] *Coast-to-Coast* 7, "The Day We Are Properly Ready," 1–2; *TAT Plane Talk* 1, no. 6, "Inauguration of Service."

[57] Serling, 10.

[58] "The Day We Are Properly Ready," *TAT Plane Talk* 1, no. 7, July 1929, 1–4.

[59] *Coast-to-Coast* 7.

[60] *I'll Take the High Road*, by Marguerite Salomon as told to Douglas Ingells (undated manuscript in the TWA Archive, Collection M-234 of the St. Louis Mercantile Library), 6.

[61] Salomon, 9.

[62] Salomon, 11.

[63] Salomon, 12–13.

[64] Salomon, 16–17.

[65] Kirk, 34.

[66] Anne Morrow Lindbergh, 46.

[67] Rust, 51.

[68] Anne Morrow Lindbergh, 48–49.

[69] Salomon, 18.

[70] Salomon, 19.

[71] Salomon, 20.

[72] Salomon, 20–21.

[73] Kirk, 53.

[74] Kirk, 54–55.

[75] Kirk, 55–60.

[76] Mark Thompson, "Transcontinental Air Transport Plane Crash 1929," *New Mexico History*, July 22, 2015.

[77] Kirk, 62.

[78] Thompson.

[79] Frankum, 43.

[80] Davies, *TWA*, 27.

[81] Frankum, 43; Serling, 12–13.

[82] Ralph S. Damon, *TWA: Three Decades in the Air* (address given to the Newcomen Society, December 4, 1952), 15.

CHAPTER 2

[1] Robert J. Serling, *Howard Hughes' Airline: An Informal History of TWA* (New York: St. Martin's/Marek, 1983), 14.

[2] R.E.G. Davies, *Airlines of the United States Since 1914* (Washington, DC: Smithsonian Institution Scholarly Press, 1998), 110–111.

[3] Serling, 16.

[4] Davies, *Airlines*, 116–117.

[5] Serling, 14.

[6] Serling, 16–17.

[7] Edward Betts, *TWA: The Making of an Airline* (TWA Master Executive Council, 1981), 52; R. E. G. Davies, *TWA: An Airline and Its Aircraft* (McLean, VA: Paladwr Press, 2000), 28.

[8] Serling, 18; J. E. Frankum, *Legacy of Leadership: A Pictorial History of Trans World Airlines* (Marceline, MO: Walsworth Publishing Company, 1971), 45; Davies, Airlines, 116.

[9] Davies, *Airlines*, 91–93; Serling, 18.

[10] TWA board minutes, October 3, 1930; Davies, TWA, 28–29.

[11] TWA executive committee minutes, October 28, 1930.

[12] J. Cheever Cowdin, letter to Keys, Hanshue, and Shaeffer, January 31, 1931.

[13] Serling, 22–23.

[14] Julius A. Karash and Rick Montgomery, *TWA: Kansas City's Hometown Airline* (Kansas City, MO: Kansas City Star Books, 2001), 15–17.

[15] Serling, 24.

[16] Serling, 25.

[17] Serling, 25–26.

[18] Serling, 26; Betts, 68.

[19] Davies, *TWA*, 36–37.

[20] Serling, 34.

[21] TWA board minutes, June 23, 1932.

[22] Bill of sale from TWA to US Department of Commerce, February 11, 1932.

[23] Henry R. Lehrer, *Flying the Beam: Navigating the Early US Airmail Airways, 1917–1941* (West Lafayette: Purdue University Press, 2014), 123–124; 147.

[24] TWA executive committee minutes, November 4, 1932; Davies, TWA, 28.

[25] TWA schedule, November 5, 1932.

[26] Davies, *Airlines*, 180–183.

[27] TWA executive committee minutes, April 22, 1932.

[28] Davies, *TWA*, 33.

[29] Arthur Pearcy, *Douglas Propliners* (London: Airlife Publishing Ltd., 1995), 26.

[30] Pearcy, 26.

[31] Serling, 34–35.

[32] Douglas J. Ingells, *The Plane That Changed the World: A Biography of the DC-3* (Fallbrook, CA: Aero Publishers, 1966), 36.

[33] Ingells, 36–40.

[34] Pearcy, 27–28.

[35] Pearcy, 28.

[36] TWA board minutes, February 2, 1934.

[37] United States Senate Historical Office, "Special Committee to Investigate Airmail and Ocean Mail Contracts," Notable Senate Investigations, 2.

[38] Davies, *Airlines*, 155–156.

[39] TWA board minutes, February 18, 1934.

[40] Ibid.

[41] Frankum, 76.

[42] Serling, 42.

[43] Frankum, 75–77.

[44] Betts, 76.

[45] Betts, 76.

[46] Robert L. Scott, *God Is My Co-Pilot* (New York: Charles Scribner's Sons, 1943), 32–34.

[47] Scott, 35–37.

[48] Ibid.

[49] Serling, 61.

[50] Davies, *TWA*, 35.

[51] *TWA Line Squalls*, August 1934, 3.

[52] *TWA Line Squalls*, August 1934, 2.

[53] Daniel L. Rust, *Flying Across America: The Airline Passenger Experience* (Norman: University of Oklahoma Press, 2009), 100–102.

[54] Serling, 49.

[55] Frankum, 79–81.

[56] Robert N. Buck, *North Star Over My Shoulder: A Flying Life* (New York: Simon & Schuster, 2002), 74–75; 108–109.

[57] *TWA Line Squalls*, August 1933, 72.

[58] *TWA Line Squalls*, August 1934, 2–3.

[59] Serling, 51.

[60] TWA board minutes, July 26, 1935.

[61] Serling, 51.

[62] Donna Steele, *TWA Cabin Attendants Wings of Pride: A Pictorial History, 1935–1985* (Marceline, MO: Walsworth Publishing Company, 1985), 26.

[63] Steele, 27–29.

[64] Steele, 31.

[65] Steele, 31–33.

[66] Steele, 33.

[67] Steele, 34.

[68] Steele, 39.

[69] Serling, 51–52.

[70] Steele, 49.

[71] Frankum, 89.

[72] TWA board minutes, July 26, 1935.

[73] Stanley R. Mohler and Bobby H. Johnson, *Wiley Post, His* Winnie Mae, *and the World's First Pressure Suit* (Washington, DC: Smithsonian Institution Scholarly Press, 1971), 67.

[74] Mohler and Johnson, 97–102.

[75] Frankum, 91.

[76] D. W. Tomlinson, "High Altitude Flying Observations" (undated manuscript in the TWA Archive, Collection M-234 of the St. Louis Mercantile Library), 5.

[77] Tomlinson, 21.

[78] Theresa L. Kraus, *Celebrating 75 Years of Federal Air Traffic Control* (n.p.: Federal Aviation Administration, 2011), 4.

[79] Lehrer, 151–152.

[80] "The Beginning of Air Traffic Control," *Aviation Online Magazine*, http://avstop.com/history/atc/air_traffic_control_begins.htm; "A Short History of Air Traffic Control," http://imansolas.freeservers.com/ATC/short_history_of_the_air_traffic.html.

[81] Lehrer, 152.

[82] Serling, 57.

[83] TWA board minutes, August 21, 1935.

[84] Serling, 58.

[85] Peter M. Bowers, *The DC-3: Fifty Years of Legendary Flight* (New York: TAB Books, 1986), 43.

[86] TWA board minutes, September 24, 1936.

[87] Serling, 58–59.

[88] Davies, *TWA*, 38–39.

[89] Rust, 103.

[90] Davies, *Airlines*, 202.

[91] Davies, *Airlines*, 675.

[92] R. E. G. Davies, *Airlines of the Jet Age: A History* (Washington, DC: Smithsonian Institution Scholarly Press, 2011), 139.

[93] Serling, 59–60.

[94] Rust, 103.

[95] *TWA Skyliner News*, September 1937, 3, 7.

[96] Ibid.

[97] Buck, 147–150.

[98] Buck, 152.

[99] Buck, 140–142.

[100] Serling, 61.

[101] TWA board minutes, October 26, 1937.

[102] TWA annual report, 1937, 2.

[103] Serling, 72–73.

[104] TWA board minutes, July 1, 1938.

[105] Serling, 74.

[106] Serling, 74.

[107] *Skyliner*, September 1937, 5.

[108] Lindbergh, letter to the TWA board of directors, January 21, 1935.

[109] A. Scott Berg, *Lindbergh* (New York: G. P. Putnam's Sons, 1998), 358.

[110] Berg, 361.

[111] Berg, 362.

[112] Berg, 367–368.

[113] Anne Morrow Lindbergh, *The Flower and the Nettle: Diaries and Letters, 1936–1939* (New York: Harcourt Brace Jovanovich, 1976), 379.

[114] Charles A. Lindbergh, *The Wartime Journals of Charles A. Lindbergh* (New York: Harcourt Brace Jovanovich, 1970), 99–100.

[115] Lindbergh, *Wartime Journals*, 108.

[116] Lindbergh, *Wartime Journals*, 115.

[117] Berg, 379.

[118] *New York Times*, December 5, 1938, 15; December 6, 1938, 25.

[119] Charles Barton, *Howard Hughes and His Flying Boat* (Fallbrook, CA: Aero Publishers, 1982), 23.

[120] "Hughes Spans U. S. in 7 Hours, 28 Minutes," Associated Press, January 20, 1937; Barton, 37.

[121] Barton, 44.

[122] Richard Hack, *Hughes: The Private Diaries, Memos and Letters* (Beverly Hills: New Millennium Press, 2001), 112–114.

[123] Hack, 115–119.

[124] "Wiley Post's Flight Best, Says Hughes," Associated Press, July 15, 1938.

[125] "Hughes Sets Mark Across Continent," Associated Press, August 21, 1938; "Airliners Will Replace Ships as Safest, Cheapest Way of Travel," *Kansas City Star*, July 21, 1938.

[126] Associated Press, December 12, 1938.

[127] Serling, 74–76.

[128] TWA board minutes, June 23, 1939.

[129] TWA board minutes, September 29, 1939.

[130] TWA board minutes, December 15, 1939.

CHAPTER 3

[1] J. E. Frankum, *Legacy of Leadership*: *A Pictorial History of Trans World Airlines* (Marceline, MO: Walsworth Publishing Company, 1971), 108.

[2] Robert J. Serling, *Howard Hughes' Airline: An Informal History of TWA* (New York: St. Martin's/Marek, 1983), 84.

[3] Daniel L. Rust, *Flying Across America: The Airline Passenger Experience* (Norman: University of Oklahoma Press, 2009), 123.

[4] TWA board minutes, May 10, 1940; R. E. G. Davies, *Airlines of the United States Since 1914* (Washington, DC: Smithsonian Institution Scholarly Press, 1982), 203.

[5] Robert W. Rummel, *Howard Hughes and TWA* (Washington, DC: Smithsonian Institution Scholarly Press, 1991), 58.

[6] Rummel, 58.

[7] Rummel, 59.

[8] Rummel, 61.

[9] Serling, 86–92; Will Hawkins, "Creating Connie," *Air Classics* 50 no. 2 (February 2014), 19–21.

[10] Rummel, 61.

[11] TWA board minutes, November 11, 1941.

[12] Rummel, 62.

[13] Jack Frye, letter to Julius Eysmans, January 29, 1942.

[14] Rummel, 65.

[15] Rummel, 67–68.

[16] TWA annual report, 1940, 10.

[17] TWA board minutes, June 11, 1940.

[18] Frankum, 111.

[19] Serling, 94.

[20] Frankum, 114–115.

[21] Edward Betts, *TWA: The Making of an Airline* (TWA Master Executive Council, 1981), 101–102.

[22] Serling, 107–110.

[23] Betts, 107.

[24] TWA board minutes, June 8, 1944.

[25] Serling, 92.

[26] Rust, 127.

[27] Rust, 128.

[28] Serling, 103–105.

[29] TWA board minutes, September 14, 1942.

[30] Rummel, 69.

[31] Davies, *TWA*, 52.

[32] Jon Proctor, *Airways Classics: TWA 1925–2001* (Sandpoint, ID: Airways International, 2012), 21.

[33] Buck, 222–223.

[34] Buck, 225–227.

[35] Buck, 236–244.

[36] Buck, 245–256.

[37] Charles Barton, *Howard Hughes and His Flying Boat* (Fallbrook, CA: Aero Publishers, 1982), 86.

[38] Donald L. Barlett and James B. Steele, *Howard Hughes: His Life and Madness* (New York: W. W. Norton & Company, 2004), 118.

[39] Barlett and Steele, 125–126.

[40] Barlett and Steele, 126–127.

[41] Barton, *TWA*, 70–71.

[42] Barlett and Steele, 129–130.

[43] Serling, 122–123.

[44] Barlett and Steele, 132–134.

[45] Frankum, 132–133.

[46] Davies, *Airlines*, 366–367.

47 Peter W. Brooks, *The World's Airliners* (New York: G. P. Putnam's Sons, 1962), 299.

48 Rummel, 93.

49 Rummel, 90.

50 Rummel, 90–91.

51 Rummel, 99–100.

52 Rummel, 101–103.

53 Rummel, 96–100.

54 Frankum, 140.

55 Davies, *Airlines*, 329.

56 Davies, *TWA*, 50.

57 Barton, 133–135.

58 Barton, 136.

59 Barton, 136–137.

60 Barlett and Steele, 143.

61 Barton, 143.

62 Barton, 131–142; Barlett and Steele, 137–145.

63 Barton, 125.

64 Rummel, 115–119.

65 Serling, 129–131; Frankum, 147–149.

66 Serling, 135–136.

67 Rummel, 119–120.

68 Rummel, 114–115; Davies, *TWA*, 73.

69 TWA board minutes, December 11, 1946.

70 TWA board minutes, December 27, 1946.

71 TWA board minutes, January 8, 1947.

72 TWA board minutes, January 9, 1947.

73 Rummel, 124.

74 TWA board minutes, January 9, 1947.

75 Ibid.

76 Associated Press, "Frye Forced Out in TWA Policy Fight," February 22, 1947.

77 TWA board minutes, February 25, 1947; April 11, 1947.

78 Barlett and Steele, 145.

79 Barton, 151–152.

80 Barton, 174.

81 Barton, 175.

[82] Barton, 180.

[83] Barton, 181.

[84] Barton, 184–185.

[85] Barton, 193.

[86] Barton, 220–221.

[87] Barlett and Steele, 157.

[88] Barton, 221–223.

[89] Barlett and Steele, 161–162.

[90] TWA board minutes, April 11, 1947.

[91] Rummel, 134–137.

[92] TWA annual report, 1948.

[93] TWA board minutes, January 28, 1948; March 24, 1948.

[94] TWA special stockholders meeting minutes, August 10, 1948; Rummel, 127.

[95] Rummel, 145–147.

[96] Rummel, 138.

[97] TWA annual report, 1948.

[98] Davies, *Airlines*, 367.

[99] Serling, 170–171.

[100] Serling, 171.

[101] Rummel, 151–152.

[102] TWA annual report, 1948.

[103] TWA annual report, 1949.

[104] TWA annual report, 1949.

CHAPTER 4

[1] Donald L. Barlett and James B. Steele, *Howard Hughes: His Life and Madness* (New York: W. W. Norton & Company, 2004), 212.

[2] Barlett and Steele, 212–214.

[3] Robert Serling, *Howard Hughes' Airline: An Informal History of TWA* (New York: St. Martin's/Marek, 1983), 175.

[4] Serling, 181–182.

[5] Serling, 175.

[6] Serling, 152–153.

[7] Richard Hack, *Hughes: The Private Diaries, Memos and Letters, the Definitive Biography of the First American Billionaire* (Beverly Hills: New Millennium Press, 2001), 239–240.

[8] TWA annual shareholders meeting minutes, April 27, 1950.

9 Robert N. Buck, *North Star Over My Shoulder: A Flying Life* (New York: Simon & Schuster, 2002), 318–319.

10 Buck, 327.

11 Civil Aeronautics Board Accident Investigation Report 5A-220, file no. 1-0114, "Trans World Airlines, Inc., Near Cairo, Egypt, August 30, 1950," adopted May 25, 1951.

12 Robert W. Rummel, *Howard Hughes and TWA* (Washington, DC: Smithsonian Institution Scholarly Press, 1991), 171–172.

13 J. E. Frankum, *Legacy of Leadership*: *A Pictorial History of Trans World Airlines* (Marceline, MO: Walsworth Publishing Company, 1971), 167.

14 Ibid.

15 Ibid.

16 Davies, *Airlines*, 336–338.

17 Daniel L. Rust, *Flying Across America: The Airline Passenger Experience* (Norman: University of Oklahoma Press, 2009), 173.

18 Rummel, 173–174.

19 Rummel, 177–179.

20 Rummel, 180.

21 *News from TWA*, "TWA's First Non-Stop Transcontinental Airliner arrives at New York," October 20, 1953.

22 Davies, *Airlines*, 349–350; Frankum, 172.

23 Rummel, 181–182.

24 Rummel, 183–184.

25 Rummel, 189–190.

26 Rummel, 192–194.

27 Rummel, 196–197.

28 *News from TWA*, "TWA's New Hostess Uniforms Keyed to Color Scheme of Super-G Connie," 1955.

29 News From TWA, "TWA's New Super-G Constellations Offer Luxury Service to 9 Cities," August 4, 1955.

30 Ibid.

31 TWA internal memorandum, March 1, 1955.

32 "The Original Mickey Mouse Club Show," http://www.originalmmc.com/whatwant.html.

33 Rummel, 244–245.

34 Rummel, 244–245.

35 Verhovek, 109–110.

36 Rummel, 301–302.

37 Rummel, 302.

[38] Rummel, 219.

[39] TWA board minutes, January 13, 1955.

[40] Rummel, 213–214.

[41] Rummel, 305.

[42] Rummel, 306.

[43] Rummel, 311–312.

[44] Rummel, 315–322.

[45] Rummel, 323.

[46] Rummel, 306–307.

[47] Barlett and Steele, 220.

[48] Barlett and Steele, 220–221.

[49] Barlett and Steele, 221.

[50] Civil Aeronautics Board, Accident Investigation Report, file no. 1-0090, "Trans World Airlines, Inc., Lockheed L1049A, N6902C, and United Air Lines, Inc., Douglas DC-7, N6324C, Grand Canyon, Arizona. June 30, 1956," released April 17, 1957, 9.

[51] CAB accident report, 8, 18–19.

[52] Rummel, 329–331.

[53] Serling, 207–208.

[54] Serling, 214–215.

[55] Barlett and Steele, 222–223.

[56] Barlett and Steele, 228.

[57] Barlett and Steele, 228–229.

[58] Barlett and Steele, 228–229.

[59] Rummel, 274.

[60] Rummel, 280–281.

[61] TWA annual report, "Finance," 1957.

[62] Serling, 230.

[63] Serling, 230–231.

[64] Serling, 232–233.

[65] Serling, 245.

[66] TWA board minutes, February 27, 1959.

[67] TWA annual report, 1959, 3.

[68] Rummel, 346.

[69] "$200 Million Gateway to Europe," *Popular Mechanics*, December 1945.

[70] Ibid.

[71] "TWA Firsts at JFK," *News from TWA*, July 23, 1968.

[72] Kornel Ringli, *Designing TWA: Eero Saarinen's Airport Terminal in New York* (Zurich: Park Books, 2015), 79.

[73] Ringli, 84.

[74] Ringli, 93, 103.

[75] Mark Lamster, *The TWA Terminal* (Princeton: Princeton Architectural Press, 1999), 2–3.

[76] "Workmen Begin Pouring 1¼ Acre Concrete Shell Over New TWA Terminal," *News from TWA*, August 26, 1960, 1.

[77] TWA board minutes, March 31, 1959.

[78] Ringli, 81.

CHAPTER 5

[1] Robert W. Rummel, *Howard Hughes and TWA* (Washington, DC: Smithsonian Institution Press, 1991), 351–353.

[2] Robert W. Serling, *Howard Hughes' Airline: An Informal History of TWA* (New York: St. Martin's/Marek Press, 1983), 246–247.

[3] Donald L. Barlett and James B. Steele, *Howard Hughes: His Life and Madness* (New York: W. W. Norton & Company, 2004), 248–249; 362–363.

[4] Serling, 249.

[5] TWA board minutes, August 31, 1960.

[6] Rummel, 364–365.

[7] Rummel, 366–367.

[8] Rummel, 369–370.

[9] Barlett and Steele, 249.

[10] Serling, 249.

[11] Barlett and Steele, 249.

[12] Rummel, 370.

[13] Daniel L. Rust, *Flying Across America: The Airline Passenger Experience* (Norman: University of Oklahoma Press, 2009), 190.

[14] Donna Steele, *TWA Cabin Attendants Wings of Pride: A Pictorial History, 1935–1985* (Marceline, MO: Walsworth Publishing Company, 1985), 166.

[15] Steele, 163–164.

[16] Rust, 192.

[17] Serling, 282.

[18] U. S. Civil Aeronautics Board Aircraft Accident Report SA-361, file no. 1-0083, "United Airlines, Inc. DC-8, N8013U and Trans World Airlines, Inc. Constellation 1049A, N6907C, Near Staten Island, New York, December 16, 1960," 16–17.

[19] Serling, 282.

[20] CAB accident report, 9.

[21] CAB accident report, 26.

[22] Serling, 283.

[23] Rummel, 377–378.

[24] Serling, 255.

[25] Rummel, 379.

[26] Rummel, 380.

[27] Rust, 198–199.

[28] Rummel, 382–383.

[29] Rummel, 384.

[30] Rummel, 386.

[31] Rummel, 386–387.

[32] Rummel, 390.

[33] Serling, 272–273.

[34] Serling, 273–274.

[35] Rummel, 395–396.

[36] Serling, 276–277.

[37] Kornel Ringli, *Designing TWA: Eero Saarinen's Airport Terminal in New York* (Zurich: Park Books, 2018), 159.

[38] "Complexities of TWA Flight Center Best Realized by Builders," *News from TWA*, May 5, 1962.

[39] "TWA Terminal's Beauty Is Enhanced by Expanse of Detailed Glasswork," *News from TWA*, November 10, 1961.

[40] "Designer Sought Spirit of Travel in Design of Trans World Flight Center," *News from TWA*, May 15, 1962.

[41] Ringli, 24.

[42] "The Story of the Trans World Fight Center from TWA Public Relations Department," May 28, 1962, 4.

[43] Ringli, 111–112.

[44] Ringli, 114–115.

[45] Rummel, 392.

[46] Rummel, 392–393.

[47] TWA board minutes, October 16, 1963.

[48] TWA annual report, 1963.

[49] Serling, 277.

[50] Serling, 278.

[51] Rummel, 399–400.

[52] *Trans World Airlines, Inc. v. Hughes*, 312 F. Supp. 478, 485 (S.D.N.Y. 1970).

[53] Civil Aeronautics Board Aircraft Accident Investigation Report SA-389, file no. 1-0033, adopted December 13, 1965.

[54] National Transportation Safety Board Aircraft Accident Investigation Report SA-396, file no. 1-0002, "Trans World Airlines, Inc. DC-9, Tann Company Beech Baron B-55 In-Flight Collision Near Urbana, Ohio, March 9, 1967," adopted June 19, 1968, 42.

[55] Ringli, 116.

[56] *Newest wonder in the world of flight . . . TWA Star Stream*, Brochure #4-5260, April 1962.

[57] Pamphlet, *TWA Wings for the World* (September 1965).

[58] Jon Proctor, "TWA—Trans World Airlines," http://jonproctor.net/twa-trans-world-airlines.

[59] Jerry W. Cosley, TWA interoffice correspondence, "Royal Party of Monaco," August 15, 1967.

[60] William Stadiem, *Jet Set: The People, the Planes, the Glamour and the Romance in Aviation's Glory Years* (New York: Ballantine Books, 2014), xii–xiii; 24–25.

[61] Stadiem, xiii.

[62] Ringli, 80.

[63] Serling, 285.

[64] Jon Proctor, "1966—Kennedy Space Center," http://jonproctor.net/1966-kennedy-space-center/.

[65] R. E. G. Davies, *TWA: An Airline and its Aircraft* (McLean, VA: Paladwr Press, 2000), 51; 54–57; 61–62.

[66] J. E. Frankum, *Legacy of Leadership: A Pictorial History of Trans World Airlines* (Marceline, MO: Walsworth Publishing Company, 1971), 210.

[67] Davies, *TWA*, 75.

[68] Davies, *TWA*, 77.

[69] Davies, *TWA*, 74.

[70] TWA board minutes, October 16, 1963.

[71] Edward Betts, *TWA: The Making of an Airline* (TWA Master Executive Council, 1981), 159.

[72] Serling, 305–306.

[73] Steele, 177.

[74] Frankum, 205.

[75] Steele, 216.

[76] Serling, 52.

[77] Serling, 305–306.

7

[78] TWA board minutes, June 21, 1972.

[79] TWA board minutes, December 21, 1966.

[80] TWA board minutes, February 28, 1967.

[81] Frankum, 209.

[82] National Transportation Safety Board, Aircraft Accident Report SA-401, file no. 1-0029, "Trans World Airlines, Inc. B707 N742TW, the Greater Cincinnati Airport, Erlanger, Kentucky, November 6, 1967."

[83] National Transportation Safety Board, Aircraft Accident Report SA-402, file no. 1-0033, Trans World Airlines, Inc. Convair 880, November 20, 1967.

[84] Frankum, 219.

[85] Davies, *TWA*, 72.

[86] "Skyjacking of TWA's Flight 840 to Damascus Branded as Piracy," *Skyliner*, September 8, 1969.

[87] "TWA Doing All Possible to Free Two Passengers Still Detained by Syria," *Skyliner*, September 2, 1969.

[88] Statement by F. C. Wiser, *News from TWA*, December 5, 1969.

[89] *Newsweek*, November 10, 1969, 42.

[90] *Newsweek*, 43.

[91] Roland Hughes, "TWA 85: The World's Longest and Most Spectacular Hijacking," BBC News, October 26, 2019.

CHAPTER 6

[1] R. E. G. Davies, *TWA: An Airline and Its Aircraft* (McLean, VA: Paladwr Press, 2000), 82.

[2] Bill Norton, Lockheed Martin C-5 Galaxy (North Branch, MN: Specialty Press, 2003), 8–11.

[3] Robert Redding and Bill Yenne, *Boeing: Planemaker to the World* (San Diego: Crescent Books, 1983), 192.

[4] J. E. Frankum, *Legacy of Leadership: A Pictorial History of Trans World Airlines* (Marceline, MO: Walsworth Publishing Company, 1971), 222.

[5] Robert J. Serling, *Howard Hughes' Airline: An Informal History of TWA* (New York: St. Martin's/Marek Press, 1983), 311.

[6] TWA annual report, 1970.

[7] Kornel Ringli, *Designing TWA: Eero Saarinen's Airport Terminal in New York* (Zurich: Park Books, 2019), 123.

[8] Annual report, 1970.

[9] Ibid.

[10] Ibid.

[11] TWA board minutes, December 16, 1970.

[12] TWA board minutes, June 23, 1971.

[13] "Flight 802 Hijacked to Beirut," *Skyliner*, January 9, 1970; "Hijacked Aircraft Departs Beirut," *News from TWA*, January 10, 1970.

[14] William Stadiem, *Jet Set: The People, the Planes, the Glamour, and the Romance of Aviation's Glory Years* (New York: Ballantine Books, 2014), 292–293.

[15] Stadiem, 294–295.

[16] Stadiem, 296–297.

[17] Stadiem, 297–298.

[18] *Time*, May 29, 1971; Eric M. Conway, *High-Speed Dreams: NASA and the Technopolitics of Supersonic Transportation, 1945–1999* (Baltimore: Johns Hopkins University Press, 2005), 118–139.

[19] TWA board minutes, February 23, 1972.

[20] TWA annual report, 1971.

[21] Ibid.

[22] TWA board minutes, August 10, 1973.

[23] TWA annual report, 1972.

[24] Edward Betts, *TWA: The Making of an Airline: (*TWA Master Executive Council, 1981), 162.

[25] Serling, 318.

[26] Betts, 162.

[27] *Trans World Airlines v. Hughes*, 449 F.2d 51 (2d Cir. 1971).

[28] Robert W. Rummel, *Howard Hughes and TWA* (Washington, DC: Smithsonian Institution Scholarly Press, 1991), 400–401.

[29] *Hughes Tool Company, et al. v. Trans World Airlines, Inc. et al.*, 409 U.S. 363 (1973).

[30] *Hughes v. Trans World Airlines, Inc.*, 336 A.2d 572 (Del. 1975).

[31] Donna Steele, *TWA Cabin Attendants Wings of Pride: A Pictorial History, 1935–1985* (Marceline, MO: Walsworth Publishing Company, 1985), 200–201.

[32] Steele, 207.

[33] Elizabeth Rich, *Flying High: What It's Like to Be an Airline Stewardess* (New York: Stein and Day, 1970), 167–171.

[34] Rich, 30.

[35] Christopher Hearne Jr., "Life After Waddell & Reed for TWA's Breech Academy," *KC Confidential*, October 9, 2019.

[36] Steele, 223.

[37] Barbara Rosewicz, "TWA Moms Can Take Wing Again," United Press International, February 24, 1982.

[38] TWA board minutes, December 5, 1973.

[39] National Transportation Safety Board Aircraft Accident Report no. NTSB-AAR-75-7, "Trans World Airlines, Inc. Boeing 707-331B N8734 in the Ionian Sea, September 8, 1974," adopted March 26, 1975, 7–8.

[40] Ibid., 21–22.

[41] Ibid., Appendix H.

[42] National Transportation Safety Board Aircraft Accident Report no. NTSB-AAR-75-16, "Trans World Airlines, Inc. Boeing 727-231, N54328, Berryville, Virginia, December 1, 1974," issued November 26, 1975, 15.

[43] Ibid., 39–40.

[44] Ibid., 52.

[45] Ibid., 41.

[46] TWA annual report, 1973.

[47] TWA annual report, 1974.

[48] TWA annual report, chairman's letter, 1974.

[49] TWA annual report, 1974.

[50] TWA board minutes, June 12, 1975.

[51] Serling, 321.

[52] Richard Witkin, "Wiser, Who Quit TWA, Named Pan Am President," *New York Times*, December 17, 1975.

[53] TWA annual report, 1976.

[54] Ibid.

[55] Ibid.

[56] Julius Karesh and Rick Montgomery, *TWA: Kansas City's Hometown Airline* (Kansas City: *Kansas City Star* Books, 2001).

[57] Serling, 318.

[58] TWA board minutes, September 21, 1977.

[59] TWA annual report, 1978.

[60] Davies, *TWA*, 68.

[61] Davies, *TWA*, 80.

[62] TWA board minutes, October 17, 1978.

[63] Ibid.

[64] Ibid.

[65] Davies, *TWA*, 82.

[66] TWA board minutes, April 26, 1978.

[67] TWA board minutes, September 20, 1978.

[68] TWA board minutes, October 19, 1977.

[69] TWA annual report, 1977.

[70] TWA board minutes, August 12. 1978.

[71] Proxy statement, September 7, 1978.

[72] R. E. G. Davies, *Airlines of the Jet Age: A History* (Washington, DC: Smithsonian Institution Scholarly Press, 2011), 139.

[73] John W. Barnum, "What Prompted Airline Deregulation 20 Years Ago? What Were the Objectives of that Deregulation and How Were They Achieved?" (Presentation to the Aeronautical Law Committee of the Business Law Section of the International Bar Association, September 15, 1998), http://corporate.findlaw.com/law-library/what-prompted-airline-deregulation-20-years-ago-what-were-the.html#sthash.dSsd5RJX.dpuf.

[74] Barnum, Ibid.

[75] *The Travel Insider*, "A History of US Airline Deregulation, Part 3: The 1970s: Seven Reasons Why Airline Regulation Was Removed" (2010), http://thetravelinsider.info/airlinemismanagement/airlinederegulation1.htm.

[76] Davies, *Airlines of the Jet Age,* 140.

[77] Barnum, Ibid.

[78] TWA board minutes, October 22, 1975.

[79] TWA annual report, 1975.

[80] Jagdeth N. Sheth, Fred C. Allvine, Can Uslay and Ashutosh Dixit, *Deregulation and Competition: Lessons from the Airline Industry* (Thousand Oaks, CA: SAGE Publications, 2007), 26–27.

[81] Testimony of Charles E. Meyer Jr. before the Senate Aviation Subcommittee, March 24, 1977.

[82] Alfred E. Kahn, "Airline Deregulation," http://www.econlib.org/library/Enc1/AirlineDeregulation.html.

[83] Davies, *Airlines of the Jet Age*, 141.

[84] Betts, 176.

[85] TWA annual report, 1978.

[86] TWC annual report, 1979.

[97] TWA board minutes, September 19, 1979.

[88] TWC special meeting of stockholders minutes, October 18, 1979.

[89] TWC annual report, 1979.

[90] Karash and Montgomery, 52.

[91] TWA board minutes, December 5, 1979.

[92] Davies, *TWA*, 89.

[93] Davies, *TWA*, 88.

[94] TWA board minutes, December 5, 1979.

[95] TWA board minutes, January 23, 1980.

[96] "Aircraft Configuration, TWA Boeing 727, U.S. Visit of His Holiness Pope Paul II, October 2–6, 1979"; "Aircraft Configuration TWA Boeing 747, Washington, D.C.–Rome Flight of His Holiness Pope Paul II, October 7, 1979," Trans World Airlines Archives, Collection M-234, Mercantile Library, St. Louis, Box 1-64.

[97] National Transportation Safety Board Aircraft Accident Report no. NTSB-AAR-81-8, "Trans World Airlines, Inc. Boeing 727-31, N740TW, Near Saginaw, Michigan, April 4, 1979," June 9, 1981, 2–3.

[98] Ibid., 34–35.

[99] Ibid., 36

[100] H. G. Bissenger, "Eleven Years after Plane Took a Dive, Pilot Tries to Clear His Reputation," *Chicago Tribune*, October 14, 1990.

[101] TWA board minutes, December 10, 1980.

[102] Davies, *TWA*, 82.

[103] Davies, *TWA*, 66–68; 76.

[104] TWA board minutes, October 27, 1982.

[105] Davies, *TWA*, 78.

[106] "#8778-What a Workhorse!" *Skyliner*, January 2, 1984; Jon Proctor, "'Grand Old Lady' Retires," *Skyliner*, October 24, 1983; Captain Ed Betts, "'One of the Finest Aircraft Ever,'" *Skyliner*, October 10, 1983; "TWA Retires Last 707s on October 30," *Skyliner*, October 10, 1983.

[107] TWA annual report, 1982.

[108] Sheth et al., 60–61.

[109] Daniel L. Rust, Lambert–St. Louis International Airport's Alternative W-1W: A Case Study (Business History Conference, 2011), thebhc.org/BEHonline/2011/rust, 6.

[110] Bob Blanchard, "TWA's New Service to Benefit St. Louis," *St. Louis Globe-Democrat*, September 9, 1982.

[111] Rick Stoff, "FAA Studies Lambert Delays," *St. Louis Globe-Democrat*, March 18, 1984.

[112] Rick Stoff, "TWA Unveils New Concourse at Lambert," *St. Louis Globe-Democrat*, July 20, 1983.

[113] Ann Saunders, "Commuters: Taking Off," *Skyliner*, November 10, 1980.

[114] Davies, *TWA*, 99–101.

[115] Thomas D. Pagano, "15 Military Controllers Arrive at Lambert," *St. Louis Globe-Democrat*, August 13, 1981.

[116] *St. Louis Globe-Democrat*, August 24, 1981.

[117] Rick Stoff, "Last of Airport Limits to Go Soon, Official Says," *St. Louis Globe-Democrat*, April 14, 1983.

[118] TWC annual report, 1981.

[119] Ibid.

[120] TWA annual report, 1982.

[121] TWA board minutes, December 7, 1982.

[122] TWA board minutes, January 26, 1983.

[123] TWA annual report, 1983.

[124] Letter to shareholders, TWA annual report, 1983; "Spin-Off Voted," *Skyliner*, January 16, 1984.

[125] Ibid.

[126] Ibid.

[127] TWA annual report, letter to shareholders, 1984.

[128] Form 10-K, 1984, 3.

[129] TWA annual report, letter to shareholders, 1984.

CHAPTER 7

[1] R. E. G. Davies, *Airlines of the United States Since 1914* (Washington, DC: Smithsonian Institution Scholarly Press, 1982), 389.

[2] Bill Bourne and Rich Roberts, *Ozark Airlines Contrails* (Mission, KS: Inter-Collegiate Press, 1983), 15.

[3] R. E. G. Davies, *TWA—An Airline and Its Aircraft* (McLean, VA: Paladwr Press, 2000), 92.

[4] Bourne and Roberts, 18.

[5] Frederick W. Roos, "Ozark: Our Hometown Airline," *American Institute of Aeronautics and Astronautics Gateway News* (July 1981), 4.

[6] Bourne and Roberts, 39.

[7] Bourne and Roberts, 89.

[8] *Skyliner*, October 30, 1958, 4.

[9] Davies, *Airlines*, 399.

[10] Bourne and Roberts, 91.

[11] Davies, *Airlines*, 406–407.

[12] Bourne and Roberts, 39.

[13] Bourne and Roberts, 45.

[14] David H. Stringer, *America's Local Service Airlines* (Huntington Beach, CA: American Aviation Historical Society, 2016), 69.

[15] Bourne and Roberts, 94.

[16] Bourne and Roberts, 65.

[17] Bourne and Roberts, 95–97.

[18] Bourne and Roberts, 62.

[19] Bourne and Roberts, 62.

[20] Rick Stoff, "TWA, Ozark Set Boarding Records," *St. Louis Globe-Democrat*, June 9, 1982.

[21] *St. Louis Globe-Democrat*, February 20, 1985.

[22] Carolyn Callison, "TWA Expansion to Boost Lambert Flights 17.5%," *St. Louis Globe-Democrat*, February 5, 1985.

[23] Margaret Sheppard, "British Caledonian to Soon Depart from Lambert," *St. Louis Globe-Democrat*, October 12, 1984.

[24] *Los Angeles Times*, February 28, 1986.

[25] Ozark Holdings Inc. proxy statement, annual meeting of stockholders to be held August 8, 1986, 8.

CHAPTER 8

[1] Carolyn Callison, "TWA Expansion to Boost Lambert Flights 17.5%," *St. Louis Globe-Democrat*, February 5, 1985.

[2] Rick Stoff, "TWA Bid Worries Lambert," *St. Louis Globe-Democrat*, May 23, 1985.

[3] TWA board minutes, May 20, 1985.

[4] C. E. Meyer, letter to the Honorable Richard Gephardt, May 30, 1985.

[5] Carl A. Icahn, letter to the Honorable Richard Gephardt, June 3, 1985.

[6] "TWA Law Ruled Unconstitutional," *St. Louis Globe-Democrat*, June 26, 1985.

[7] Albert L. Schweitzer and Roger McGrath, "Judge Dissolves Order Barring Icahn's TWA Bid," *St. Louis Globe-Democrat*, June 13, 1985.

[8] "Icahn Wins Round in Battle with TWA," *St. Louis Globe-Democrat*, June 11, 1985.

[9] "The Summer of 1985: How It Was—An Interview with MEC Chairman Harry Hoglander," *Lancet Flight Forum of the TWA MEC*, October/November 1985, 3.

[10] TWA board minutes, June 13, 1985.

[11] Ibid.

[12] *Lancet Flight Forum* Hoglander interview, 3.

[13] Connie Bruck, "Kamikaze: How Texas Air's Frank Lorenzo Wrecked His Own Chance to Acquire TWA—and Carl Icahn Picked up the Pieces," *American Lawyer*, December 1985, 75–76.

[14] Associated Press, "He's Pulled a Grenade Pin," *New York Times*, June 15, 1985.

[15] Except as noted, the following account of the hijacking is based on John Testrake and David J. Wimbish in *Triumph over Terror on Flight 847* (Grand Rapids, MI: Fleming H. Revell Company, 1987), and B. Christian Zimmermann, *Hostage in a Hostage World* (St. Louis: Concordia Publishing House, 1985).

[16] "49 Still Held on Airliner in Algiers," *St. Louis Globe-Democrat*, June 16, 1985.

[17] Harry Hoglander, "Recollections of a Year Past," *Lancet Flight Forum*, February 1986, 4.

[18] Ibid.

19 "Beleaguered TWA Says Strike Vote by Flight Attendants Was 'Bad Timing,'" UPI, June 21, 1985.

20 *TWA Newsgram* 59, August 13, 1985.

21 TWA board minutes, August 20, 1985.

22 Harry Hoglander, "An Open Letter to the TWA Board of Directors," *Wall Street Journal*, August 16, 1985.

23 Ibid.

24 Hoglander, "Recollections," 4.

25 *Lancet Flight Forum*, Hoglander interview, 5–6.

26 Ibid.

27 *TWA Newsgram* 61, August 20, 1985.

28 Bruck, 82.

29 TWA board minutes, September 27, 1985.

30 Paul Wagman, "Icahn: His Personal Game of Monopoly Has Made Him One of the Wealthiest People in America," *St. Louis Post-Dispatch*, November 10, 1985.

31 Ibid.

32 TWA press release, "Who Is Carl Icahn?" May 30, 1985.

33 Ibid.

34 Ibid. Interview with Paul Wagman, May 16, 2022.

35 Ibid.

36 Ibid.

37 William A. Carley and Daniel Hertzberg, "TWA Is Said to Be Seeking Bidders Again," *Wall Street Journal*, December 18, 1985.

38 William A. Carley, "TWA's Auction Is Set Back as 2 Unions Vehemently Object to Sale to Texas Air," *Wall Street Journal*, December 19, 1985.

39 Hoglander, "Recollections," 5.

40 *The Tale's End: OZA Council 106 Newsletter*, Final Edition, May 1987, 6.

41 Form 10-K, 1985, 2.

42 Christopher Carey, "Icahn Era Ends," *St. Louis Post-Dispatch*, January 6, 1993.

43 Wagman interview.

44 "On This Day, 2 April 1986: Bomb Tears Hole in Aircraft over Greece," BBC News, http://news.bbc.co.uk/onthisday/hi/dates/stories/april/2/newsid_4357000/4357159.stm.

45 Ibid.

46 *Los Angeles Times*, February 28, 1986.

47 Esperon Martinez Jr., "Mergers: Vexing Consolidations," *Airline Pilot*, August 1986, 14.

[48] Martinez, 15–16.

[49] Mike J. O'Toole, September 5, 1986, letter to Henry A. Duffy and attached "Chronology of Events."

[50] Ibid.

[51] Angelo Marchione, August 25, 1986, letter to Henry Duffy.

[52] *The Tale's End*, 17.

[53] Ibid., 11–12.

[54] Ibid., 17.

[55] Jean T. McKelvey, Ed., *Cleared for Takeoff: Airline Labor Relations Since Deregulation* (Ithaca, NY: ILR Press, 1988), 157–158.

[56] Interview with Linda Kunz, August 16, 2018.

[57] Trans World Airlines, Securities and Exchange Commission Form 10-K for the Year Ended December 31, 1986, 36.

[58] Ibid., 2–3.

[59] Ibid., 5.

[60] Ibid., 2.

[61] Angelo Marchione, letter to all TWA pilots, September 22, 1987.

[62] Paul Wagman, "TWA Says Icahn Buyout May Be Scrapped," *St. Louis Post-Dispatch*, October 2, 1987.

[63] Wagman, "Icahn Withdraws Bid to Take TWA Private," *St. Louis Post-Dispatch*, October 21, 1987.

[64] "TWA Is Buying 12 Million Shares of Texaco's Stock," *St. Louis Post-Dispatch*, November 26, 1987.

[65] "TWA, ALPA Agree Until '92," *Skyliner*, January 15, 1987, 1.

[66] TWA MEC negotiating committee, "Letter to All TWA Pilots," December 22, 1987.

[67] Wagman, "Pilots Show TWA by Not Showing TWA," *St. Louis Post-Dispatch*, January 6, 1988.

[68] TWA board minutes, January 13, 1988.

[69] TWA board minutes, January 18, 1988.

[70] TWA board minutes, April 26, 1988.

[71] TWA board minutes, May 6, 1988.

[72] SEC Form 10-K for the year ended December 31, 1988, 1.

[73] "Union Calls for U.S. Investigation of TWA," *Aviation Week & Space Technology*, September 5, 1988, 229.

[74] Paul Wagman, "TWA Pilots' Union Head Steps Down," *St. Louis Post-Dispatch*, 77June 27, 1988.

[75] Associated Press, "TWA Stockholders OK Sale to Icahn," *St. Louis Post-Dispatch*, September 8, 1988.

[76] TWA Master Executive Council, *The Spinner*, September 1988, 9.

[77] Robert J. Cole, "COMPANY NEWS: Holders Support Plan Taking T.W.A. Private," *New York Times*, September 8, 1988.

[78] Thomas G. Donlan, "Super Pilot or Predator? Zeroing in on What Carl Icahn Has Wrought at TWA," *Barron's*, September 26, 1988, 8.

[79] Ibid.

[80] Form 10-K, 1988, F-4.

[81] Carey, "Attendants Seek Probe of Icahn's Purchases," *St. Louis Post-Dispatch*, December 14, 1988.

[82] Form 10-K, 1988, 25.

[83] "Icahn Ends Pursuit of Eastern," New York Times News Service, October 18, 1988.

[84] Christopher P. Fotos, "TWA Orders Airbus A330s to Upgrade Aging Fleet," *Aviation Week & Space Technology*, April 3, 1989, 64–65.

[85] "TWA Lost $4.4 Million in 2nd Quarter," Associated Press, August 12, 1989.

[86] Todd Vogel, "Carl Icahn Has Lots of Cash. Will He Spend It on TWA?" *Business Week*, July 17, 1989, 86–87.

[87] TWA board minutes, June 13, 1989.

[88] Carey, "Rumors Fly as TWA Seeks Partner," *St. Louis Post-Dispatch*, August 13, 1989.

[89] Carey, "TWA Pilots in Dispute about Chairman," *St. Louis Post-Dispatch*, September 15, 1989.

[90] David Lawler, "Pilots Take Aim at Icahn," *St. Louis Sun*, December 5, 1989.

[91] James T. McKenna, "TWA Unions Attempt to Shape Strategy for Gaining Leverage Over Airline Sale," *Aviation Week & Space Technology*, December 4, 1989.

[92] David Lawler and Christy Marshall, "Icahn Selling London Route," *St. Louis Sun*, December 19, 1989.

[93] Carey, "TWA Pilots Blast Sale of Route," *St. Louis Post-Dispatch*, December 19, 1989.

[94] Carey, "TWA's Fate in Icahn's Hands," *St. Louis Post-Dispatch*, December 26, 1989.

[95] Kent T. Scott, letter to all TWA pilots, February 6, 1990.

[96] Form 10-K, 1989, 22.

[97] Carey, "TWA Loss Frees Icahn to Sell Assets," *St. Louis Post-Dispatch*, February 2, 1990; "Summary of Icahn Agreements," Lancet Flight Forum, January 1990, 4–5.

[98] David Lawler, "Icahn: Union Breaks Will Make TWA fly," *St. Louis Sun*, February 6, 1990; Carey, "Silence Broken in Icahn Battle with Pilots," *St. Louis Post-Dispatch*, February 13, 1990.

[99] Lawler, "Unions Hold Key to Airline's Direction," *St. Louis Sun*, February 9, 1990.

[100] Daniel J. Kadlec, "Icahn Pledge to TWA Pilots," *St. Louis Sun*, February 15, 1990.

[101] Lawler, "Union's Course: Keep 'Em Flying," *St. Louis Sun*, February 15, 1990.

[102] Carey, "Civic Leaders Frustrated in Efforts to Help TWA," *St. Louis Post-Dispatch*, February 22, 1990.

[103] Robert L. Koenig, "Danforth Protests on TWA," *St. Louis Post-Dispatch*, February 24, 1990.

[104] Koenig, "Travelers Called Losers in Airline Deregulation," *St. Louis Post-Dispatch*, March 29, 1990.

[105] Ibid.

[106] Form 10-K, 1989, 1–2.

[107] "Pilots' Chief: 'No Concessions,'" *St. Louis Sun*, February 21, 1990.

[108] Kadlec and Lawler, "Pilots Resist Concessions," *St. Louis Sun*, March 1, 1990.

[109] Lawler, "Icahn Tries a New Line," *St. Louis Sun*, April 6, 1990.

[110] Phil Linsalata, "TWA May Give Up Routes," *St. Louis Post-Dispatch*, May 3, 1990.

[111] Phillip Dine, "Work Slowdown Hits TWA in KC," *St. Louis Post-Dispatch*, May 12, 1990.

[112] Carey and Linsalata, "Icahn's Wealth Soars, TWA's Falls," *St. Louis Post-Dispatch*, May 20, 1990.

[113] Ibid.

[114] Carey, "TWA to Cut 5 Planes and 7 Cities," *St. Louis Post-Dispatch*, June 26, 1990.

[115] Carey, "TWA Loses Three Senior Vice Presidents," *St. Louis Post-Dispatch*, October 11, 1990; "TWA Laying Off 24 New Pilots," *St. Louis Post-Dispatch*, October 13, 1990.

[116] Carey, "TWA Cutting Capacity 10 Percent," *St. Louis Post-Dispatch*, October 23, 1990.

[117] Carey, "TWA Lays Off 390, About 50 Here," *St. Louis Post-Dispatch*, November 14, 1990.

[118] Carey, "Airlines Improve Performance; TWA at Back of Pack," *St. Louis Post-Dispatch*, November 7, 1990.

[119] Carey, "Air Lock," *St. Louis Post-Dispatch*, November 13, 1990.

[120] Reuters News Service, "TWA Agrees to Sell Routes to London," *St. Louis Post-Dispatch*, December 17, 1990.

[121] Koenig and Carey, "U. S. Plans to Review TWA Deal," *St. Louis Post-Dispatch*, December 21, 1990.

[122] Carey, "Many Demands on TWA's Cash," *St. Louis Post-Dispatch*, December 23, 1990.

[123] Form 10-K, 1990, 36.

[124] TWA board minutes, February 5, 1991.

[125] Carey, "TWA Feeling Weight of Debt Load," *St. Louis Post-Dispatch*, February 10, 1991.

[126] Koenig, "Effort to Get Buyer for TWA Falls Short," *St. Louis Post-Dispatch*, March 21, 1991; Carey and Koenig, "TWA Buyout Package Set," *St. Louis Post-Dispatch*, March 30, 1991.

[127] Carey and Koenig, "American Warns Against TWA Deal," *St. Louis Post-Dispatch*, April 5, 1991.

[128] Carey and Koenig, "Airline Adamant on Routes," *St. Louis Post-Dispatch*, April 17, 1991.

[129] Carey and Patricia Corrigan, "American to Buy Three TWA Routes," *St. Louis Post-Dispatch*, May 3, 1991.

[130] Adam Goodman, "TWA Offers to Buy Back Its Debt," *St. Louis Post-Dispatch*, May 16, 1991.

[131] William Flannery, "TWA Averts Showdown," *St. Louis Post-Dispatch*, July 26, 1991.

[132] Allan Sloan, "Icahn Hopes to Pull Off a Great Escape at TWA," *Los Angeles Times*, July 31, 1991.

[133] Kent T. Scott, letter to all TWA pilots, August 26, 1991.

[134] William F. Compton, letter to all TWA pilots, September 10, 1991.

[135] Koenig, "Amendment Would Keep Icahn from Bailing Out," *St. Louis Post-Dispatch*, November 22, 1991; "TWA Safeguard Approved," *St. Louis Post-Dispatch*, November 28, 1991.

[136] Compton, letter to all TWA pilots, December 18, 1991.

[137] Form 10-K, 1991, 40, F-3, F-31.

[138] Koenig, "Agency to Protect TWA Pensions," *St. Louis Post-Dispatch*, February 5, 1992.

[139] Carey, "TWA Will Fly to Moscow," *St. Louis Post-Dispatch*, February 28, 1992.

[140] Carey, "TWA Makes Deeper Cut in Fares," *St. Louis Post-Dispatch*, April 13, 1992.

[141] Carey, "TWA Shows Loss of $86.8 Million for First Quarter," *St. Louis Post-Dispatch*, May 18, 1992.

[142] Jim Gallagher, "Icahn Blamed in TWA Talks," *St. Louis Post-Dispatch*, August 11, 1992.

[143] William Compton, "TWA: Surviving the Raid," *Airline Pilot,* March/April 1993, 15.

[144] Allison Frankel, "Getting the Other to Blink," *American Lawyer,* April 1993.

[145] David A. Vise, "Pension Struggle Puts TWA Chief's Fortune on Line," *Washington Post*, October 25, 1992.

[146] Frankel, ibid.

[147] Letter, Christopher S. Bond and John C. Danforth to the Honorable Lynn Martin, October 8, 1992.

[148] Adam Goodman and Carey, "The Deal That Saved TWA," *St. Louis Post-Dispatch*, December 13, 1992.

[149] Frankel, Ibid.; Compton, 16; "It's a Deal: Agreement with PBGC Clears Way for TWA to File Reorganization Plan," *Skyliner*, December 18, 1992.

[150] Richard A. Gephardt, letter to Robin Wilson, October 23, 1992.

CHAPTER 9

[1] Trans World Airlines, Securities Exchange Commission Form 10-K for the year ended December 31, 1992, 56.

[2] "Focus on TWA," *Skyliner*, October 16, 1992.

[3] "TWA Markets New Image with Advertising Campaign," *Skyliner*, January 22, 1993.

[4] Robert Sanford, "Less Is More as TWA Removes Seats," *St. Louis Post-Dispatch*, January 29, 1993.

[5] "Co-Chief Executives Explain Business Plan for the 'New' TWA," *Skyliner*, March 26, 1993.

[6] Christopher Carey, "Flying into the Future," *St. Louis Post-Dispatch*, February 28, 1993.

[7] Patricia Miller, "Travelers spot more smiles at 'new' TWA," *St. Louis Business Journal*, March 22–28, 1993.

[8] Michael Mecham and Anthony Velocci, "First Chinese-Built MD-83s Find Home with TWA," *Aviation Week & Space Technology*, May 3, 1993; *TWA St. Louis Weekly*, April 30, 1993.

[9] Carey, "TWA Soars to Top Spot in U.S. On-Time Survey," *St. Louis Post-Dispatch*, March 12, 1993.

[10] Carey, "TWA Will Announce New HQ Next Month," *St. Louis Post-Dispatch*, March 26, 1993.

[11] "Zander Rejects TWA Employment Offer," *Bloomberg Business News,* August 19, 1993.

[12] "Up, Up and Away: Flying Out of Bankruptcy," *Skyliner*, August/September 1993.

[13] Form 10-K, 1993, 41.

[14] Carey, "TWA's Cool Summer May Portend Cold Winter," *St. Louis Post-Dispatch*, November 17, 1993; Anthony L. Velocci, "Losses Shake Faith in TWA," *Aviation Week & Space Technology*, November 22, 1993.

[15] TWA annual report, 1993, 32.

[16] Velocci, "TWA Taps 'Outsider' to Heal Ailing Carrier," *Aviation Week* & Space Technology, January 10, 1994.

[17] *Kansas City Star*, April 1, 1994.

[18] "Board Names Craib Chairman, CEO," *Skyliner*, January 28, 1994.

[19] Victoria Lee Frankovich, letter to "Dear Fellow Flight Attendants and Friends," April 26, 1993.

[20] Form 10-K, 1993, F-4

[21] Carey, "TWA Adds Summer Flights at Lambert," *St. Louis Post-Dispatch*, March 18, 1994.

[22] Compton, letter to all TWA pilots, April 21, 1994.

[23] David Berkley, "Cultural Change at TWA Culminates with the Appointment of the Reengineering Team," *Lancet Flight Forum*, August 1994, 1.

[24] TWA pilots' master executive council, "Handouts for Visits with the Membership," June 1994.

[25] Compton, letter to all TWA pilots, July 15, 1994.

[26] Carey, "TWA Is Laying Off 500 Workers," *St. Louis Post-Dispatch*, August 4, 1994.

[27] William Flannery, "Layoffs Prompt Analysts to Question TWA's Future," *St. Louis Post-Dispatch*, August 5, 1994; "TWA President, Pilots Meet on Restructuring," *St. Louis Post-Dispatch*, August 6, 1994.

[28] "The Message Is Clear: TWA Making Radical Changes to Ensure Survival," *Skyliner*, August 26, 1994.

[29] Carey, "TWA Pilots Land Cost-Cutting Deal," *St. Louis Post-Dispatch*, September 2, 1994.

[30] Danielle Bochove, "TWA Employees Seek Silver Lining in a Cloud-Filled Sky; All 3 Unions Reach Agreements," *St. Louis Business Journal*, September 26–October 2, 1994.

[31] Ibid.

[32] "TWA Stock Nosedives after Talk about Debt," *Bloomberg Business News*, September 29, 1994.

[33] Carey, "TWA Has First Operating Profit in 4 Years," *St. Louis Post-Dispatch*, November 2, 1994.

[34] Carey, "Trading in TWA Stock Grounded," *St. Louis Post-Dispatch*, November 3, 1994.

[35] Carey, "TWA's Chief Is Hopeful," *St. Louis Post-Dispatch*, November 11, 1994.

[36] Compton, "Three Down and One to Go," *Lancet Flight Forum*, December 1994, 4.

[37] Robert Manor, "TWA Pilots Picket Offices of Investors Opposed to Debt Plan," *St. Louis Post-Dispatch*, January 12, 1995.

[38] Form 10-K, 1994, 39.

[39] Tim O'Neil, "The Pilot Averted a Catastrophe—Smaller Plane Called Cause of Collision," *St. Louis Post-Dispatch*, November 24, 1994.

[40] National Transportation Safety Board Aircraft Accident Report NTSB/AAR-95/05, adopted August 30, 1995, 48.

[41] Carey, "Icahn May Get Role in TWA Overhaul," *St. Louis Post-Dispatch*, January 13, 1995.

[42] TWA board minutes, February 28, 1995, 6; Form 10-K, 1995, 6.

[43] Richard A. Gephardt and Richard K. Armey, letter to Honorable Federico Peña, June 8, 1995.

[44] Richard Gephardt, letter to His Excellency Tony Blair, February 5, 1998.

[45] Form 10-K, 1995, 13–14.

[46] Elaine X. Grant, "TWA—Death of a Legend," *St. Louis Magazine*, July 2006.

[47] TWA board minutes, April 18, 1995, 10; July 20, 1995, 8.

[48] Form 10-K, 1996, 5.

[49] Unless otherwise stated, all factual information concerning the crash is from the National Transportation Safety Board Aircraft accident report "In-flight Breakup Over the

Atlantic Ocean, Trans World Airlines Flight 800, Boeing 747-131, N93119, Near East Moriches, New York," NTSB Number AAR-00/03, Adopted August 23, 2000 (the "NTSB Report").

[50] Julius A. Karash and Rick Montgomery, *TWA: Kansas City's Hometown Airline* (Kansas City: *Kansas City Star* Books, 2001), 77.

[51] NTSB report, 326.

[52] NTSB report, 178.

[53] "Federal Agencies Deny TWA Flight 800 Shot down by Missile," CNN, November 8, 1996.

[54] "Pierre Salinger Syndrome and the TWA 800 conspiracies," CNN, July 17, 2006.

[55] Lydia Saad and Frank Newport, "Cause of TWA Flight 800 Crash Not Settled in Americans' Minds," Gallup News Service, May 29, 1997.

[56] Donaldson, "Interim Report on the Crash of TWA Flight 800 and the Actions of the NTSB and the FBI," July 17, 1998.

[57] Elaine Scarry, "The Fall of Flight 800: The Possibility of Electromagnetic Interference," *New York Review of Books*, April 9, 1998.

[58] International Association of Machinists and Aerospace Workers: "Analysis and Recommendations Regarding T.W.A. Flight 800."

[59] NTSB report, 87–89.

[60] NTSB report, 93.

[61] Pat Milton, "FBI Denies Newsman's Claim Navy Missile Shot Down TWA Flight 800," Associated Press, November 8, 1996.

[62] NTSB report, 248.

[63] NTSB report, 251.

[64] NTSB report, 258–289.

[65] NTSB report, 271–294.

[66] "NTSB Denies Petition on 1996 Crash of TWA Flight 800," NTSB news release, July 2, 2014, https://www.ntsb.gov/news/press-releases/Pages/PR20140702.aspx.

[67] Thomas Petzinger Jr., *Hard Landing: The Epic Contest for Power and Profits That Plunged the Airlines into Chaos* (New York: Three Rivers Press, 1996), 50.

[68] Carey, "TWA Moves to Downsize in New York," *St. Louis Post-Dispatch*, December 23, 1996.

[69] Carey, "TWA Future Is Focused on Lambert—Travelers Here May Get to Choose from More Flights, Destinations," *St. Louis Post-Dispatch*, December 29, 1996; Davies, *TWA*, 103–104.

[70] Form 10-K, 1996, 15.

[71] Form 10-K, 1997, 2–5.

[72] Carey and Dine, "TWA Union Wants CEO Removed," *St. Louis Post-Dispatch*, February 4, 1997.

[73] Phillip Dine, "TWA Attendants to Join Machinists," *St. Louis Post-Dispatch*, February 28, 1997.

[74] Form 10-K, 1997, 19.

[75] Kyong M. Song, "TWA Pilots Replace Union Chief Joe Chronic," *St. Louis Post-Dispatch*, March 17, 1999.

[76] Song, "TWA Reports $120.5 Million Loss for 1998," *St. Louis Post-Dispatch*, February 18, 1999.

[77] TWA board minutes, May 25, 1999.

[78] TWA board minutes, July 27, 1999.

[79] R. Thomas Buffenbarger, letter to the editor, *St. Louis Post-Dispatch*, June 16, 1999.

[80] Form 10-K, 1998, 1, 5.

[81] Daniel L. Rust, *The Aerial Crossroads of America*: *St. Louis's Lambert Airport* (St. Louis: Missouri History Museum Press, 2016), 233–235.

[82] Ibid.

[83] Carolyn Tuft, "Airport Decides; Bridgeton in Way—Growth Targets Third of Municipality; Foes Vow Fight," *St. Louis Post-Dispatch*, July 7, 1995.

[84] Kyung M. Song, "TWA Hopes Improvements Help Its Business by Cutting Delays," *St. Louis Post-Dispatch*, October 1, 1998.

[85] Ken Leiser, "Lambert Drops from List of 10 Busiest Airports—Those Who Oppose Expansion Say This Bolsters Their Cause—Ranking Is Now No. 11," *St. Louis Post-Dispatch*, February 15, 2000.

[86] *City of Bridgeton, et al., v. FAA, et al.*, 212 F.3d 448 (8th Cir. 2000).

[87] *City of Bridgeton v. City of St. Louis*, 18 S.W.3d 107 (Mo. App. E. D. 2000).

[88] Tim O'Neil, "1999: The Pope's Trip to St. Louis Was a 31-Hour Whirlwind Visit," *St. Louis Post-Dispatch*, January 26, 2020.

[89] William F. Compton, "Employee-Ownership, a Union Appointed Director, and Profits: the TWA Story," undated address to the National Academy of Arbitrators.

[90] Form 10-Q, June 30, 2000, 11.

[91] Cynthia Wilson, "NewJets Might be TWA's Ticket to Regional Success," *St. Louis Post-Dispatch*, August 10, 2000.

[92] "TWA Misses Some Payments to Worker Retirement Funds," Bloomberg News, December 23, 2000.

[93] Wilson, "Icahn-Owned Firm Will Terminate Two TWA Pension Funds," *St. Louis Post-Dispatch*, December 2, 2000.

CHAPTER 10

[1] "Credit-Rating Agency Places TWA's Debt on Its Watch List," Bloomberg News, January 6, 2001.

[2] Tom Johnson and Kim Kahn, "AMR Takes TWA Aboard," *CNN Money*, January 10, 2001, http://money.cnn.com/2001/01/10/deals/amr_twa.

[3] Compton, letter to the employees and retirees of TWA, January 10, 2001.

[4] Philip Dine, "American Is Buying Jets, Gates from U.S. Airways," *St. Louis Post-Dispatch*, January 11, 2001.

[5] Jim Gallagher and Chern Yeh Kwok, "American May Have Trouble Combining Work Forces," *St. Louis Post-Dispatch*, January 11, 2001.

[6] Gallagher, "Icahn Lawyer Says TWA Rejected Deal to Avoid Bankruptcy," *St. Louis Post-Dispatch*, January 13, 2001.

[7] Dine, "TWA Plan for Managers' Incentives Is Criticized," *St. Louis Post-Dispatch*, January 27, 2001.

[8] Wilson and Dine, "Deal between American, TWA Draws Objections," *St. Louis Post-Dispatch*, January 25, 2001.

[9] Dine, "TWA Chief Gets Stuck in Courthouse Elevator," *St. Louis Post-Dispatch*, January 28, 2001.

[10] Dine, "TWA, American Deal Spurs Bill to Limit Mergers," *St. Louis Post-Dispatch*, January 30, 2001.

[11] Statement of Donald Carty, Hearing before the Committee on Commerce, Science and Transportation, United States Senate, "Effects of the American Airlines/TWA Transaction and Other Airline Industry Consolidation on Competition and the Consumer," S. Hrg. 107-1094, February 1, 2001.

[12] Statement of William F. Compton, S. Hrg. 107-1094, February 1, 2001.

[13] Deirdre Shesgreen, "Key Senators Support Plan to Sell TWA," *St. Louis Post-Dispatch*, February 8, 2001.

[14] Wilson, "American Airlines Chief Says Company Isn't Taking Competing Offer for TWA Seriously," *St. Louis Post-Dispatch*, February 16, 2001.

[15] Dine and Wilson, "American Runs into Competition in Bidding for TWA," *St. Louis Post-Dispatch*, March 1, 2001.

[16] Wilson and Dine, "Icahn Group, 4 Others Bid for TWA's Assets," *St. Louis Post-Dispatch*, March 6, 2001.

[17] Wilson and Dine, "TWA's Top Union Wants American to Tell More about Jobs," *St. Louis Post-Dispatch*, March 9, 2001; "Bankruptcy Judge Calls Icahn's Offer to Buy TWA 'a Joke,'" *St. Louis Post-Dispatch*, March 10, 2001.

[18] Wilson and Dine, "Judge Puts off Ruling on TWA Sale until Monday," *St. Louis Post-Dispatch*, March 11, 2001.

[19] Wilson and Dine, "Judge Clears Way for American," *St. Louis Post-Dispatch*, March 13, 2001.

[20] Tim O'Neil, "Kansas City Celebration Is Delayed by Balky Tug at Airport," *St. Louis Post-Dispatch*, April 10, 2001.

[21] *Bensel, et al. v. Allied Pilots Association, et al.*, 387 F.3d 298, 302 (3d Cir. 2004).

[22] Ibid.

[23] Wilson, "TWA Pilots Don't Like Plan to Put Them into American Seniority List," *St. Louis Post-Dispatch*, November 10, 2001.

[24] Leiser, "Leaders Launch Runway Project," *St. Louis Post-Dispatch*, July 31, 2001.

[25] Harumi Ito and Darin Lee, *Assessing the Impact of the September 11 Terrorist Attacks on U.S. Airline Demand* (Providence: Brown University Press, 2004), 3.

[26] Mark Johanson, "How 9/11 Changed the Way We Travel," *International Business Times*, September 9, 2011.

[27] Ito and Lee, 4, 22.

[28] U. S. Department of Transportation, Bureau of Transportation Statistics, "Airline Travel Since 9/11," December 2005.

[29] Lynne Marek, "AMR's Loss in 3rd Quarter Is a Record $414 Million," Bloomberg News, October 25, 2001.

[30] Cynthia Wilson, "TWA Checks Its Baggage, Begins Final Leg to American," *St. Louis Post-Dispatch*, December 2, 2001.

[31] Compton, "TWA Name Disappears from the Skies," *St. Louis Post-Dispatch*, December 2, 2001.

[32] Wilson, "American Plans to Ground 717s, Bump TWA workers," *St. Louis Post-Dispatch*, January 4, 2002.

[33] Wilson, "TWA Pilots Union Wants American to Work Harder toward Equitable Seniority Pact," *St. Louis Post-Dispatch*, December 8, 2001.

[34] John Hughes, "Carty Says American Airlines' Service Cuts Will Go Deep," Bloomberg News, September 26, 2001.

[35] Ken Moritsugu, "Airlines Try Congressional Fly-By," Knight-Ridder Newspapers, September 25, 2002.

[36] Wilson, "American Airlines Will Idle 42 More Jets to Save $100 Million," *St. Louis Post-Dispatch*, October 17, 2002.

[37] Scott McCartney, "Will AMR Join UAL, US Air in Bankruptcy?" *Wall Street Journal*, February 3, 2003.

[38] Wilson, "American Details Its Request for Saving Nearly $2 Billion," *St. Louis Post-Dispatch*, February 5, 2003.

[39] Wilson, "CEO Says Airline Is Losing Cash at the Rate of $5 Million a Day," *St. Louis Post-Dispatch*, February 6, 2003.

[40] Wilson, "Ex-TWA Workers Are Hit Hard by Concessions," *St. Louis Post-Dispatch*, April 4, 2003.

[41] Wilson, "American Airlines Asks Pilots to Trim Their Ranks by 2,500," *St. Louis Post-Dispatch*, April 3, 2003.

[42] Wilson, "Attendants' Switch Keeps American out of Bankruptcy," *St. Louis Post-Dispatch*, April 17, 2003.

[43] McCartney, Theo Francism and Joann S. Lublin, "Carrier Created Protections for Executives in Event of Reorganization Filing," *Wall Street Journal*, April 17, 2003.

[44] Trebor Banstetter and Bob Cox, "American Airlines Unions Protest Plan for Executive Pay," Knight-Ridder Newspapers, April 18, 2003.

[45] "Watching out for No. 1," *St. Louis Post-Dispatch*, April 22, 2003.

[46] Andrea Ahiles, "Arpey Grew up with Airlines in the Family," Knight Ridder Newspapers, April 27, 2003.

[47] Wilson, "American Sends out Layoff Notices," *St. Louis Post-Dispatch*, April 30, 2003.

[48] Dine, "American Broke Promises, Ex-TWA Workers Testify," *St. Louis Post-Dispatch*, June 13, 2003.

[49] Wilson, "Judge Denies TWA Attendants' Request to Delay Furloughs," *St. Louis Post-Dispatch*, July 1, 2003.

[50] *Bensel v. Allied Pilots Association*, 271, F. Supp.2d 616 (D. N. J., 2003).

[51] Todd Frankel, "UMSL Drops Plan to Honor Former TWA Chief," *St. Louis Post-Dispatch*, May 1, 2003.

[52] Wilson, "Airline Hints at Threat to Hub Here," *St. Louis Post-Dispatch*, July 2, 2003.

[53] Leiser, "Slay, Holden Get No Reassurance from Airline," *St. Louis Post-Dispatch*, July 12, 2003.

[54] Terry Mason, "American Airlines Battles a History of Unsuccessful Mergers," *Dallas Morning News*, January 26, 2013.

[55] Wilson, "Cuts Are All about Money, Airline Chief Tells Analysts," *St. Louis Post-Dispatch*, July 17, 2003.

[56] Ibid.

[57] Shane Graber, "Lambert Field Leads Nation's Large Hubs in Loss of Flights—Airport Handles 2,028 Fewer Flights Weekly, Industry Data Shows," *St. Louis Post-Dispatch*, January 12, 2004.

[58] Leiser, "AA Slashes Operations Here (Airport Authority)—Airport Authority Freezes Spending, Runway Work Goes On," *St. Louis Post-Dispatch*, July 17, 2003.

[59] Lambert–St. Louis International Airport Historical Passenger Statistics and Historical Operations Statistics Since 1985.

[60] Leiser, "Airport Expansion Is Ahead of Schedule—Finishing Work Early Should Help Keep Airport Competitive, Officials Say," *St. Louis Post-Dispatch*, April 30, 2004.

[61] Elisa Crouch, "So Far, Lambert's New Runway Is a Model for Such Projects," *St. Louis Post-Dispatch*, June 12, 2005.

[62] Tim McLaughlin and Elisa Crouch, "Lambert Boardings Hit 20-Year Low," *St. Louis Post-Dispatch*, January 14, 2005; "Lambert's Debt Rating Is Cut amid Service Concerns," *St. Louis Post-Dispatch*, June 7, 2005.

[63] "Boldly Going Nowhere . . . Yet," *St. Louis Post-Dispatch*, April 13, 2006.

[64] Herbert Muschamp, "Stay of Execution for a Dazzling Airline Terminal," *New York Times*, November 6, 2004.

[65] David W. Dunlap, "BLOCKS: Unusual Planning Duel over Kennedy Terminal," *New York Times*, November 28, 2002.

[66] Carol Vogel, "Port Authority Shuts Art Exhibit in Aftermath of Rowdy Party," *New York Times*, October 7, 2004.

[67] Amy Plitt, "TWA Terminal Hotel Celebrates Groundbreaking with a New Rendering," *Curbed New York*, December 15, 2016.

[68] Dante Mazza, "TWA Flight Center at JFK Airport," *American Landmarks*, https://www.americanlandmarks.org/post/2019/07/14/twa-terminal-at-jfk-airport.

[69] *Bensel, et al. v. Allied Pilots Association, et al.*, 387 F.3d at 311-312.

[70] Terry Maxon, "ALPA, ex-TWA Pilots Agree to $53 Million Settlement in American Airlines Seniority Dispute," *Dallas Morning News*, January 23, 2014.

[71] "A Timeline of Events in American Airlines' History," *Dallas Morning News*, February 14, 2013.

[72] United States Department of Justice, Office of Public Affairs, "Justice Department Files Antitrust Lawsuit Challenging Proposed Merger Between US Airways and American Airlines," August 13, 2013, http://www.justice.gov/opa/pr/justice-department-files-antitrust-lawsuit-challenging-proposed-merger-between-us-airways-and.

[73] Jad Wouwad and Christopher Drew, "Justice Dept. Clears Merger of 2 Airlines," *New York Times*, November 12, 2013.

[74] Terry Maxxon, "The Biggest Airline Has the Biggest Profit," *Dallas Morning News*, January 28, 2015, http://www.dallasnews.com/business/airline-industry/20150127-american-airlines-reports-4-billion-in-2014-profit.ece.

[75] Federal Aviation Administration, FAA Aerospace Forecast: Fiscal Years 2015–2035, 15.

[76] FAA Aerospace Forecast, 1.

[77] Mark Johanson, "How 9/11 Changed the Way We Travel," *International Business Times*, September 9, 2011.

[78] Mark Gerchick, *Full Upright and Locked Position: Not-So-Comfortable Truths about Air Travel Today* (New York: W. W. Norton & Company, 2013), 135–136.

[79] Gerchick, 203–204.

[80] United States Department of Transportation Bureau of Transportation Statistics, 2019 Annual and 4th Quarter U.S. Airline Financial Data.

[81] The State of the Aviation Industry: Examining the Impact of the COVID-19 Pandemic, Statement of Airlines for America (A4A) before the United States Commerce, Science and Transportation Committee, May 6, 2020.

[82] Coronavirus Aid, Relief, and Economic Security (CARES) Act (H.R. 748, Public Law 116-136), https://www.govinfo.gov/content/pkg/PLAW-116publ136/html/PLAW-116publ136.htm.

SELECTED BIBLIOGRAPHY

Barlett, Donald L., and James B. Steele. *Howard Hughes: His Life and Madness*. New York: W. W. Norton & Company, 2004.

Barton, Charles. *Howard Hughes and His Flying Boat*. Fallbrook, CA: Aero Publishers, 1982.

Berg, A. Scott. *Lindbergh*. New York: G. P. Putnam's Sons, 1998.

Betts, Edward, and the TWA Master Executive Council. *TWA: The Making of an Airline*. Mission, KS: Inter-Collegiate Press, 1981.

Bowers, Peter M. *The DC-3: Fifty Years of Legendary Flight*. New York: TAB Books, 1986.

Brooks, Peter W. *The World's Airliners*. New York: G. P. Putnam's Sons, 1962.

Buck, Robert N. *North Star Over My Shoulder: A Flying Life*. New York: Simon & Schuster, 2002.

Burgess, George H., and Miles C. Kennedy. *Centennial History of the Pennsylvania Railroad Company*. N.p.: Pennsylvania Railroad Company, 1949.

Conway, Erik M. *High-Speed Dreams: NASA and the Technopolitics of Supersonic Transportation, 1945–1999*. Baltimore: Johns Hopkins University Press, 2005.

Davies, R. E. G. *Airlines of the Jet Age: A History*. Washington, DC: Smithsonian Institution Scholarly Press, 2011.

_____. *Airlines of the United States Since 1914*. Washington, DC: Smithsonian Institution Scholarly Press, 1998.

_____. *Charles Lindbergh: An Airman, His Aircraft, and His Great Flights*. McLean, VA: Paladwr Press, 1997.

_____. *TWA: An Airline and Its Aircraft*. McLean, VA: Paladwr Press, 2000.

Frankum, J. E., and the Trans World Airlines Flight Operations Department. *Legacy of Leadership: A Pictorial History of Trans World Airlines*. Marceline, MO: Walsworth Publishing Company, 1971.

Gerchick, Mark. *Full Upright and Locked Position: Not-So-Comfortable Truths About Air Travel Today*. New York: W. W. Norton & Company, 2013.

Hack, Richard. *Hughes: The Private Diaries, Memos and Letters*. Beverly Hills: New Millennium Press, 2001.

Hoffman, Alan B. *Up There with the Biggest: The Story of Ozark Airlines*. Phoenix: TheBookPatch, 2019.

Horgan, James J. *City of Flight: The History of Aviation in St. Louis*. Gerald, MO: Patrice Press, 1984.

Ingells, Douglas J. *The Plane That Changed the World: A Biography of the DC-3*. Fallbrook, CA: Aero Publishers, 1966.

Jordanoff, Assen. *Through the Overcast: The Weather and the Art of Instrument Flying*. New York: Funk & Wagnalls Company, 1943.

Karash, Julius A., and Rick Montgomery. *TWA: Kansas City's Hometown Airline*. Kansas City: *Kansas City Star* Books, 2001.

Kirk, Robert F. *Flying the Lindbergh Line: Then and Now*. Bloomington, IN: AuthorHouse, 2013.

Kraus, Theresa L. *Celebrating 75 Years of Federal Air Traffic Control*. Washington, DC: Federal Aviation Administration, 2011.

Lamster, Mark. *The TWA Terminal*. Princeton: Princeton Architectural Press, 1999.

Lehrer, Henry R. *Flying the Beam: Navigating the Early US Airmail Airways, 1917–1941*. West Lafayette: Purdue University Press, 2014.

Lindbergh, Anne Morrow. *Hour of Gold, Hour of Lead: Diaries and Letters of Anne Morrow Lindbergh, 1929–1932*. New York: Harcourt Brace Jovanovich, 1973.

_____. *Locked Rooms and Open Doors: Diaries and Letters of Anne Morrow Lindbergh, 1933–1935*. New York: Harcourt Brace Jovanovich, 1974.

_____. *The Flower and the Nettle: Diaries and Letters, 1936–1939*. New York: Harcourt Brace Jovanovich, 1976.

___. *North to the Orient*. New York: Harcourt, Brace & Company, 1935.

Lindbergh, Charles A. *Autobiography of Values*. New York: Harcourt Brace Jovanovich, 1977.

___. The *Spirit of St. Louis*. New York: Charles Scribner's Sons, 1953.

___. *The Wartime Journals of Charles A. Lindbergh*. New York: Harcourt Brace Jovanovich, 1970.

Lyon, Thoburn C. *Practical Air Navigation*. Washington, DC: US Government Printing Office, 1940.

Minton, David H. *The Boeing 747*. Blue Ridge Summit, PA: TAB Aero, 1991.

Mohler, Stanley R., and Bobby H. Johnson. *Wiley Post, His* Winnie Mae*, and the World's First Pressure Suit*. Washington, DC: Smithsonian Institution Scholarly Press, 1971.

Morgan, Len, and Terry Morgan. *The Boeing 727 Scrapbook*. Fallbrook, CA: Aero Publishers, 1978.

Norton, Bill. *Lockheed Martin C-5 Galaxy*. North Branch, MN: Specialty Press, 2003.

Pearcy, Arthur. *Douglas Propliners: DC-1–DC-7*. London: Airlife Publishing Ltd., 1995.

____. *McDonnell Douglas: MD-80 & MD-90*. Osceola, WI: MBI Publishing Company, 1999.

Peterson, Barbara Sturken, and James Glab. *Rapid Descent: Deregulation and the Shakeout in the Airlines*. New York: Simon & Shuster, 1994.

Petzinger, Thomas Jr. *Hard Landing: The Epic Contest for Power and Profits That Plunged the Airlines into Chaos*. New York: Three Rivers Press, 1996.

Proctor, Jon. *Convair 880 and 990*. Miami: World Transport Press, 1996.

____. *TWA, 1925–2001*. Spokane, WA: Airways International Inc., 2012.

Proctor, Jon, and Jeff Kreindler, eds. *Trans World Airlines: A Book of Memories*. St. Augustine, FL: BluewaterPress, 2016.

Redding, Robert, and Bill Yenne. *Boeing: Planemaker to the World*. San Diego: Crescent Books, 1983.

Rich, Elizabeth. *Flying High: What It's Like to Be an Airline Stewardess*. New York: Stein and Day, 1970.

Ringli, Kornel. *Designing TWA: Eero Saarinen's Airport Terminal in New York*. Zurich: Park Books, 2015.

Rummel, Robert W. *Howard Hughes and TWA*. Washington, DC: Smithsonian Institution Scholarly Press, 1991.

Rust, Daniel L. *The Aerial Crossroads of America: St. Louis's Lambert Airport*. St. Louis: Missouri History Museum Press, 2016.

____. *Flying Across America: The Airline Passenger Experience*. Norman: University of Oklahoma Press, 2009.

Schiff, Barry J. *The Boeing 707*. New York: Arco Publishing Company, 1967.

Schwartz, Vanessa R. *Jet Age Aesthetic: The Glamour of Media in Motion*. New Haven: Yale University Press, 2020.

Scott, Robert L. *God Is My Co-Pilot*. New York: Charles Scribner's Sons, 1943.

Serling, Robert. *Howard Hughes' Airline: An Informal History of TWA*. New York: St. Martin's/Marek, 1983.

Shaw, Robbie. *Boeing 757 & 767: The Medium Twins*. Oxford: Osprey Publishing, 1999.

Sheth, Jagdeth N., Fred C. Allvine, Can Uslay, and Ashutosh Dixit. *Deregulation and Competition: Lessons from the Airline Industry*. New Delhi: Response Books, 2007.

Simons, Graham M. *Comet! The World's First Jet Airliner*. Barnsley, South Yorkshire: Pen & Sword Aviation, 2013.

Solberg, Carl. *Conquest of the Skies: A History of Commercial Aviation in America*. Boston: Little, Brown and Company, 1979.

Stadiem, William. *Jet Set: The People, the Glamour, and the Romance in Aviation's Glory Years*. New York: Ballantine Books, 2014.

Steele, Donna. *TWA Cabin Attendants Wings of Pride: A Pictorial History, 1935–1985*. Marceline, MO: Walsworth Publishing Company, 1985.

Stringfellow, Curtis K., and Peter M. Bowers. *Lockheed Constellation*. Osceola, WI: Motorbooks International, 1992.

Testrake, John, and David J. Wimbish. *Triumph over Terror on Flight 847*. Grand Rapids, MI: Fleming H. Revell Company, 1987.

Verhovek, Sam Howe. *Jet Age: The Comet, the 707, and the Race to Shrink the World*. New York: Avery, 2010.

Wegg, John (ed.). *Remembering That Wonderful Airline—TWA*. Sandpoint, ID: Airways International Inc., 2005.

Zimmermann, Christian. *Hostage in a Hostage World*. St. Louis: Concordia Publishing House, 1985.

INDEX

oil crisis of 1973, 157, 159, 184

Orteig Prize, 16

Ovington, Earle, 7

Ozark Air Lines, 4, 173, 174, 178, 179–187, 200–203, 241, 243, 255, 257, 260, 263; fleet, *183*

Ozark Midwest, 186

Palestine Liberation Organization, 150

Pan American Airways, 58, 59, 69, 70, 72, 76, 77, 79, 85, 86, 90, 92, 103, 104, 110, 111, 115, 129, 130, 143, 146, 149, 152, 157, 160, 164, 185, 213, 214, 216, 250

Pan Am Express, 217

Parks, Oliver, 179

Parks Air Lines, 179

Parrish, Wayne, 46, 68

Parsons, Louella, 93

Pearson, Richard D., 194, 196, 200

Pennsylvania Railroad, 18

Pension Benefit Guaranty Corporation (PBGC), 216, 218, 219, 221, 250

pensions, 219, 220, 250, 261

People Express Airlines, 172, 239

Pickford, Mary, 24

pilots, 207, 210, 211, 212, 213, 216, 249, 255, 259, 260, 262, 263, 266; strike, 82–83

Pittsburgh Aviation Industries Corporation (PAIC), 32–34

Pope John Paul II, 169, 247

Popular Front for the Liberation of Palestine (PFLP), 143, 148–150

Portair, 26

Post, Wiley, 50, 63

Professional Air Traffic Controllers Organization (PATCO), 175

profitability, 10, 29, 54, 91, 93, 95, 111, 115,130, 143, 148, 151–152, 159, 160, 161, 164, 167–169, 175, 176–178, 185–186, 187, 200, 204, 207, 208–210, 214, 218, 224, 226, 230, 232, 240, 268

"Project Dynamite," 98

Project Greenland, 106

publicity, 29, 35, 43, 62, 68, 72, 82, 96, 99, 101, 112–114, 123, 127–128, 132–135, 161, 165, 223, 228, 261

Raymond, Arthur, 39, 40

Reconstruction Finance Corporation (RFC), 83

regional carriers, 174, 186, 232, 248, 249

Richter, Paul, 13, 17, *33*, 44, 46, 58, 59, 65, 66, 67, *84*, 269

Rickenbacker, Eddie, 42, 43

Robbins, Richard, 34, 39, 42, 44, 47

Robertson, Bill, 18

Robertson Aircraft Corporation, 15, 16

Rockne, Knute, 12, 17, *35*

Roosevelt, Elliott, 75

Rummel, Robert, 77, 97, 103

Ryan Airlines, 16

Saarinen, Aline, 128

Saarinen, Eero, 112, 113

safety, 12, 22, 27–29, *33*, 36–38, 43, 45, 46, 48, 51–53, 56–59, 65, 95, 106, 108, 120, 122–123, 130, 132, 154, 155, 158–159, 170, 180, 231, 236,

Salomon, Marguerite, 23, 24

Santa Fe Railway, 18

Schnall, Elliot, 194

Scott, Kent, 210, 212, 213, 217

Scott, Robert L., 44

security, 150, 158, 198, 257–258, 260, 265

seniority, 120, 156, 196, 200–203, 252, 255–257, 259, 261–263

September 11, 2001, 5, 150, 257–258, 260, 263, 264, 266, 267

Shaeffer, Daniel M., *33*, 34

Six-Day War, 141, 148, 157

skyjacking, 143–145, 148–150, 190–192, 199

Slay, Mayor Francis, 257, 263

Smart, L. Edwin, 161, 164, 167, 168, 187

Southwest Air Fast Express (SAFE), 17, *33*

Southwest Airlines, 186, 187, 258, 266

Spartan Food Services, 168

Spoils Conferences, 31, 41, 42, 44

Staggers, Ida, 139, 140

Standard Airlines, 13, 14, 17

stewardesses. *See* flight attendants *and* hostesses

St. Louis City, 52, 180, 188, 225

St. Louis headquarters, 220, 224, 225, 228

ABOUT THE AUTHORS

Daniel L. Rust is an associate professor of transportation and logistics management at the University of Wisconsin–Superior. He has served as assistant director of the Center of Transportation Studies at the University of Missouri–St. Louis. He is the author of *The Aerial Crossroads of America* (Missouri History Museum Press, 2016) and *Flying Across America* (University of Oklahoma Press, 2009).

Alan B. Hoffman is a general historian and aviation historian who practiced law for 43 years. He served in the United States Army for three years and was an active private pilot for 47 years. He is the author of *Up There with the Biggest: The Story of Ozark Airlines* (The Book Patch, 2019). He serves as the "Aviation Watch" expert analysis columnist for the *Law360* news service.